THE Wallace Nutting EXPANSIBLE CATALOG

Being Studies in America and other Lands of Aspects in the Life of the Fathers and the Country Life of to-day. The pictures are made on platinum paper and are colored by hand. This book is merely a key of the subjects.

Published by

DIAMOND PRESS

P.O. Box 167

Maple Glen, PA 19002-0767

(215) 345-6094

Wallace Nutting Expansible Catalog

Originally published by Wallace Nutting, Framingham, MA, 1915

Library of Congress Catalog Card Number: 87-070415

ISBN: 0-9615843-3-5

Published by
Diamond Press, P.O. Box 167, Maple Glen, PA 19002-0767

This book may be purchased from the publisher.
Please include $1.00 postage.

Introduction

By 1912 Wallace Nutting's picture business was booming. His reputation as a photographer and picture-maker increased demand for his pictures throughout the country. The wide variety of pictures — streams, lakes, blossoms, birches, country lanes, interiors, people, castles, houses, bridges, and animals... both American and European — often made it confusing for customers to order.

In 1912, to help eliminate this problem, Wallace Nutting produced his first picture catalog. A hard-cover, bound book approximately 75 pages in length, this catalog was used by his salesmen to help in the sale of Wallace Nutting pictures. This 1912 catalog states: "*This book is out of date even now that it is new, in the sense that is does not include all the latest work of Mr. Nutting, for he is producing new subjects every month in the year... naturally such a work cannot be revised often. It is probable that this edition de luxe will remain as the standard, and the new work will be shown only in occasional supplements.*"

By 1915, Wallace Nutting had a better idea. Rather than issue one bound book with many loose supplements, he issued a revised catalog that was not bound, but instead held together in notebook-like form. Therefore, when he 'expanded' his picture line, his catalog could be expanded too. The new supplements cound be added to, or used to replace, pages in the original catalog. Hence, the Wallace Nutting 'Expansible' catalog.

This book is an exact reprint of that catalog, including updates. It is the most complete book of its kind anywhere and Diamond Press is pleased to make this new edition available to you.

What can this book be used for?

First, it can be used as a reference tool for collectors and dealers alike. It will visually show you the wide variety of Wallace Nutting pictures that were produced by 1915... and are still obtainable today.

Second, if you are buying your Wallace Nutting pictures sight unseen or through the mail, it will allow you to see the pictures before you buy. Written descriptions may attempt to describe pictures as accurately as possible, but nothing is as good as seeing the real thing.

Finally, if you have smaller, untitled pictures in your collection or shop, this book will allow you to identify not only the title, but the location of many pictures as well.

Whether you are a Wallace Nutting collector or dealer, I'm certain you will find the 'Wallace Nutting Expansible Catalog' enjoyable, informative, and profitable reading.

Michael Ivankovich, Author
'The Price Guide to Wallace Nutting Pictures'

TABLE OF CONTENTS

SUBJECTS BY NUMBER

From 1–3999 and above 8000, America (except very few old foreign).

4000–4499 Italy (except even numbers to 4022).

4500–4999 France and Germany.

5000–5499 Holland.

5500–8000 Great Britain.

AN EXPANSIBLE CATALOG

IN order to keep our friends advised of our recent work, we are putting forth this expansible catalog, so paged that at the end of each division, Birches, Blossoms, etc., supplements may be inserted from time to time, as they are sent to the holder of this catalog. The reader will kindly take care to make these insertions at once on receiving the additions, as this is the only manner in which this catalog can be at all correct or up to date. The issuance of these books is so expensive that we cannot afford to give out additional catalogs, and it must, therefore, remain with the holder to keep all the parts together.

We believe that this is the richest setting forth of pictures which has ever been undertaken. We were told when the last list was issued that it was the best of its sort that was ever published. This book contains more than double the previous quantity of illustrations. It is not the intention, at any time, to issue any other book, but only to increase this one.

This book, unless it is sold, remains the property of the publishers, being loaned. The holders are not, of course, at liberty to cut out portions of it.

We have not retained quite all the old cuts, but most of them will be found in the following pages, some being inserted only for the sake of completeness. The entire collection of Wallace Nutting pictures consists of many thousands, not all of which can be here shown, but only a representative number.

Probably a small list, without cuts, may be issued of subjects purely architectural.

It is obvious that an index is impossible, as it would be useless after the issuance of the first supplement.

EXPLANATION

The letters before the numbers refer to the sizes of the pictures, not to the size of the mounts. Before every number appears a letter, as C 220. This means the picture 220 is sold in the C, or 8 x 10 size, on a mount 14 x 17. In order to be sure to get just what you wish, it is necessary that the letter should be placed before the number, as perhaps the same number may be issued in ten different sizes. The C size will be sent unless otherwise ordered.

The pictures are sold *only* in the sizes listed. As a rule they are not suitable to be reproduced in other sizes. If you don't trust our taste in this respect, and insist on ordering in other sizes please include one-third extra for cost of plate. We do not guarantee satisfaction in such cases.

	Plate	Mount	List
A means	5 x 7 Plate,	11 x 14 Mount,	List $1.25
Q	4 x 10	11 x 17	1.50
S	6 x 10	13 x 17	2.00
C	8 x 10	14 x 17	2.50
O	5 x 14	13 x 22	2.50
P	7½ x 14	15 x 22	4.00
E	11 x 14	18 x 22	5.00
F	14 x 17	22 x 28	6.50
T	12 x 20	22 x 30	7.00
G	16 x 20	26 x 30	8.00
H	20 x 24	29 x 36	12.00
J	20 x 28 or 30	29 x 40	15.00
W	20 x 40	30 x 52	20.00

The following sizes are signed but not titled:

	Plate	Mount	List	
R means	4 x 6 Plate,	10 x 12 Mount,	List $12.00	per doz.
K	3 x 6⅝	8 x 12	9.00	"
D	3¼ x 4	7 x 9	6.00	"
D	2½ x 5	7 x 9	6.00	"
B	2 x 3	5 x 7	3.00	"

There are several hundred subjects under each of these small sizes. Orders in any size can be made up to consist, if desired, of figures only, or of blossoms, streams, birches or cottages. We do not show cuts of any size smaller than A.

BEST SELLERS

Seven Assorted, either as A set, C set, or E set

No.	Title	Page
2530	The Coming Out of Rosa (Figure and Blossom. Also in F)	467
6063	Larkspur (Figure and Blossom)	451
73	Decked as a Bride (Blossom. Also in S, O, P, G, H, J)	109
220	The Swimming Pool (Stream. Also in Q, S, O, P, F, G, T, H, J, W)	810
3284	A Chair for John (Figure)	462
4010	A Fruit Luncheon (Figure)	453
5605	The Nest (Cottage and Blossom)	401

Second Seven Assorted, either as A set, C set, or E set

No.	Title	Page
292	Grace (Birch. Also in Q and F)	16
506	A Canopied Road (Blossom. Also in Q, F, J)	111
170	Honeymoon Drive (Blossom. Also in F, G, H)	110
437	Pine Landing (Water. Also in Q)	818
6414	Hollyhock Cottage (Cottage and Blossom)	404
4002	A Stitch in Time (Figure)	461
3082	Three Chums (Figure. Also in F)	453

Seven Assorted, either as Q set or O set

No.	Title	Page
3701	A Little River (Also in P, G, T and W)	806
5093	A Peaceful Stretch (Holland Canal)	253
158	Flowering Time (Also S, P, T, W)	112
3265	The Walpole Road (Blossom)	105
5663	Five O'Clock (English Cottage)	103
750	The Book Settle (Figure. Also in S and P)	469
3734	A Newmarket Belle (Figure. Also in S)	459

Second Seven Assorted either as Q set or O set

No.	Title	Page
3147	A Sheltered Road (Birch)	11
221	Whitsunday (Blossom)	113
57	The Beauty of the Uplands (Blossom. Also in P)	116
704	Confidences (Figure. Also in C, E, F)	468
3072	The Old Home (Figure. Also in S and P)	461
6134	The Tranquil Vale (Stream. Also in P)	653
3497	A Barre Brook (Also in C, E, P, T, W)	804

Seven Assorted as S set or P set

No.	Title	Page
247	A Berkshire Brook (Also in Q and C)	114
3247	A Keene Road (Blossom)	108
52	Christmas Jelly (Figure. Also in C)	480
3670	In John Hancock's Chair (Figure)	483
323	A Warm Spring Day (Pastoral. Also in Q, C, O, E, W)	701
985	A Fleck of Sunshine (Figure. Also in T)	487
268	Slack Water (Stream. Also in Q, O, T, W)	808

BEST SELLERS

Seven Blossoms in C set, or E set (not included in any of above sets).

No.	Title	Page
244	Where Grandma Was Wed (Also in P and J)	108
3623	The Softness of Spring	101
3107	Windsor Blossoms	101
3301	Rural Sweetness	105
27	Billows of Blossom (Also in G)	102
34	Spring in the Berkshires	114
112	A Tunnel of Bloom (Also in J)	116

Seven Figures (Colonials), in C set or E set (not included in any of above sets).

No.	Title	Page
3304	The Treasure Bag (Also in A and G)	454
703	Afternoon Tea (Also in G)	471
734	The Maple Sugar Cupboard (Also in G)	474
707	Prudence Drawing Tea	465
4008	A Virginia Reel	461
3744	A Formal Call	464
3280	An Old Colony Home Room	463

Second Seven Figures (Colonial), in C set or E set (not included in any of above sets).

No.	Title	Page
3728	Braiding a Rag Rug	473
136	At the Fender (Also in A)	467
746	An Elaborate Dinner (Also in Q, F, P, J)	481
3288	The Divining Cup	458
677	Mending (Also in G)	471
3796	Trimming the Pie Crust	459
1389	The Spinet Corner (Also in A)	478

Seven Assorted Foreign, either as A set or C set.

No.	Title	Page
5561	Mary's Little Lamb (England, Kent)	704
5010	Windings in Holland (Cottages and Canal)	254
480	The Pergola, Amalfi (Also in E and F)	606
5606	Hawthornden (Cottage in Sherwood Forest), (Also in E and G)	403
5662	Under Ivy Bridge (Devon), (Also in E)	201
4065	Little Washerwomen (Amalfi)	458
4463	Spring's First Green (Mountain, No. Italy), (Also in E and G)	654

Seven Cathedrals, as A set or C set or E set.

No.	Title	Page
6222	The Conscious Stones (Bolton Abbey)	352
5701	Wells, from the Bishop's Garden	353
6125	Stepping Stones, Bolton Abbey (Also in T)	351
4344	Venice's Chief Glory (St. Mark's)	356
5550	Canterbury Close (long vertically)	355
5853	Durham	358
4276	The Italian Spring (Seven-Domed Church, Padua)	358

As popularity varies a new sheet will be sent to substitute for pages 6 and 7.

HOW TO ORDER PICTURES

No Pictures on Commission. We do not send out pictures on commission sale, because we have always been able to sell all the pictures we could make and make well.

No Pictures Returnable. No pictures are sold with the direct, indirect, or implied obligation to receive them back if not sold. No salesman in our employ has any right to give any such assurance.

Making up Orders. Those dealers who are acquainted with our pictures can easily find by referring to the classification on page 3 the class of subjects for which they are looking. One warning should be given. A great many cuts appear in the squarer shapes, like the C and E size, which are also made in narrower panels, so that if a buyer is looking for panels it is wise for him to give heed to the notations under all the pictures in a certain class, to see whether or not they may be issued in the panel size.

Express, Freight or Mail. Unless particular instructions are sent with the order we shall forward goods by the cheapest way.

Packing. All packing is done gratis, except in case of less number of framed pictures than regularly sold, or less than seven A size or larger, when a charge of twenty-five cents is made for packing.

Claims for Injury. The forwarders are in all cases liable for injury to goods in transit.

Remounting. We remount pictures for the nominal charge of fifty cents per dozen in assorted sizes. The expense to us is considerably more than this; but it is for our interest that the pictures be kept in good condition, and we wish to stand behind the buyer in this particular.

It is, however, essential, if the buyer dismounts his pictures to return to us, that he cut out and send to us the signatures. We are obliged to make this rule as instances have not been unknown of mounting other pictures than our own above our signature. We would advise that pictures sent to us for remounting should not be dismounted, but should be cut down nearly to the size of the print.

A Variety of Specialties. We have an immense variety, some five or six hundred styles, of special goods, some, in the form of plain engraving, being invitation cards, etc., and others are special styles of menus, banquet cards, place cards, etc. Above are not illustrated.

New Small Goods. We are constantly adding to the range of our numbers in the small goods. We make at least one new subject a day of this character.

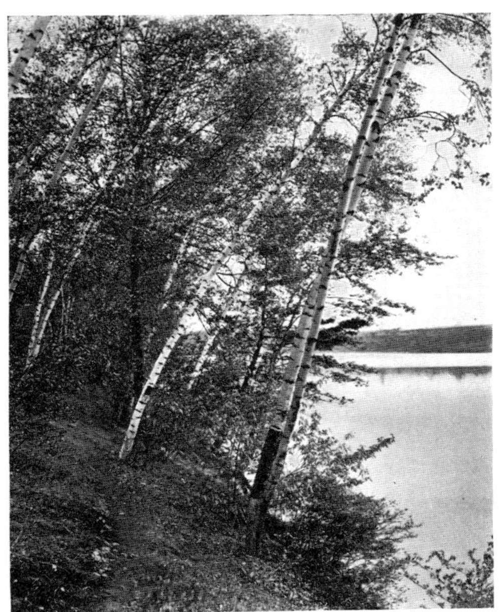

A Marlboro Shore Q and C 3459

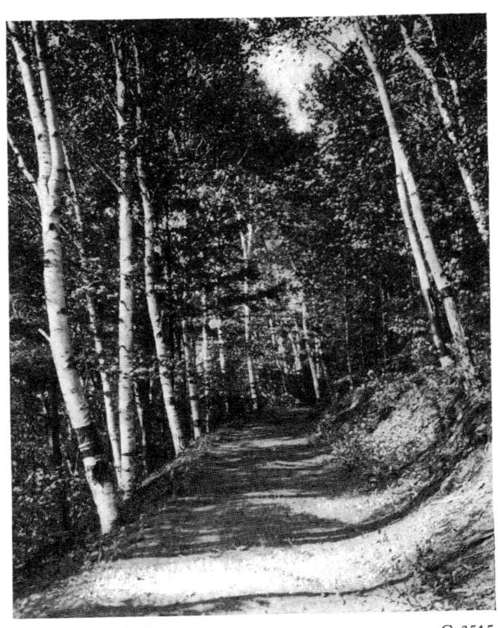

Cross Road Shadows C 3515

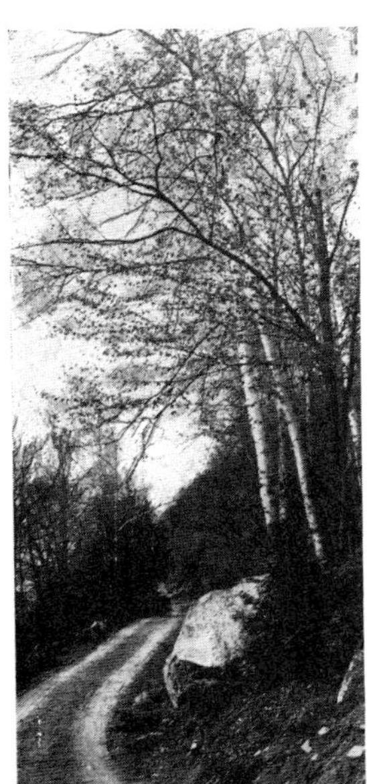

A Sheltered Road Q and O 3147

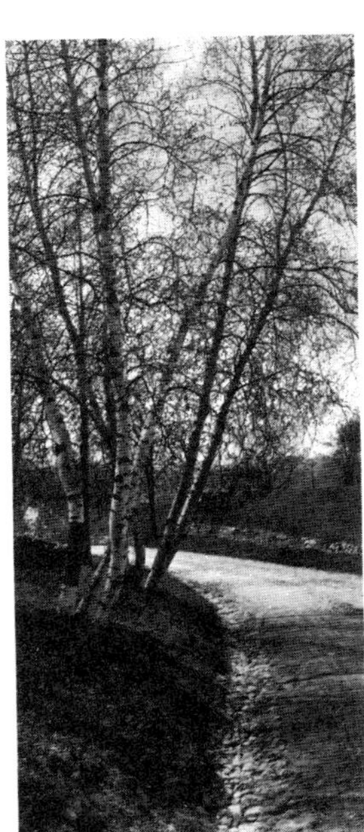

Early May Q, S and P 3067

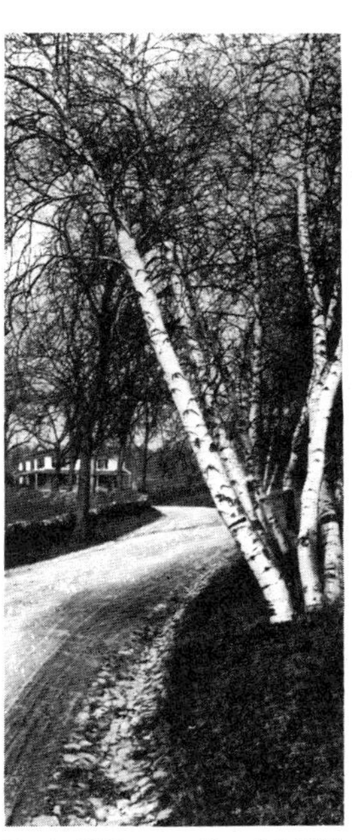

Up the Hill Q and S 3025

We have been accused of overcoloring the birch trunks. It is hard to believe that the birch is so white. We do not color the trunks at all, except where the outside bark is missing. At first the exposed bark is red brown, but turns dark gray to black.

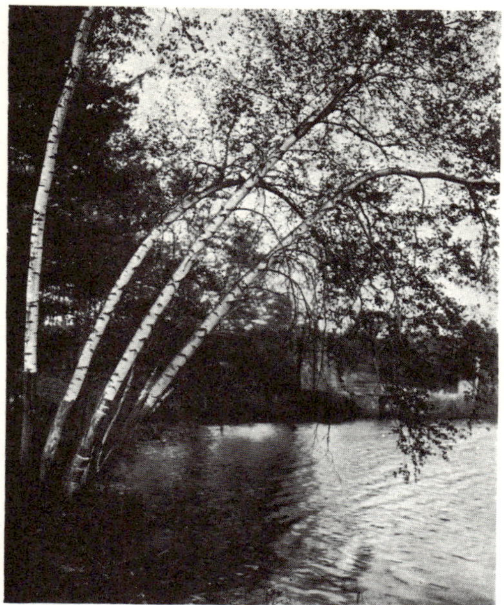

Birch Drapery C 3611

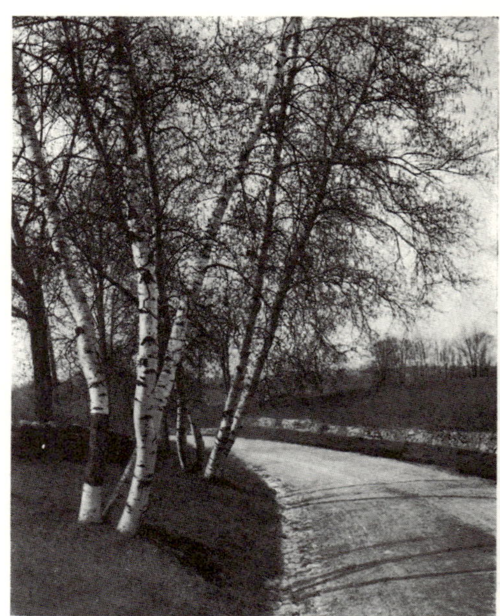

Southboro Birches 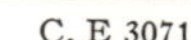 C, E 3071

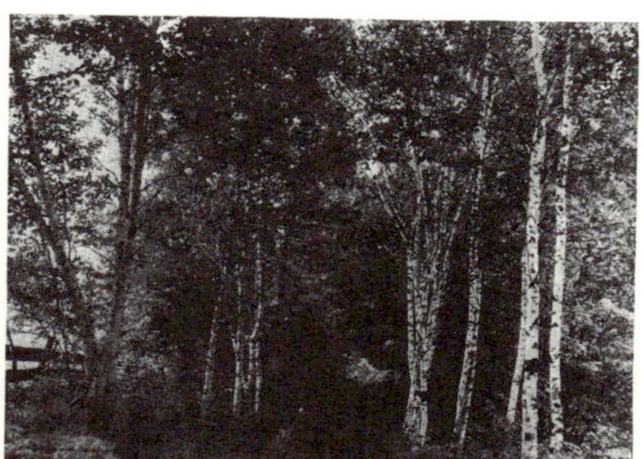

The Bridesmaids of the Wood E 61

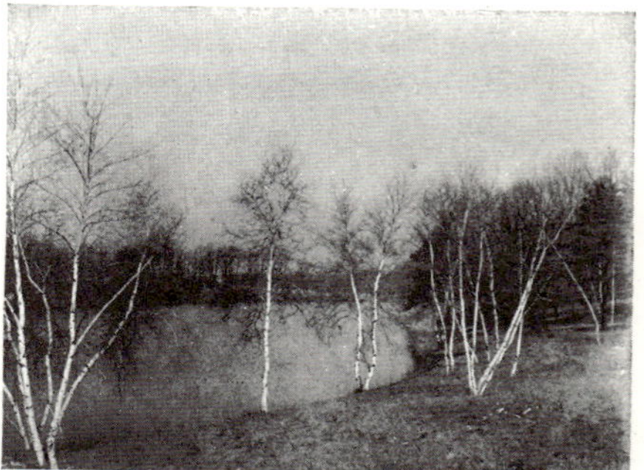

Morning Among the Birches C or E 328

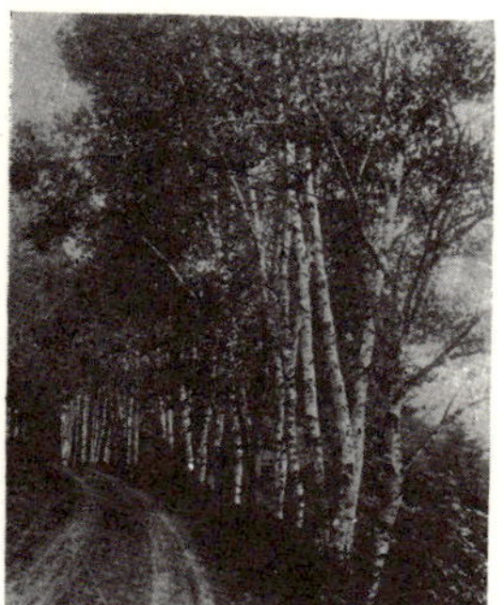

A Waterford Curve Q or C 361

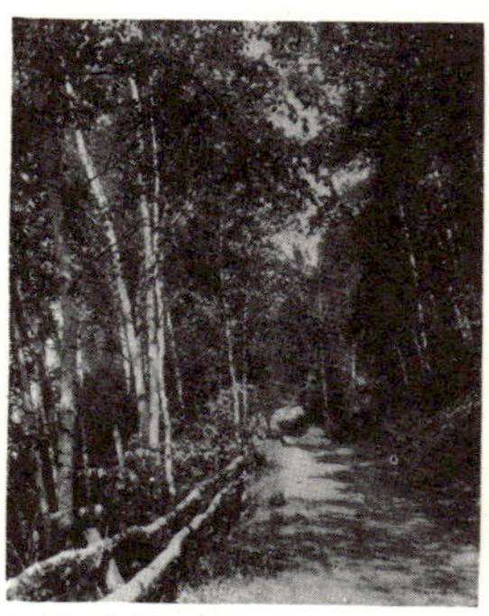

A Birch Paradise Q or C 322

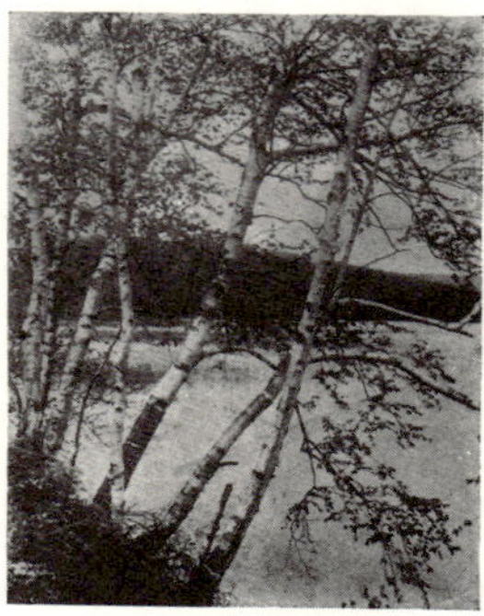

By a Berkshire Pool C 291

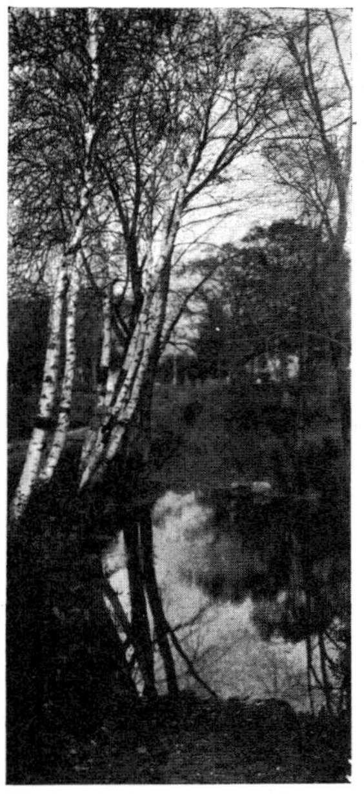

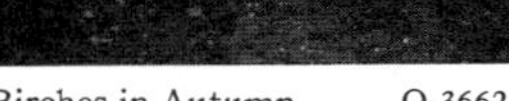

Birches in Autumn Q 3662

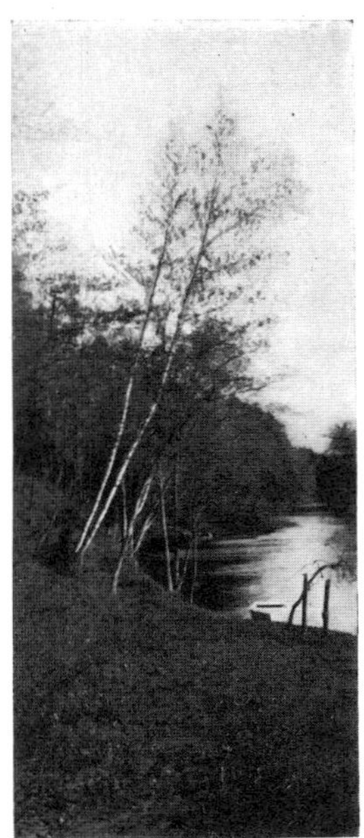

The Shore Vista Q 579

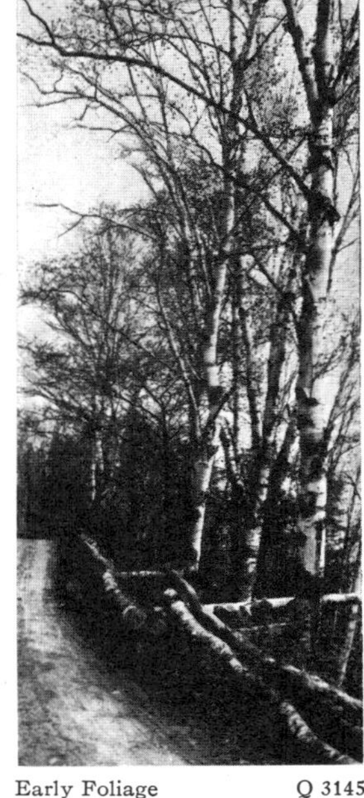

Early Foliage Q 3145

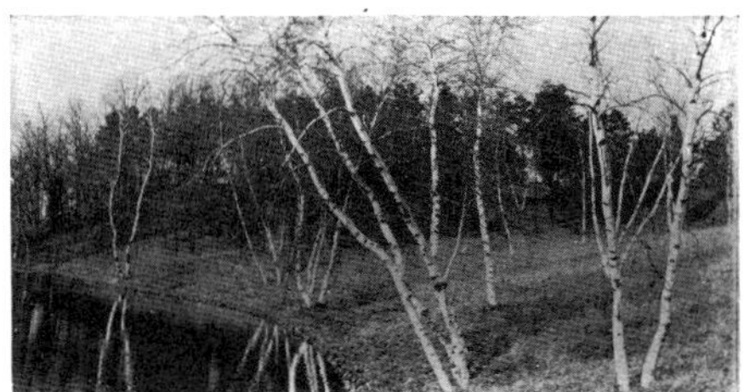

Birch Clusters P 2701

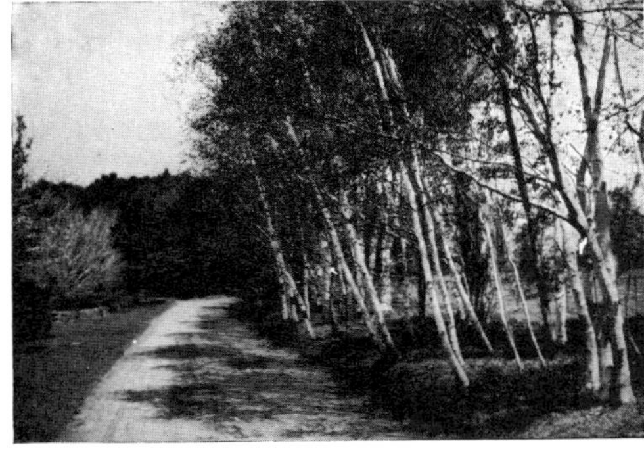

Roadside Grace A 239

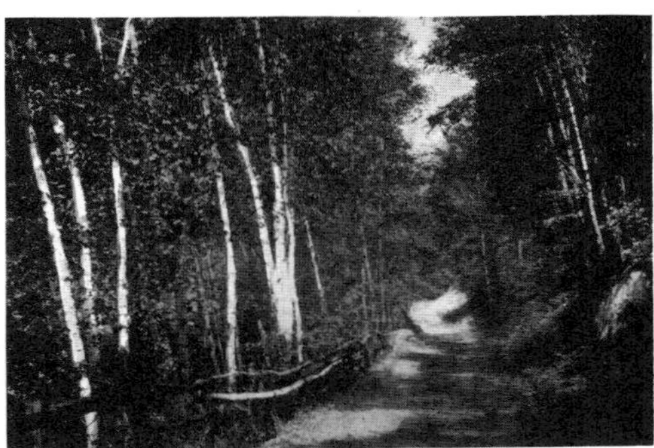

A Birch Wood A 277

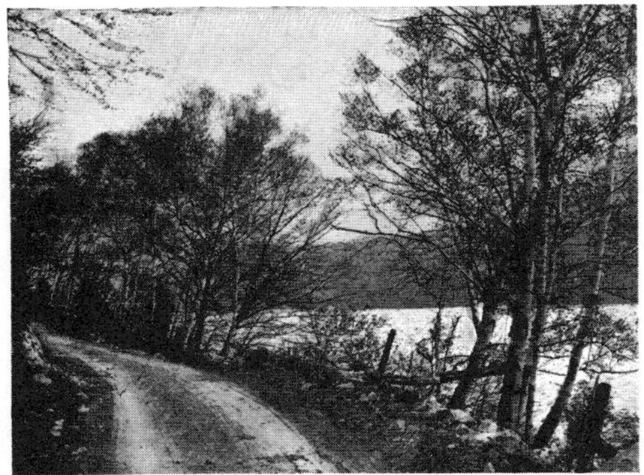

Spring at the Lake C and F 3461

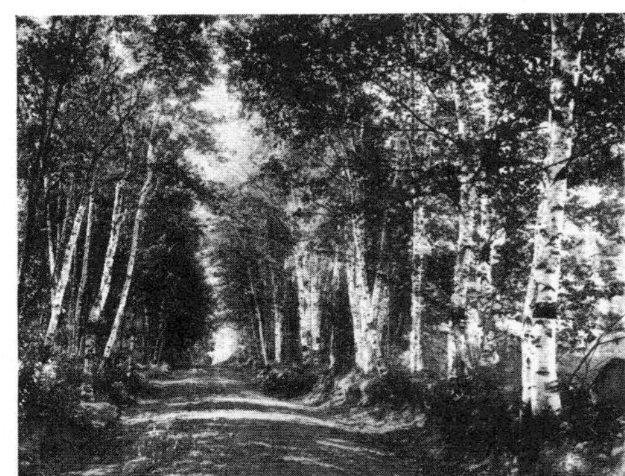

A New Hampshire Drive C, E 3575

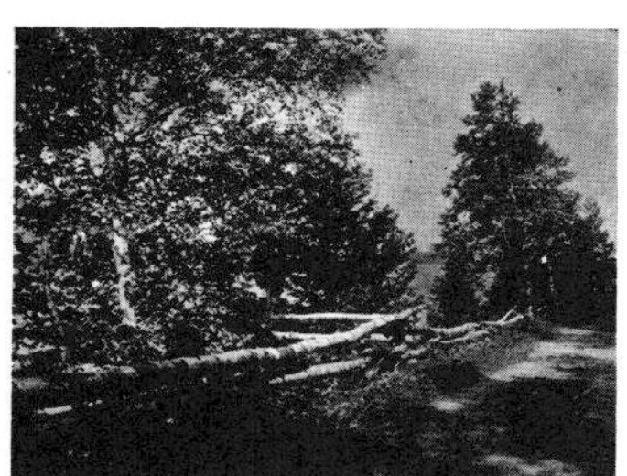

A Fence Row C 2626

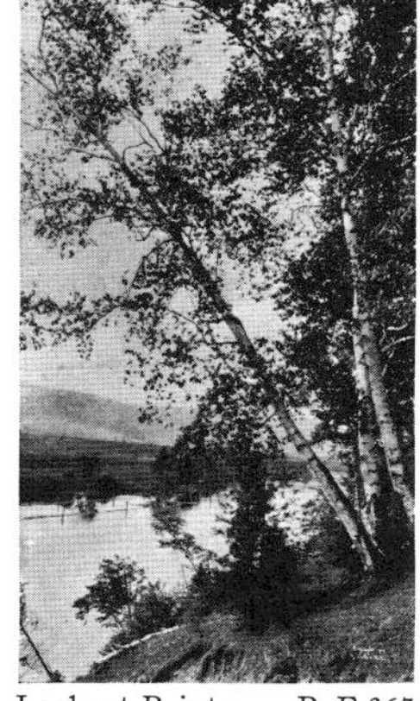

Lookout Point P, E 367

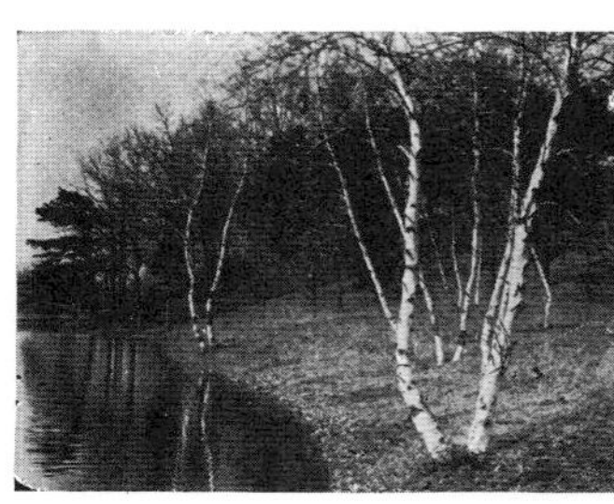

Birch Curve C 439

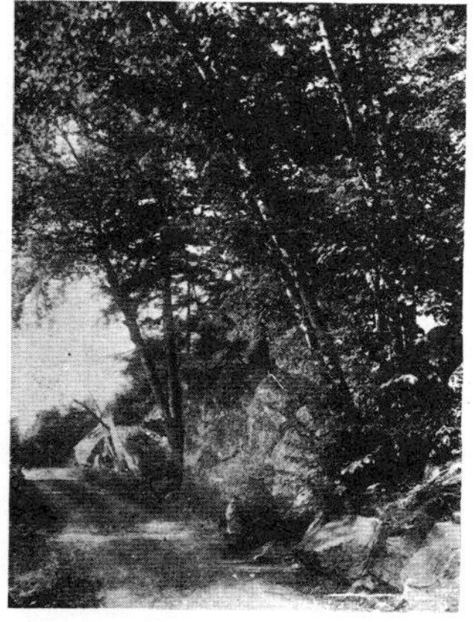

The Climax of the Road E 88

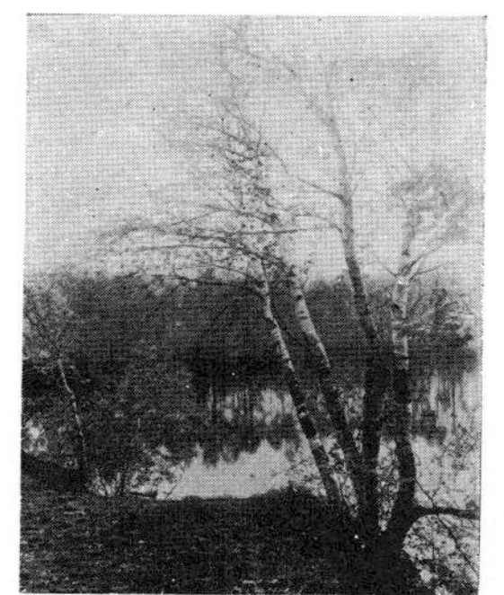
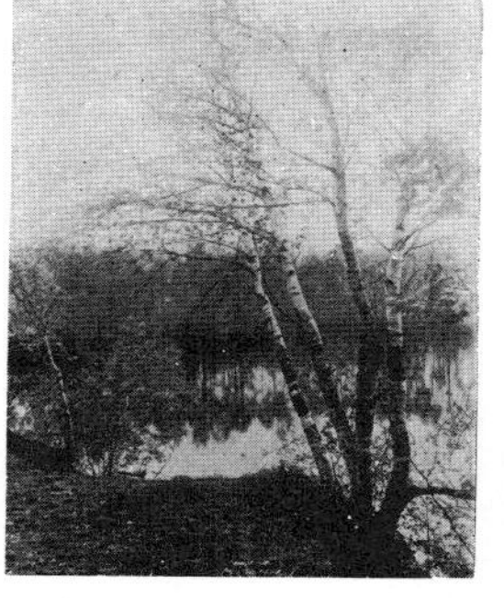

Birch Strand Q or C 296

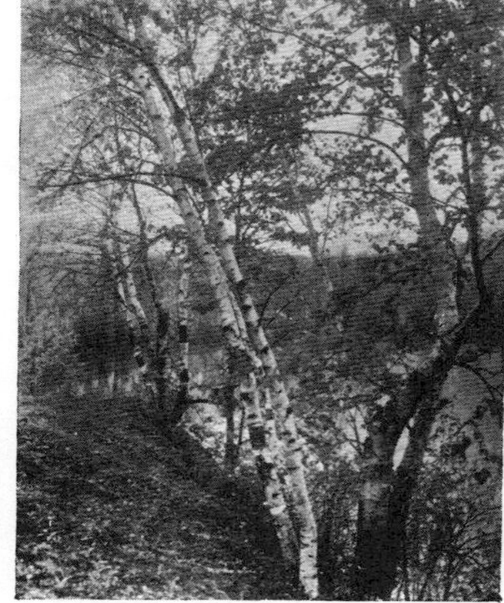

Silver Birches Q or C 278

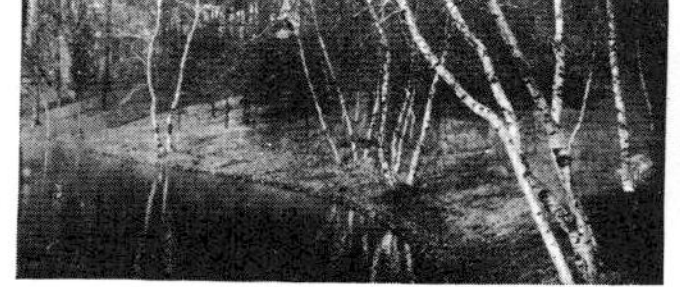

The Birch Bank Q 443

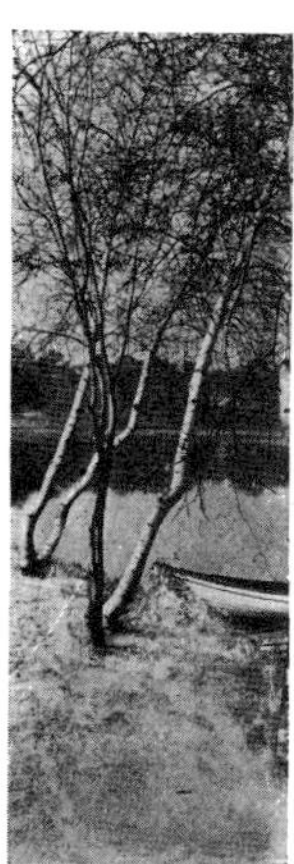

Birch Cove
O, P or E 104

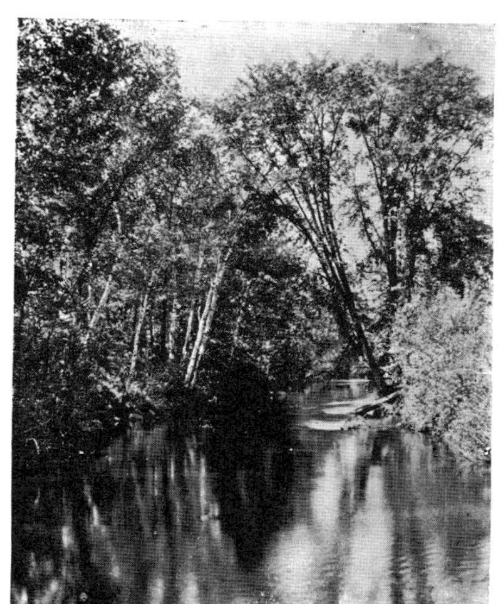

An Elm-Birch Arch O, P or E 355

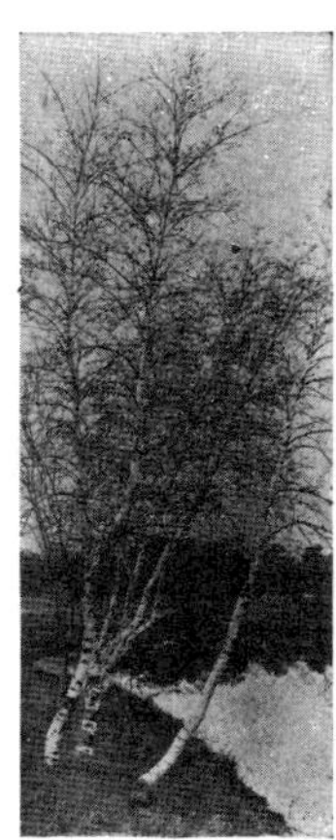

The Lake Marge
O 345

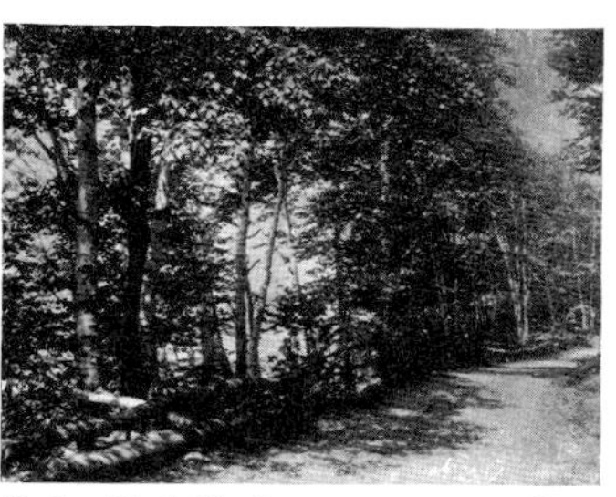

Under Birch Shadows C 289

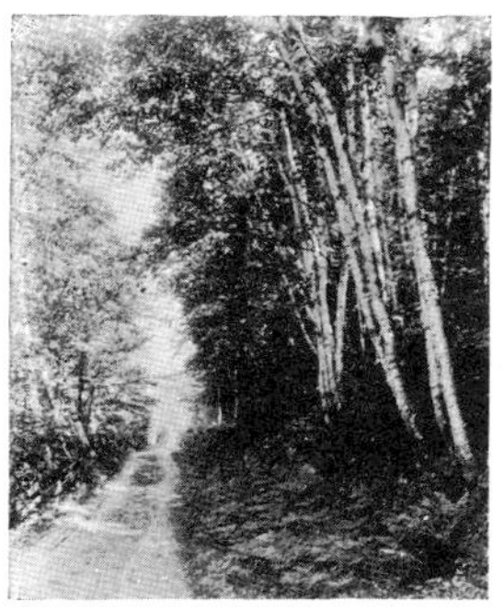

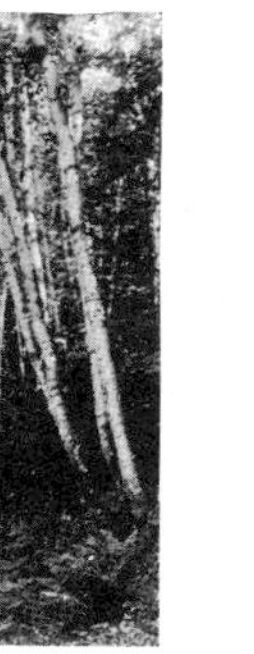

Among the Ferns C 351

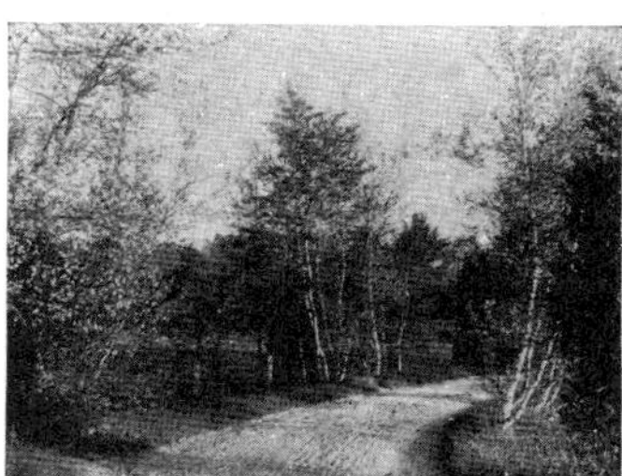

A May Drive Q, C or F 285

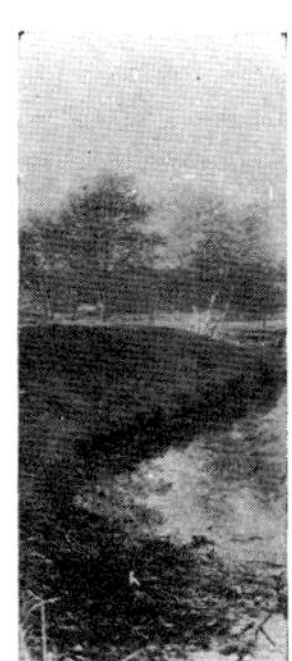

June Haze
Q 411

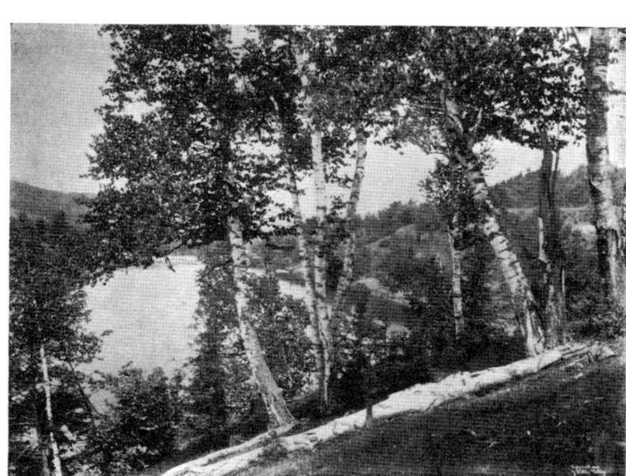

A Birch Grove A, C, E or J 370

A Roadside Brook
Q 163

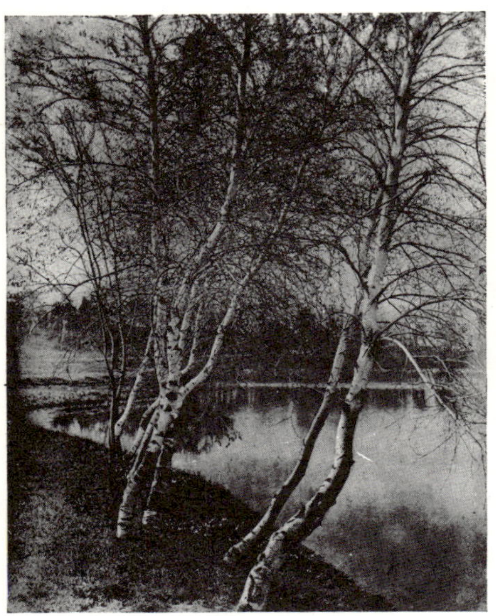
Grace A, Q, C, E or F 292

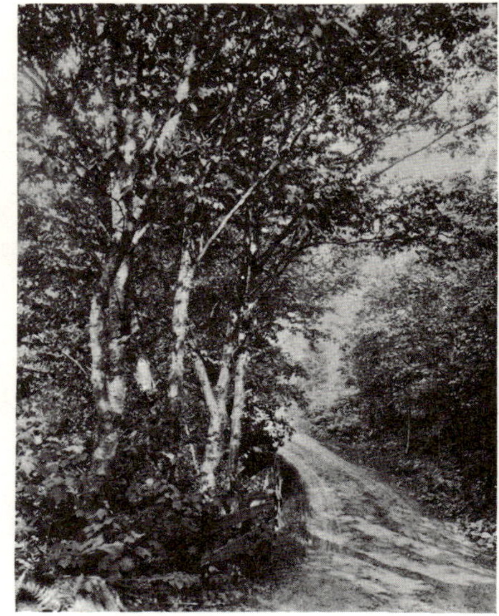
Westmore Drive A, Q, C, O or E 365

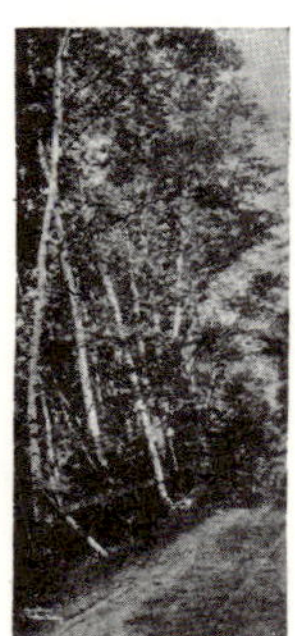
A Silver Screen
Q 350

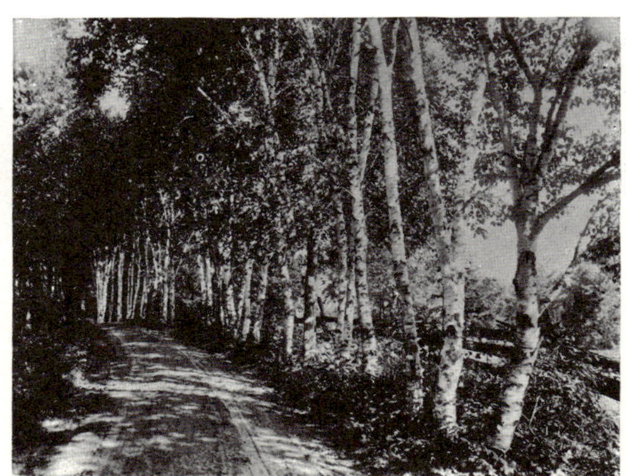
Birch Bend C, E, F 18

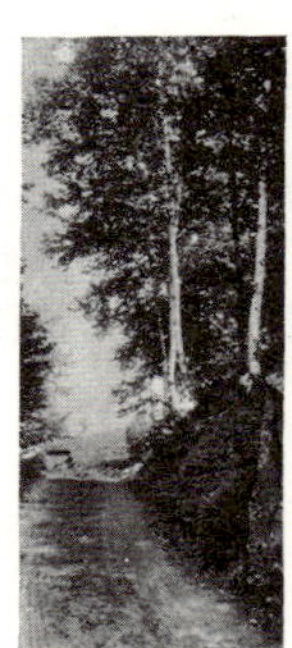
At the Hilltop
Q 2655

The following are not illustrated:

P 368 Birch Lookout
C 546 A Lincoln Drive
A 1727 Up the Path
A C 1830 The Birch Border
O P 2706 The Curve of a Hill Road
C 3001 Autumnal Birches
S 3005 A Thanksgiving Landscape
A 3063 A Downward Curve
C 3151 A Mountain Shore
C 3155 Birch Knoll
A 3163 A Passumpsic Gorge
A 3181 The May Awakening
S P E 3311 Early Birches
C 3501 A Brandon Roadside
A 3557 Lichen and Birch
C 3571 White Mountain Birches
C 3667 White Mountain Birch Road

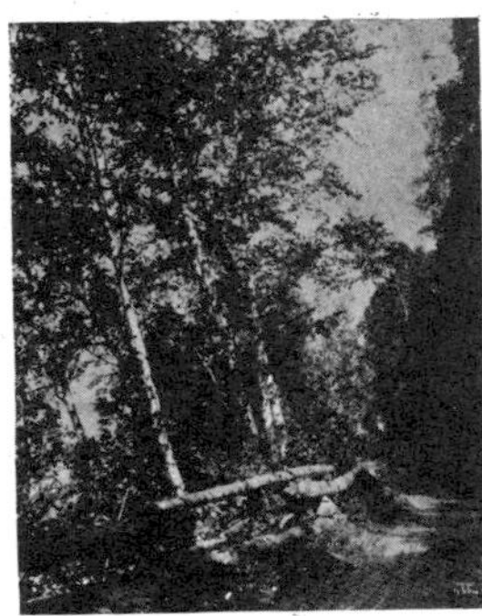

A White Rail
C 301

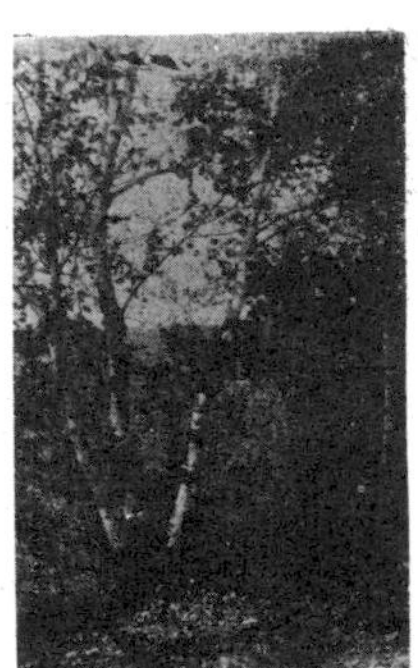

A Berkshire Path
S 264

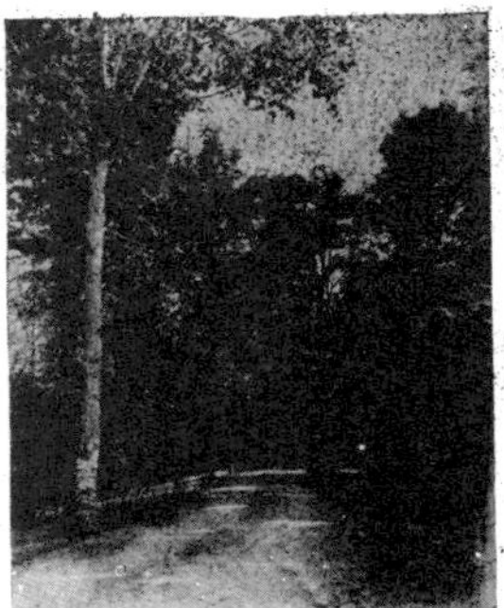

Woodland Enchantment
C 559

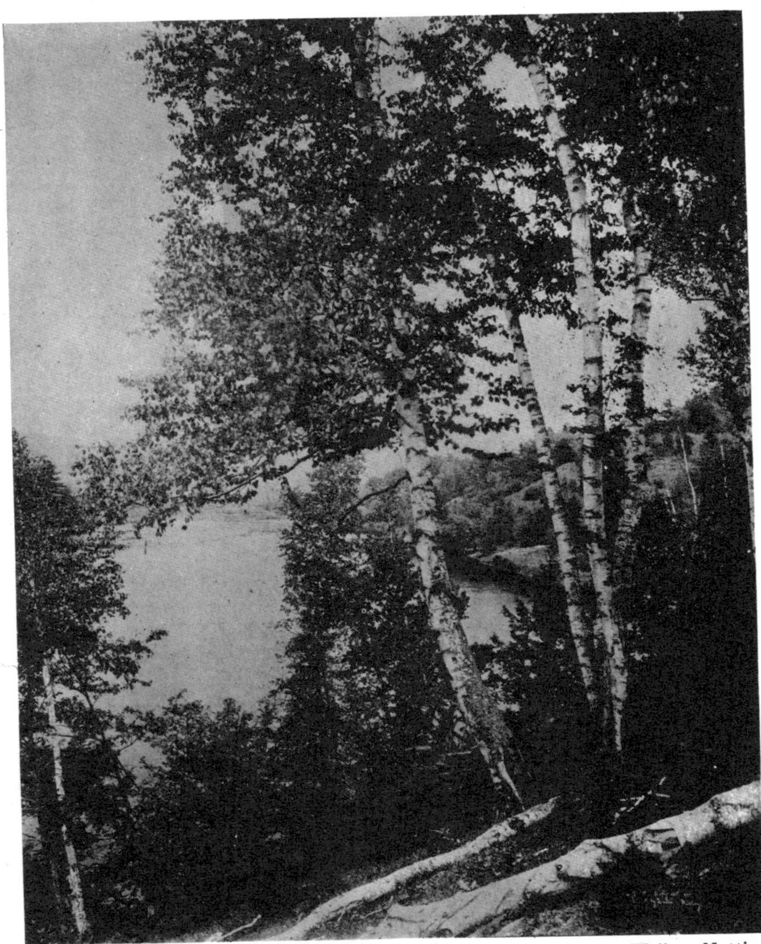

Birch Hilltop A, Q, C, O, P, E or H 382 Wallace Nutting

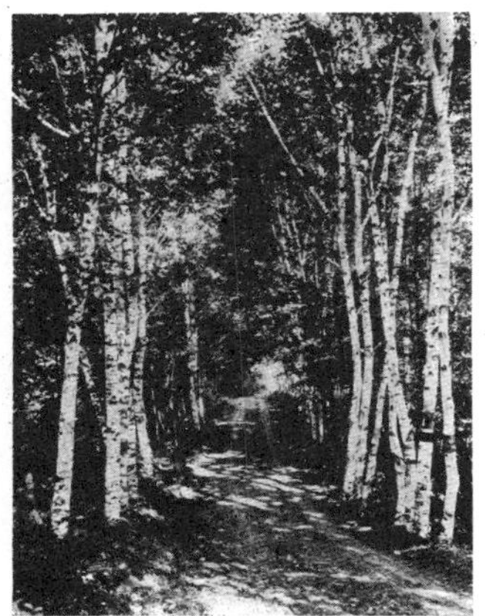

A Woodland Cathedral C, E 14

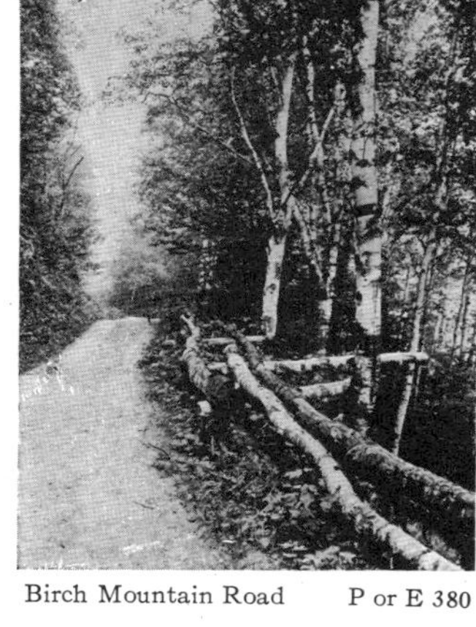

Birch Mountain Road P or E 380

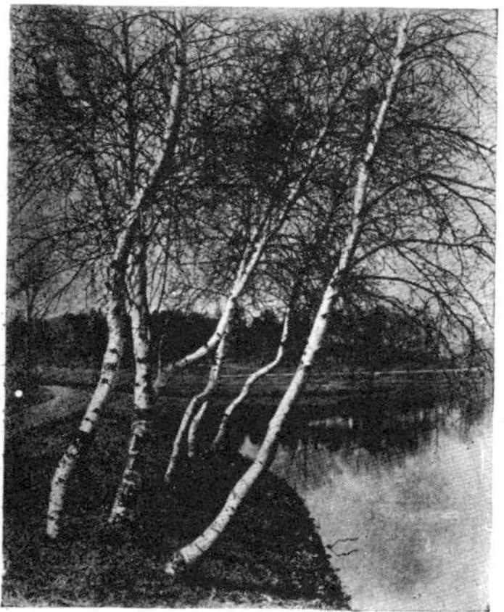

A Silent Shore Q, C, P or E 249

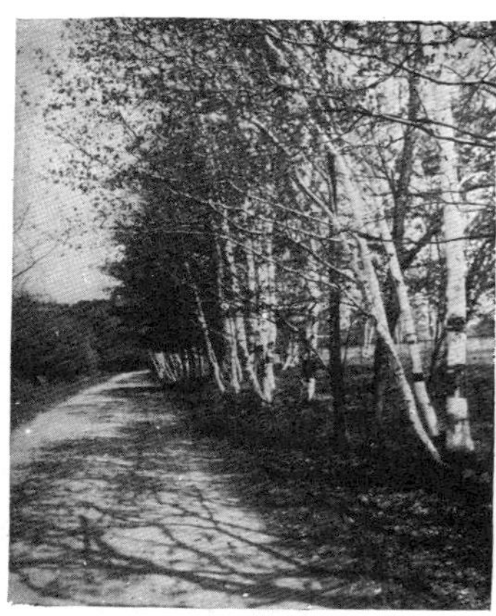

The Light Side of the Road C 238

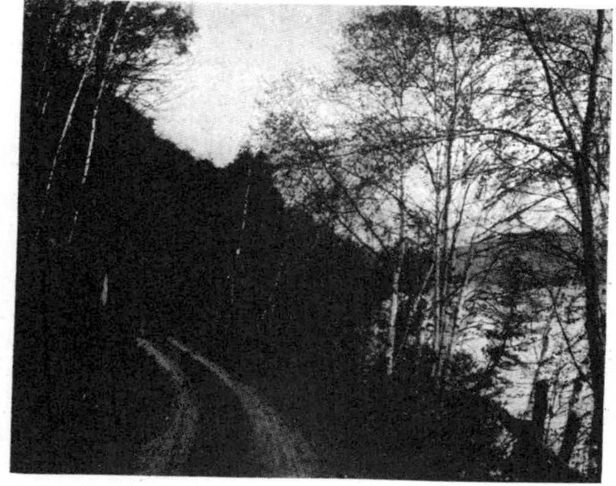

Lake Bank Birches C 1445

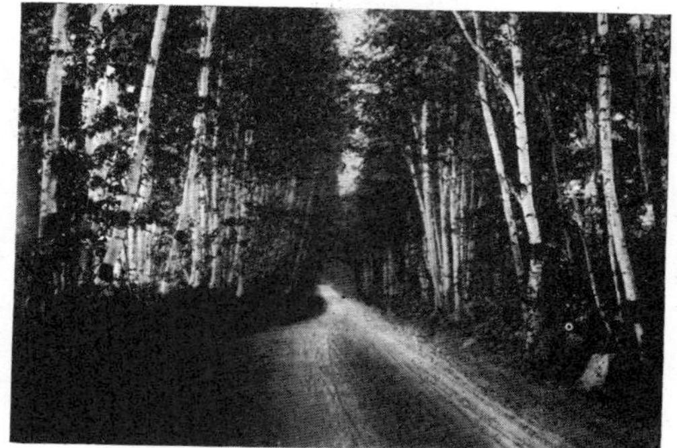

New Hampshire Birches A 371

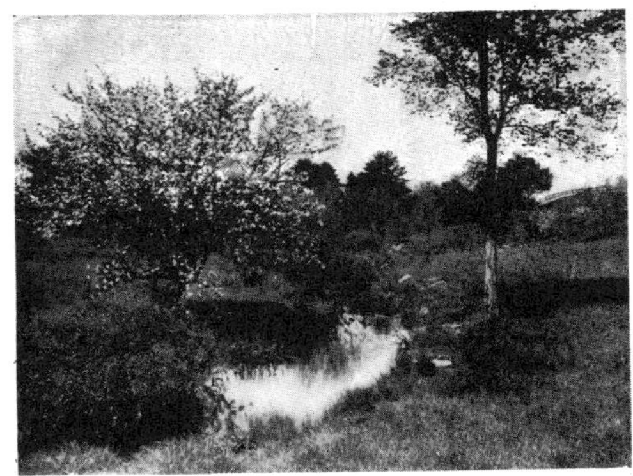

The Softness of Spring C, E 3623

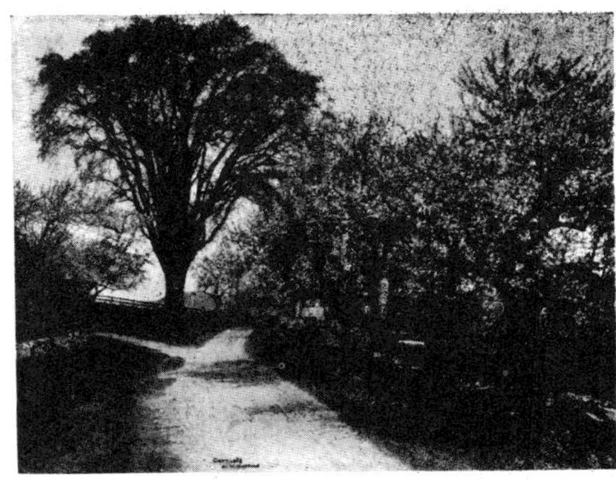

Windsor Blossoms C, E 3107

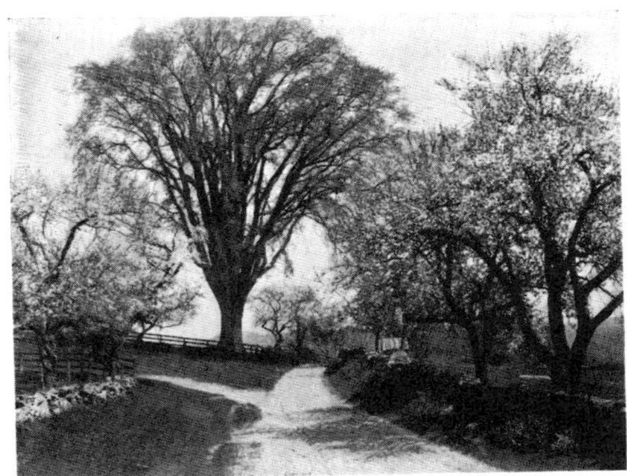

Springfield Blossoms C 3105

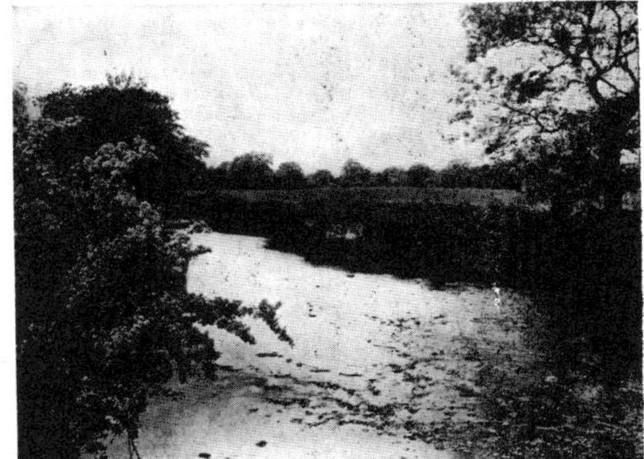

Meadow Beauty A, C and E 5653

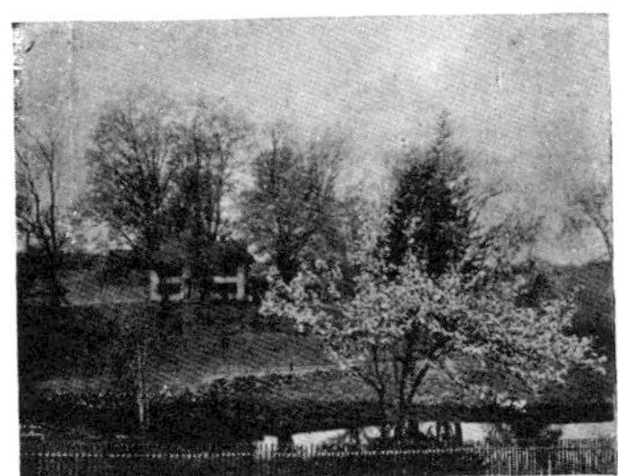

Nuttinghame Blossoms C 85

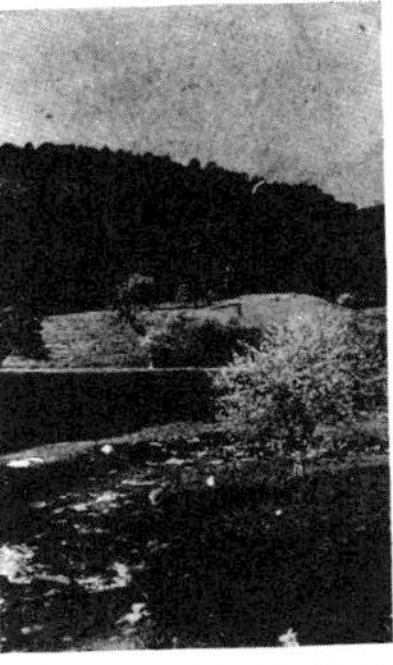

An Orchard in the Hills
S 148

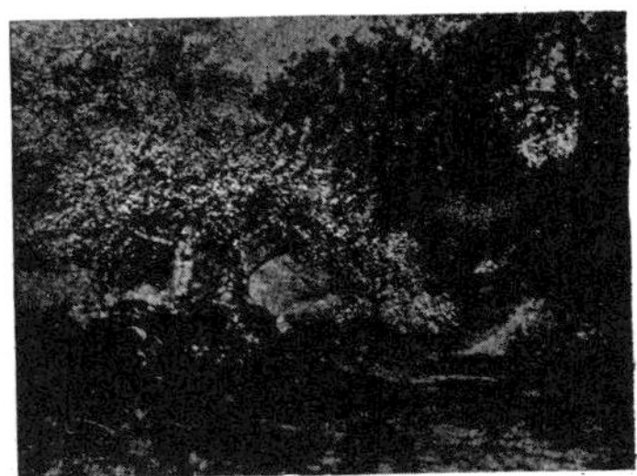

A Dell of Blossoms C 497

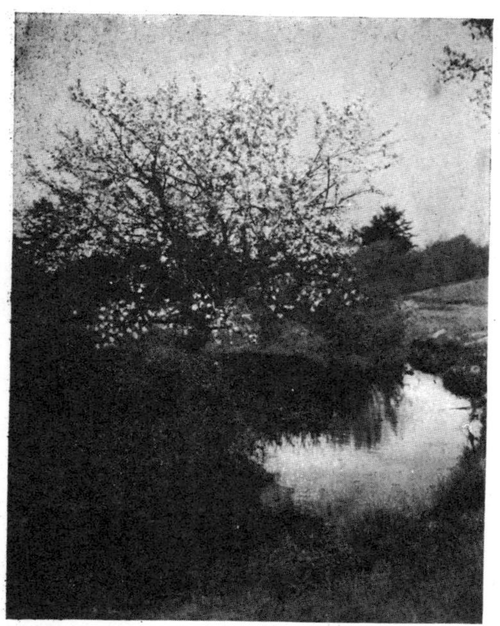

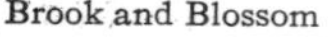

Brook and Blossom — Q and C 3617

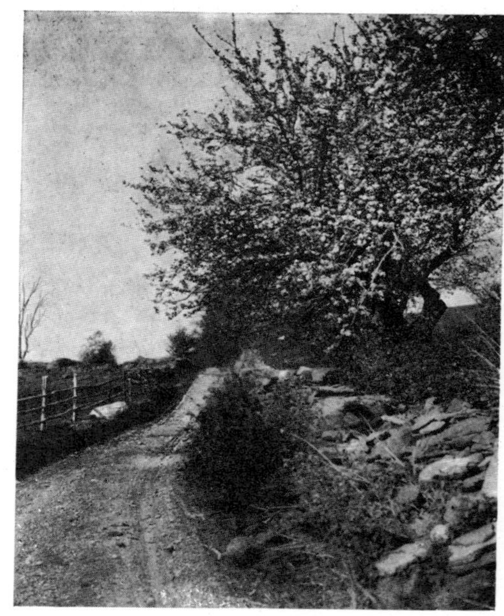

Catskill Blooms — C 3249

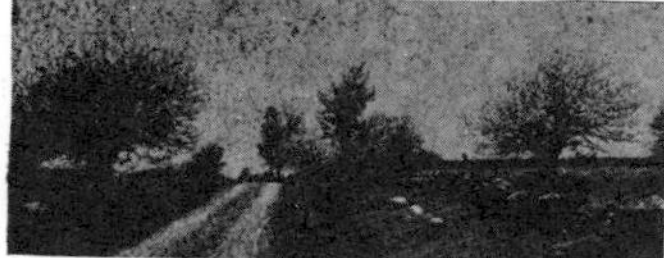

A New Hampshire Road — Q or C 659

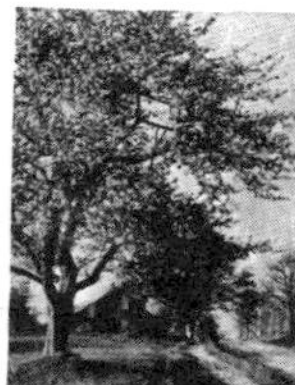

The Cottage Path
A 465

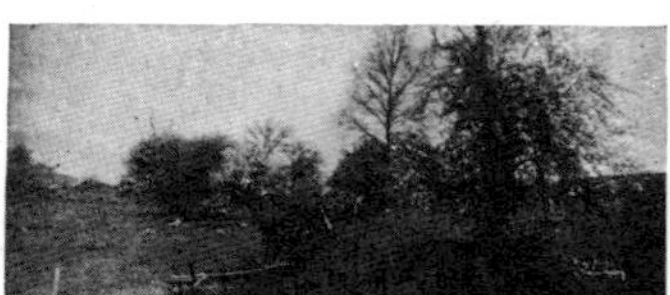

We are Young! — Q 189

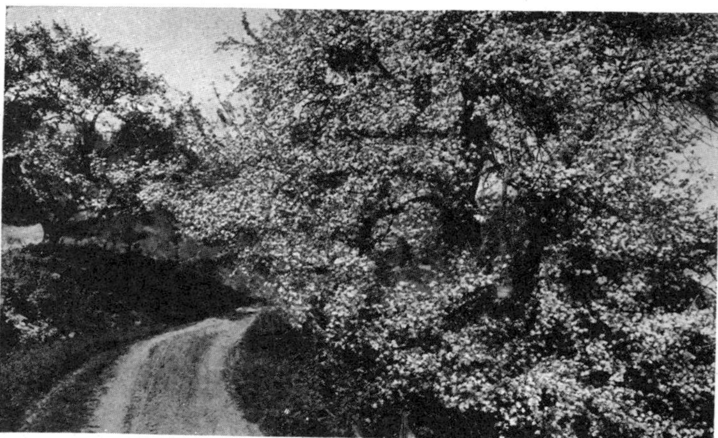

Billows of Blossom — C, E and G 27

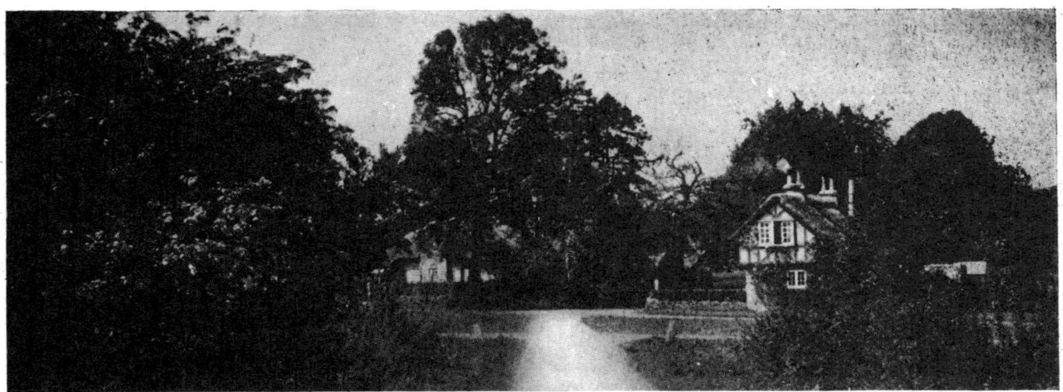

Five o'Clock O, P 5663 Wallace Nutting

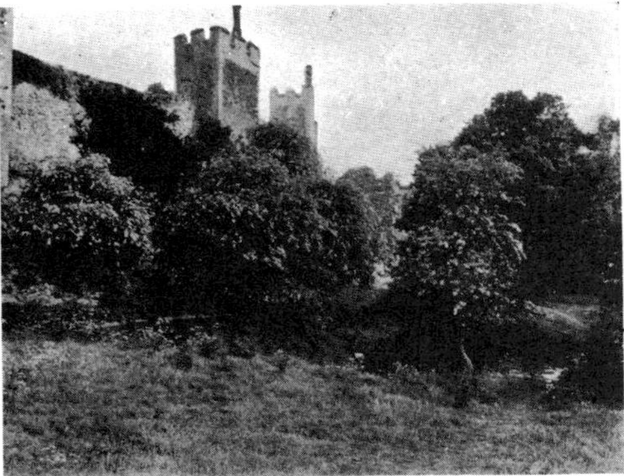

Old Framlingham A, C 5648

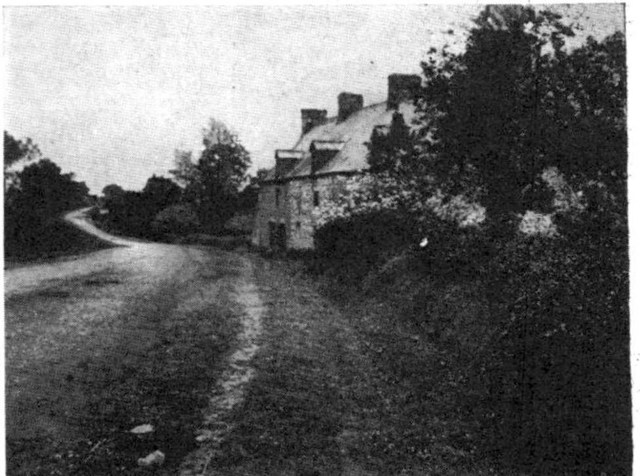

At Grandmother's A, C 4852

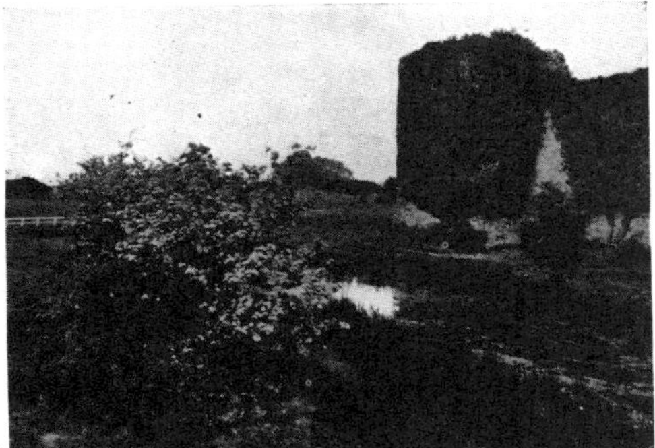

Blossom, Stream and Tower A, C 5784

BLOSSOMS

The eternal appropriateness of a blossom picture as a gift results in very great popularity for this class of subjects. They are all good for weddings. Some of them are especially titled for that purpose. Strange to say, blossoms sell at Christmas as well as at any time of the year. People wish to import the spring into the winter. For the sick, or for any place whatever in the home, even the dining-room, they find their place, and next to the figure subjects they are the most popular class of our pictures.

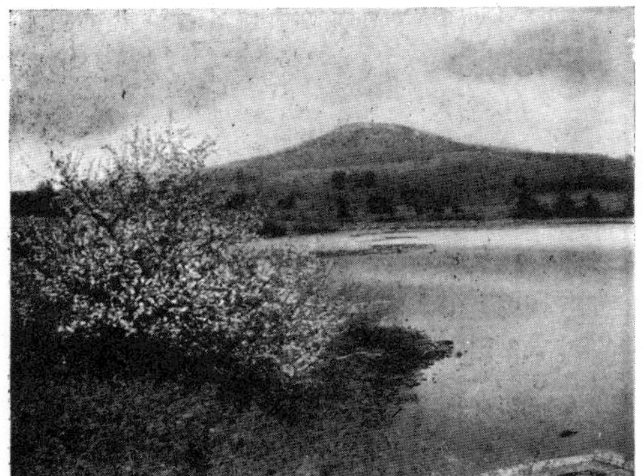
Blossoms by the Lake S, C 3235

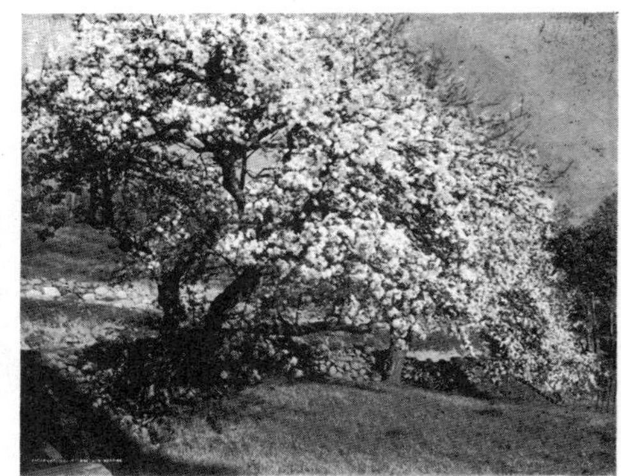
Apple Blossom by the Wall C and E 8021

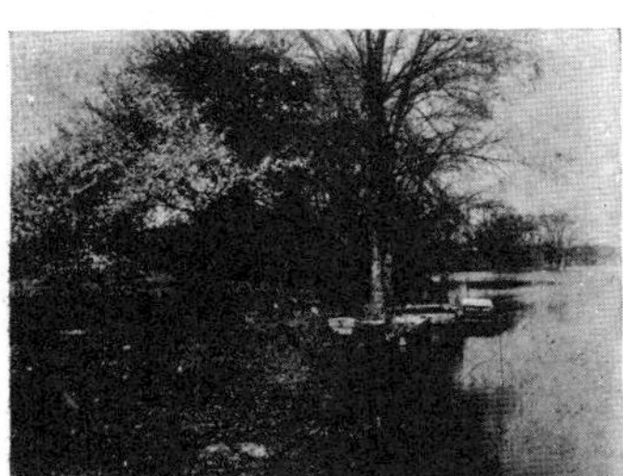
Blossom Point C 110

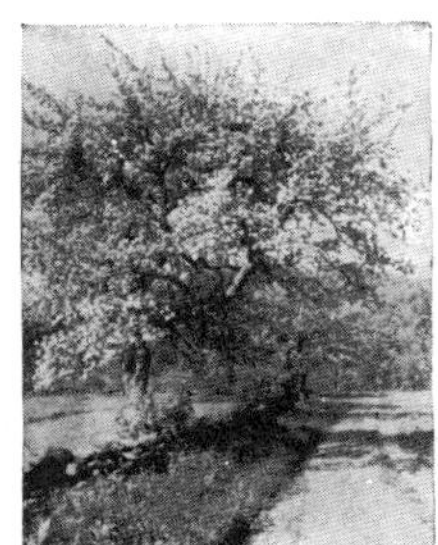
Queen of May E 38

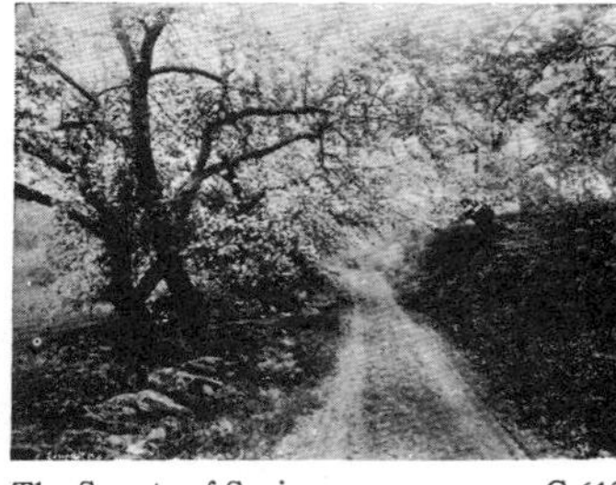
The Sweets of Spring C 612

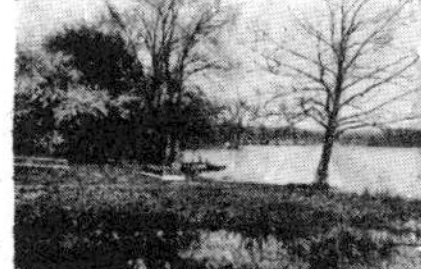
Blossom Landing
A, Q or C 436

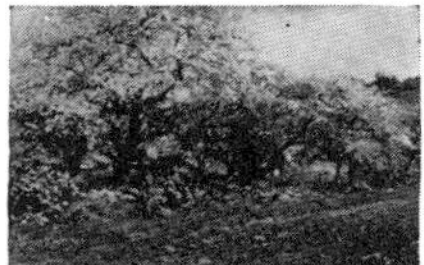
Along the Wall A 1447

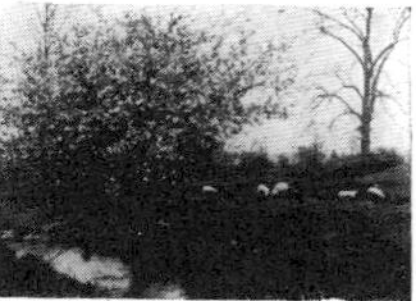
New Life A 409

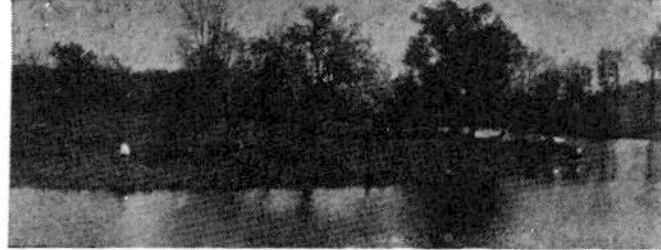
Heifers by the Stream Q 358

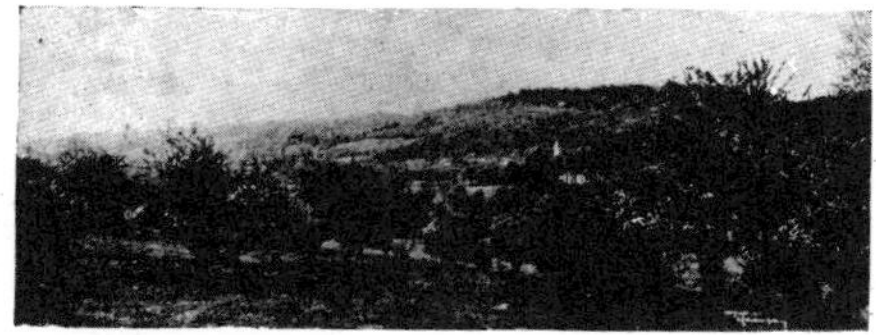
The Heart of New England O 248

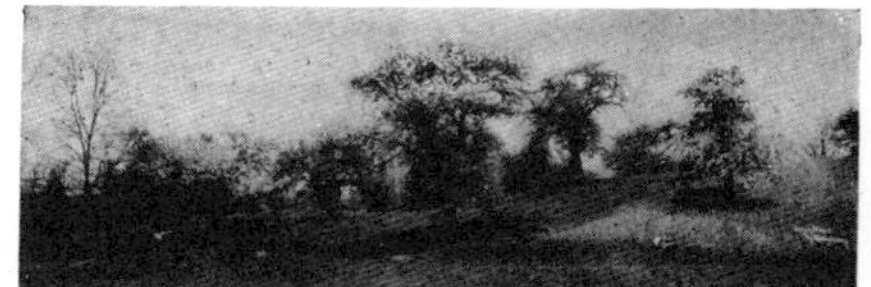
A Bridal Procession O 2679

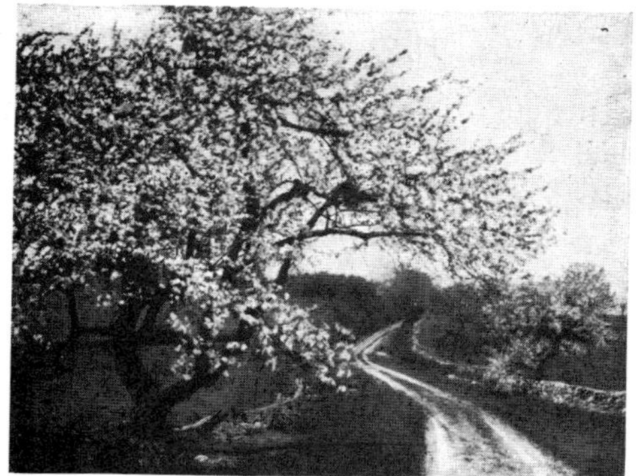
Rural Sweetness C and E 3301

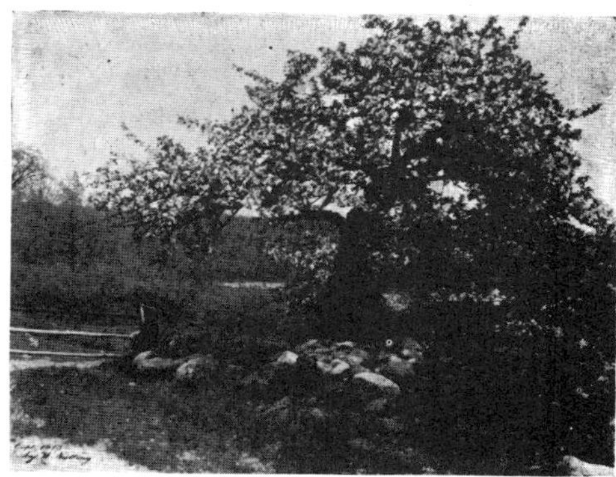
On Worcester Hills C 3429

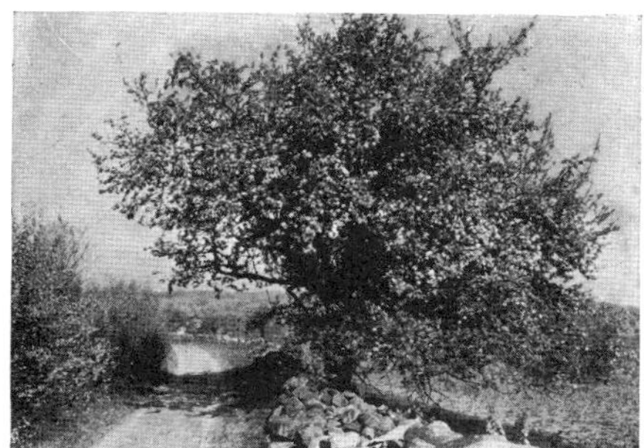
The Pride of the Lane C or E 177

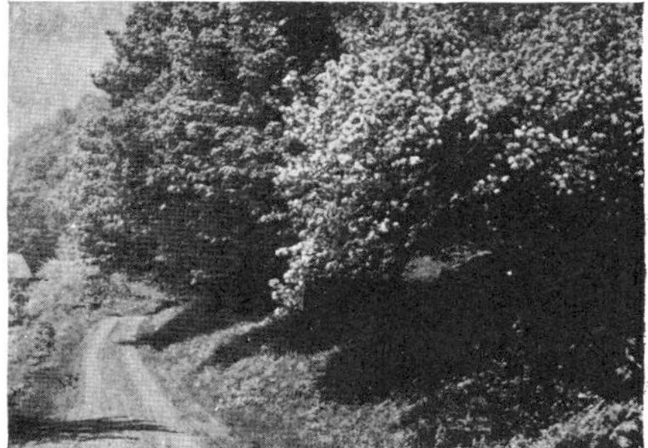
Down the Hill to School C 334

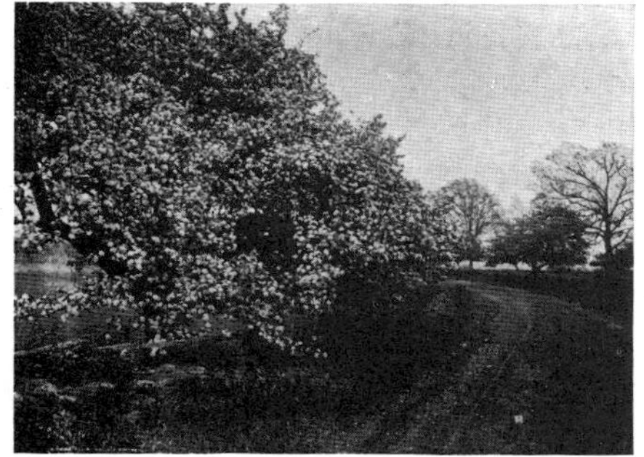
Petals in the Path E or P 137

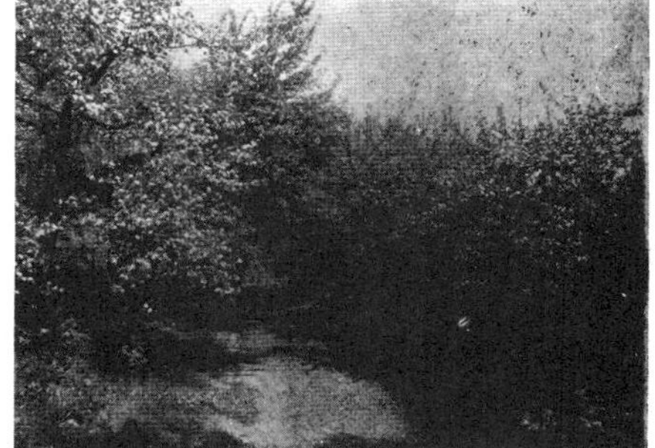
Through the Orchard Road E 109

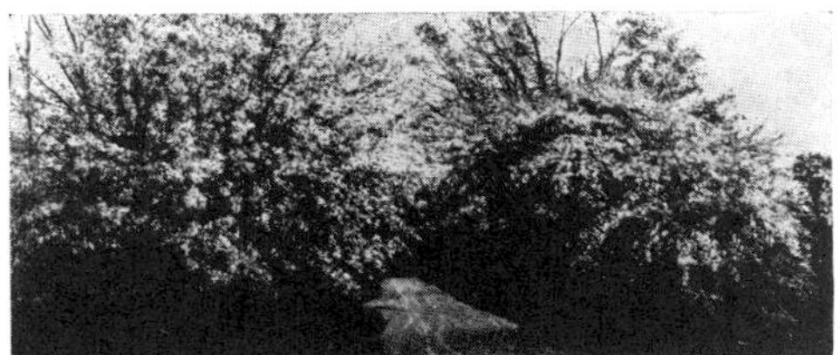
The Walpole Road Q and O 3265

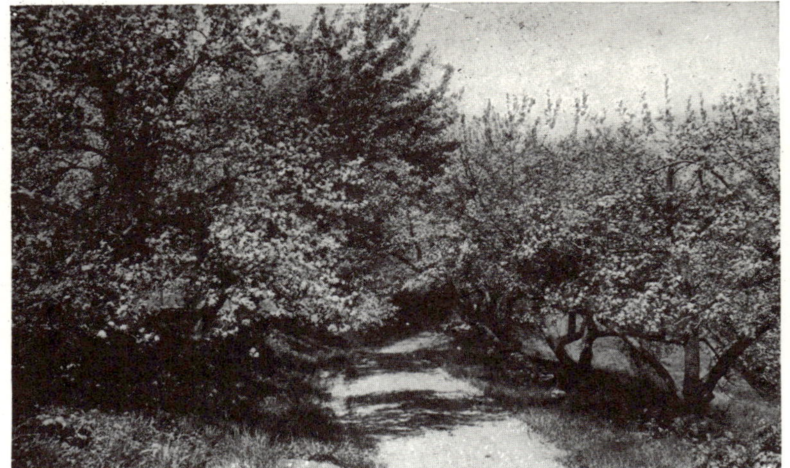

Blossom Bordered — C, E or J 58 — Wallace Nutting

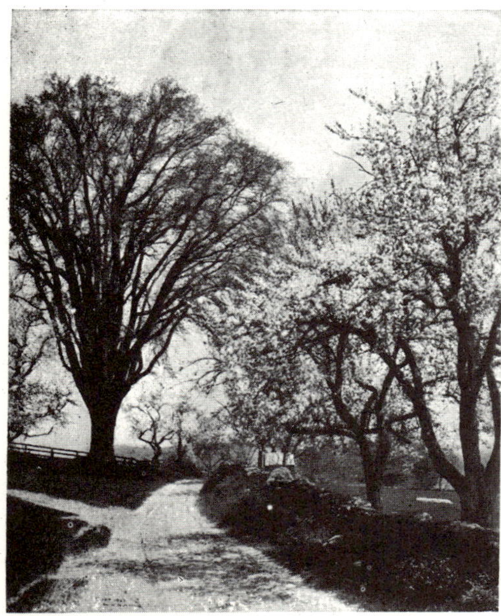

Vermont Blossoms — C 3101

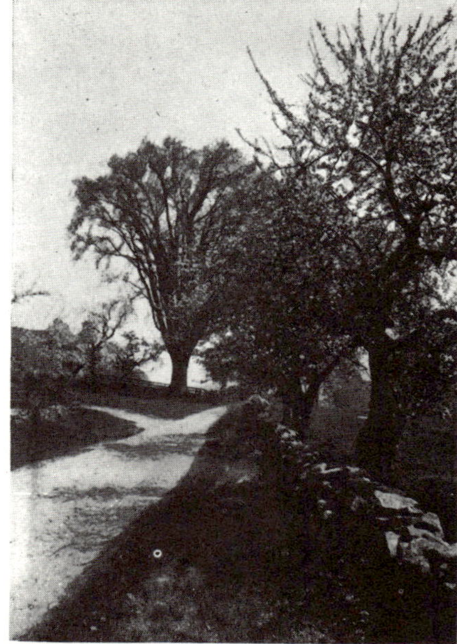

Fair May — A 3179 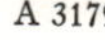

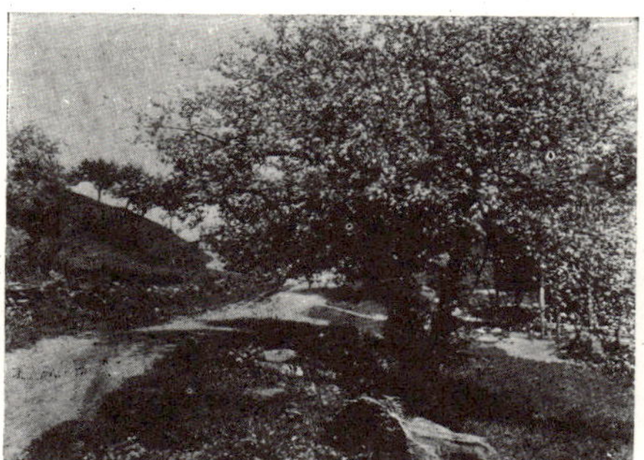

A Roadside Apple Tree — E 94

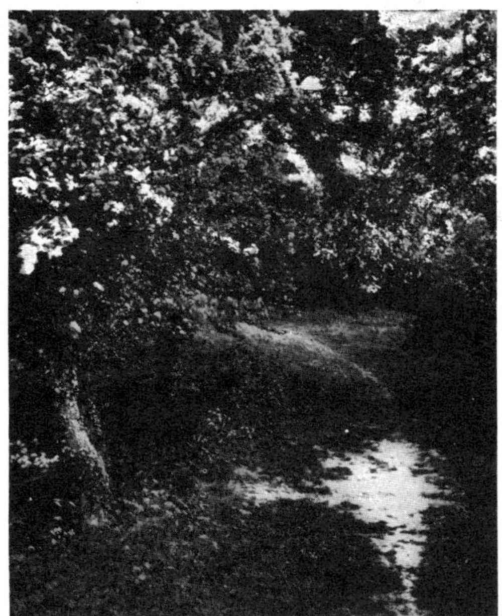

The Hawthorn Dell A, C 5627

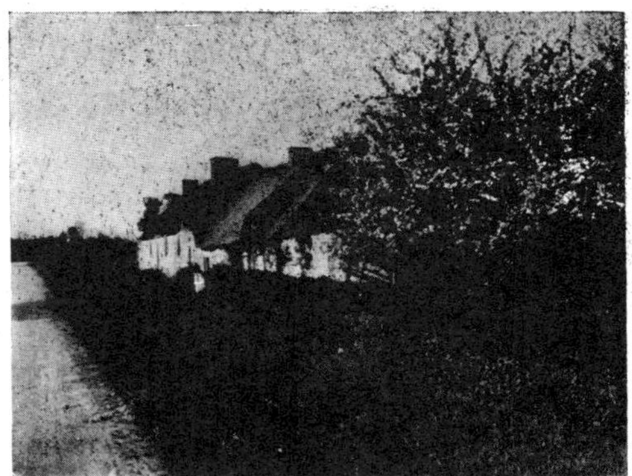

Thatched Dormers A, S, C 4826

While the apple blossom seems the favorite, we have lately learned that the English hawthorn, either white or pink, as it ornaments the hedge-row in May, is a close rival. On this page at the top appears a group of wild hawthorns blooming along a path. The second picture is a charming bit in Normandy, showing the long thatched dormers running to the peak of the roof. The bottom picture is a sweet and restful scene near Dort.

On the next page, "Orta in Blossom Time" is a view across one of the smaller Italian lakes, and is proving very attractive. Of course, "Honeymoon Drive" still remains a favorite. Probably two-thirds of all the blossoms shown are in attractive request almost every day.

The handsomest of the very large blossoms is the forty-inch picture "Flowering Time," although "The Beauty of the Uplands" is a rival.

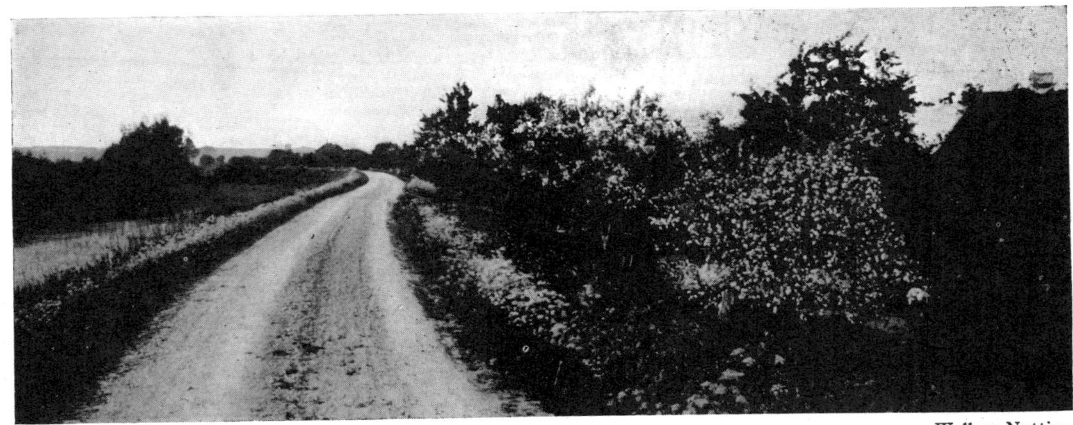

Dykeside Blossoms A, Q 5083 Wallace Nutting

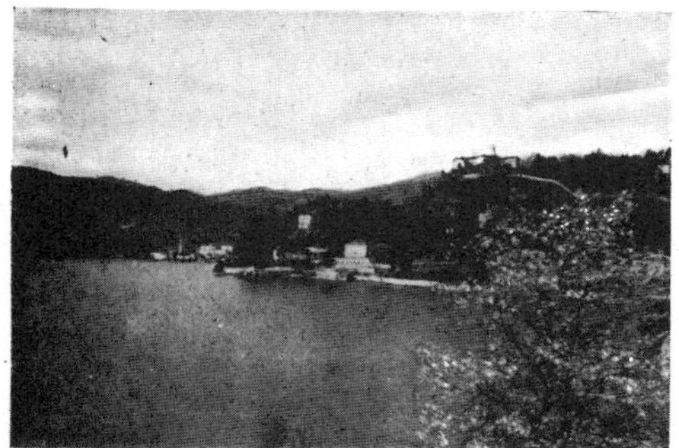

Orta in Blossom Time A and S 4460

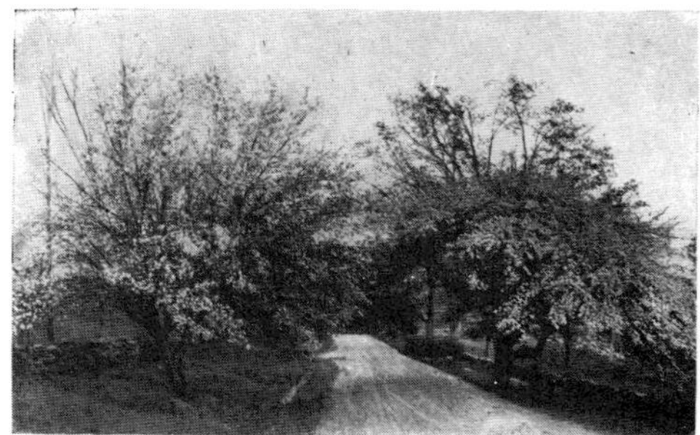

A Keene Road S and P 3247

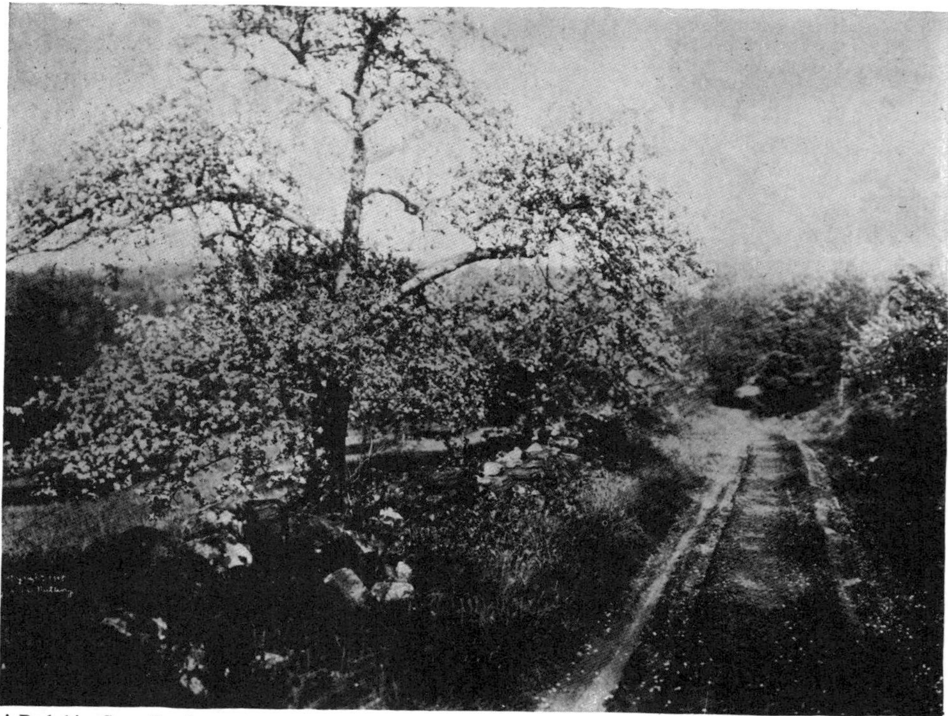

A Berkshire Cross Road C 331 Wallace Nutting

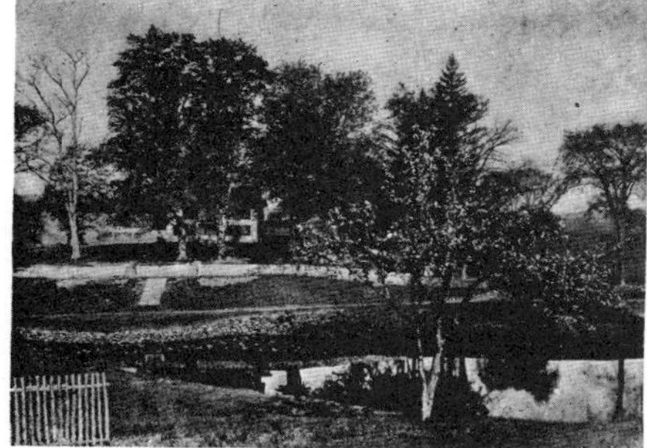

The Old Homestead C or E 1130

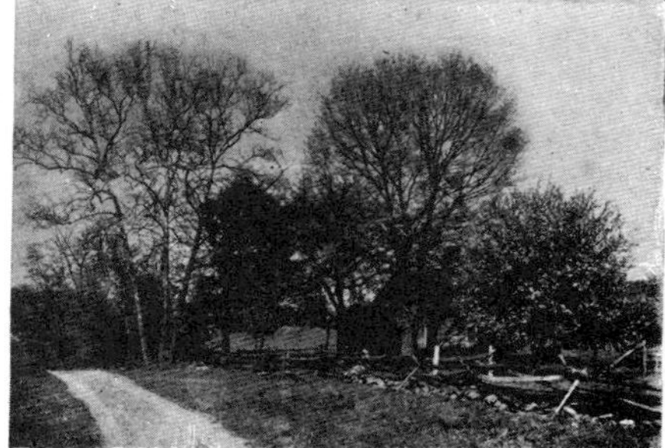

Where Grandma was Wed C or E 244

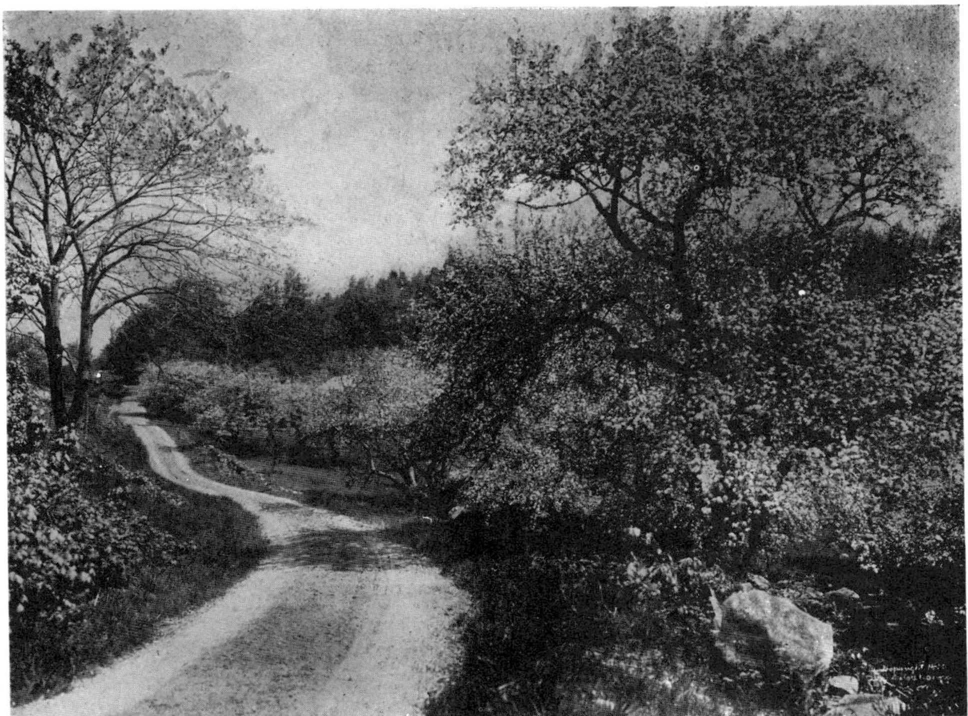

Decked as a Bride C, E or J 73 Wallace Nutting

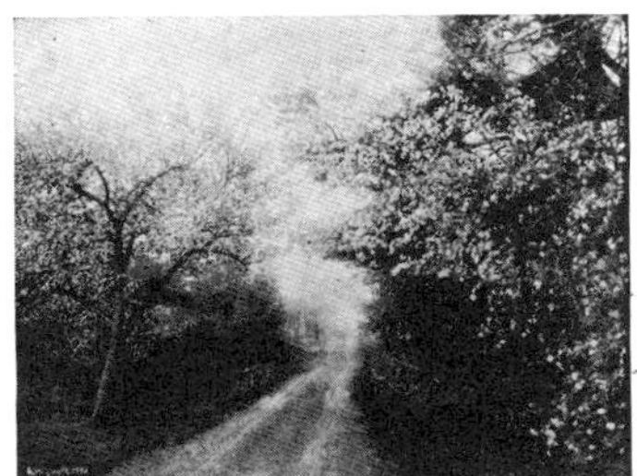

Blossoms that Meet A or C 895

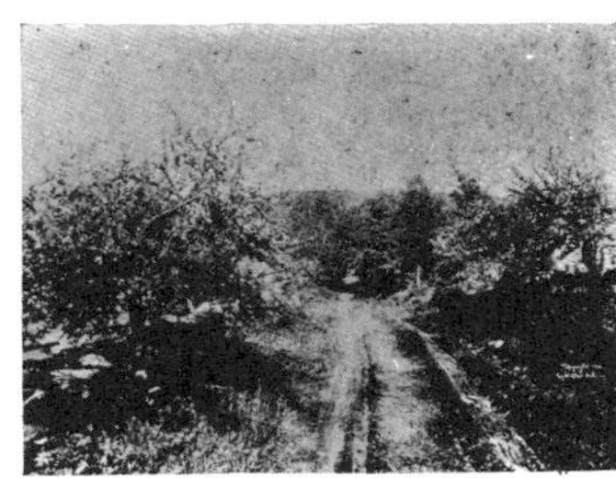

New England Uplands Q or C 332

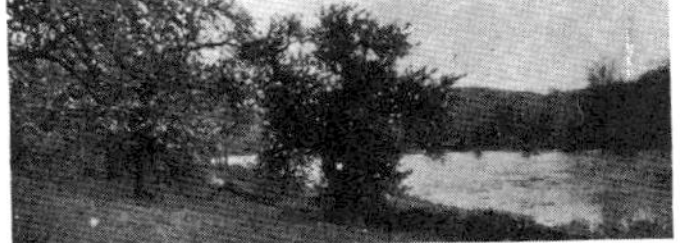

Housatonic Blossoms Q 980

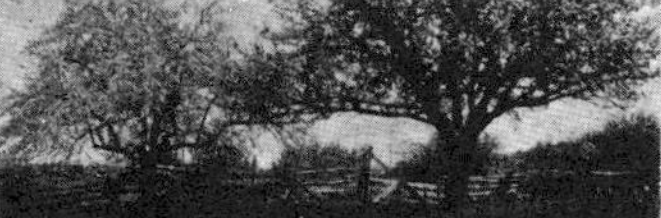

A Bee's Paradise 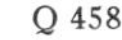 Q 458

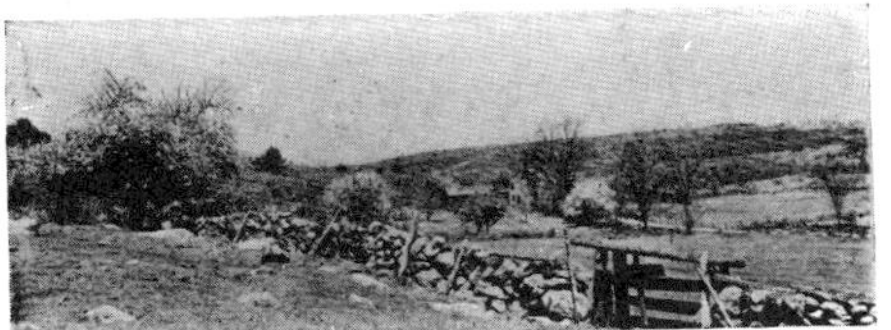

Across the Farm O 2624

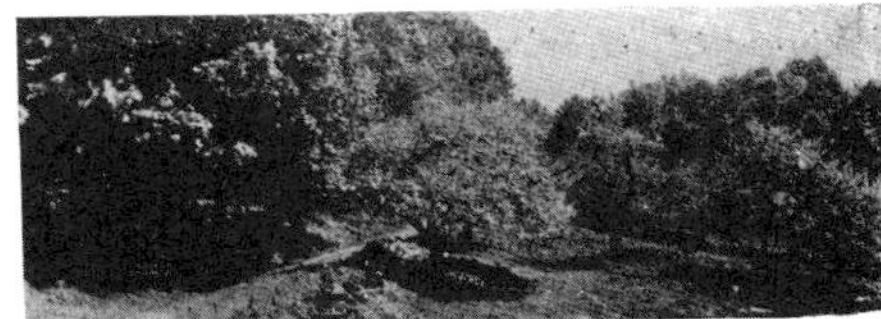

Above the Orchard Q 149

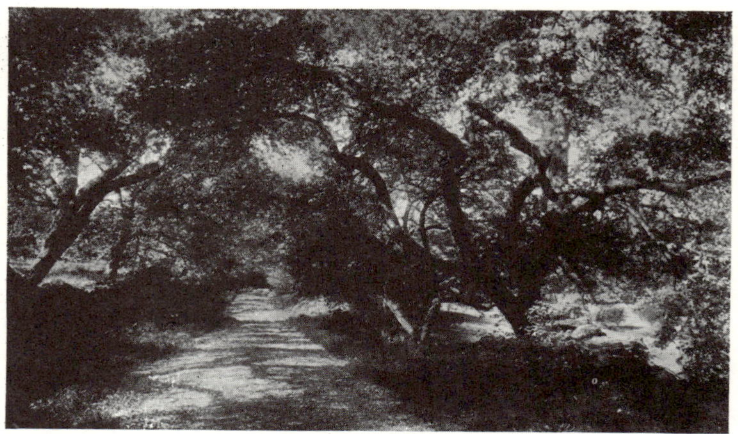

Honeymoon Drive A, C, E, F, G or H 170 Wallace Nutting

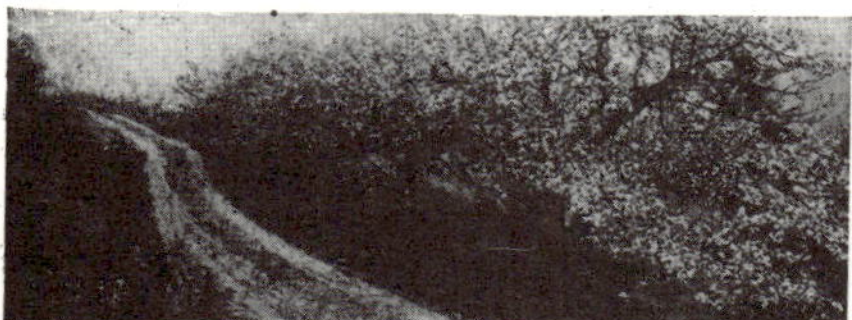

Nearing the Crest Q or S 432

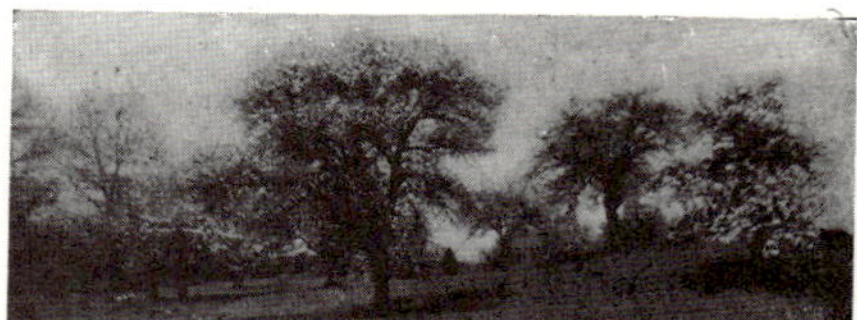

An English May Q 2694

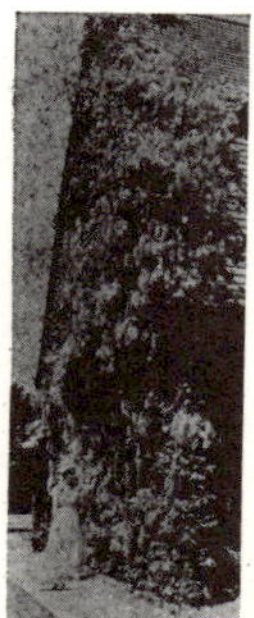

Wistaria Gables
Q 2161

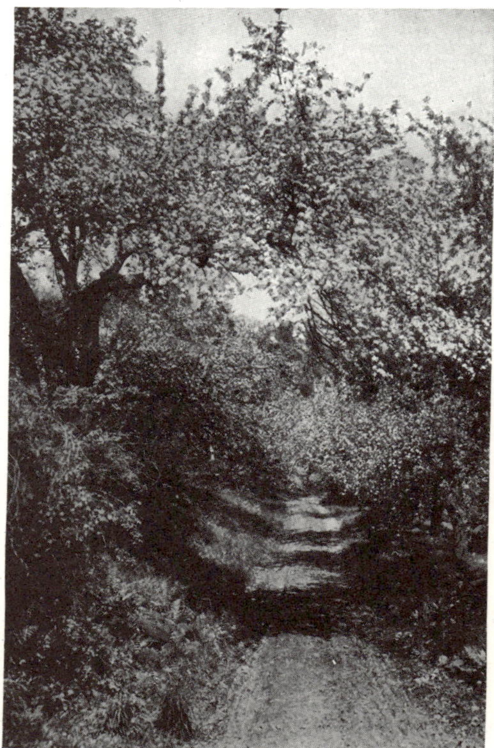

A Tunnel of Bloom C, E or J 112 Wallace Nutting

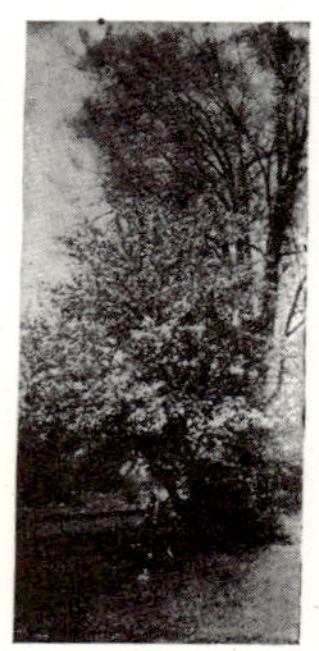

May by the Wayside
Q 489

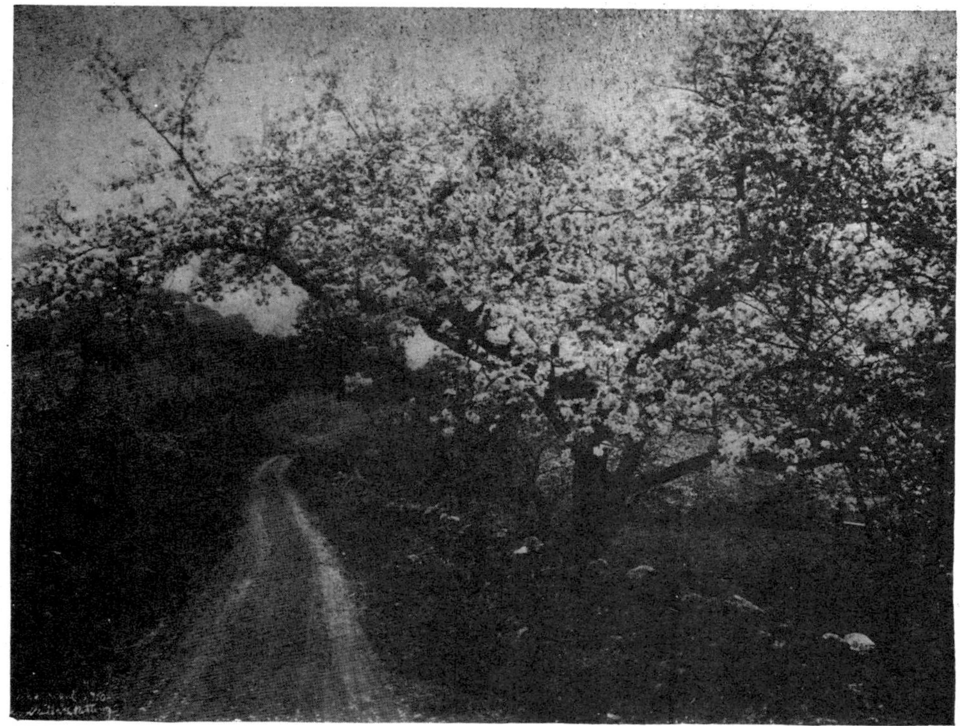

A Canopied Road | A, C, E, F or J 506 | Wallace Nutting

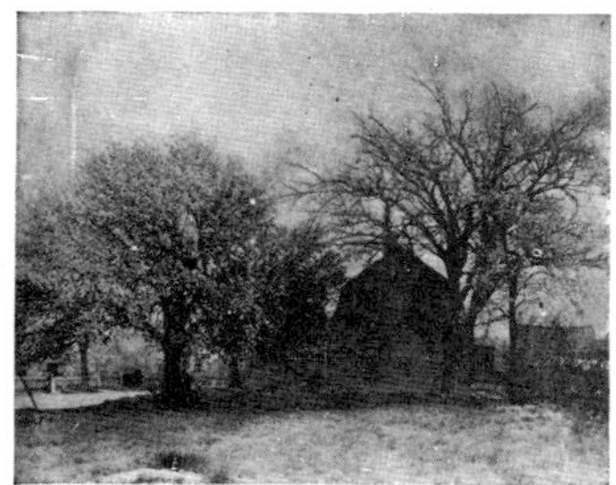

Spring Fashions | Q, S, or C 270

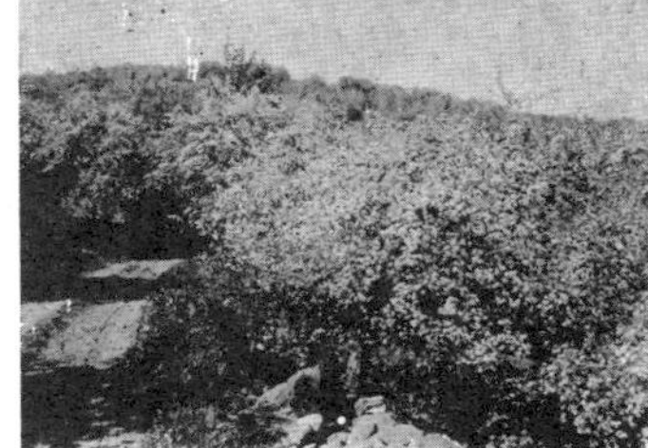

Over the Treetops | C 879

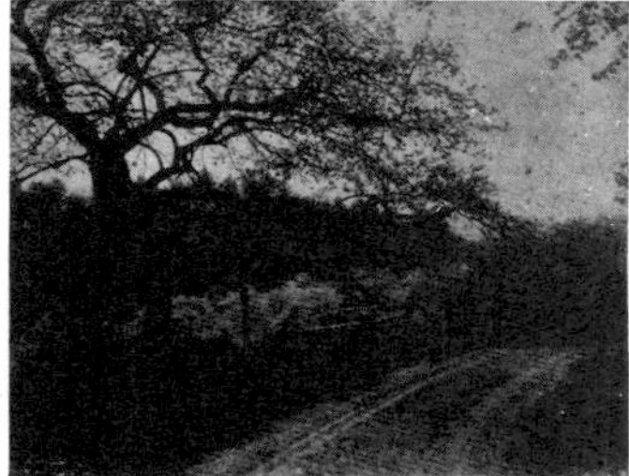

Bowered Barway | C 470

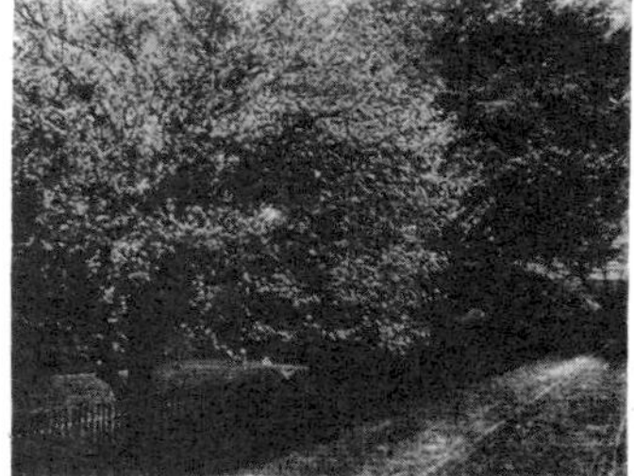

The Wealth of May | C 2601

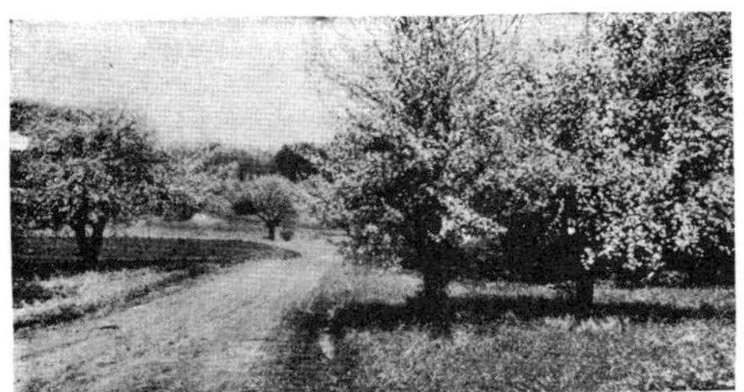

America Superba P 155

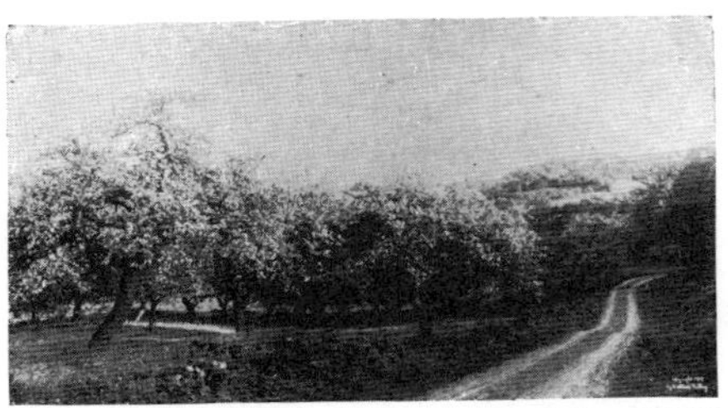

Flowering Time S, P or W 158

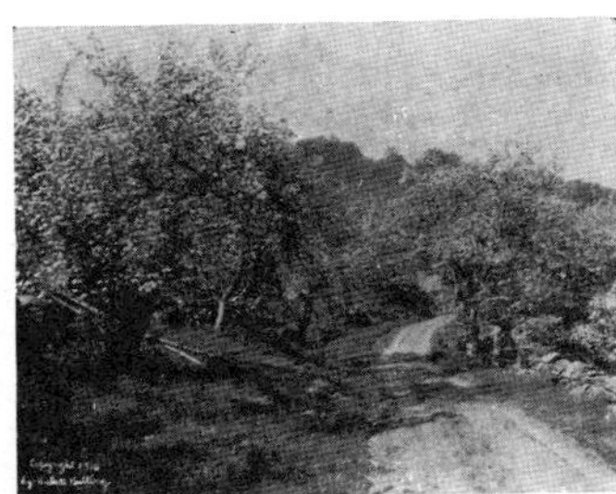

Bloom and Shadow C 487

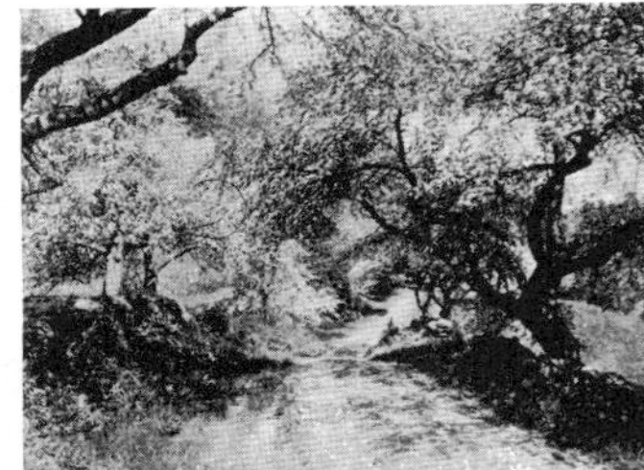

Lined with Petals C 597

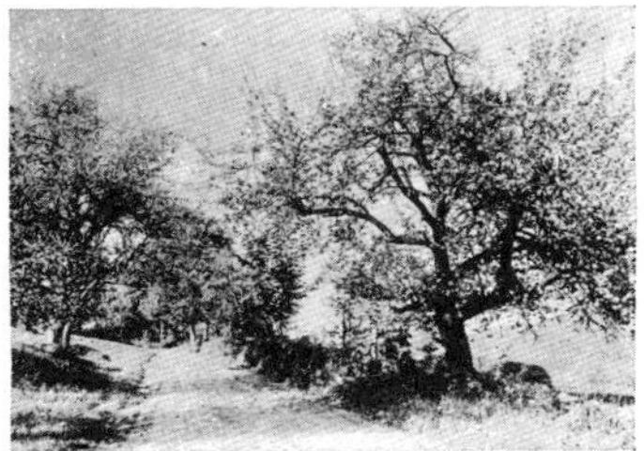

Blossom Drive Q or C 649

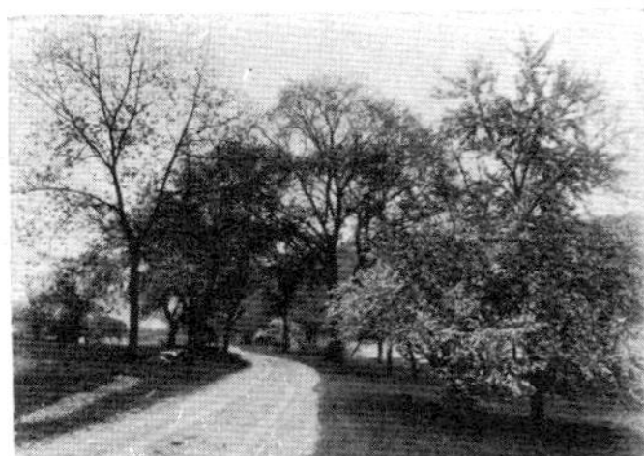

A May Countryside S and P 647

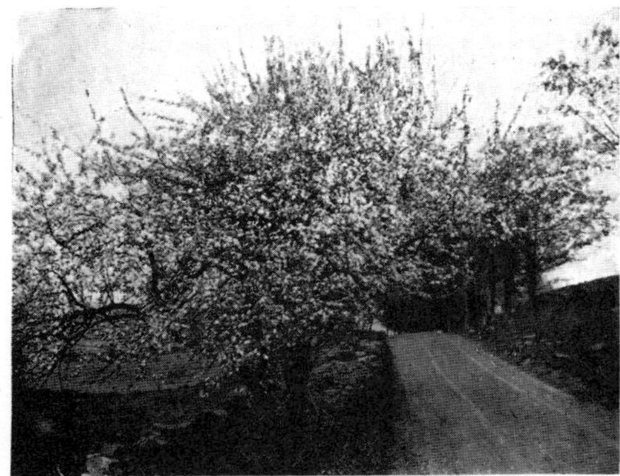

A Stamford Roadside A, C 3231

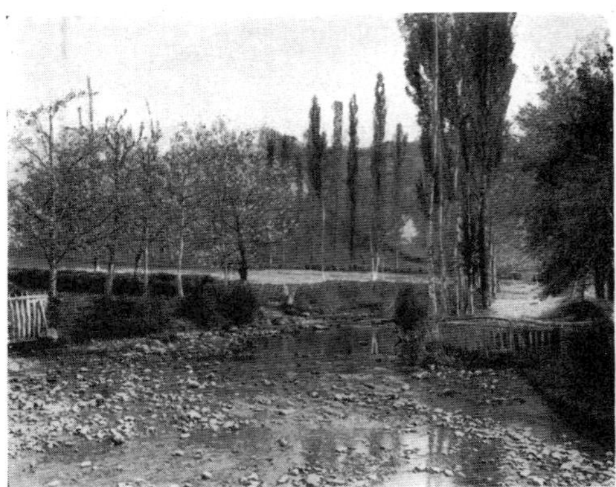

A Valley in the Pyrenees A, C 4591

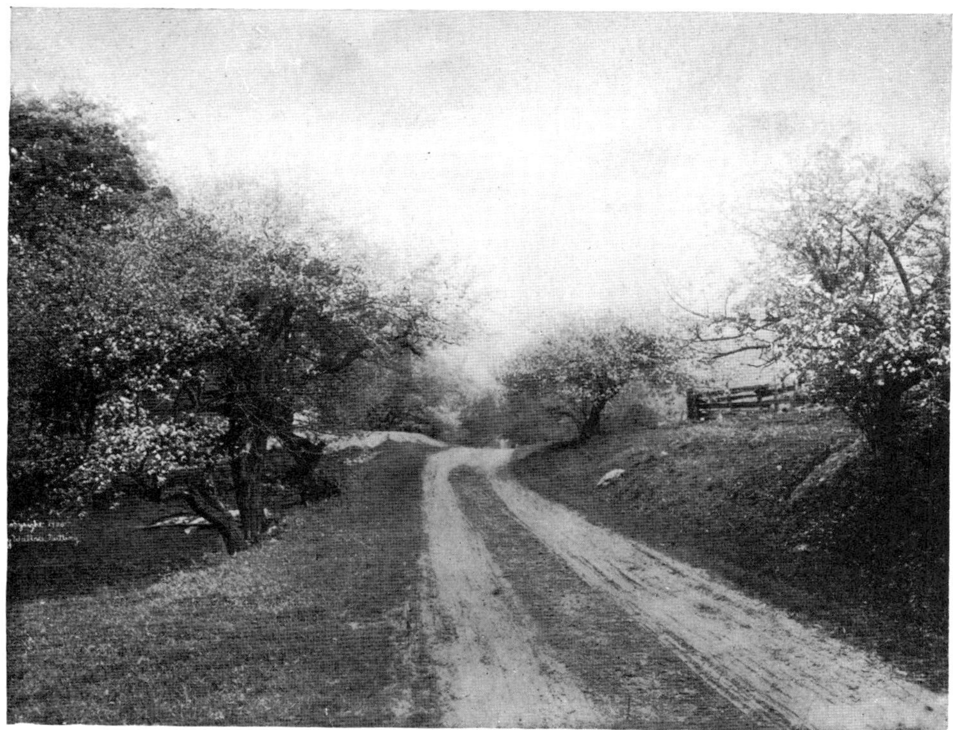

Happy Valley Road Q or C 205 Wallace Nutting

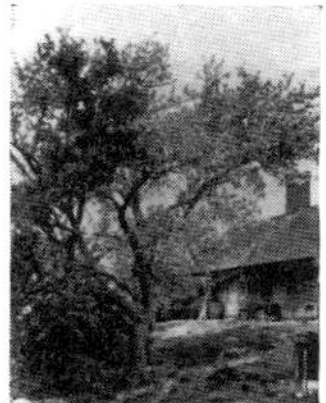

An Old Back Door
A 491

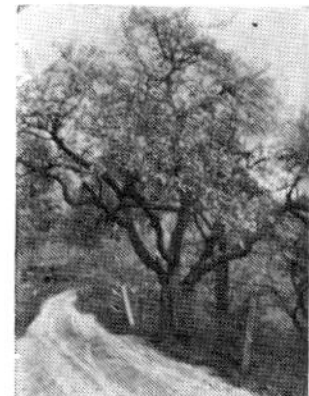

Height of Spring
A 445

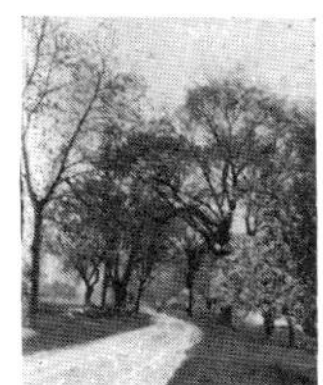

A Fragrant Highway
A 459

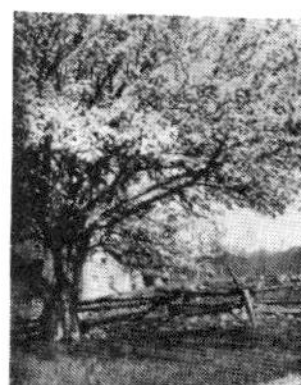

Blossom Cottage
A 2657

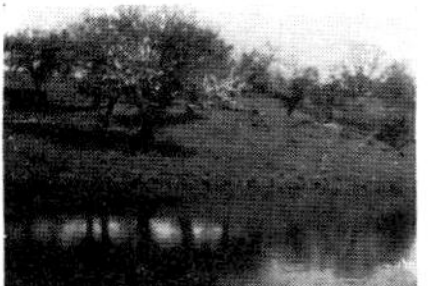

Petals Above and Below
A 164

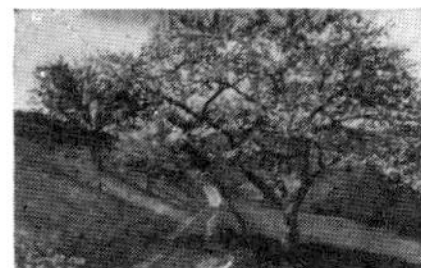

On Either Hand
A 2663

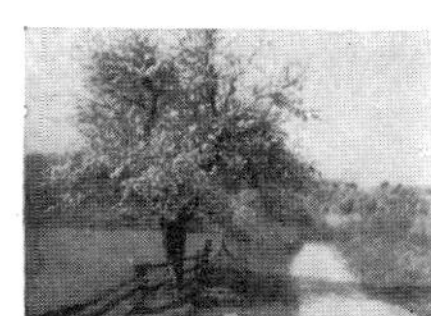

The Shadow of the Blossoms
C 165

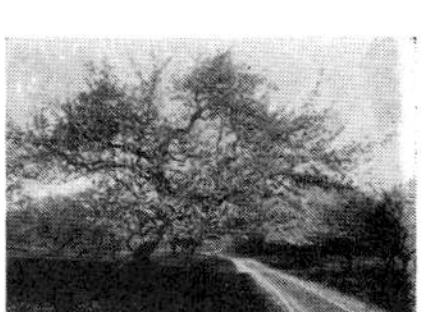

Over the Road
C 427

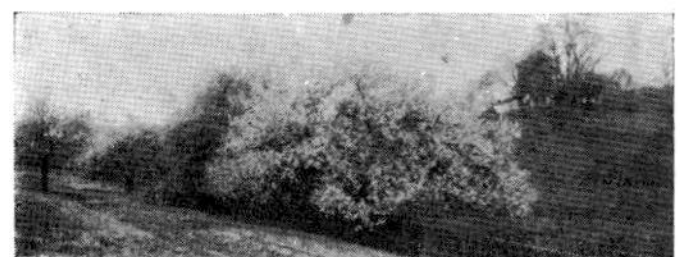

Blossom Valley Q 131

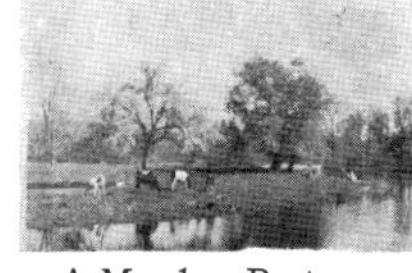

A Meadow Pasture
A 347

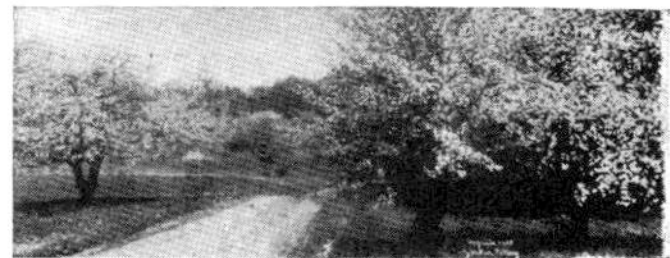

Whitsunday Q 221

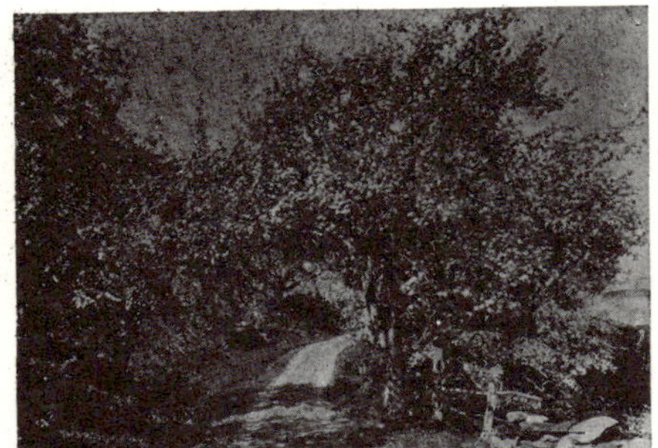

At the Barway E 33

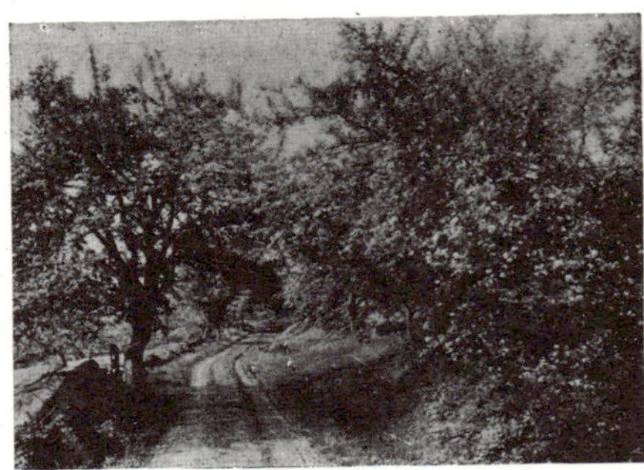

Spring in the Berkshires E 34

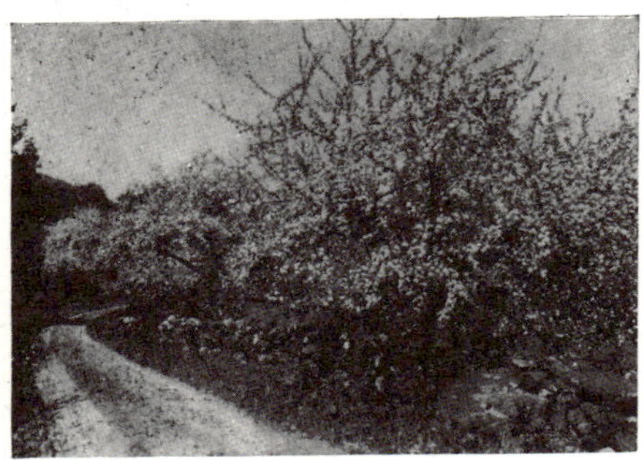

Curve, Shadow and Bloom E 64

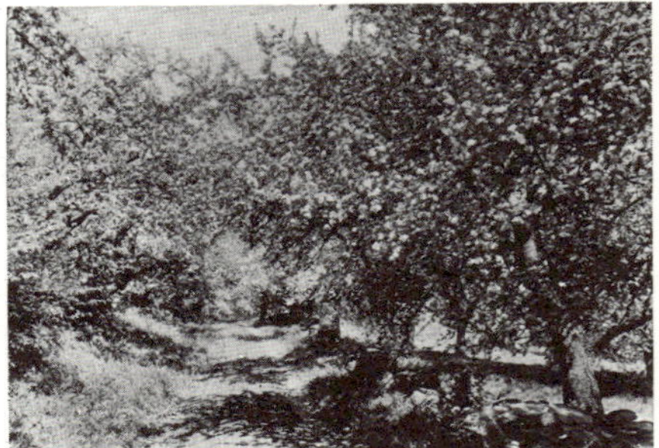

The Way of the Blessed E 105

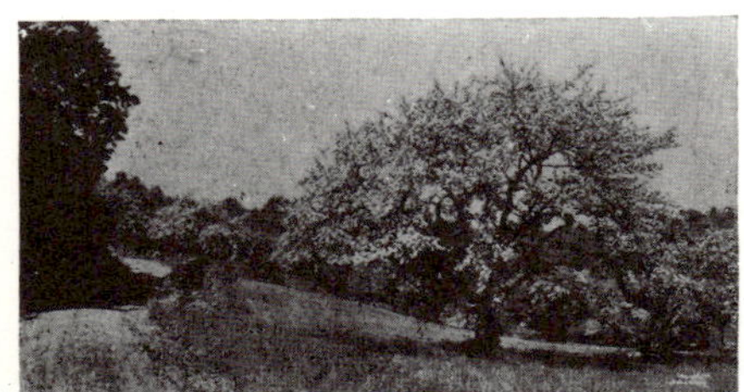

A Berkshire Bend P 87

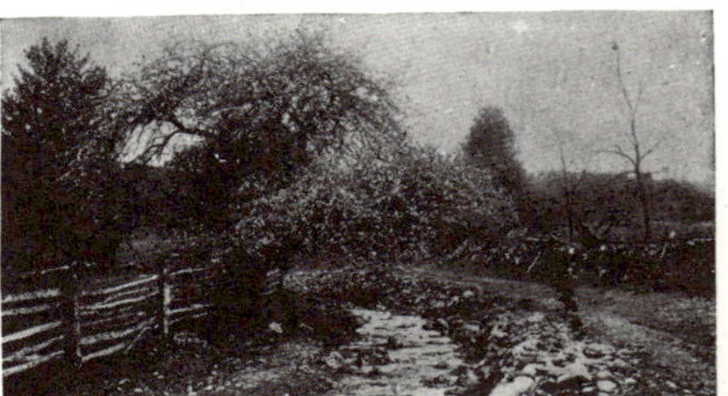

A Berkshire Brook Q, C or P 247

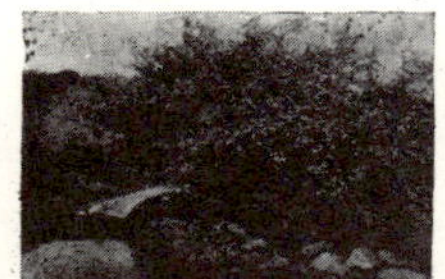

The Orchard Bend
A 457

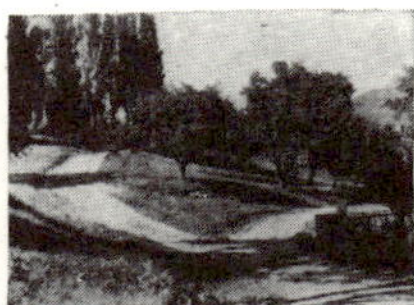

The Cross Roads in May
A 78

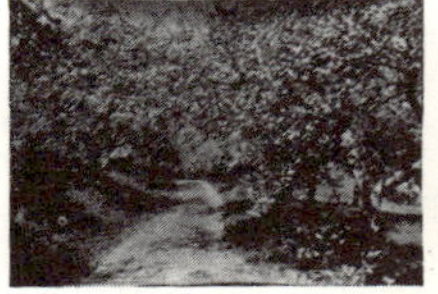

A Pink Bower
A 461

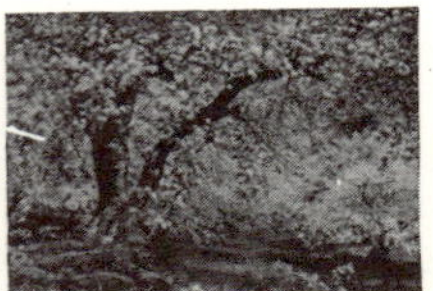

The Heart of the Orchard
A 456

EDUCATION

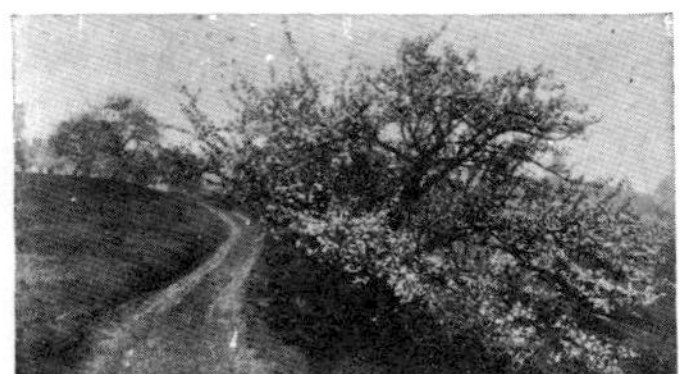
From the Foot of the Hill
S 428

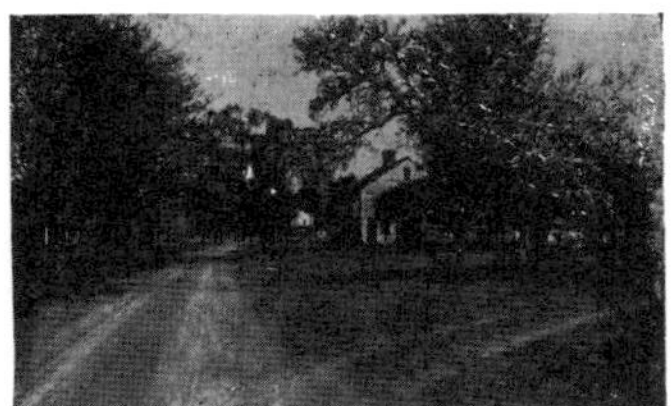
A Memory of Childhood
A or C 160

Taste in pictures develops slowly in most minds. At first the gaudy, the elaborately ornate, at last the delicate touches win. We make these pictures partly to satisfy our own feeling, and partly in the effort to lead the public taste. These colors are in some cases a trifle overdone, and in other cases are what we consider just right. Any blossom whether made by God or man will, if left long in the sun, tone down a little. If you ask, why so many roads, we reply that all pictures derive enhanced attraction from a human relation. There is more sentiment and charm in combining a path or a road with a blossom than in giving either alone. We are prepared to supply so many different styles that the taste of the customer is sure to be satisfied. Please do not order pictures in any other sizes than those listed. If the subjects were appropriate for greater enlargement they would be so listed. Satisfaction will not be guaranteed on orders of enlargements and we shall be obliged to charge for the plate.

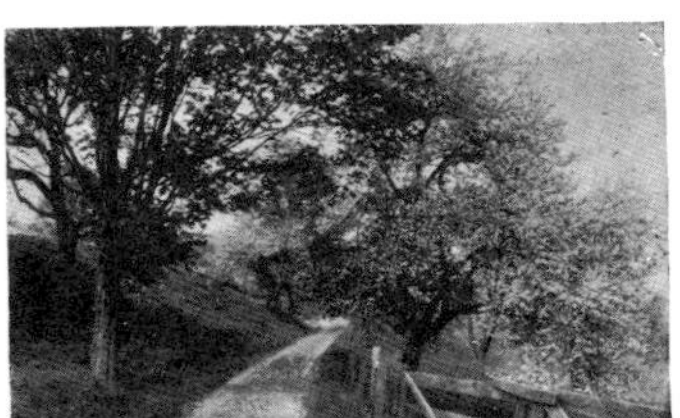
A Maple-Apple Arch
S 972

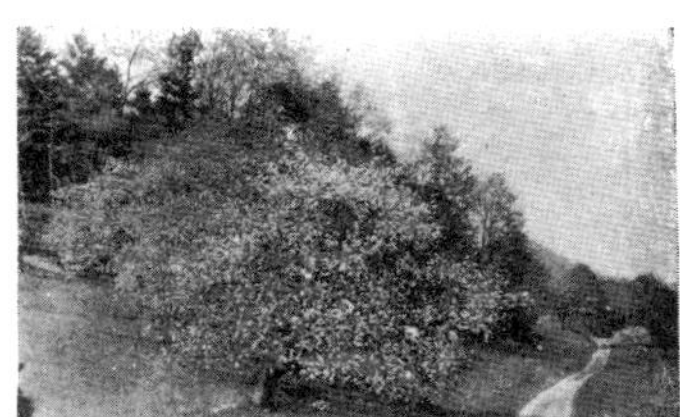
"Over the Hills and Far Away."
S 724

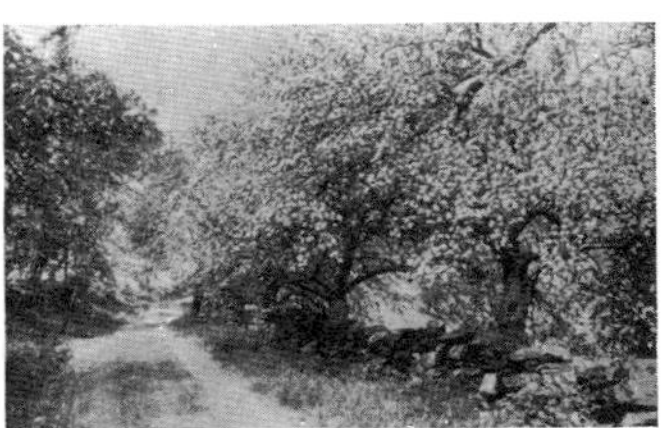
Disappearing in Blossoms
S 1111

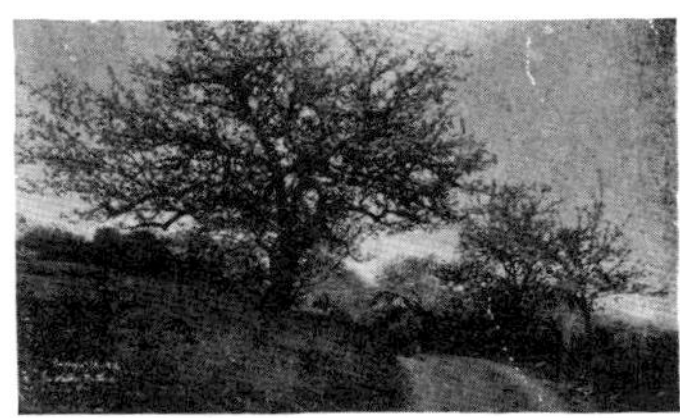
Over the Crest
Q, S or C 639

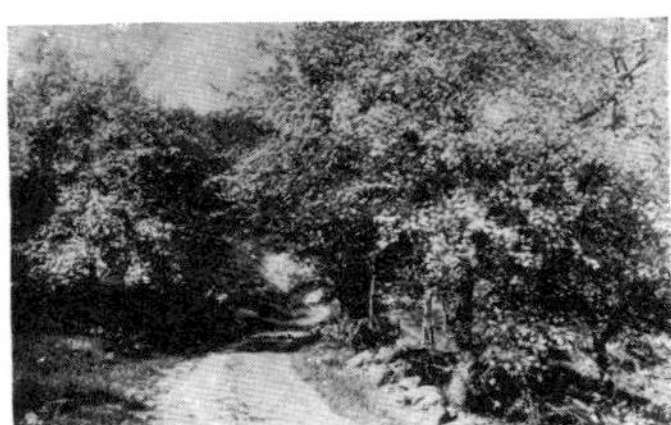
A Double Border
S 1110

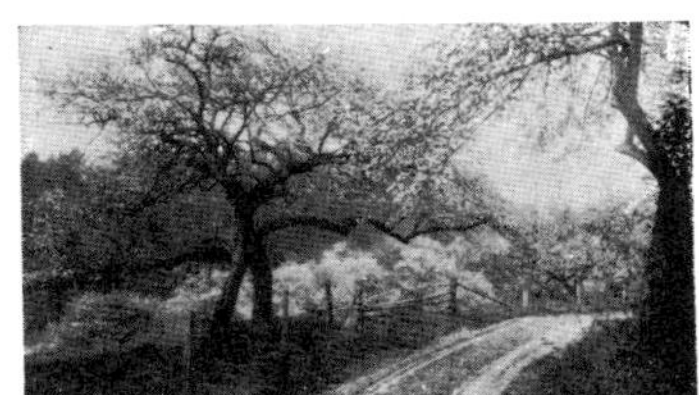
The Turn by the Bars
S 928

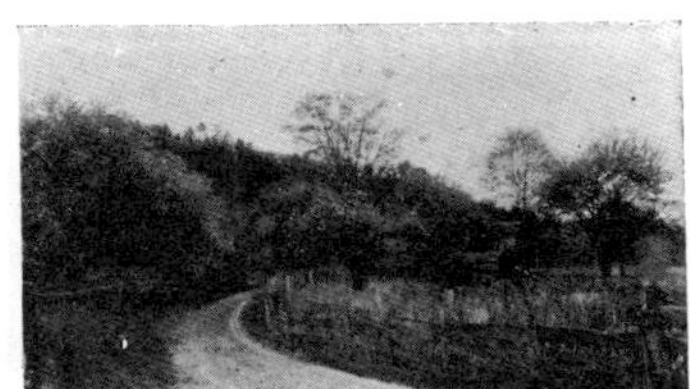
The Ancestral Cottage
S 817

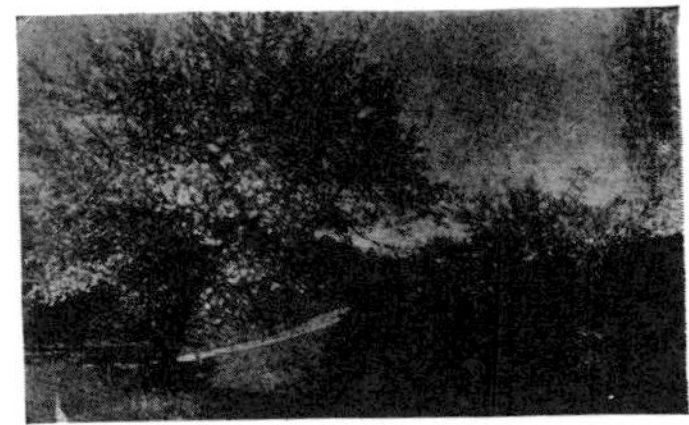
Where Bees are Humming
S 414

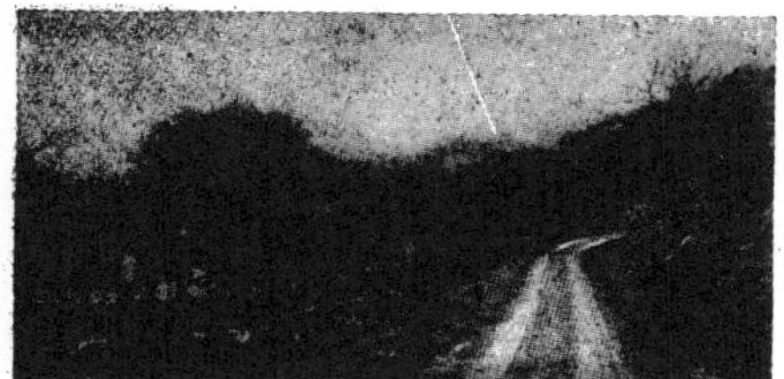
Berkshire Curves S or P 169

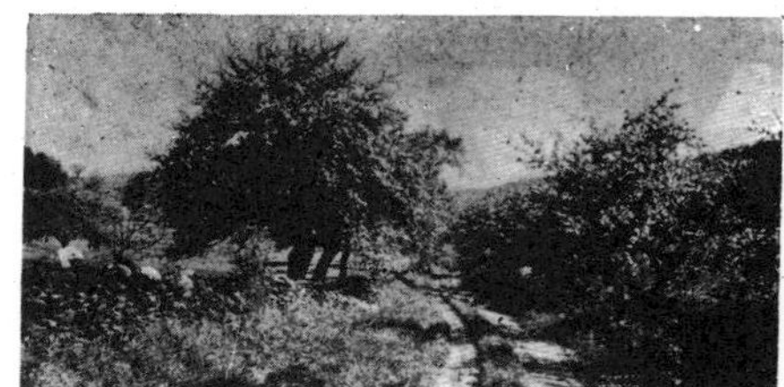
The Beauty of the Uplands S, P, W 57

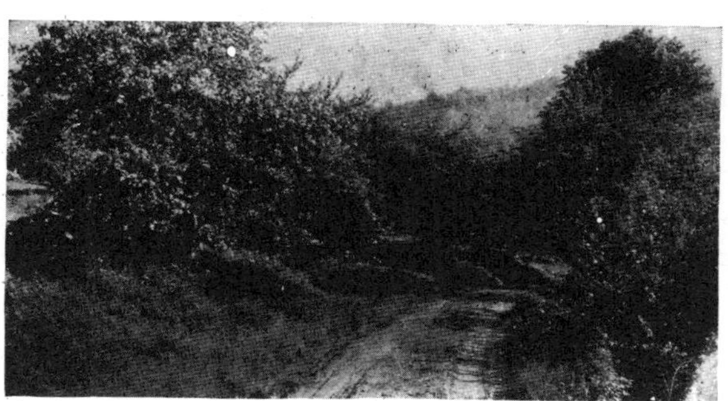
Highland Blossoms S, P, W 49

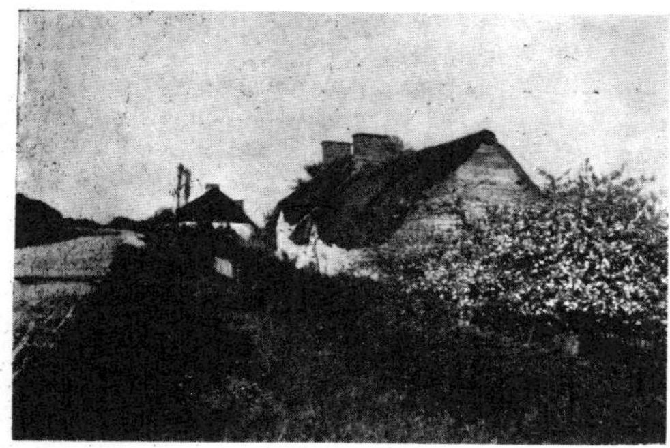
Mellow May A, S 4841

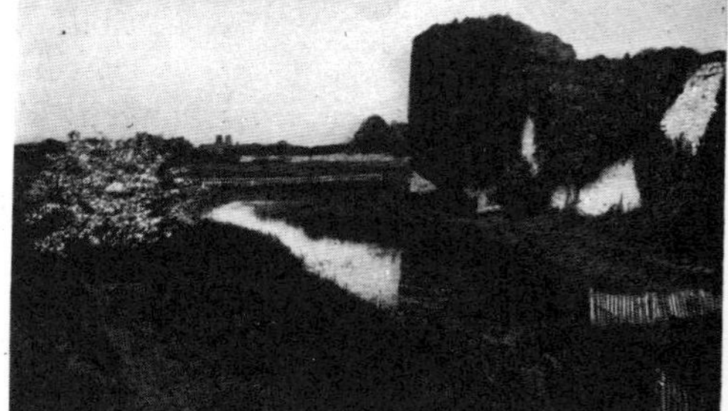
Sussex Blossoms A, S 5787

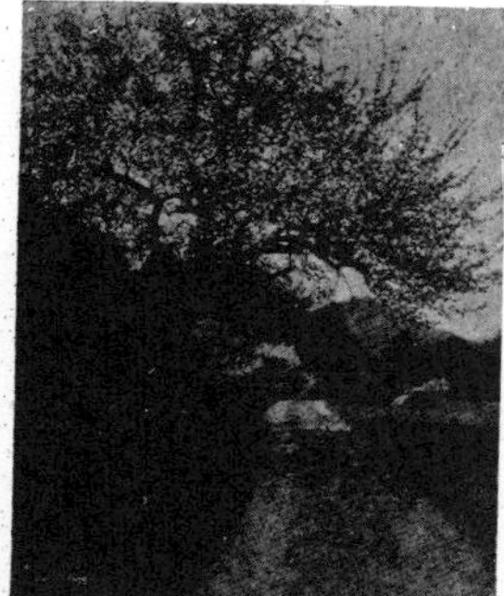
A Peep at the Hills C 476

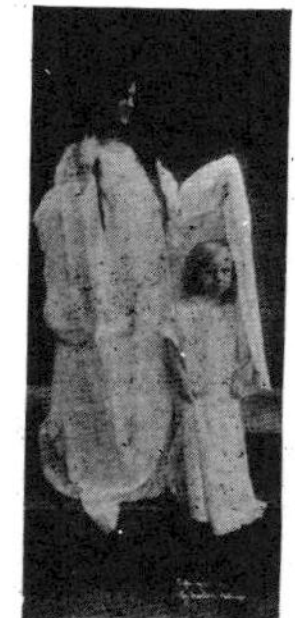
The Guardian Angel
Q 1041

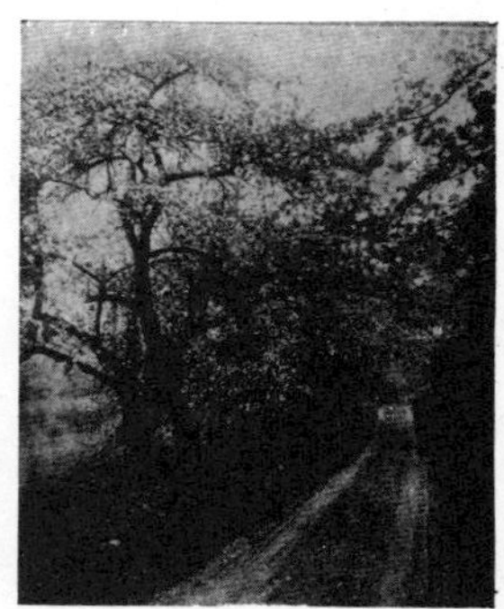
By the Stone Wall C 835

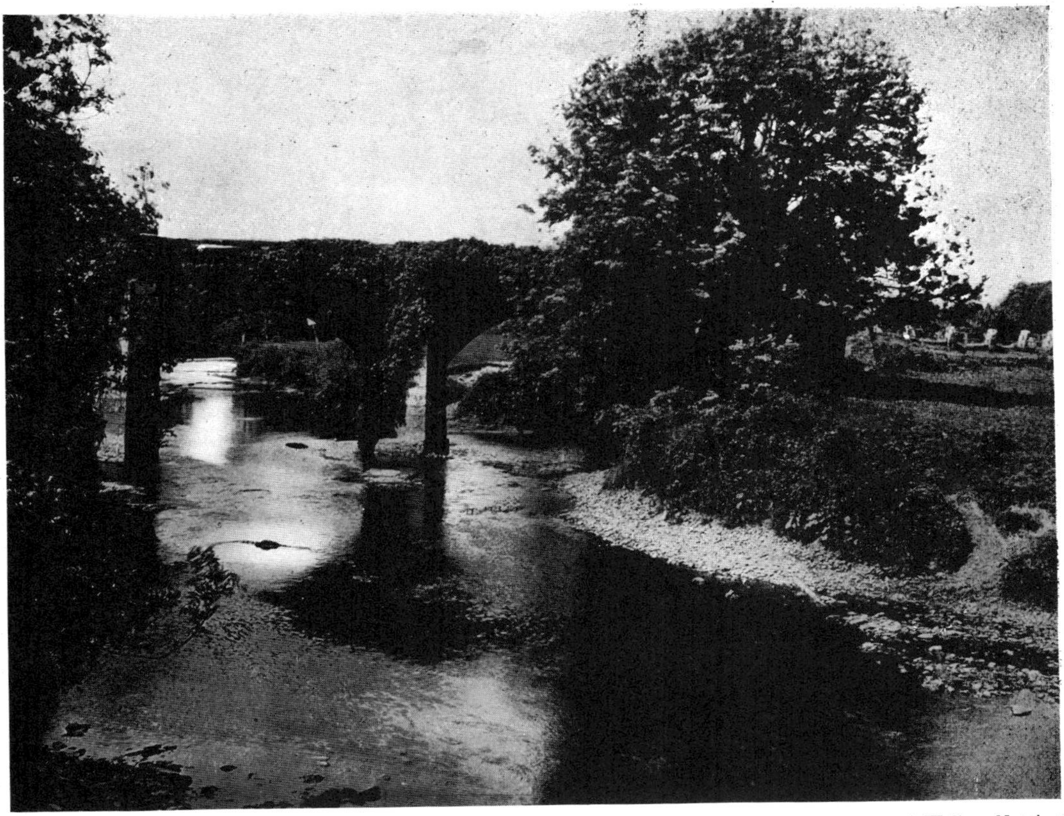

Under Ivy Bridge A, C, E, F 5656 Wallace Nutting

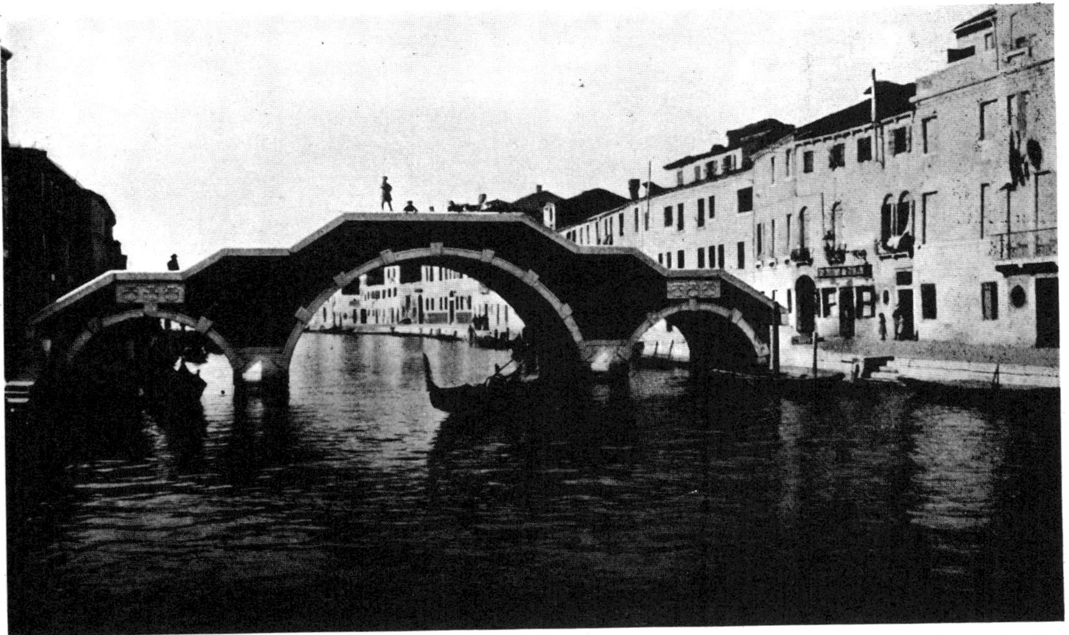

Bridge of Three Arches A, Q, S 4245 Wallace Nutting

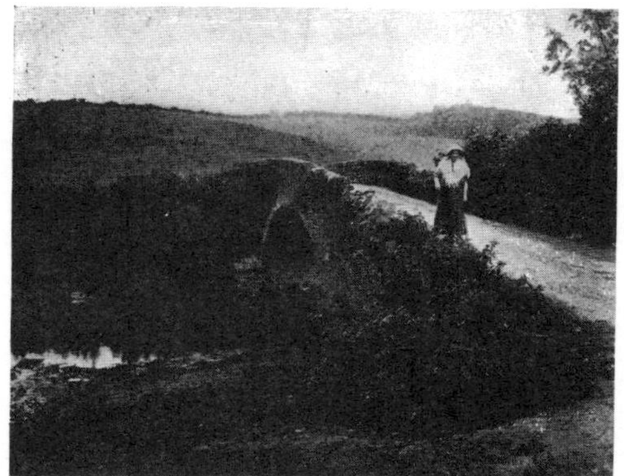

Lorna Doone A, C, E 5657

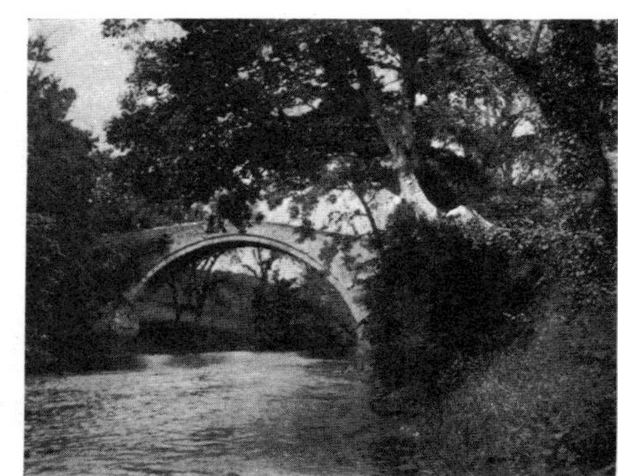

Burns's Brig o' Doon A, C 5947

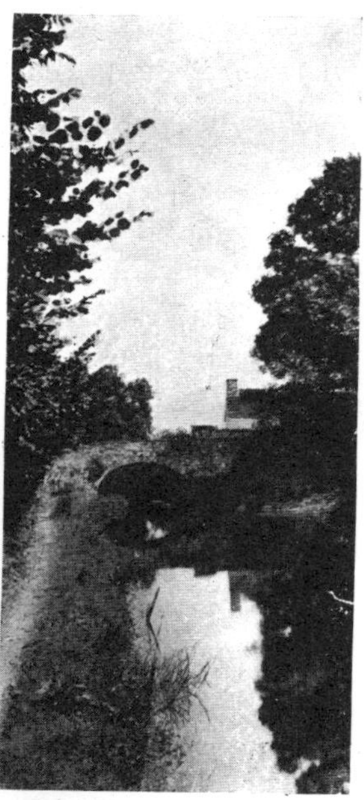

A Rural Path Q 6241

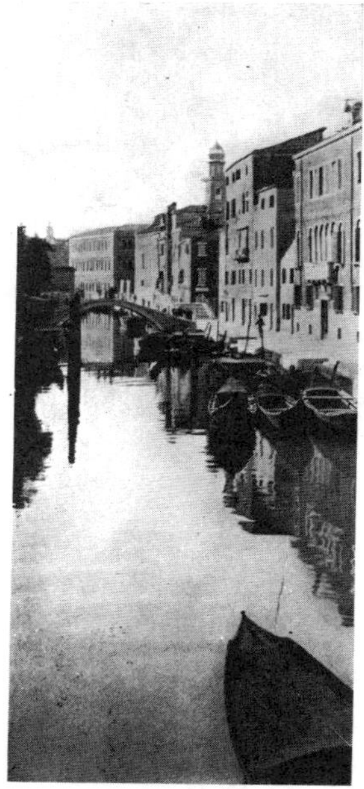

Old Venice Q 4299

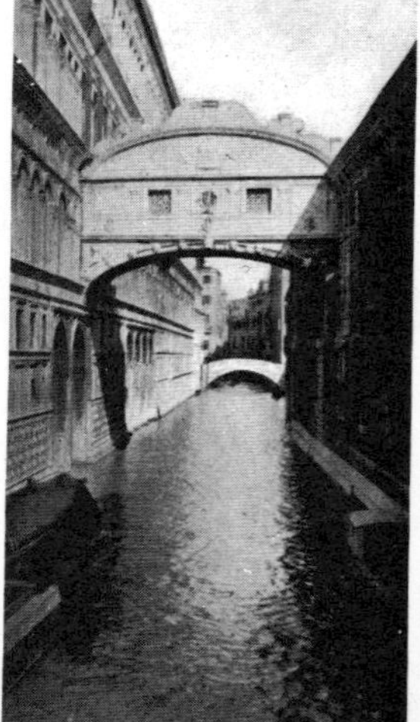

Bridge of Sighs Q 4235

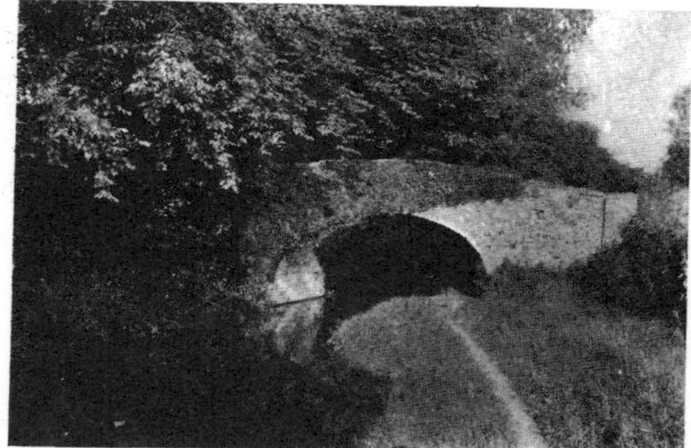

Far From Broadway A, C 6287

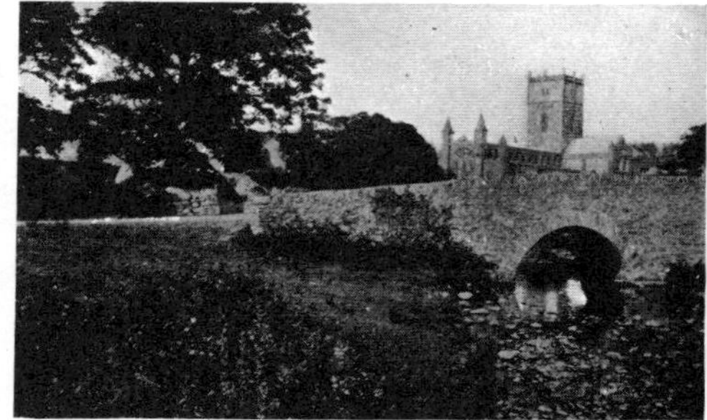

St. David's Bridge A, S 6047

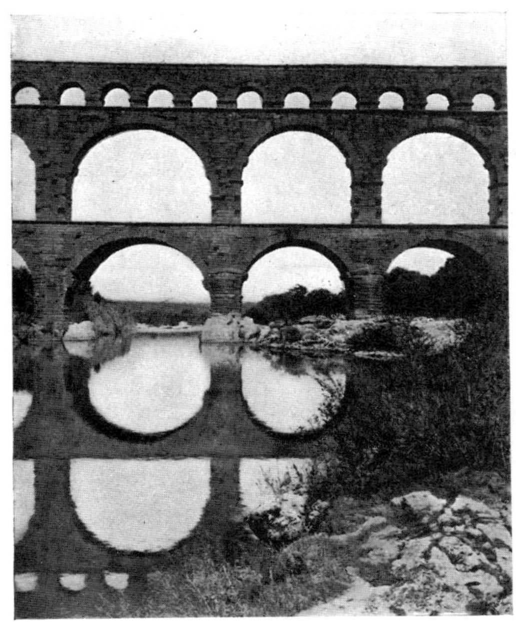

Dream Arches A, C, E 4564

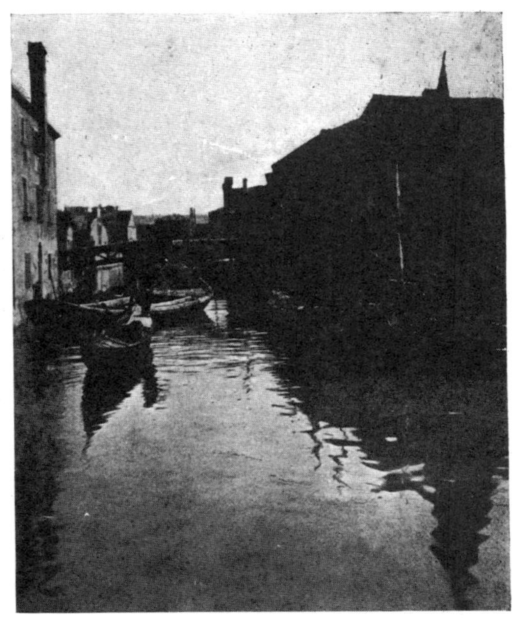

Among Saffron Sails A, C 4314

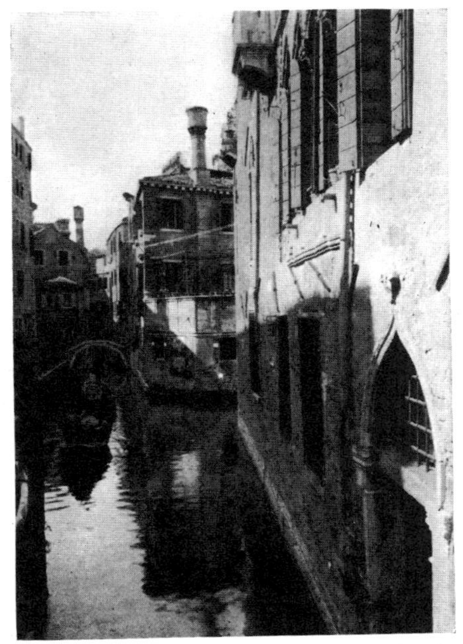

Water Paths of Venice A, Q, S, C, O, P 4253

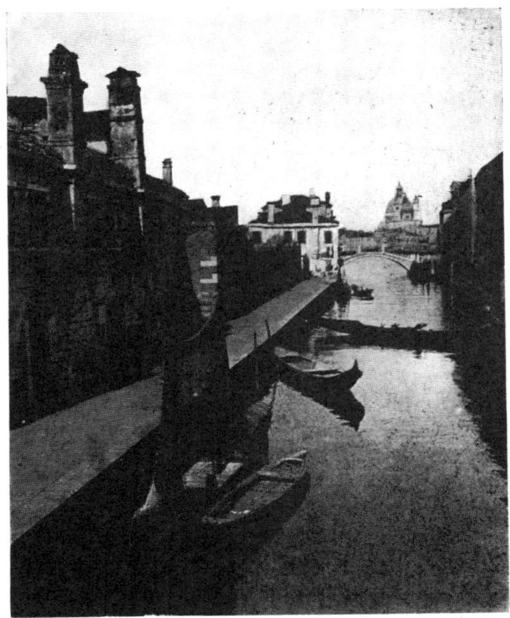

A Canal in Sunshine A, C 4325

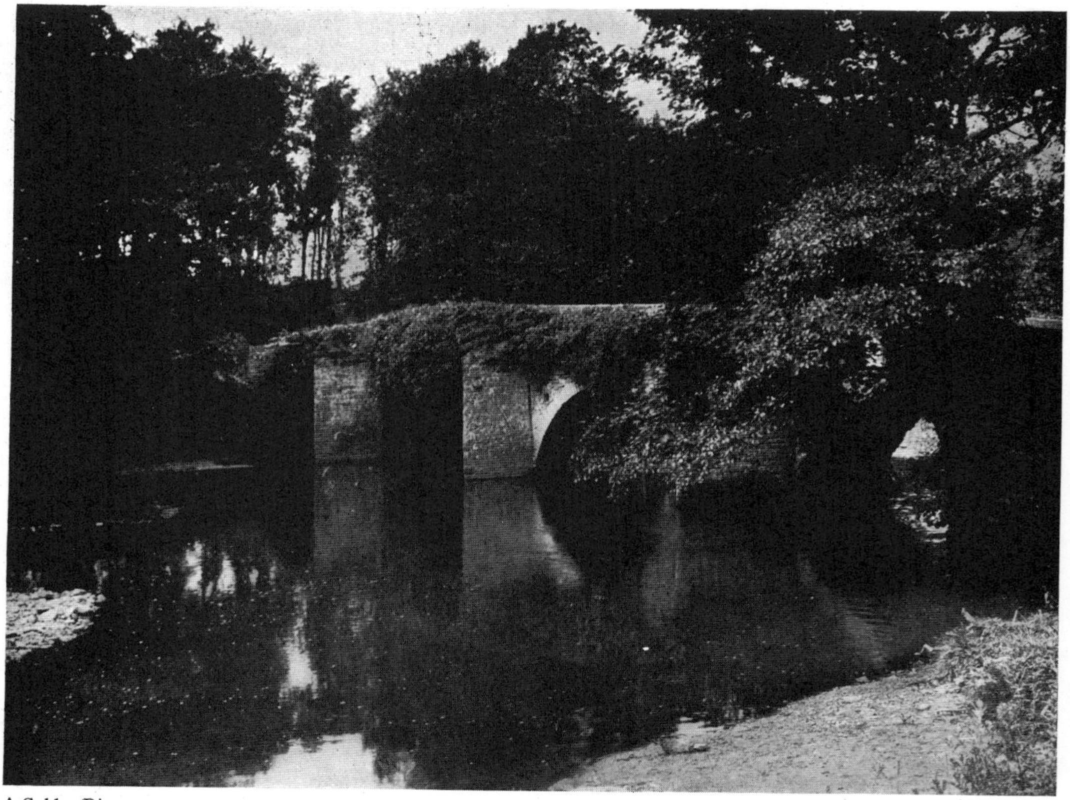

A Golden River — A, C, E 6120 — Wallace Nutting

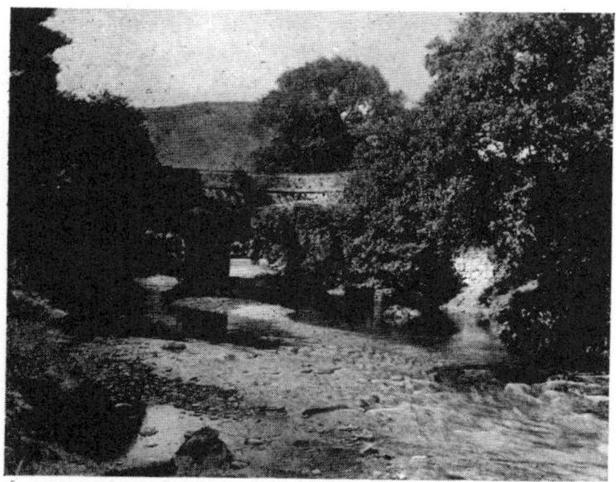

The Old Bridge and the New — A, C 6226

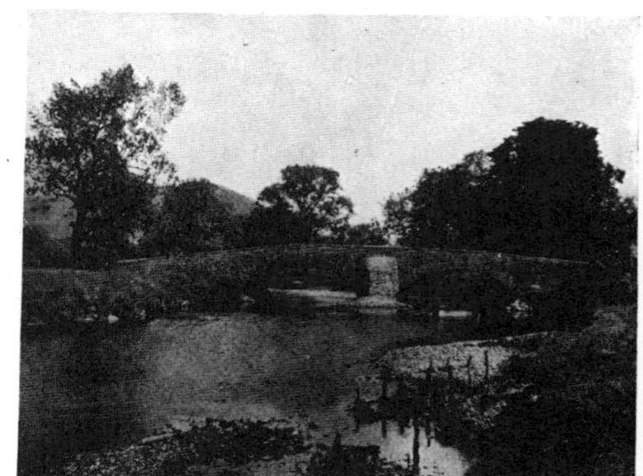

The Vale of Derwent — A, C, 6128

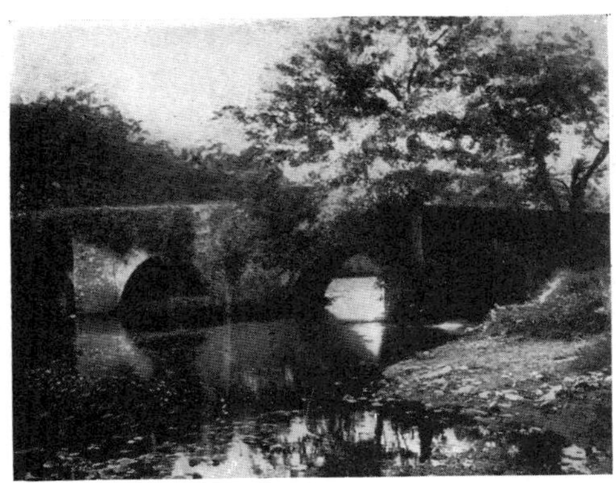

Late Twilight A, C 6089

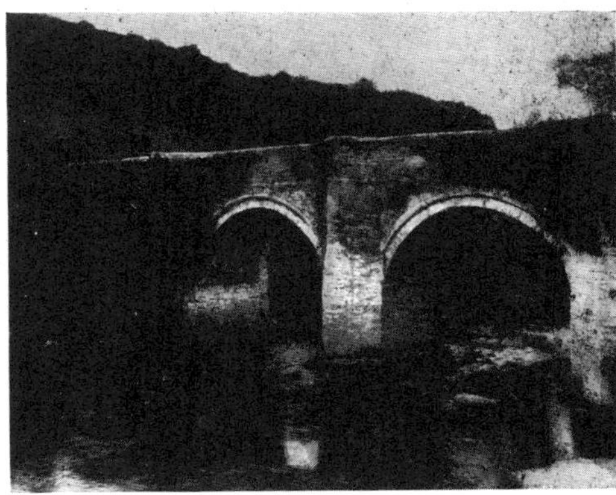

Devon Arches A, C 5692

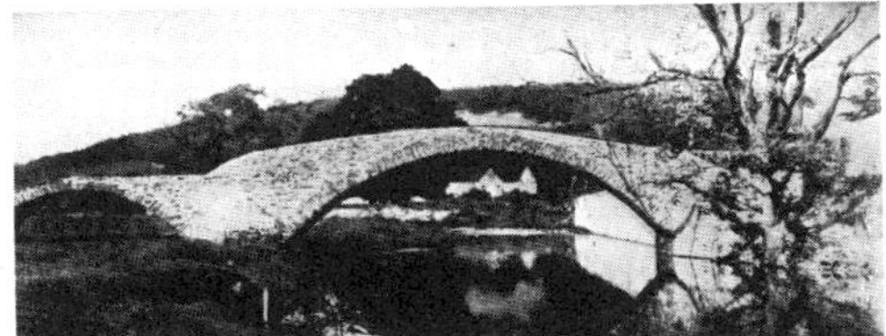

The Forgotten Bridge Q, S 5938

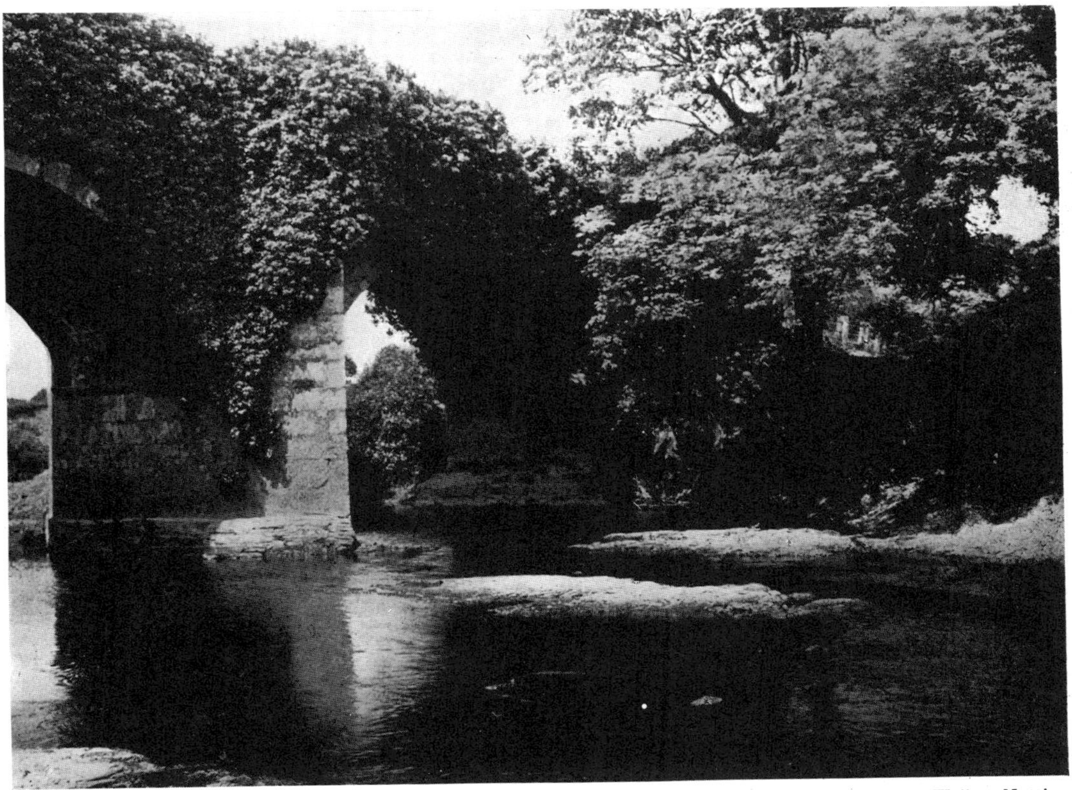

Below the Arches A, C, E 5662 Wallace Nutting

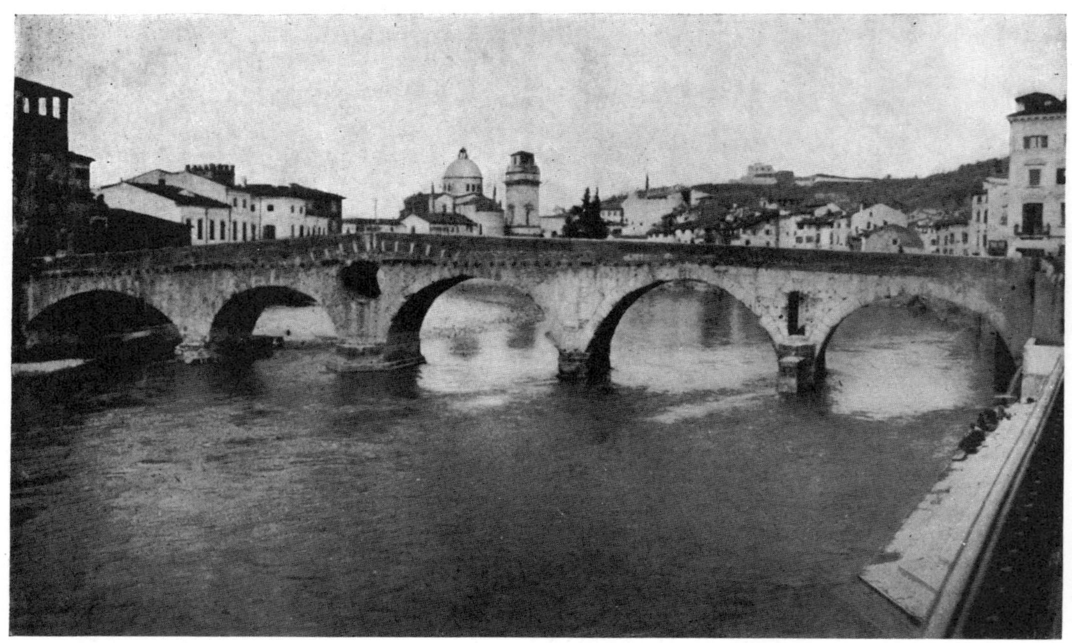
Arches and Domes (Verona) Q, S 4392 Wallace Nutting

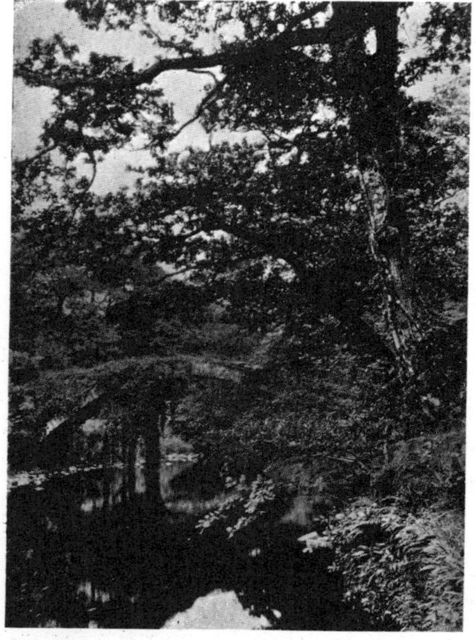
Oak Glen A, C 6422

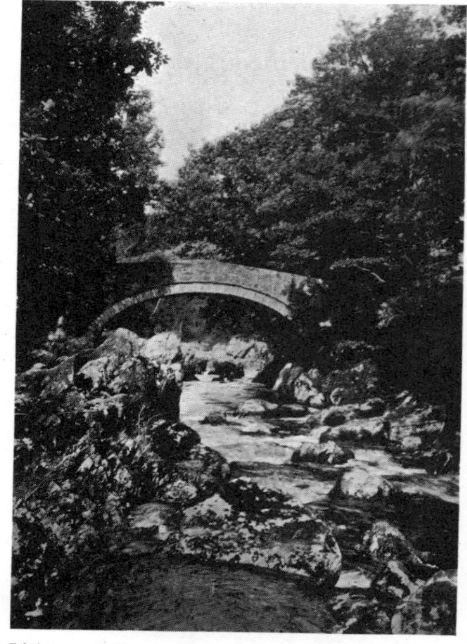
Lichen and Foam A, C 6232

BRIDGES

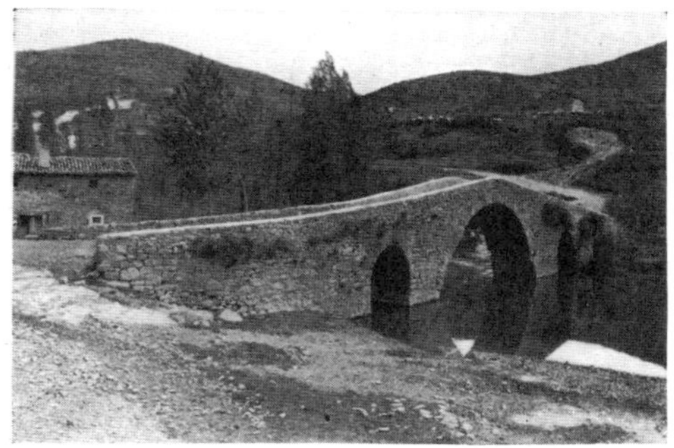

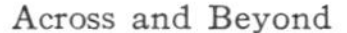

Across and Beyond A, S, P 4616

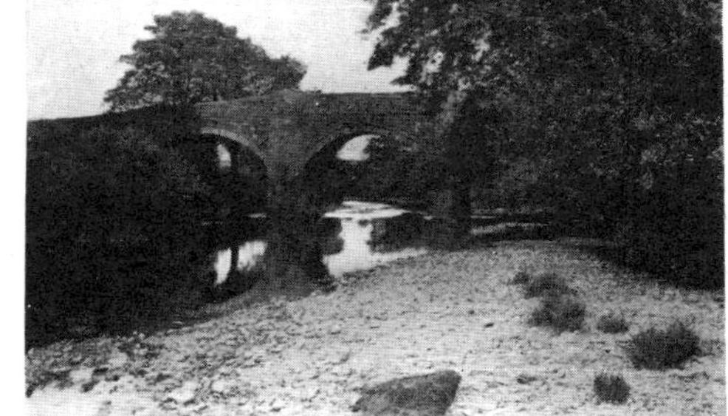

The Pebbly Strand A, S, C 5691

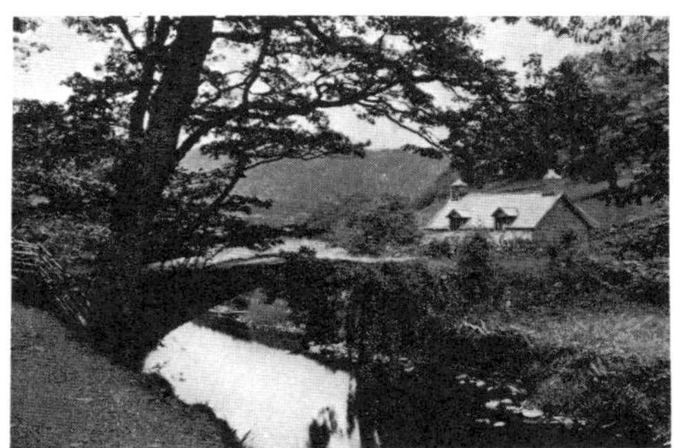

Bridge Drapery A, C 6420

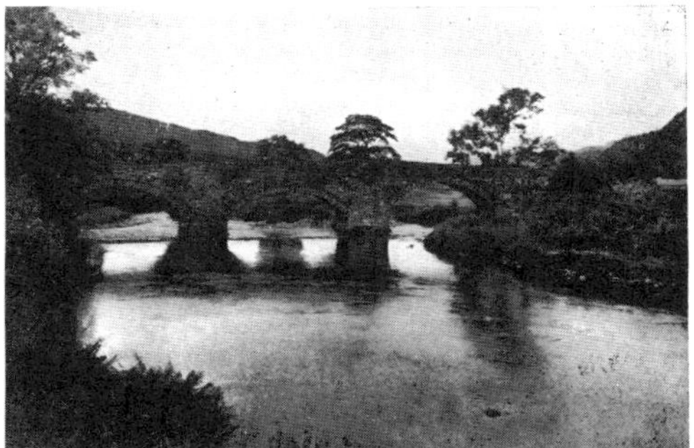

A Leisurely River A, Q 6440

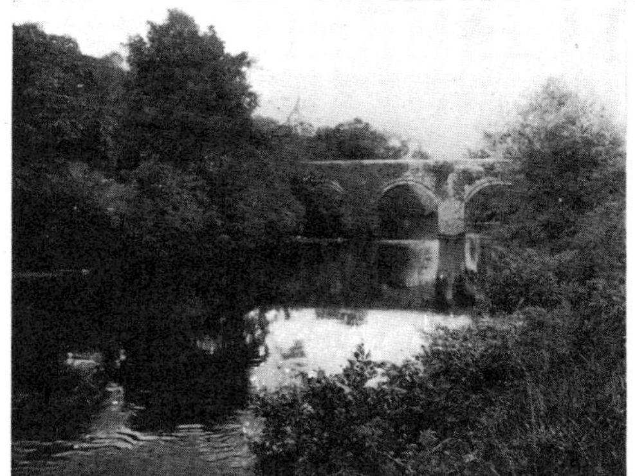

Where the Stream Rests A, C 5693

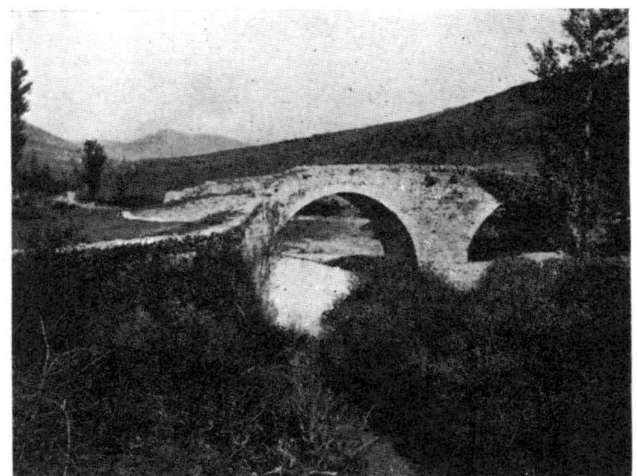

A Bridge in Spain A, C 4615

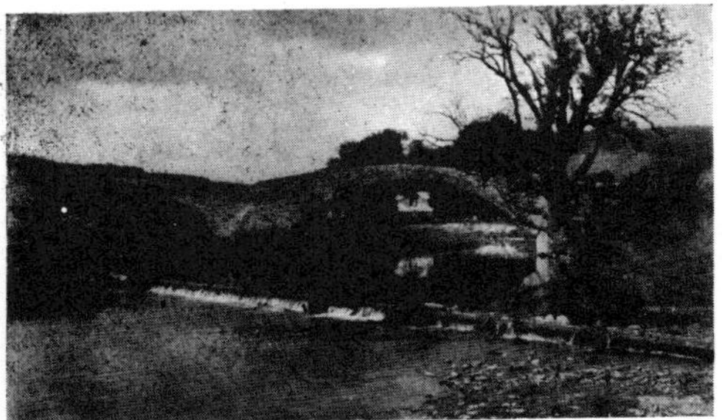
The Old Meadow Arches A, S 5936

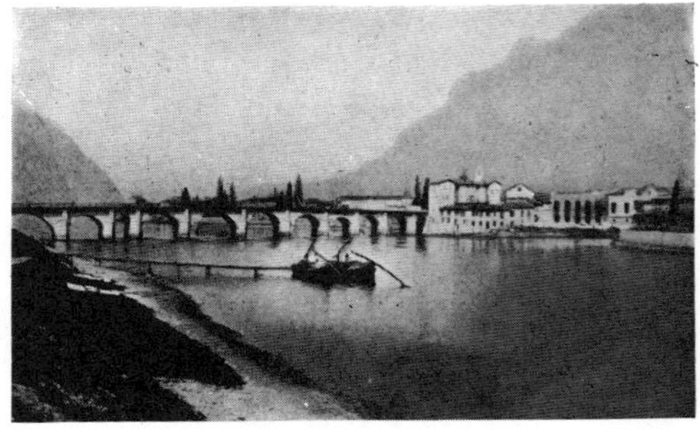
Lecco's Bridge A 4379

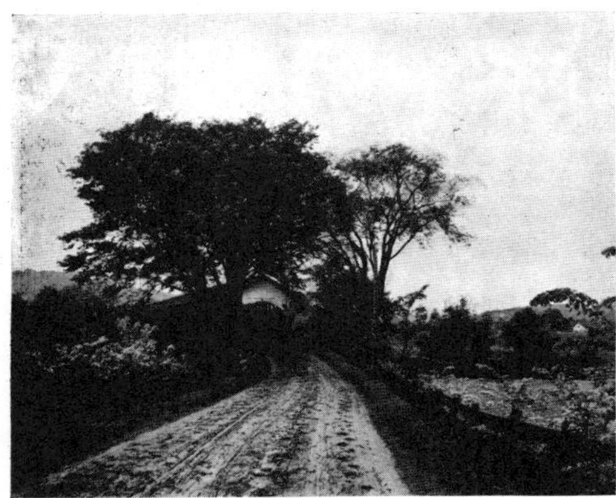
Entering the Old Bridge C 663

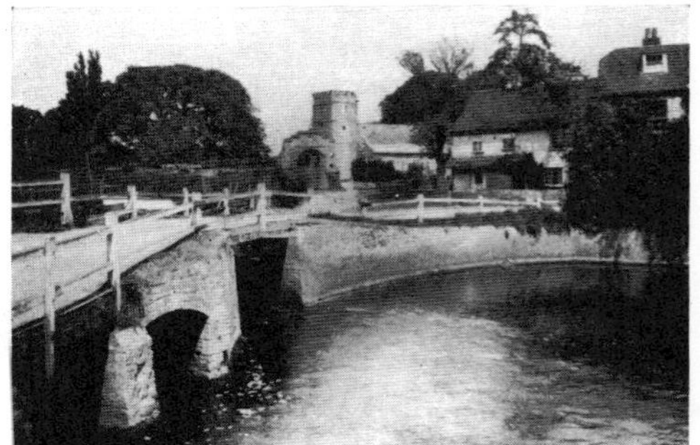
The Church and the Bridge A, C 5551

American bridges, unhappily being built of wood, are not, as a rule, very attractive. " Entering the Old Bridge " above is an agreeable exception. There is also " A Woodstock Arch " (C 151), and " The Upper Winooski " on page 803.

In England and on the Continent the bridges, being almost altogether of stone and often ivy covered, are particularly fine, and we have a list of about 300 such pictures. Those illustrated are a representative selection and include subjects made in seven foreign countries. "Dream Arches," on page 203, is the famous Roman Aqueduct near Nîmes. We have this picture in horizontal form, also a diagonal view up to E and F sizes. It will be noticed that the upper left and bottom right pictures on page 207 are Spanish. " Oak Glen " is a Roman bridge in Wales. " A Golden River " cannot fail to please.

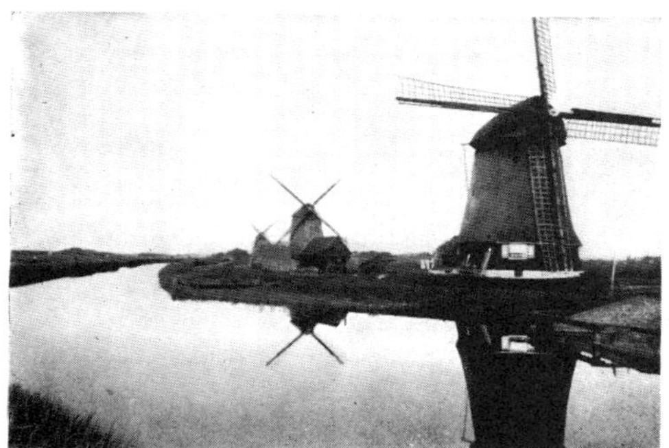
The Mills at the Turn A, S, E, F 5061

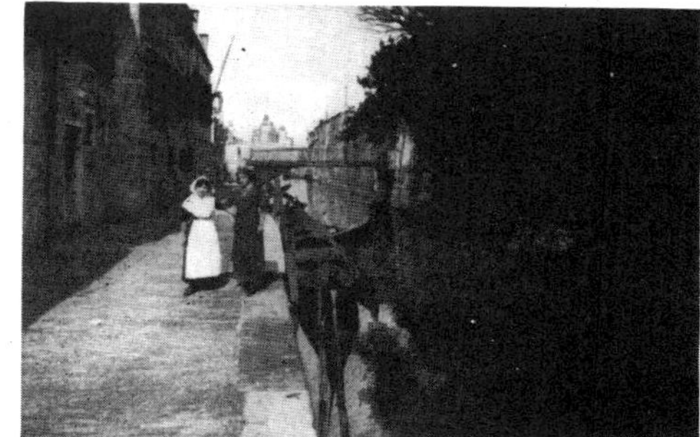
Strolling on the Quay A, C 4326

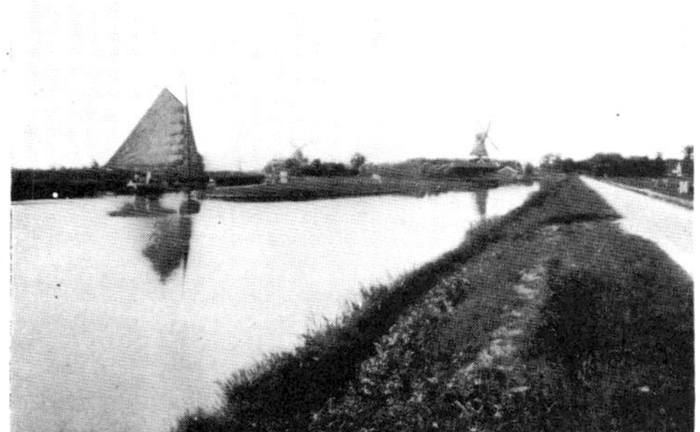
Sailing Among Windmills A, Q, S, O, P 5086

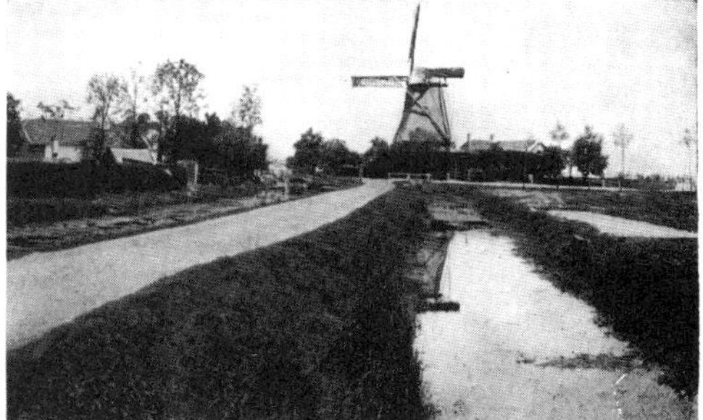
The Canal Road A, S 5100

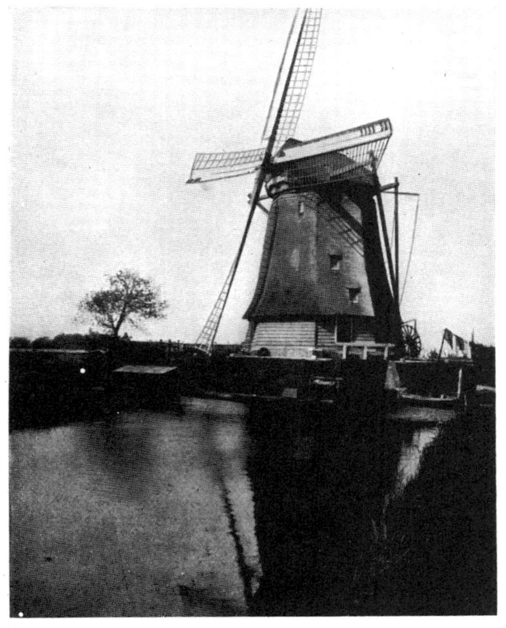
A Listless Day A, S, C 5016

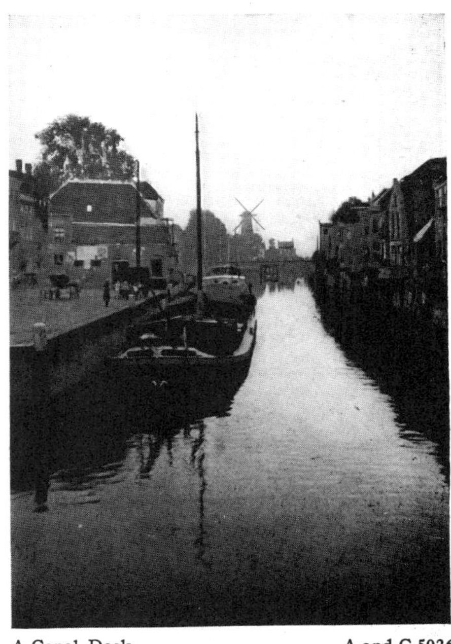
A Canal Dock A and C 5026

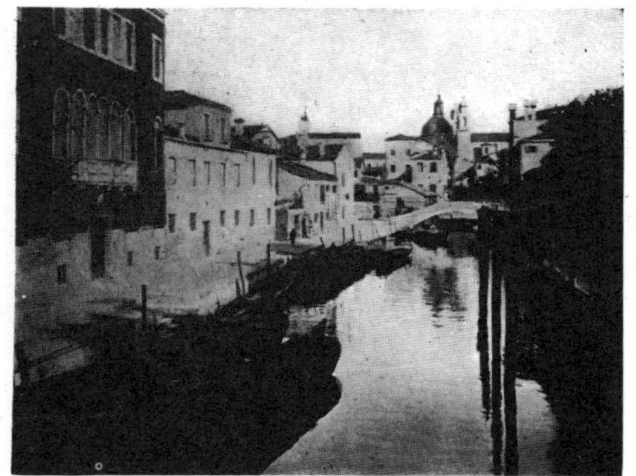
La Gindecca A, C 4298

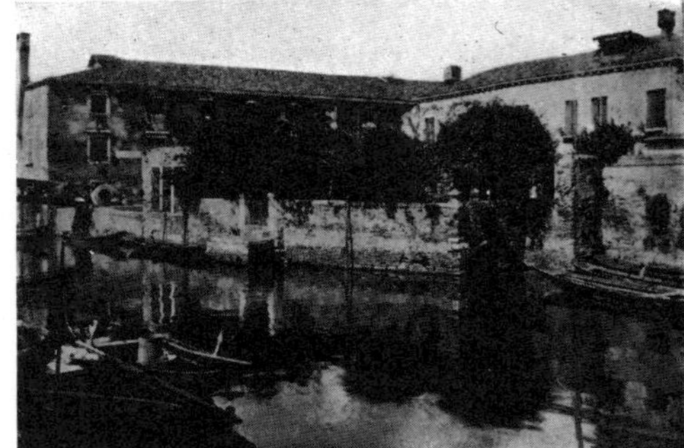
A Water Garden in Venice 4333

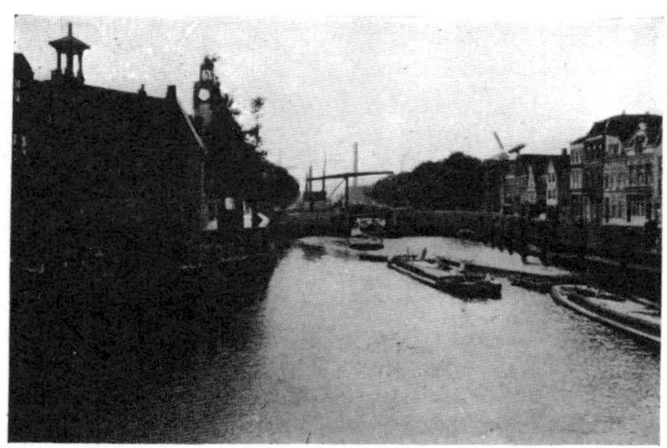
A Dutch Bridge S 5094

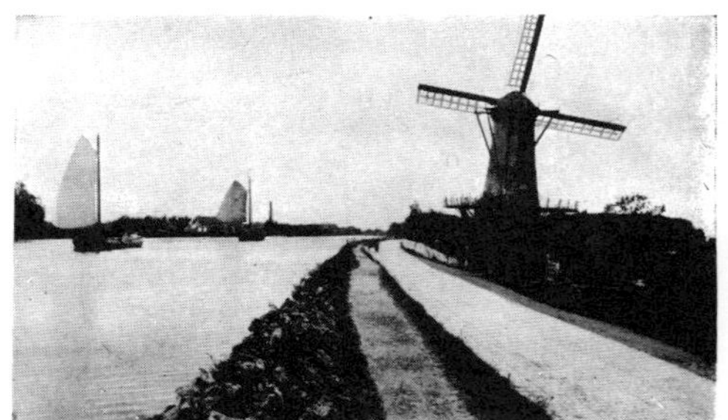
Dutch Sails Q, S 5082

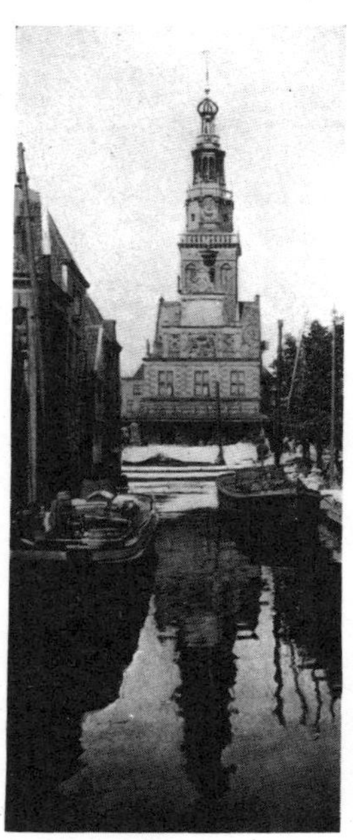
The Cheese Market A, S 5058

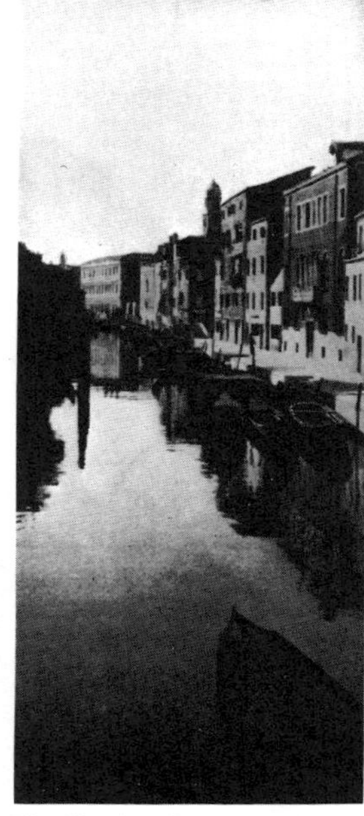
The Sleeping Canal Q 4299

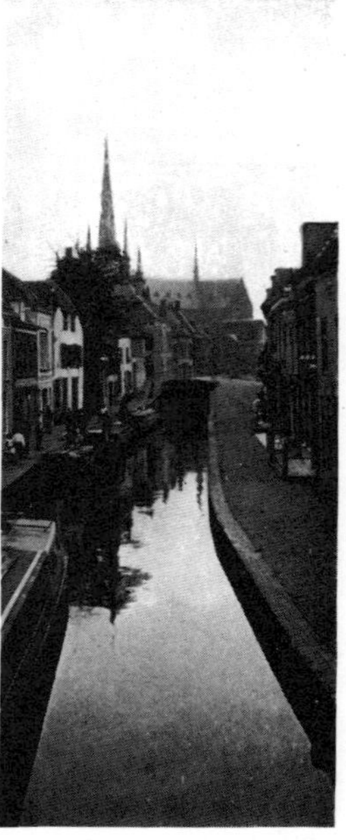
In Worden Q 5092

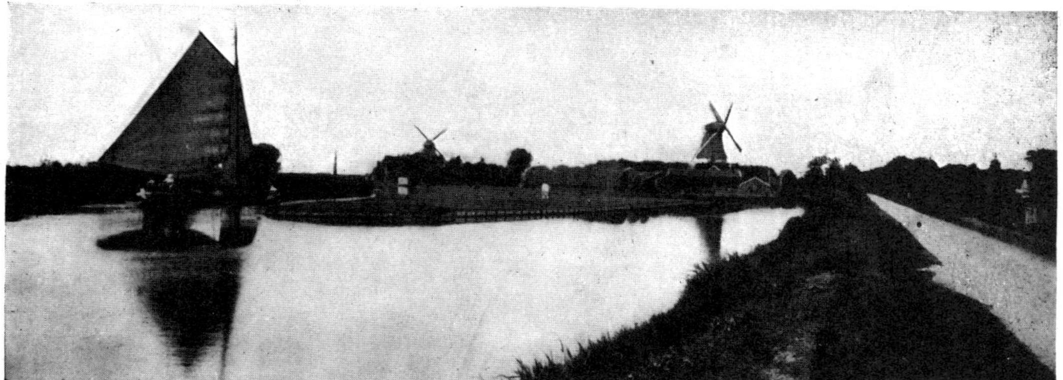

A Peaceful Stretch Q, O 5093 Wallace Nutting

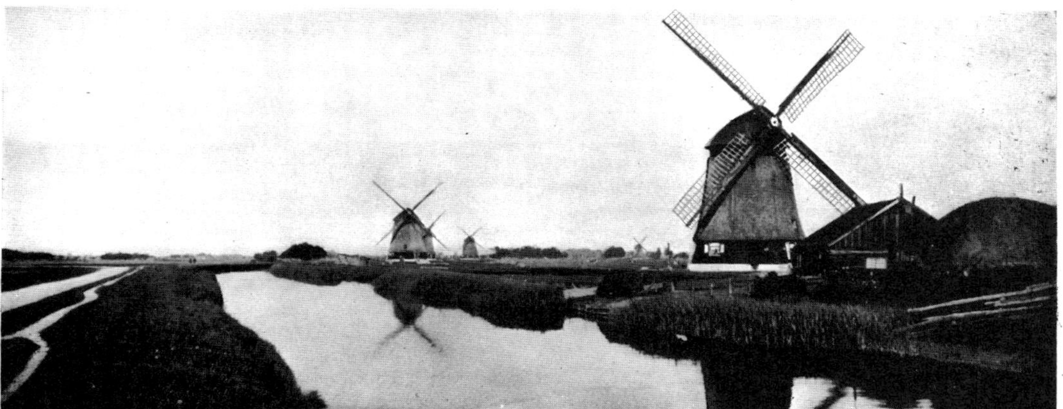

The Canal Row Q 5062 Wallace Nutting

CANALS

Please notice that a considerable number of pictures which would otherwise come under this classification are in the class of Bridges (page 201); that is to say, if canals have bridges we have for the most part placed the cuts with Bridges. There is a considerable similarity in the large number of other canal pictures which we have. The famous cheese market at Alkmaar (page 252) is one of the daintiest architectural bits in Holland.

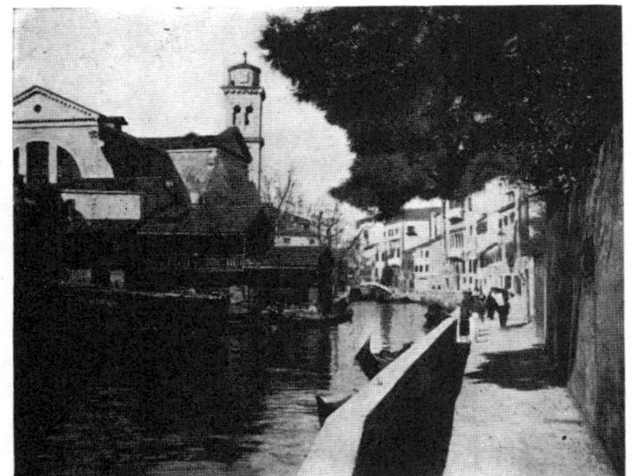
A Gondolier Dock A, C 4302

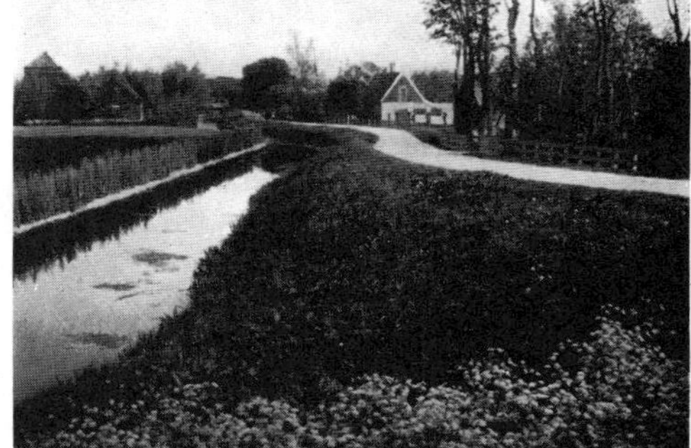
Windings in Holland A, C 5010

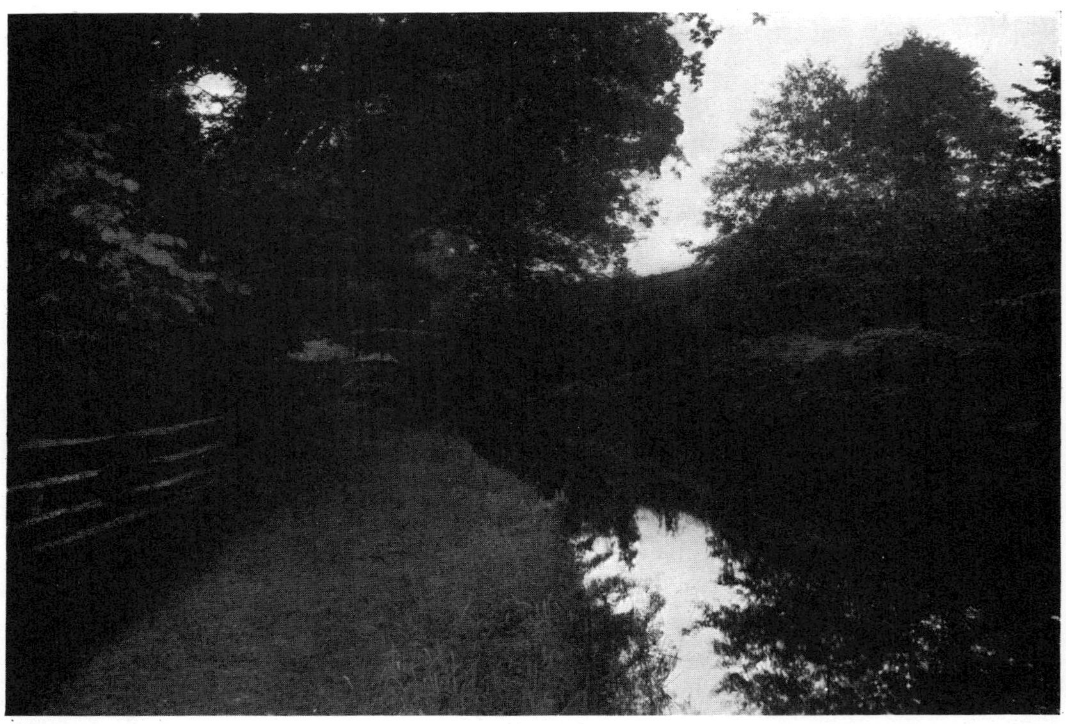
A Path to Content A, S, C 6243 Wallace Nutting

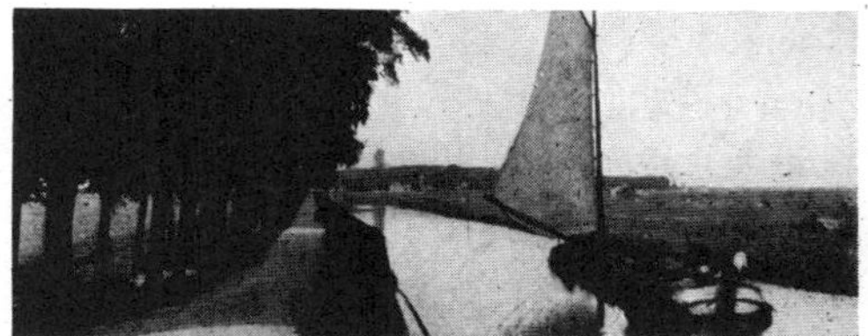
With the Wind A, Q 5024

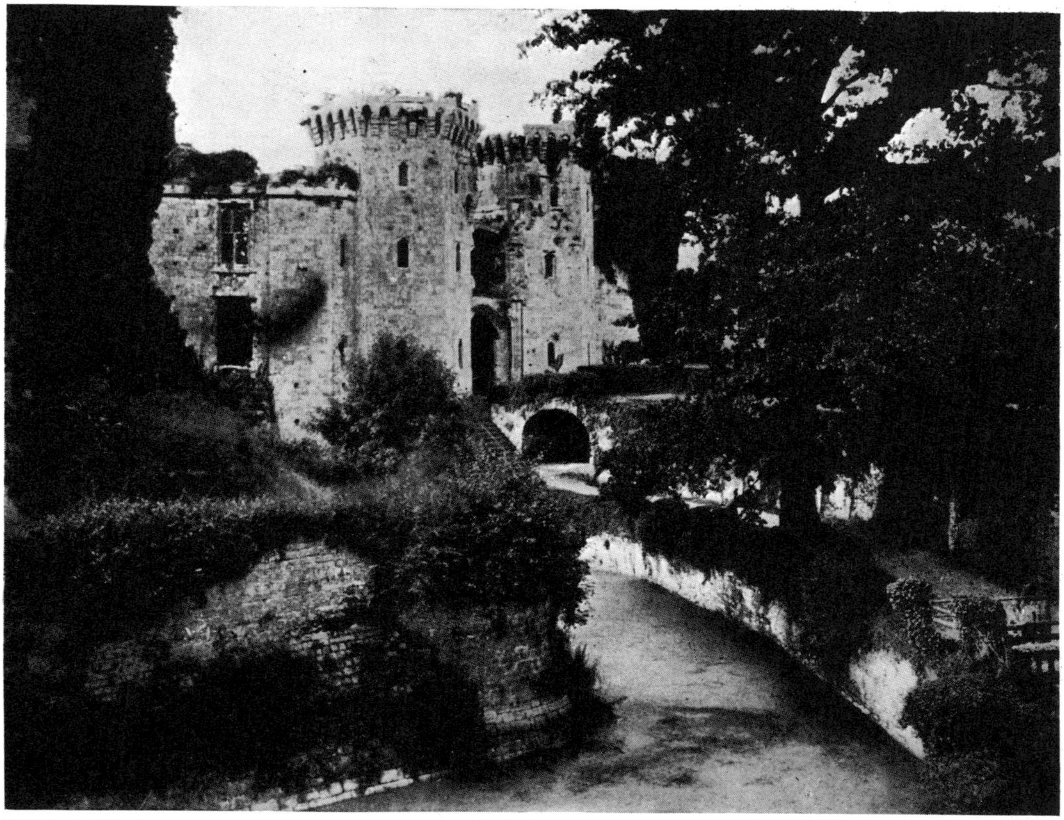

Old Moat of Raglan A, C, E 6452 Wallace Nutting
As a Vertical Picture the number is 6451 and is entitled A Castle Moat

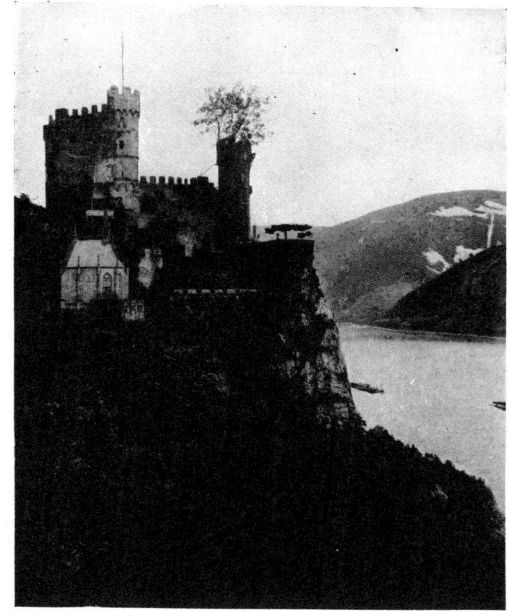

Rheinstein A, C 4892

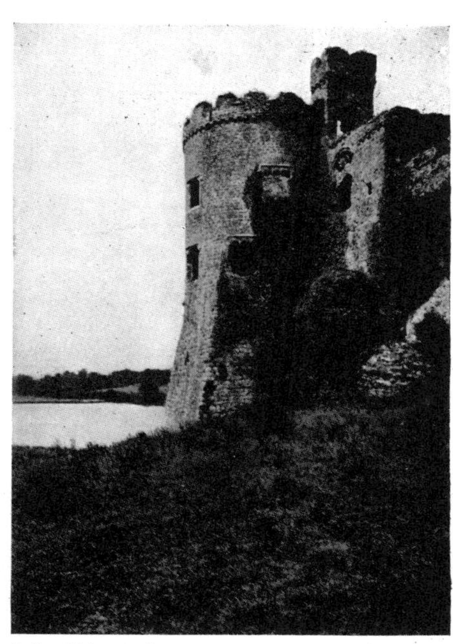

A Castle Outwork A, C 6441

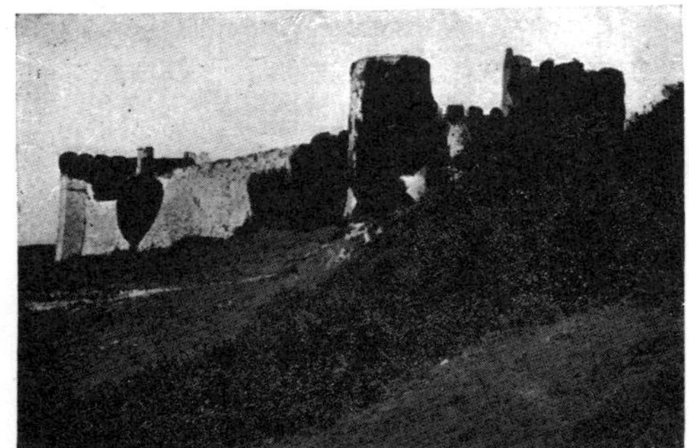

A Baron's Hold A, S 5992

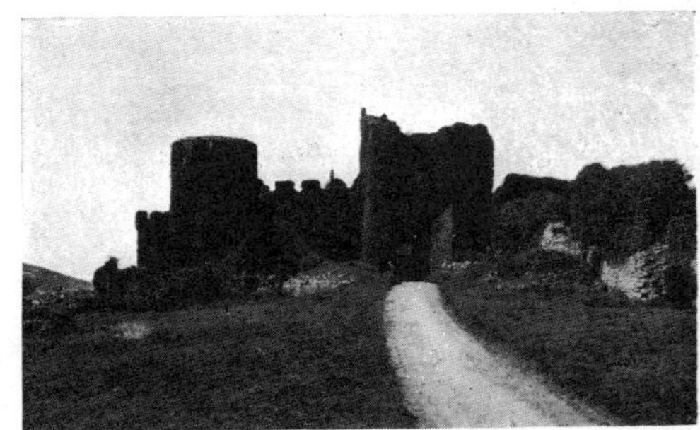

Entrance, Carew Castle A, S 6391

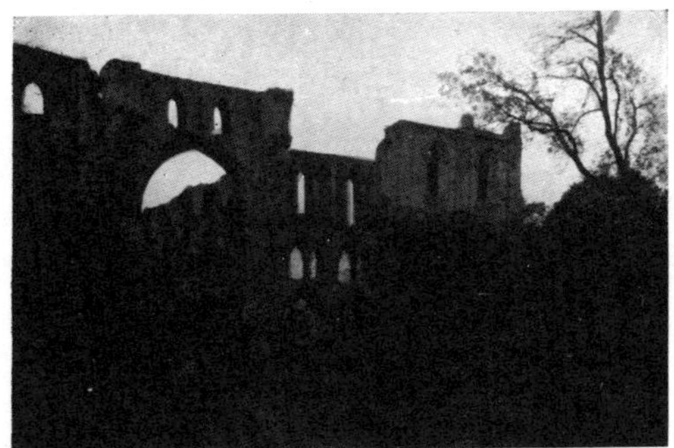

Ruins of Rievaulx A, S 5902

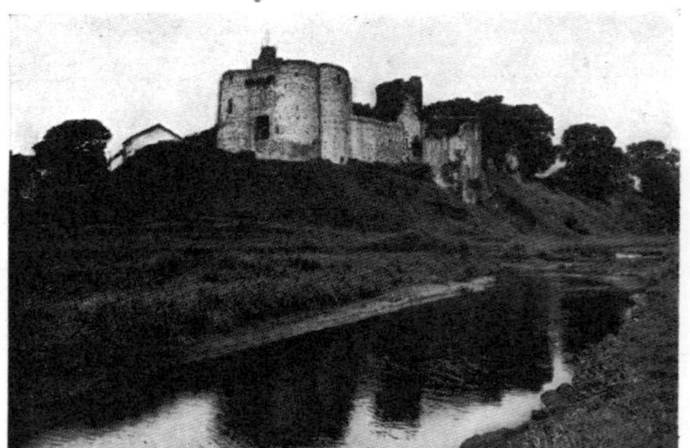

By Castle Towers A, S, C 5996

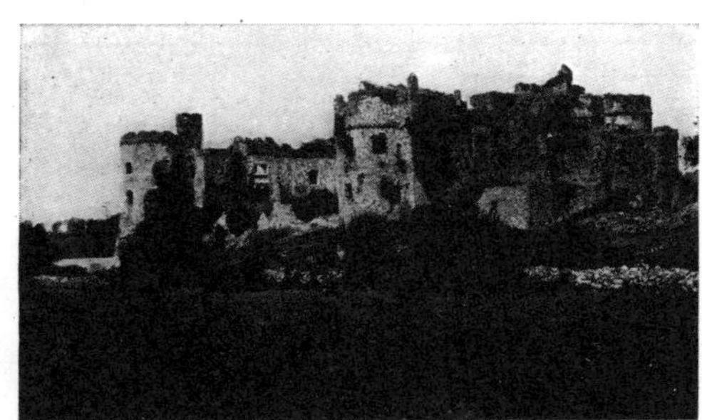

A Welsh Stronghold A, S 6394

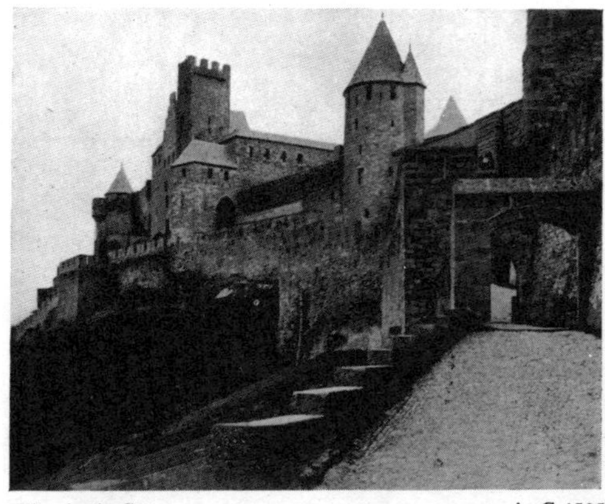

The Aude Gate A, C 4505

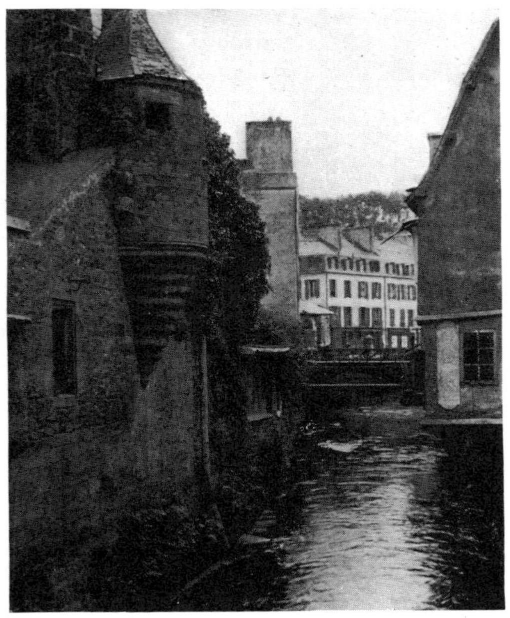

An Oriel (Quimper) A, S, C 4763

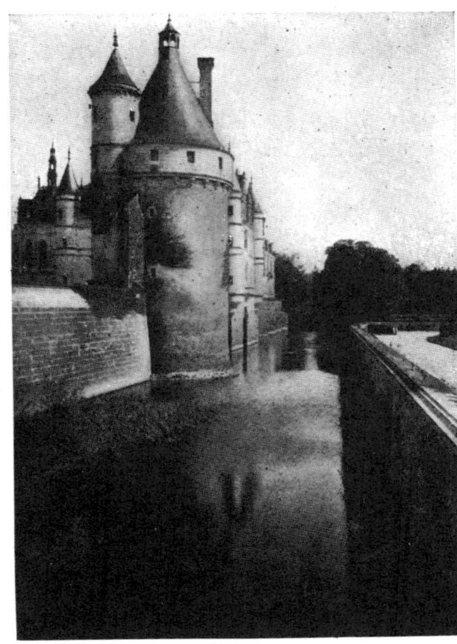

The Donjon, Chenanceau A, C, E 4651

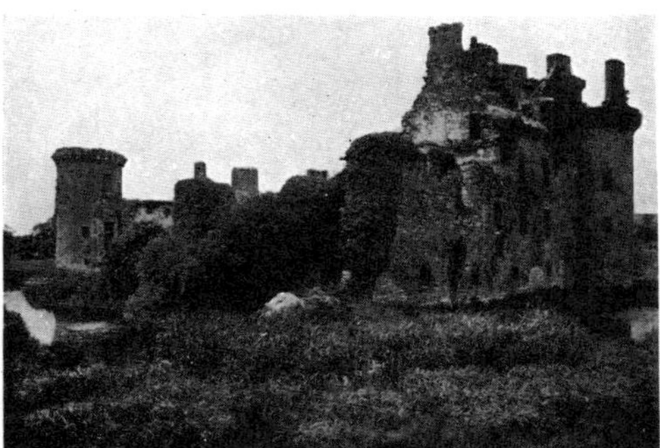

A Scottish Stronghold A, S 6223

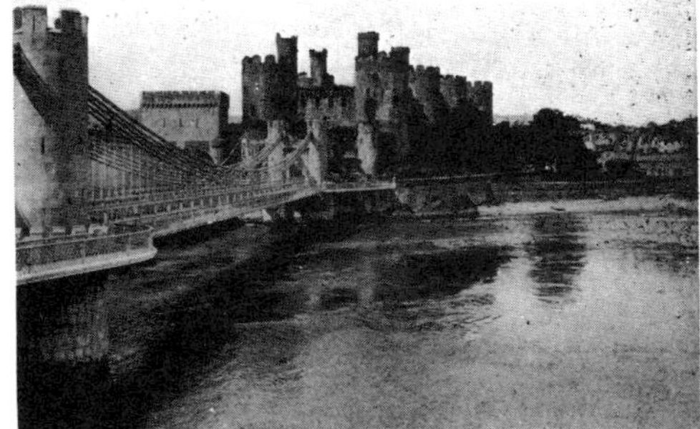

Conway Towers and Stream A, S 6365

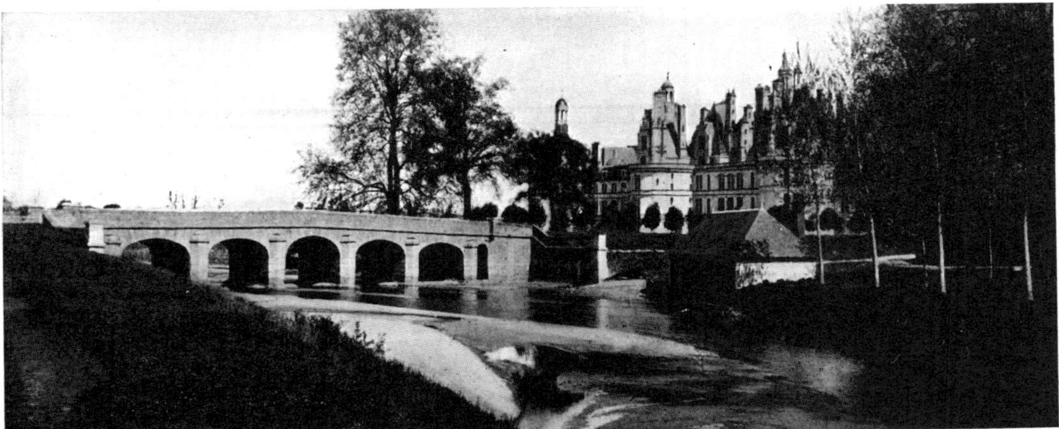

Chambord and Its Bridge Q or S 4733 Wallace Nutting

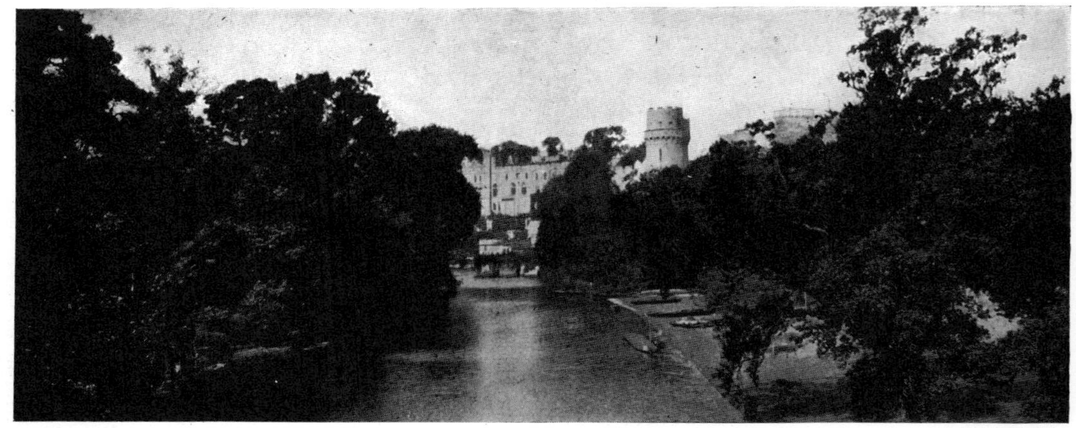

Warwick Castle A, Q, S 6275 Wallace Nutting

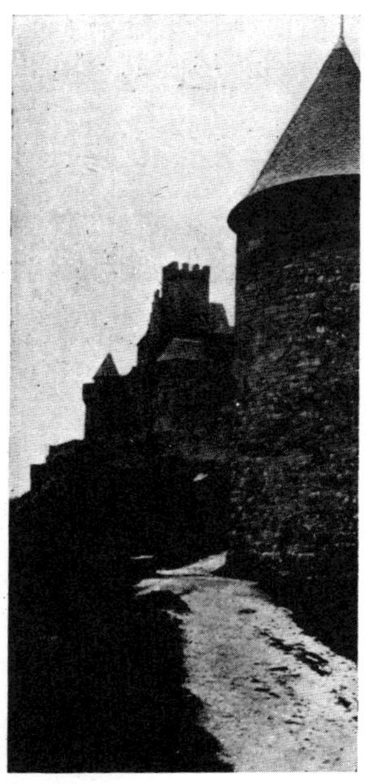

Carcassonne Q 4508

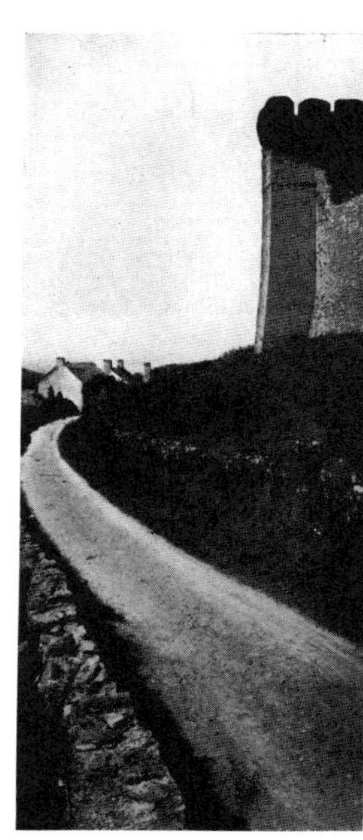

Beneath Castle Walls Q 5991

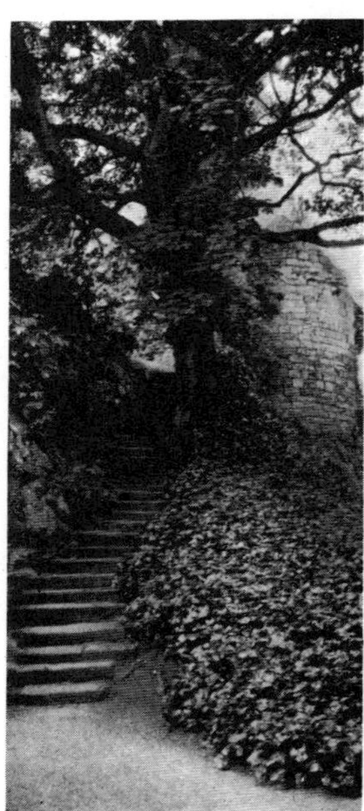

An Old Castle Stair Q 5833

CASTLES

We have besides the castles shown, a considerable number of others, such as Tantallon Hold (page 603), included with some others under Marines, and Dover Castle (no illustration). There are also Hardwick Hall, the chateaux of Loches and of Pau and various other French and British strongholds.

CASTELLATED CARCASSONNE

We have about fifty prints of Carcassonne. The one showing the whole town from the plain is attractive. There are also others that show sections of the castle wall, of the keep, of the streets, and of the noble church, and the remains of the old theatre. This is so special a subject that we have illustrated only one of these, but would be glad to furnish information on request.

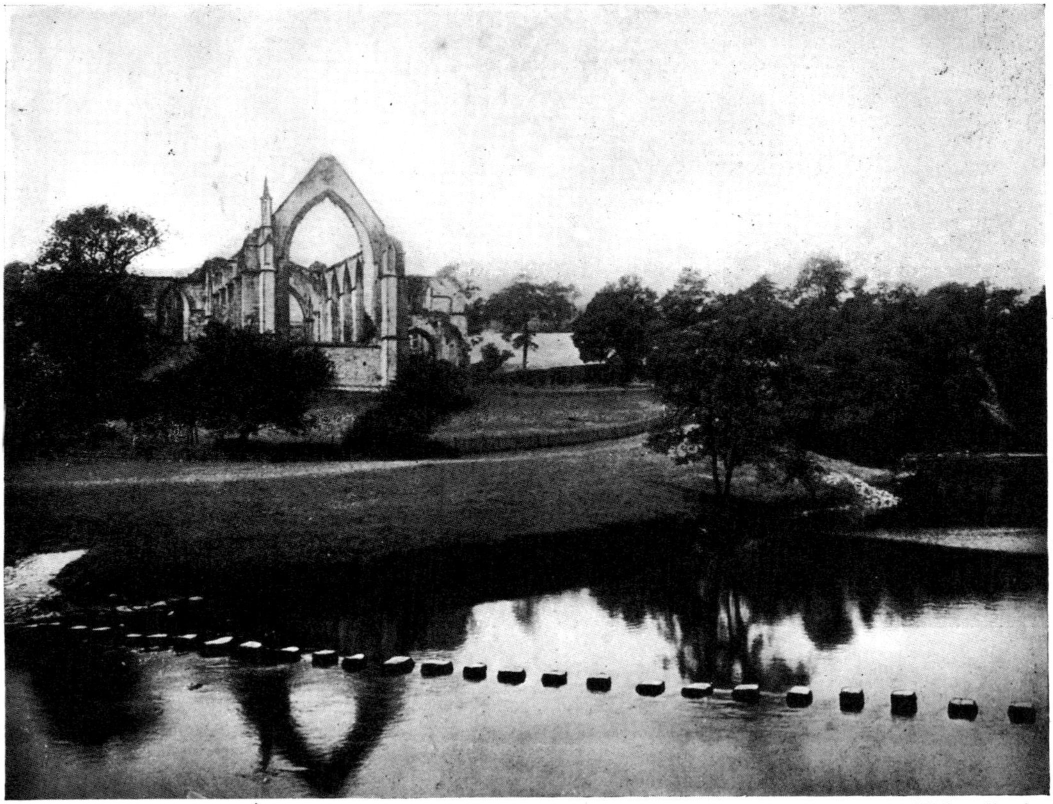

Stepping Stones at Bolton Abbey C, E, T 6125 Wallace Nutting

The picture above shows one of the most remarkable series of stepping stones in Britain. There is another series near Bridgend in Wales (page 461) and elsewhere. The combination of the stepping stones with the abbey above makes a very beautiful subject for a library or parlor wall. It will be noted that it is published in the larger sizes. Besides the illustrations we have pictures of Exeter, of Tintern Abbey (this not recommended, because being repaired), of Vendome, of Quimper, of Notre Dame, of Strasburg, and others in Italy, France and Britain. We also have some fine old American churches of the Georgian type, both interiors and exteriors.

The pictures shown are only samples of the wealth of material secured by Mr. Nutting during his recent trip abroad, when he took over two thousand pictures. He has, for example, some forty or fifty pictures of Canterbury, some fifteen or twenty of Salisbury, and the same number of Milan.

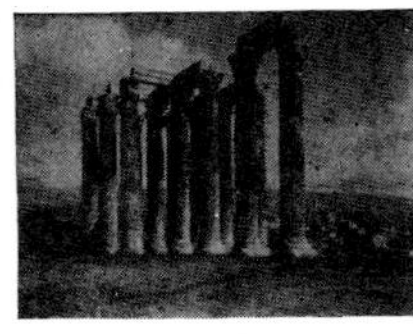
Temple of Zeus, Athens
C, E or G 36

The Milan pictures give fine bits of the exquisite detail of that famous structure. Note, for example, on page 356, the statue on the lofty tower. It is one of hundreds, and is said to be that of Christ blessing the city. On page 357 is shown another charming segment of the great cathedral.

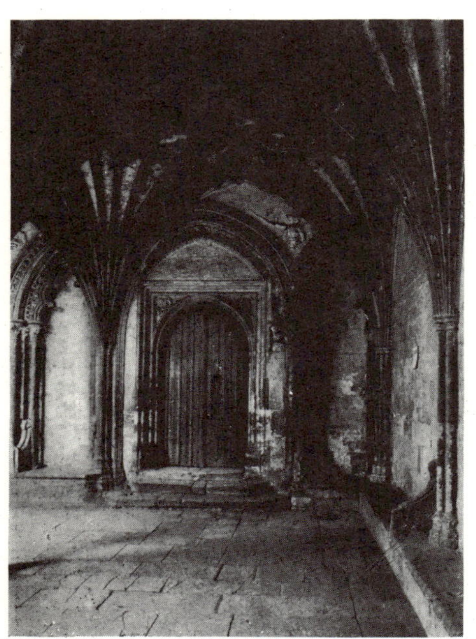

The Cloister Door (Canterbury) A, C 5795

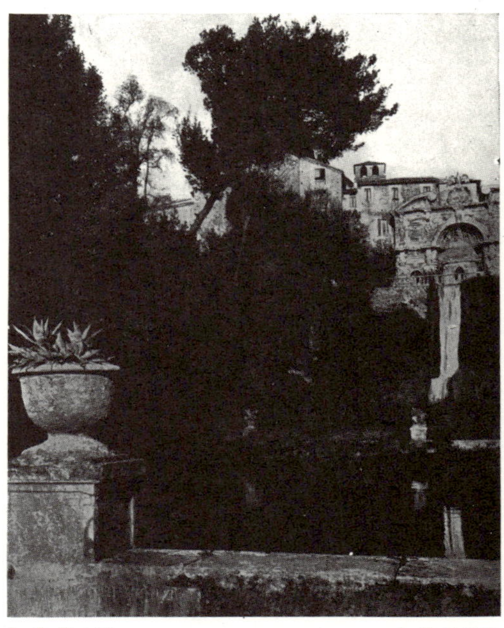

An Italian Dream A, C, E 4218

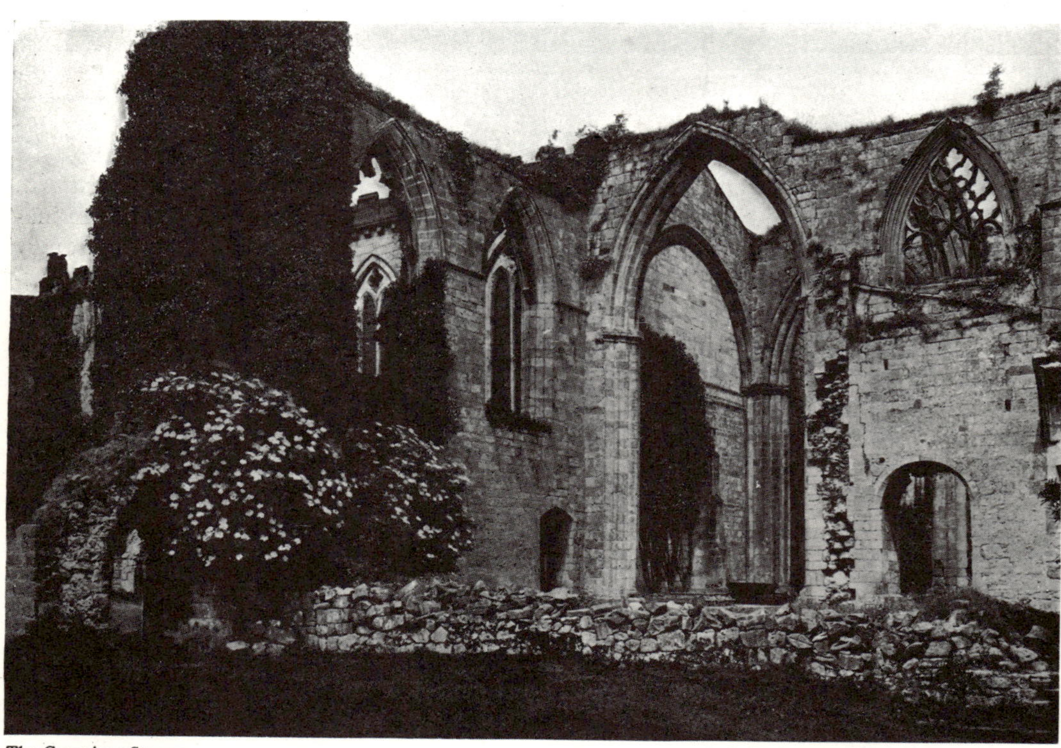

The Conscious Stones A, C, E 6222 (also A, C and E 6219 Vertical)

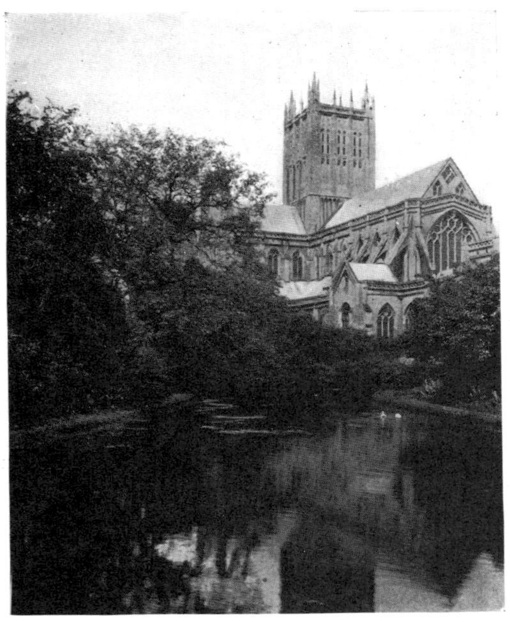
Wells, from the Palace Pool A, C, E 5700

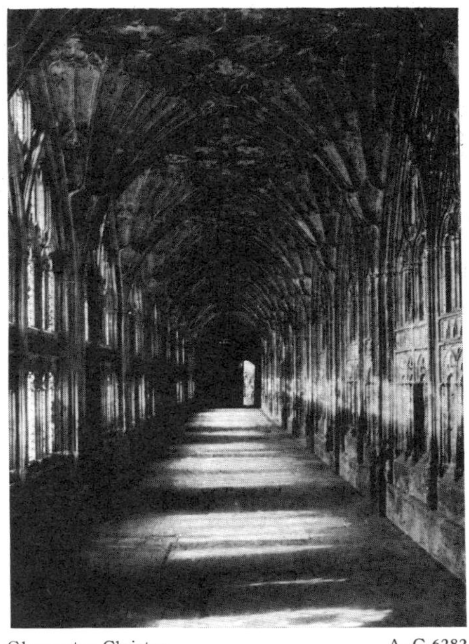
Gloucester Cloister A, C 6282

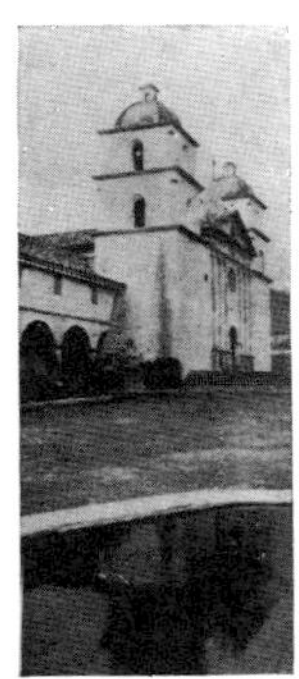
Santa Barbara Towers
Q or C 2217

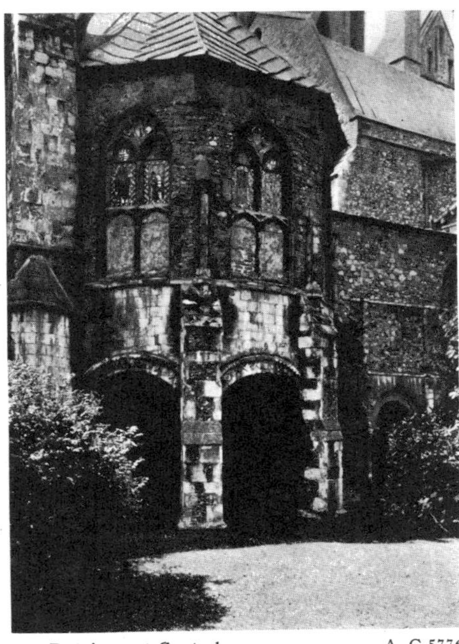
The Baptistry at Canterbury A, C 5776

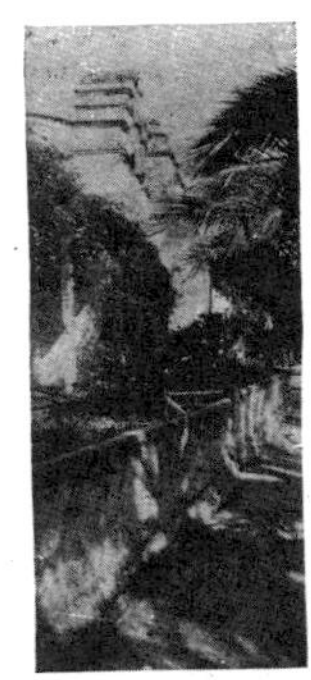
A Mission Corner
Q 2149

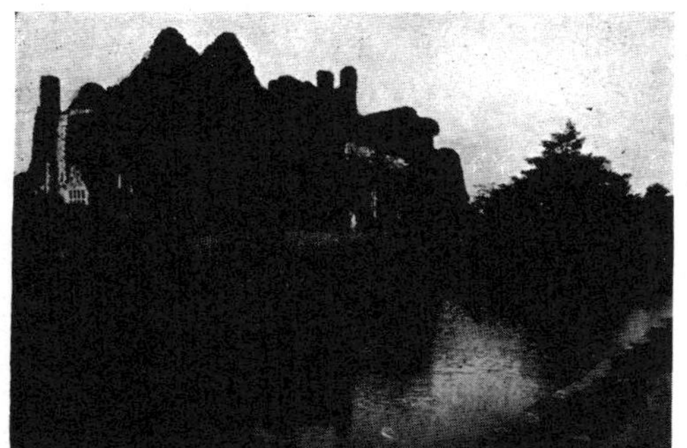

An Abbey Moat A, C 6053

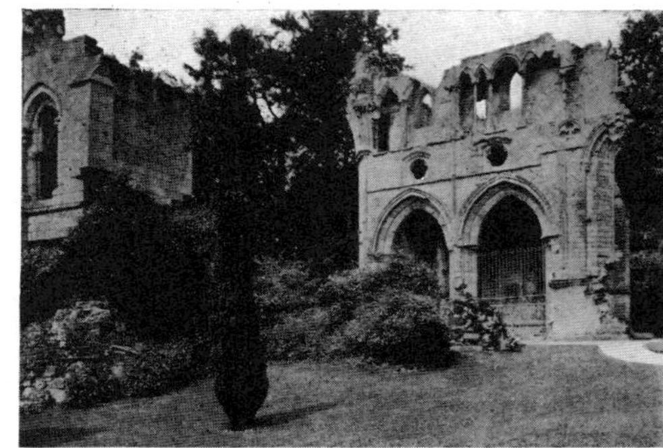

Scott's Tomb, Dryburgh A, S 5885

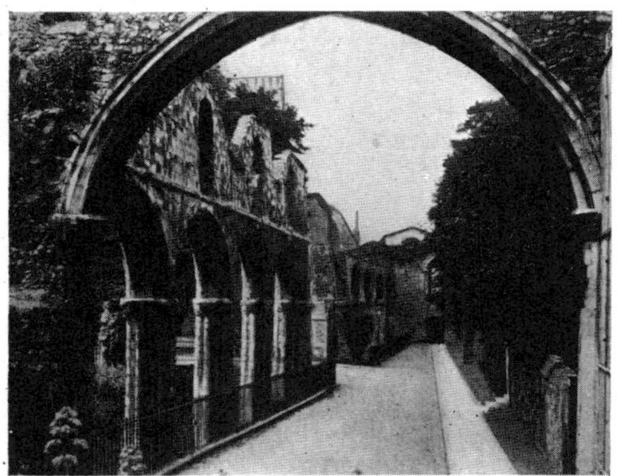

Canterbury Arches A, C 5549

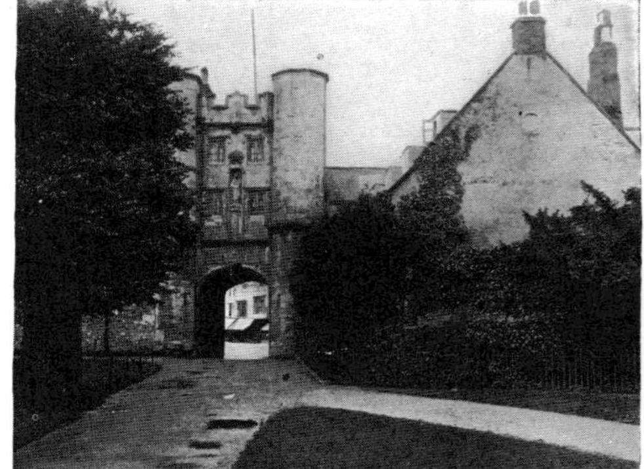

Within the Close A, C 5699

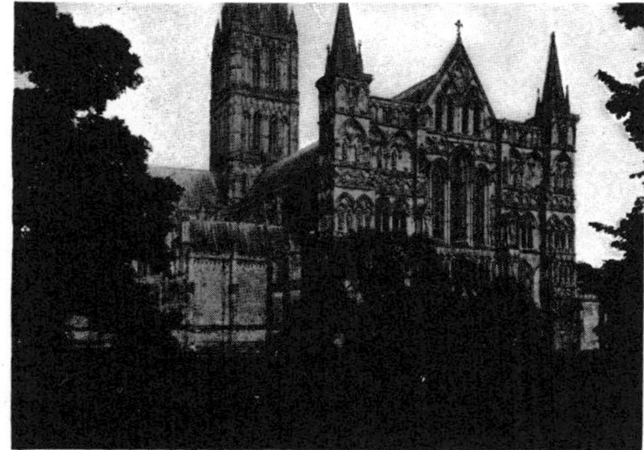

Salisbury Façade A, C 5745

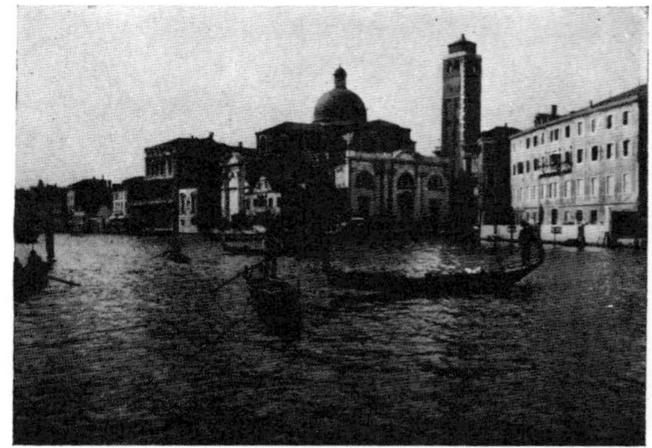

Old Venice A, S, C 4249

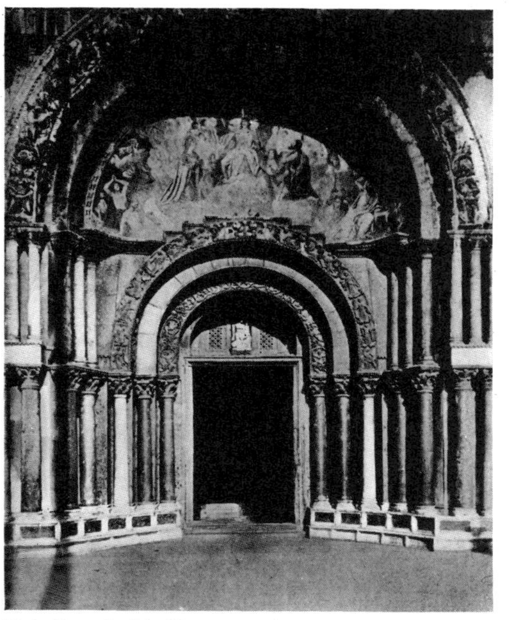

Main Door, St. Mark's A, C, E, G 4255

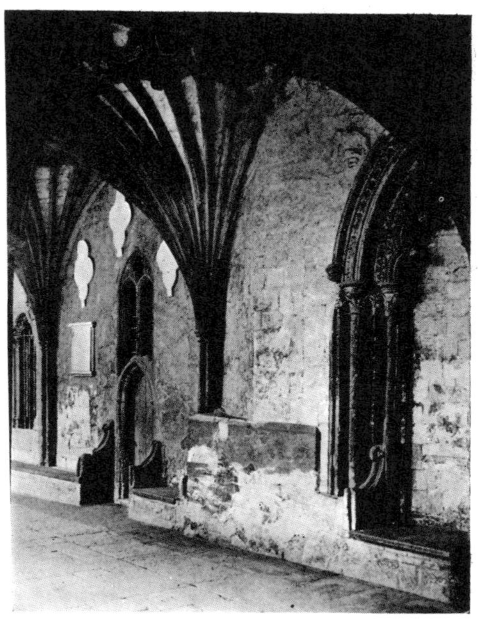

Cloister Seats, Canterbury A, C 5554

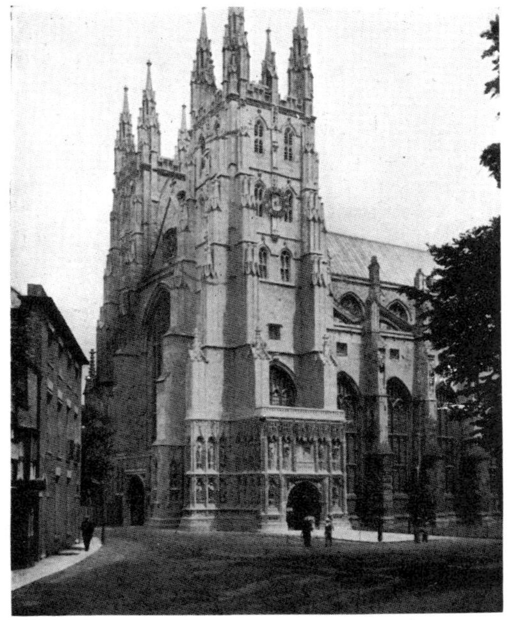

Canterbury Close A, C, E 5550

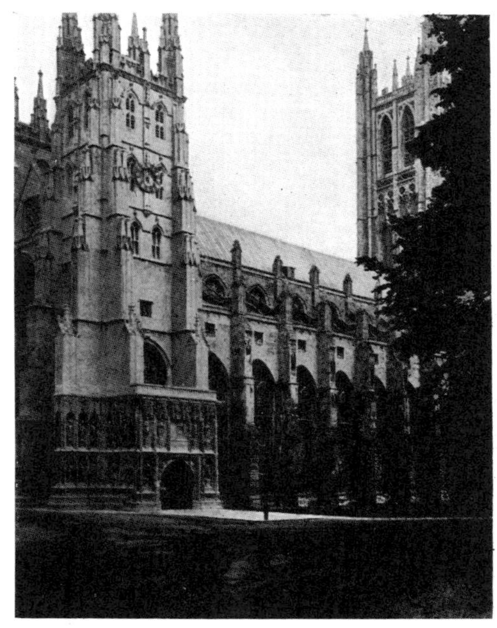

At Canterbury Gate A, C, E 5545

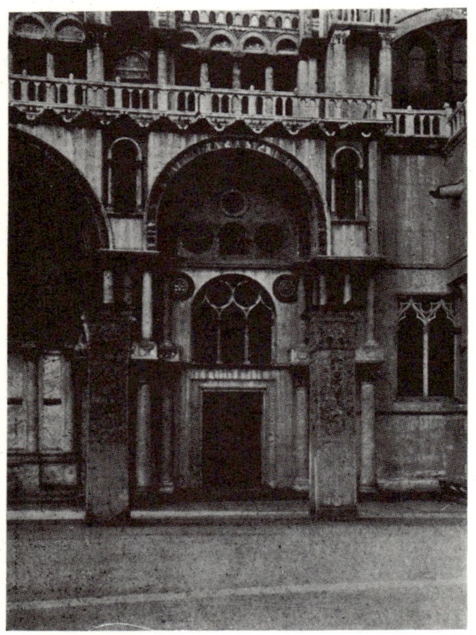

A Detail of St. Mark's A, C, E 4318

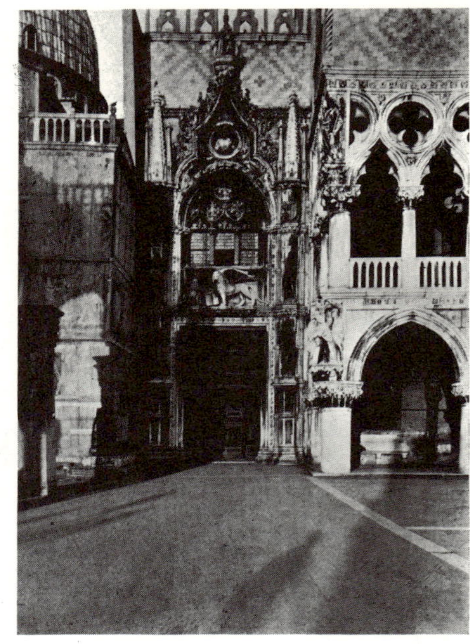

Porta Della Carta A, C, E, G 4346

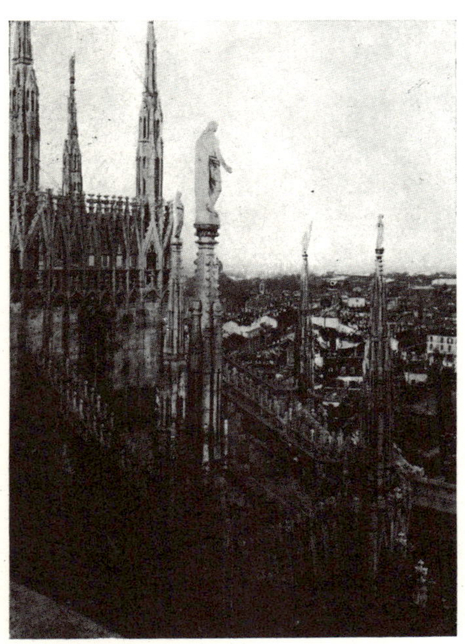

Through Milan's Spires A, C, E, 4375

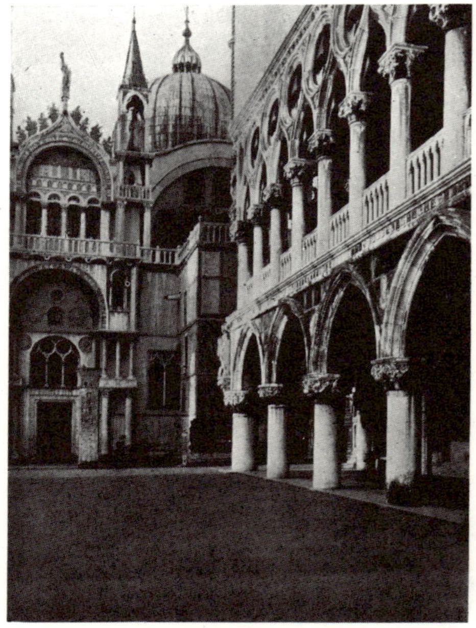

Venice's Chief Glory A, C, E 4344

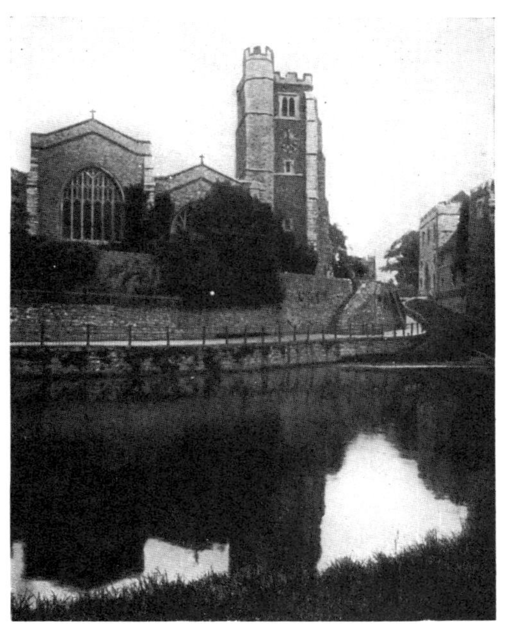
The Church by the Stream A, C 5576

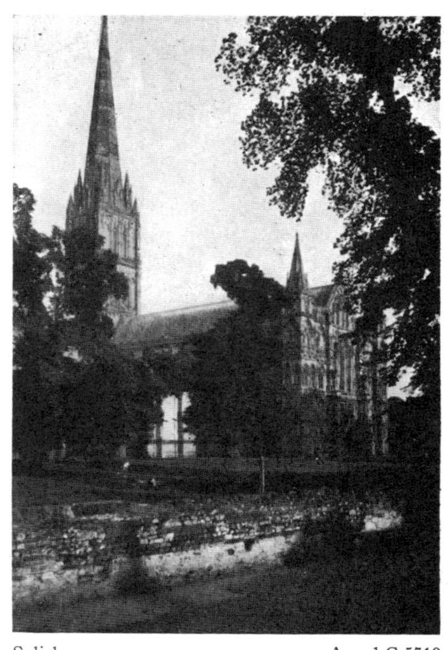
Salisbury A and C 5710

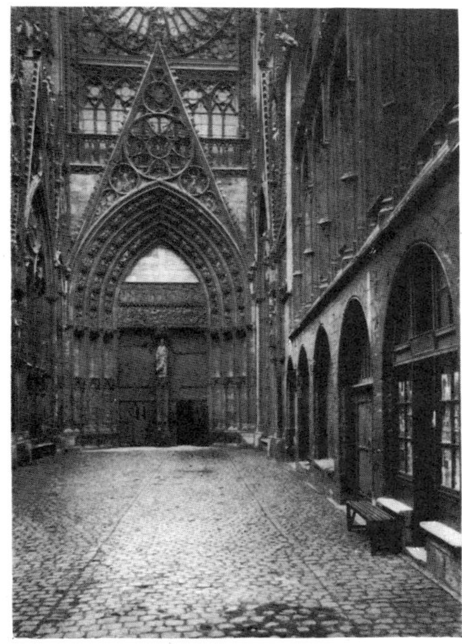
A Cathedral Close, Rouen C 4823

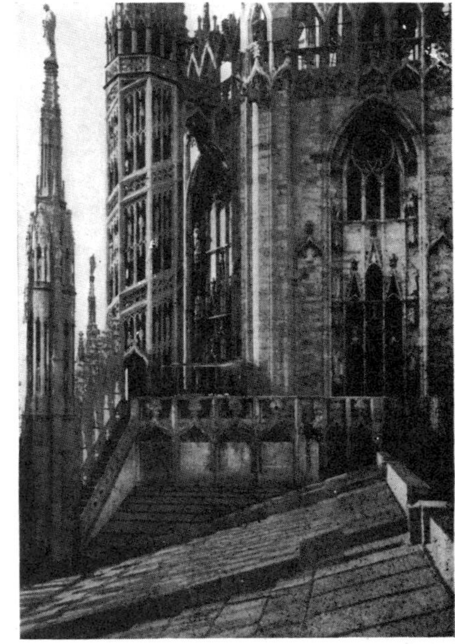
A Part of Milan's Towers A, C, E 4381

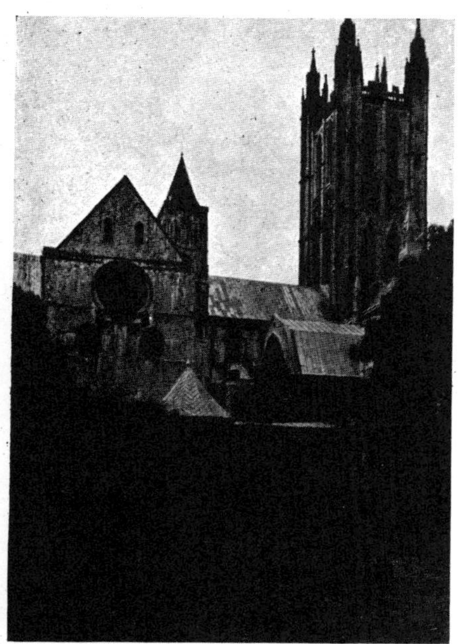

The North of Canterbury A, C 5778

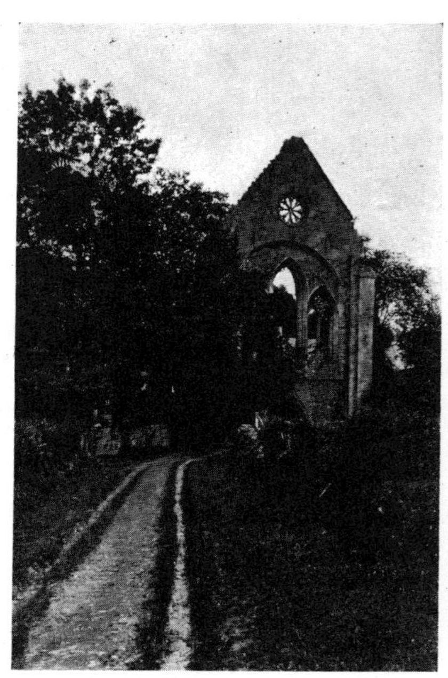

The Abbey Road A, S 6447

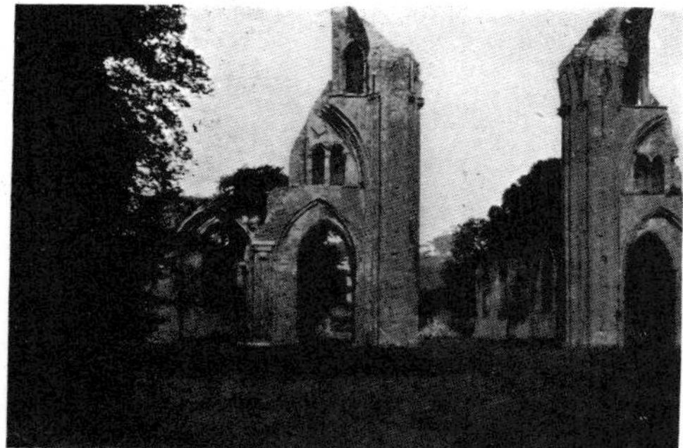

Old Glastonbury A, C 6344

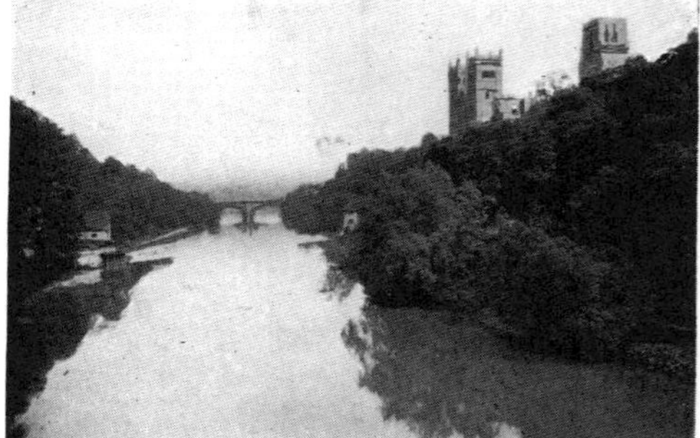

Durham A, C 5853

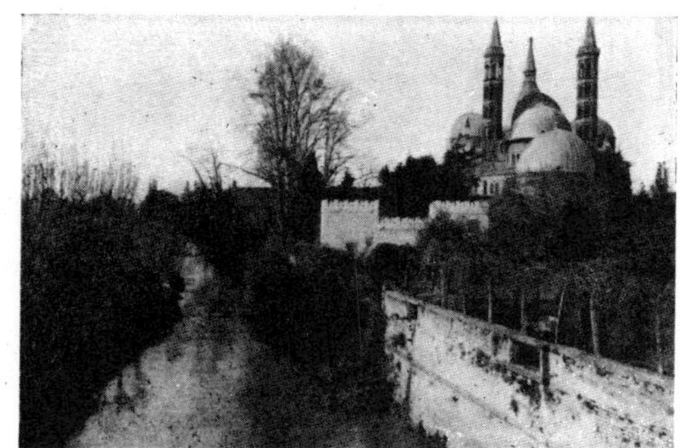

The Italian Spring A, C, E 4276

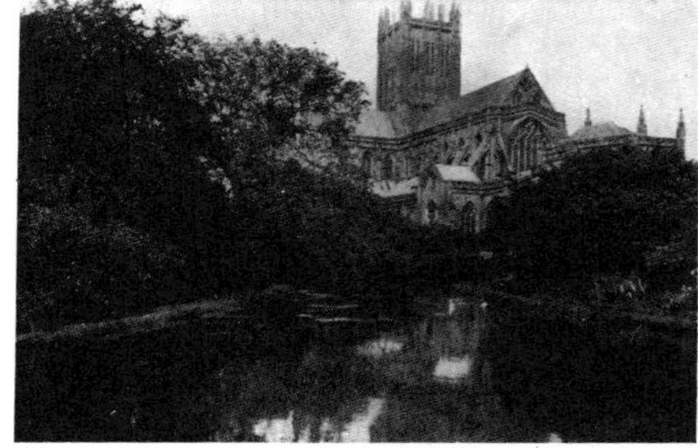

Wells, Bishop's Garden A, C, E, F 5701

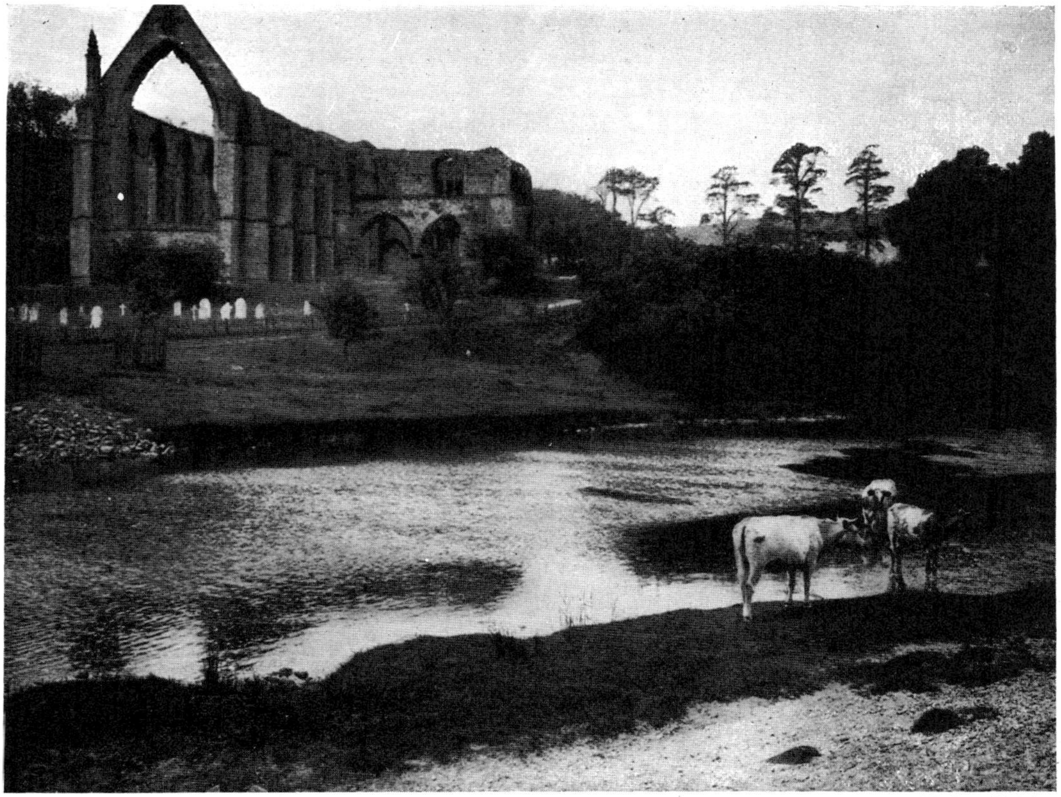

Bolton A, C, E, F, T 6216 Wallace Nutting

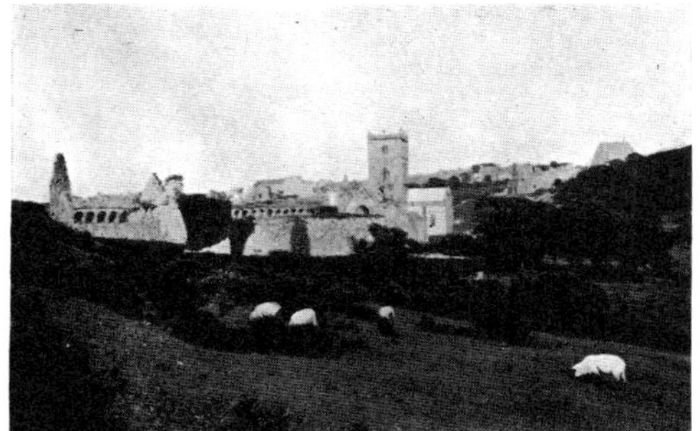

St. David's Palace A, S, P 5981

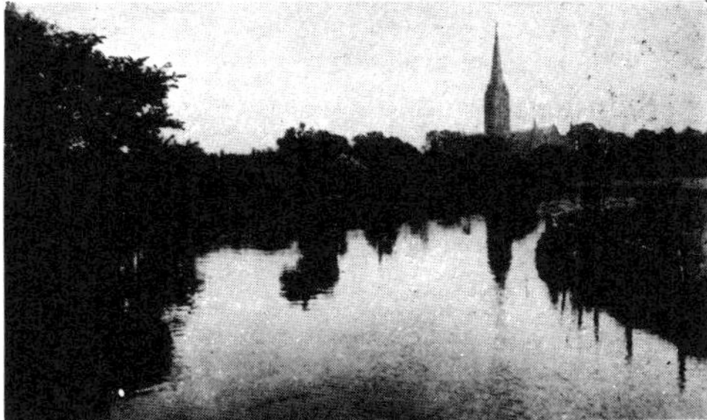

Summer on the Avon A, S, P 5708

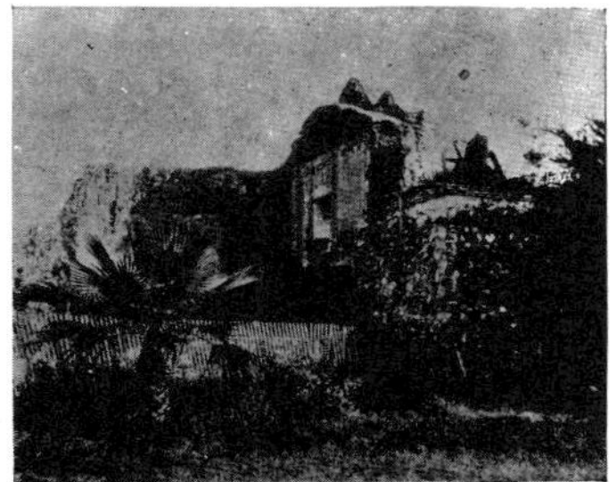

The Ruins of San Diego Mission C 2203

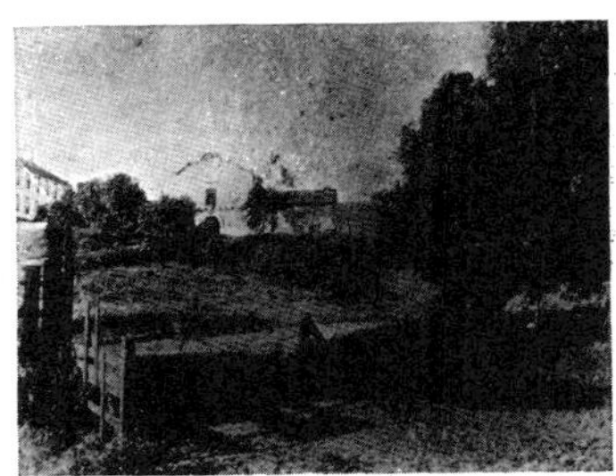

San Diego from the Highway C 2208

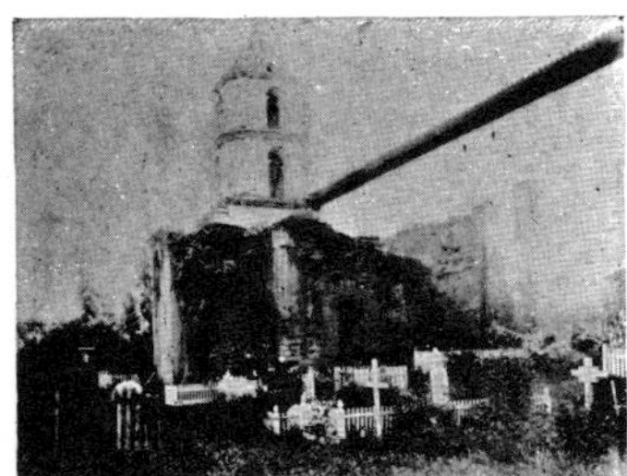
Churchyard, San Luis Rey C 2204

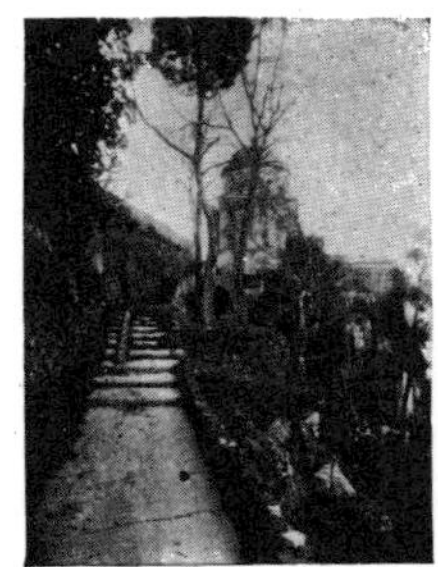
Old Italy E 31

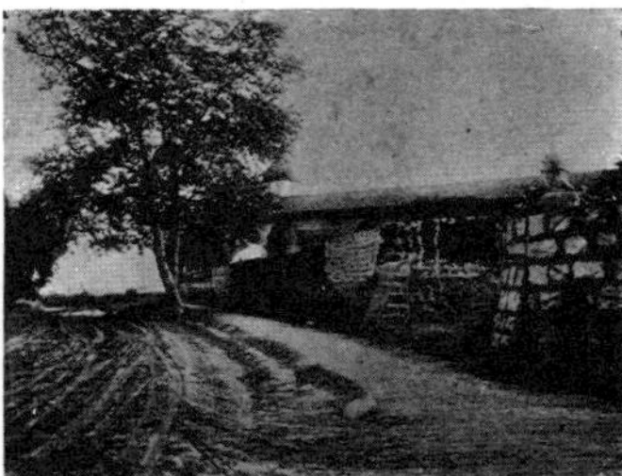
The Mission Road C 2218

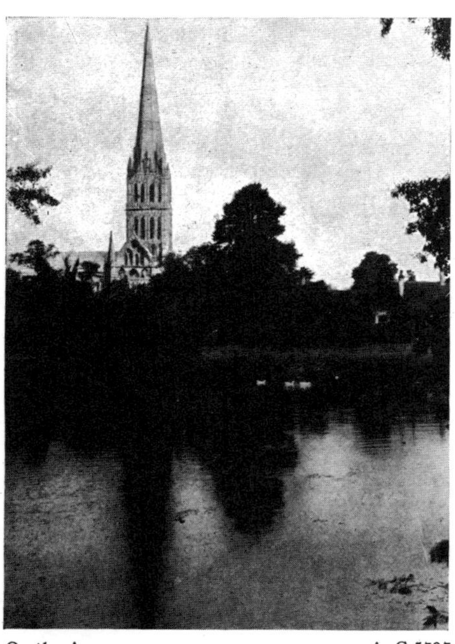
On the Avon A, C 5707

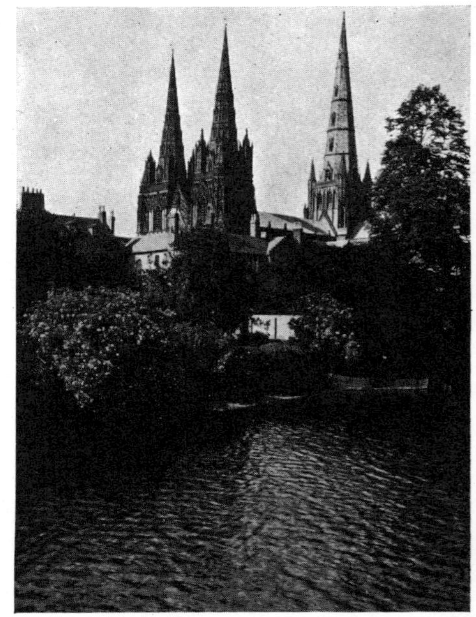
Litchfield Minster A, C, E 5845

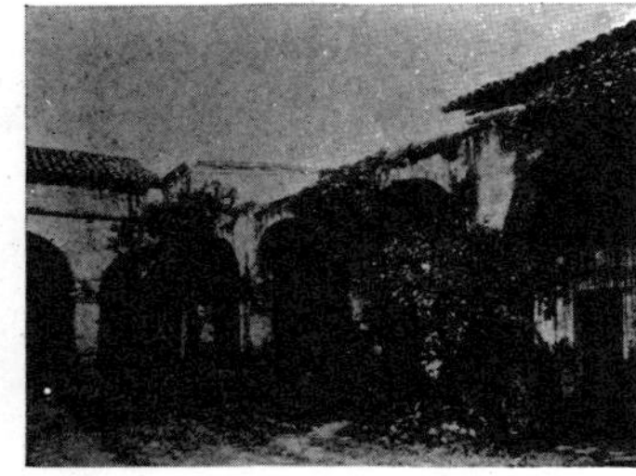
A Corner of Capistrano C 2192

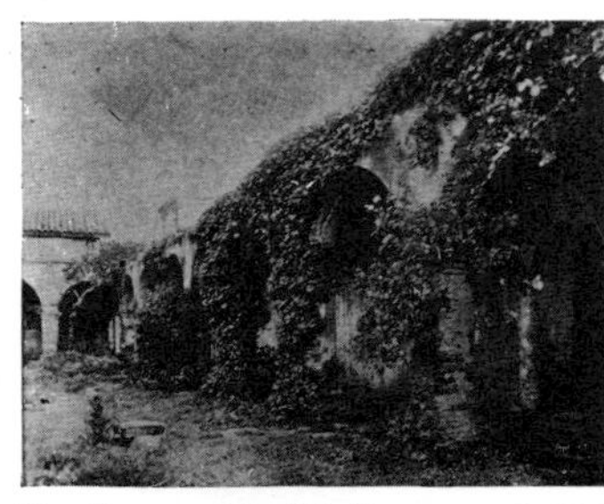
The Poetry of the Mission C 2198

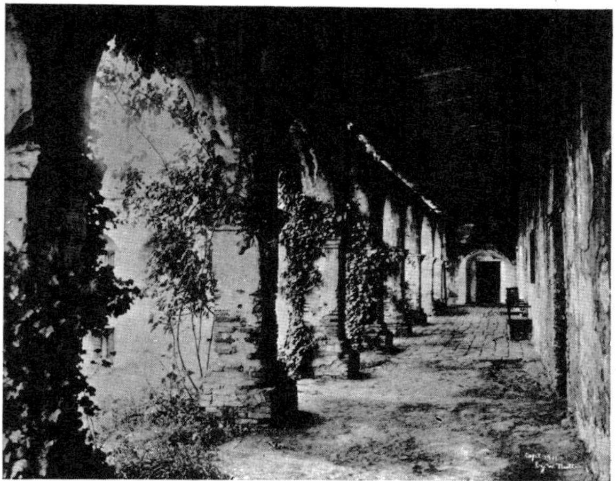

Ivy and Rose Cloisters C, E, F or J 2197

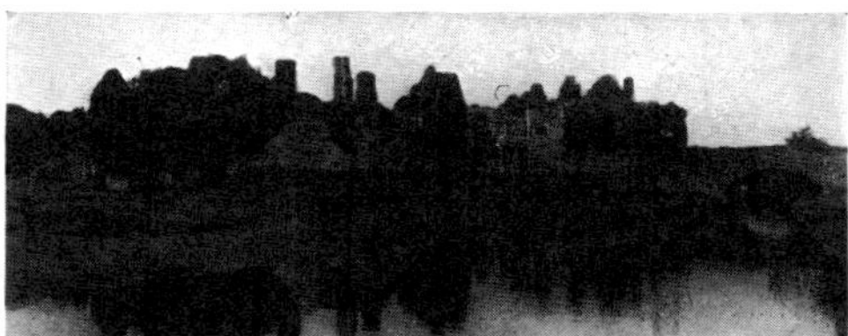

The Abbey by the Stream Q, O 6028

Neath Abbey, shown just above, is in South Wales and, with the bridge in conjunction, it affords a charming horizontal panel, but no one should buy it who does not love abbey ruins. " Summer on the Avon " (page 359) is not made at Stratford, which does not now, with its lofty trees, make a satisfactory picture. The print on page 359 is of Salisbury, of which there is another one long vertically, and various detailed views. " Litchfield Minster " (page 360) has some fine pink hawthorn blossoms just beyond the water. The rich brown tones of the spires give this subject a peculiar distinction. On page 358 " The Abbey Road " shows the Vale Crucis. " The Italian Spring " on the same page is the famous seven-domed church of Padua. " Durham Towers," shown on the same page, has a sky of a soft reddish brown and is a rich afternoon theme.

None of the Nutting negatives are ever sold, though frequent requests have come from competitors for the sale of such as we no longer use; but following the law that "The good is the enemy of the best," we constantly consign to the scrap heap subjects which have proved salable, but have been superseded by others a little better.

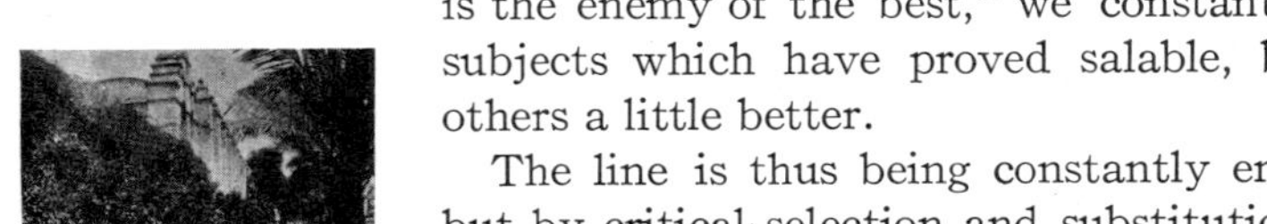

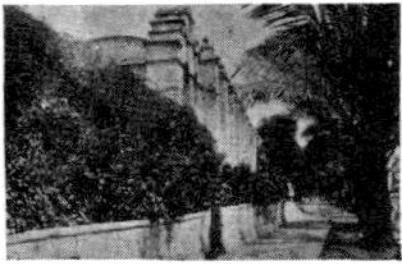

San Gabriel Mission
A 126

The line is thus being constantly enriched, not only by additions, but by critical selection and substitution. We are never content with past successes. Among the most widely popular are subjects added only within the last few months.

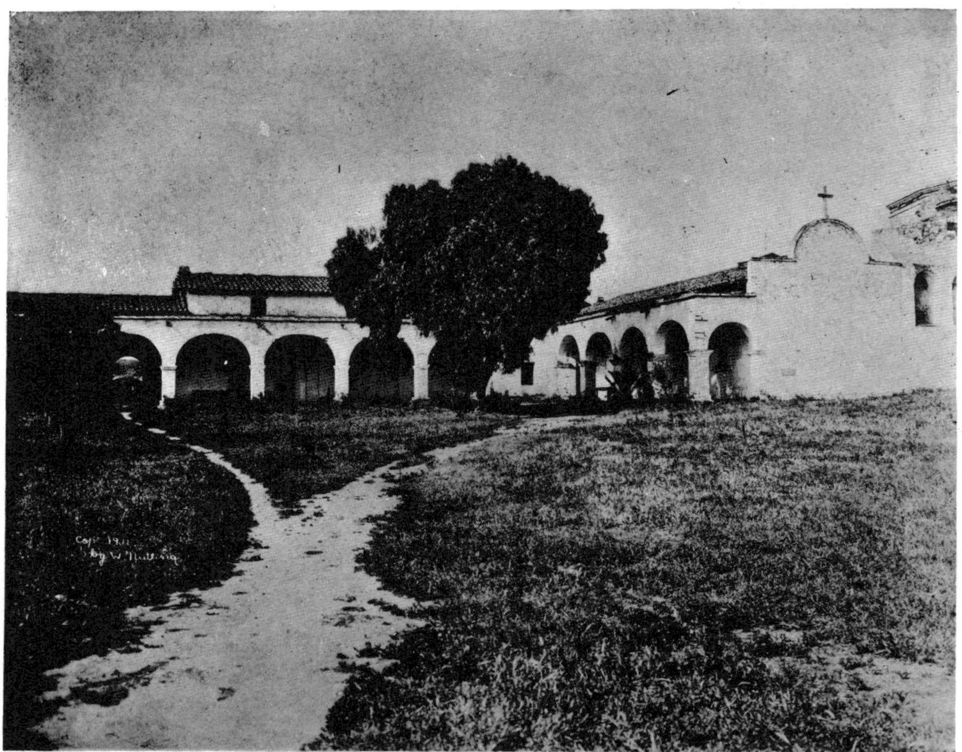

The Approach | Q, S, C, P or E 2195 | Wallace Nutting

MISSIONS

Mr. Nutting has made practically all the Californian Missions. It has always been his opinion that they are overrated architecturally. Nevertheless, that shown immediately above, especially in the panel size, is very attractive. " Ivy and Rose Cloisters " (page 361) appears in large sizes. It is especially satisfactory in the E and F sizes. We have a half-dozen aspects of San Gabriel and Santa Barbara.

If it is desired to obtain any of these ecclesiastical themes without color, they will be supplied in sepia, but long notice is required, as we use very little sepia.

Mr. Nutting is in process now of making additions to his old American churches; but the demand for them is more largely from architectural students. Mr. Nutting will make to order any American church within reasonable distance of his home, if given a little time, as he tours a great deal. He will also make arrangements to photograph private estates, if desired.

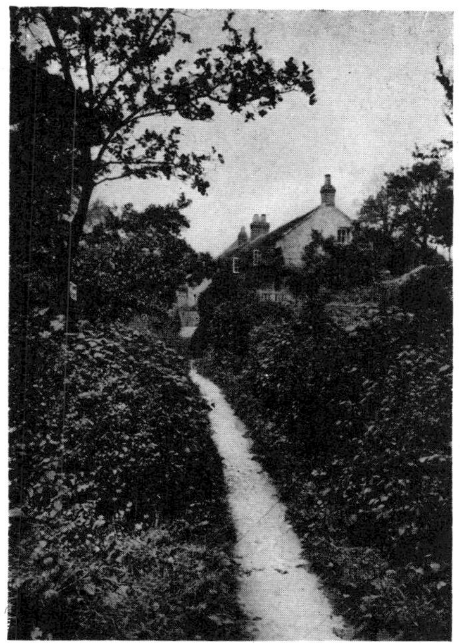

A House Lane A, S 5823

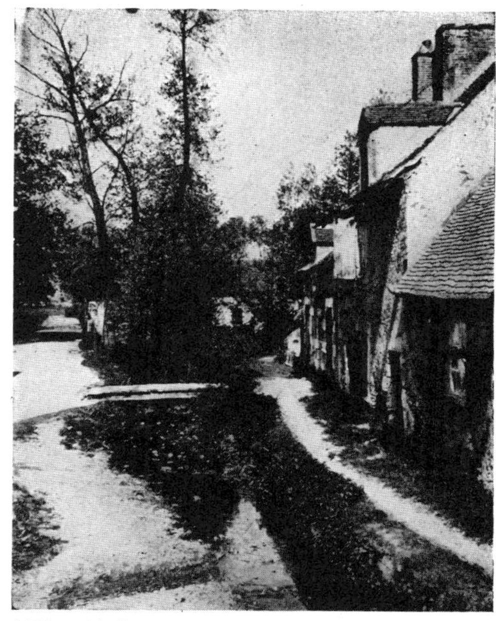

A Waterside Cottage A, C 4720

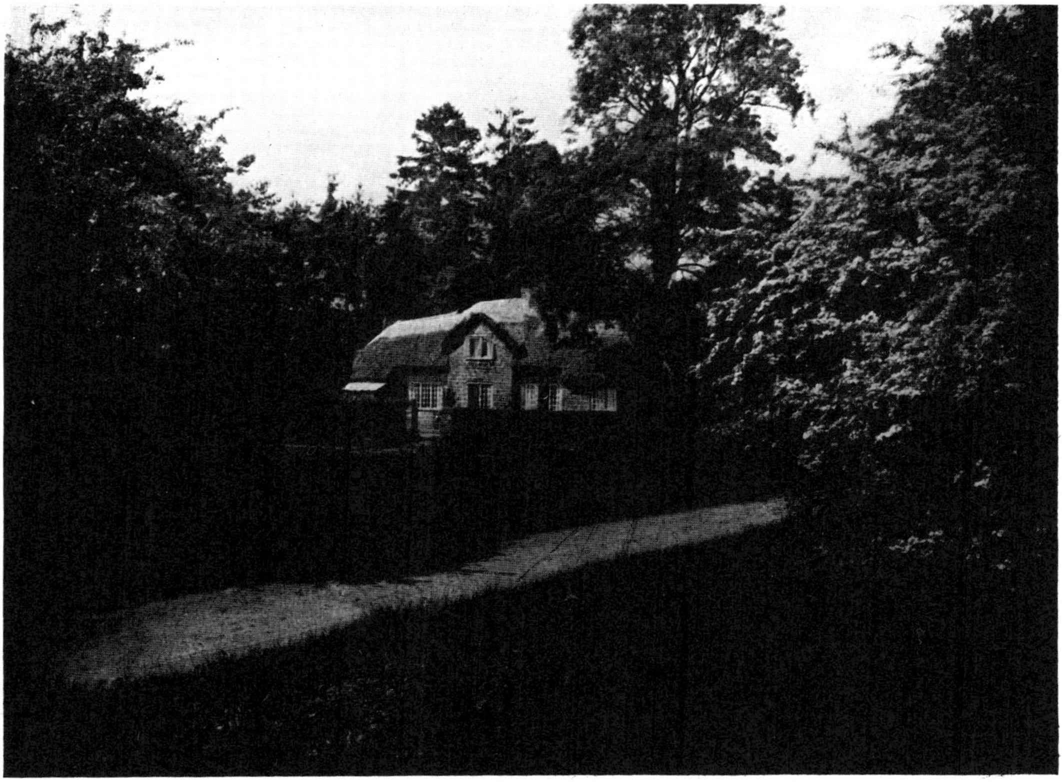

The Nest A, C, E 5605 Wallace Nutting

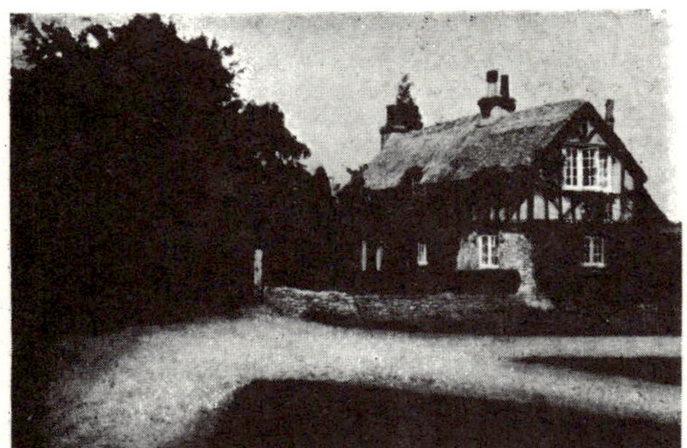
The Parsonage Drive A, S 5624

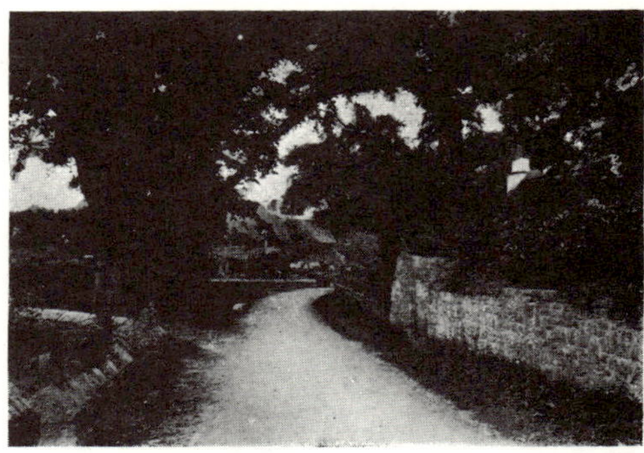
Patti's Favorite Walk A, C 6230

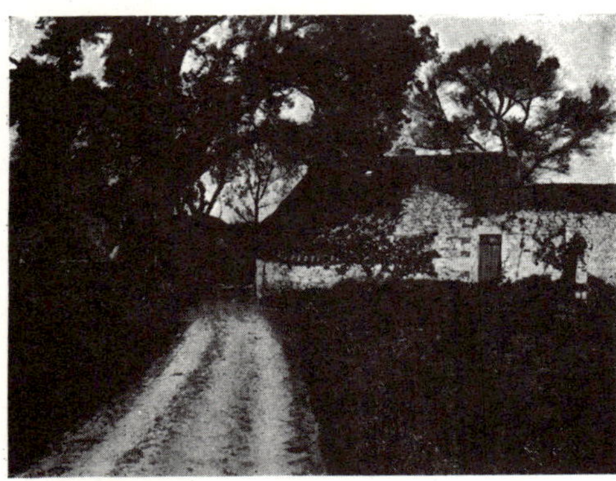
The Farmstead Entrance (France) A, C 4654

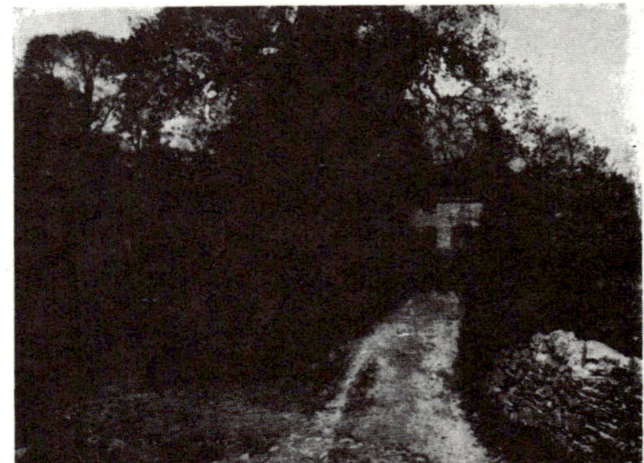
Isaac Walton Brook A, C 5804

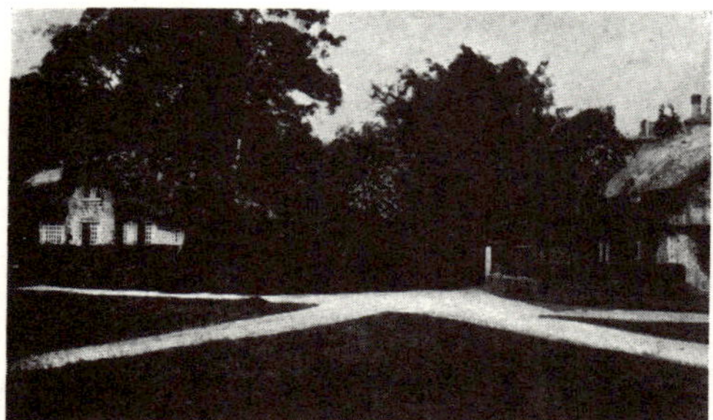
The Quiet Life A, S, P 5703

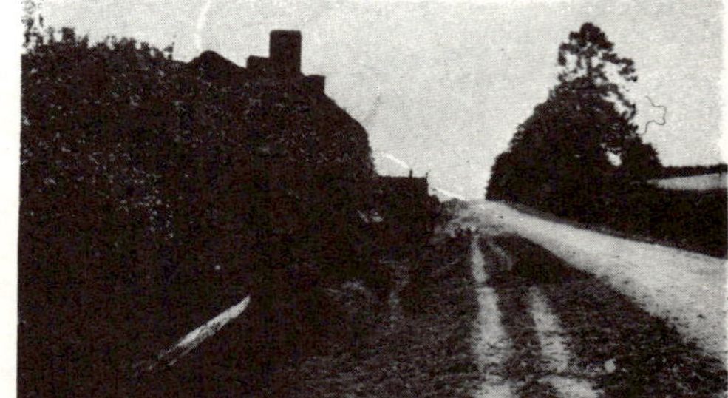
Half Hidden A, S 4848

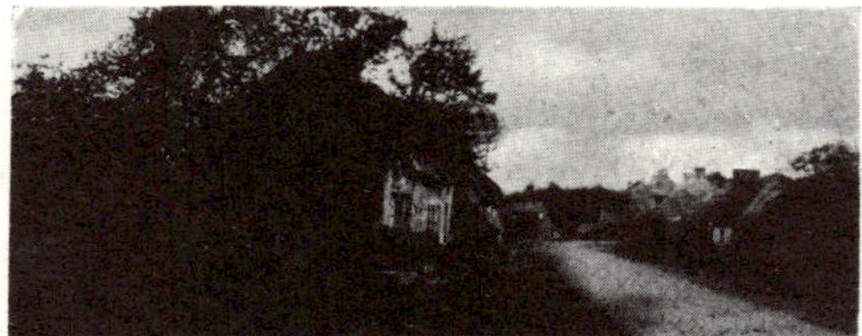
A Peaceful Village A, Q 4833

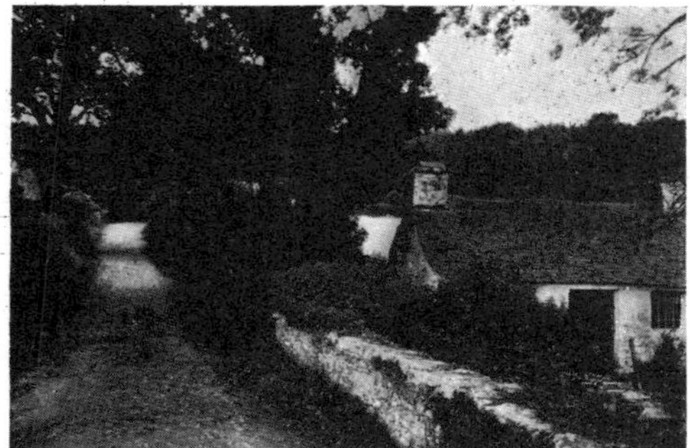

Where Grandma was Born A, C, E 6119

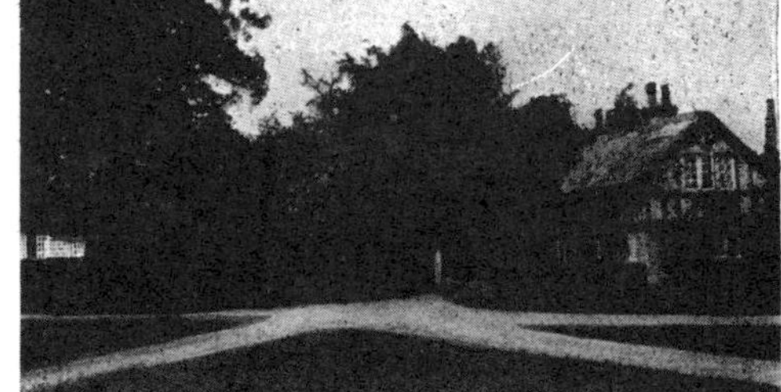

The Vicarage

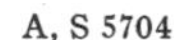

A, S 5704

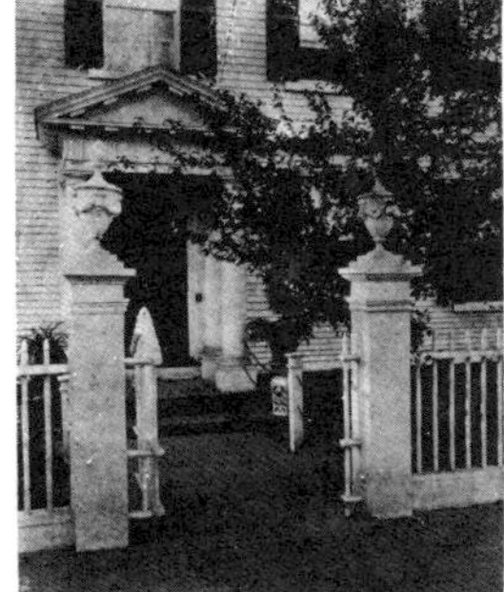

Gate with Urns C 986

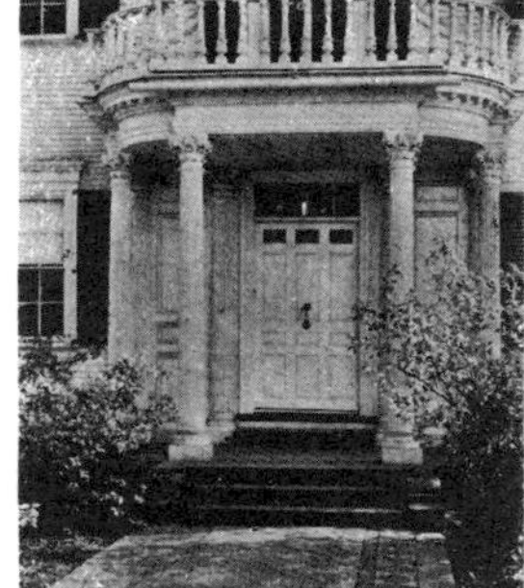

Langdon Door C 572

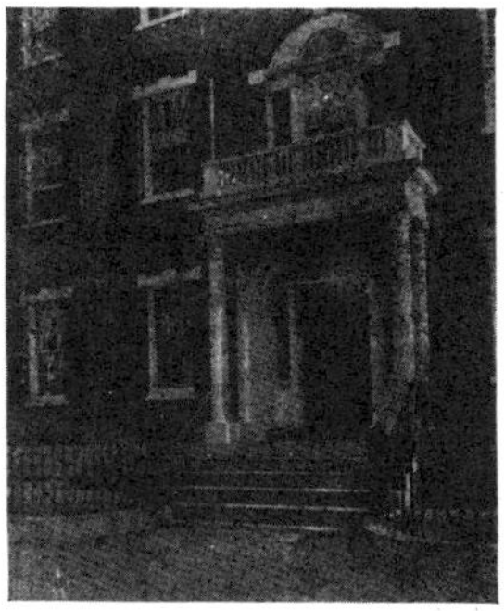

A Georgian Door S or C 989

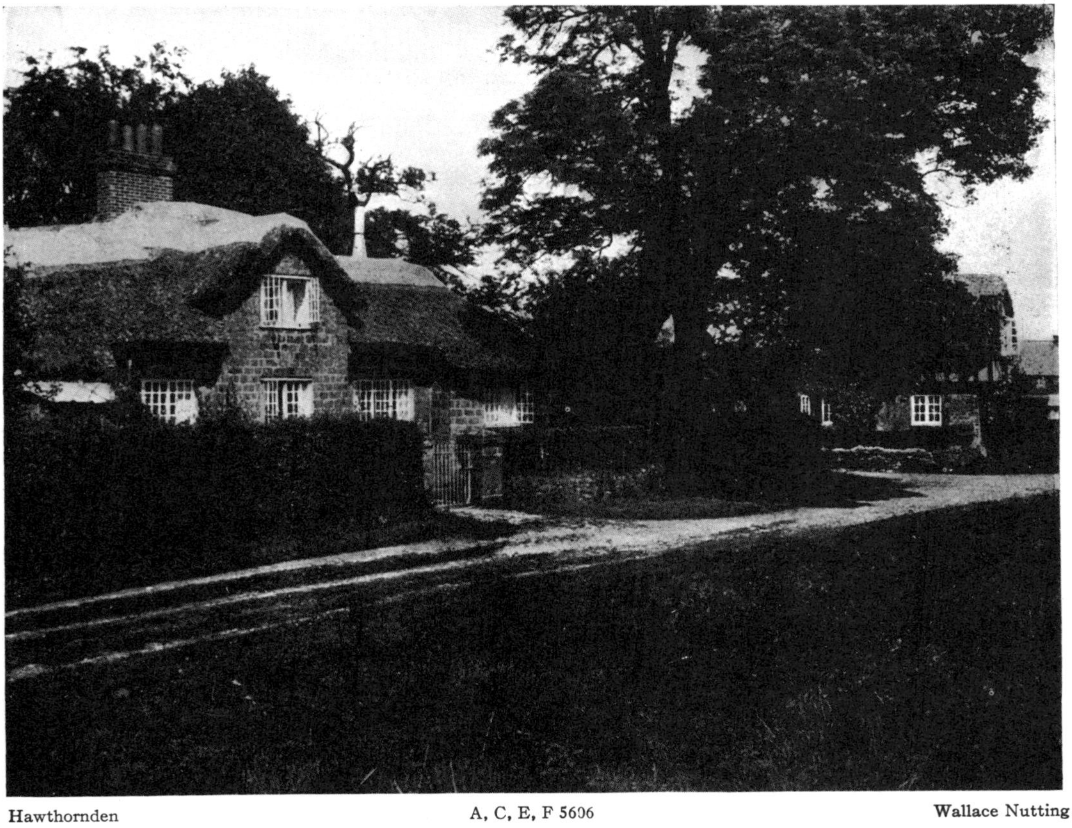

Hawthornden A, C, E, F 5606 Wallace Nutting

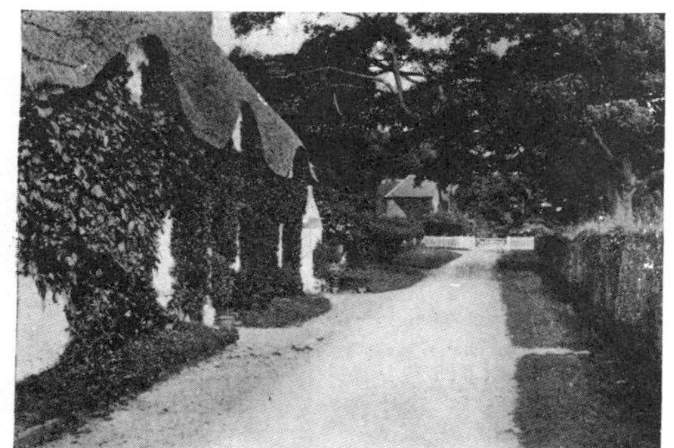

The Little Street A, C 6059

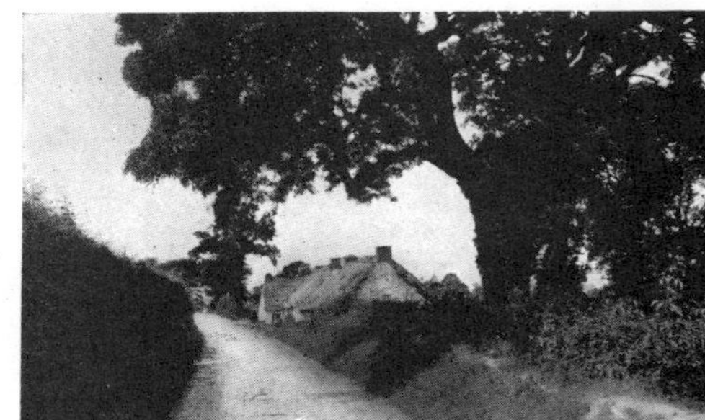

Home A, S 6220

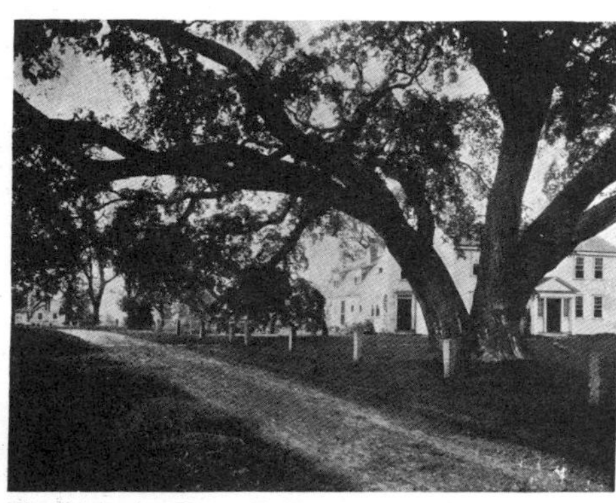

The Protecting Home Tree Wallace Nutting
C and E 1517

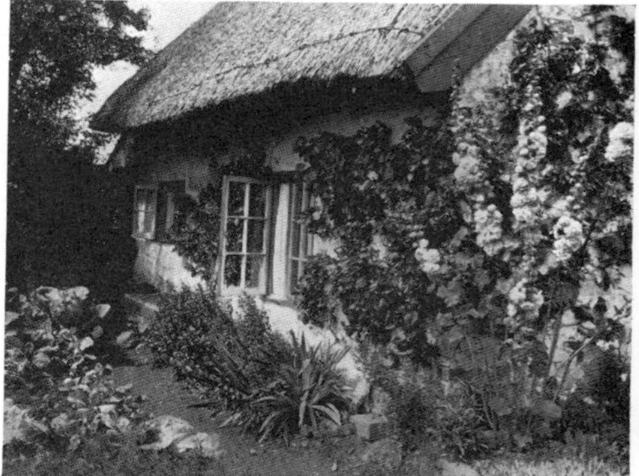

Hollyhock Cottage A, C, E 6414

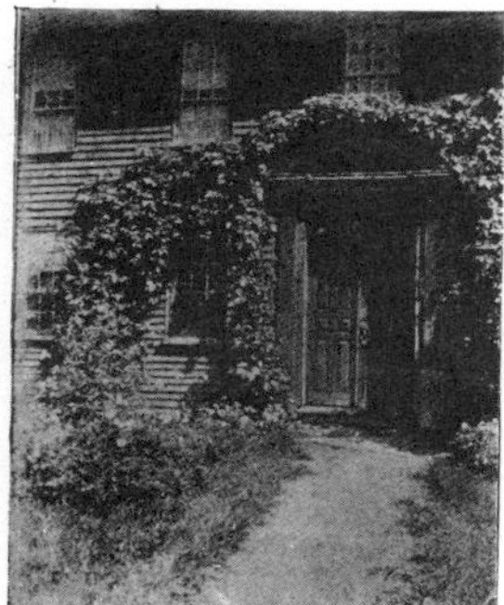

A Newbury Door S, C 991

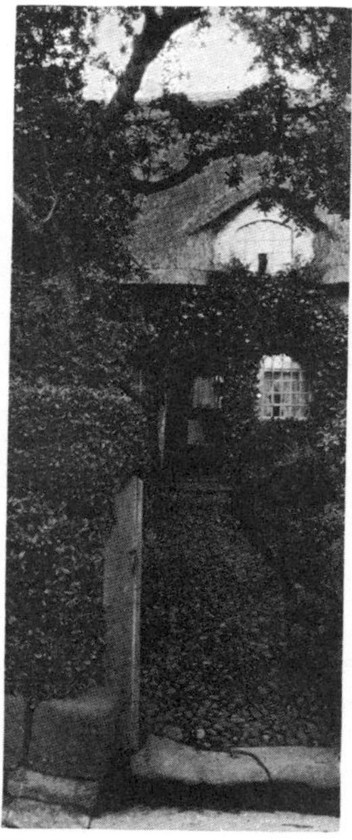

The Lure of Home Q 6410

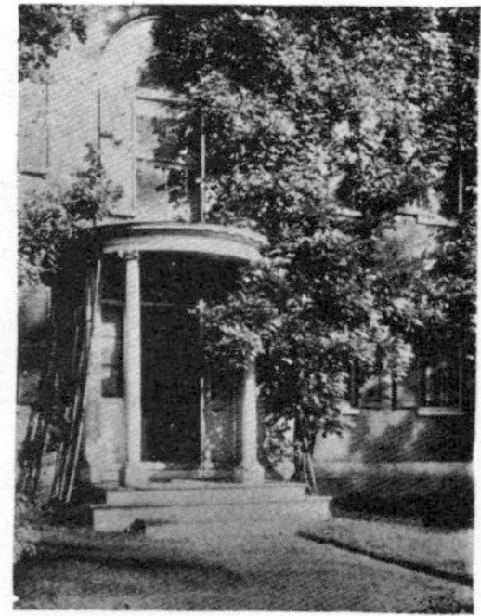

Benedict Door C 571

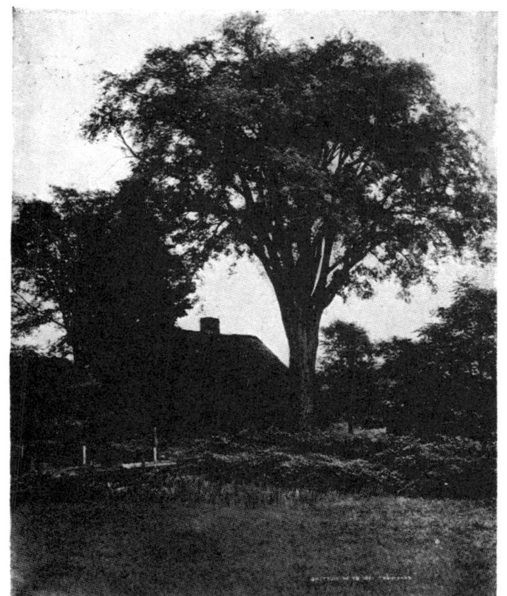

Two Centuries 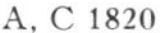 A, C 1820

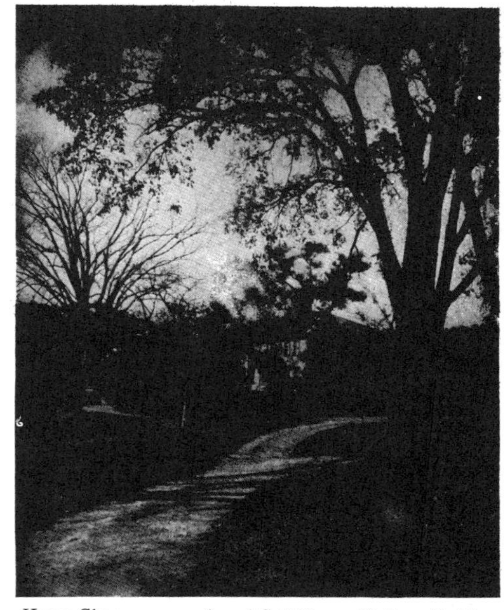

Home Charm A and C 1427 Wallace Nutting

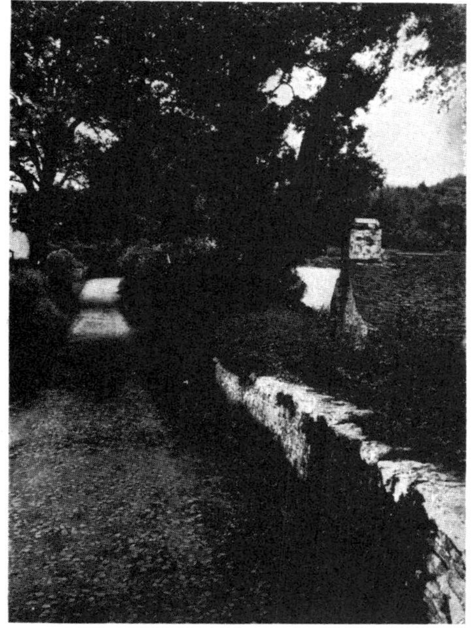

Up from the Dell A, C, E 6117

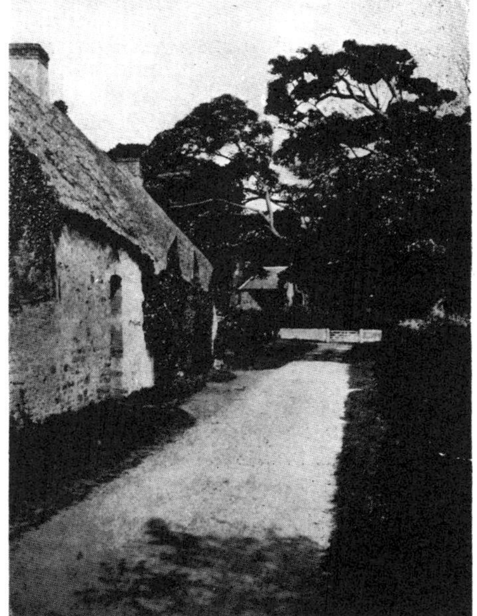

Afternoon in the Lane A, C 6057

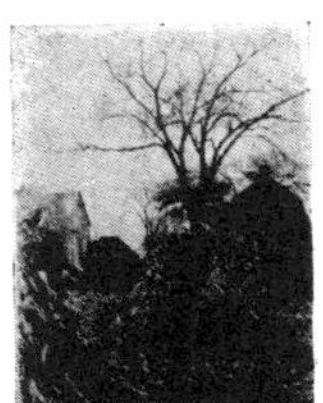

Thanksgiving
A 60

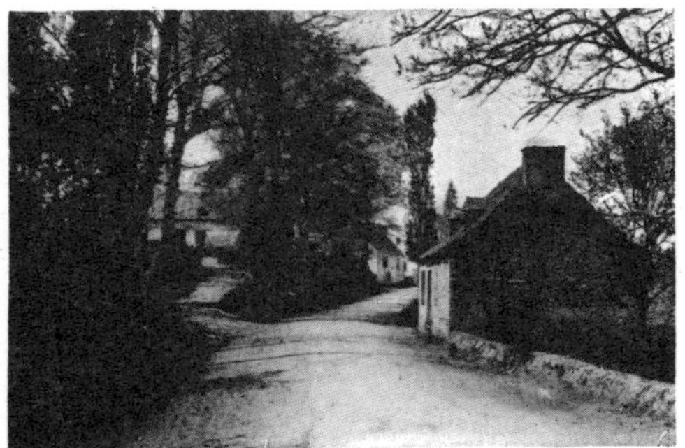

Mauvezin's Village Street A, C 4534

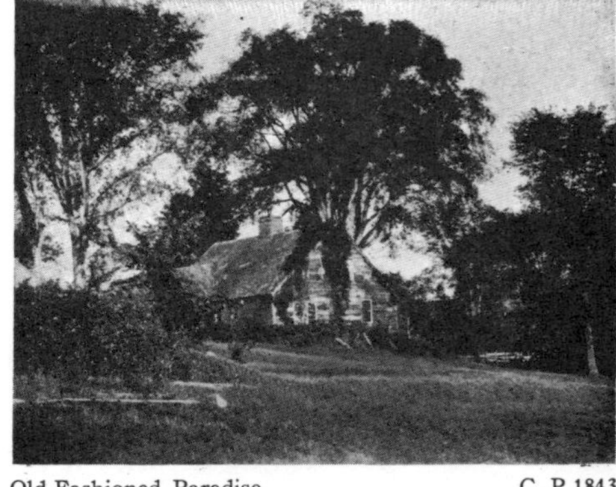

Old Fashioned Paradise C, P 1843

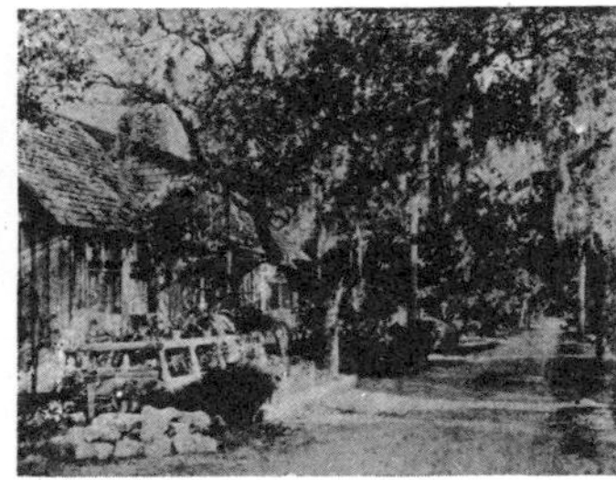

The Cottage in the Lane A or C 1127

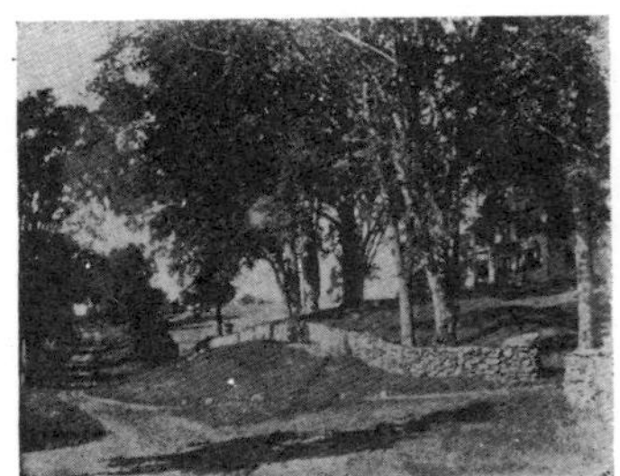

A Connecticut Homestead A or C 346

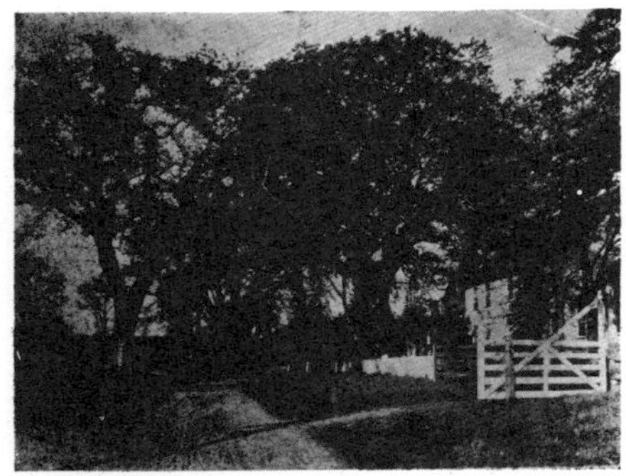

An Old Fashioned Village E 55

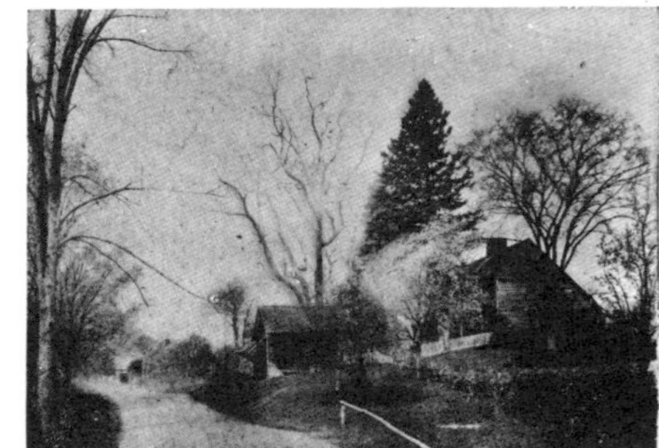

The Old Stage Road E 120

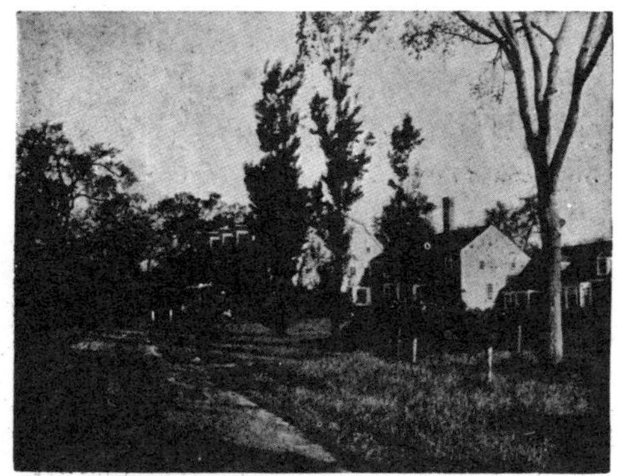

The Wayside Inn Approach Wallace Nutting
A and C 592

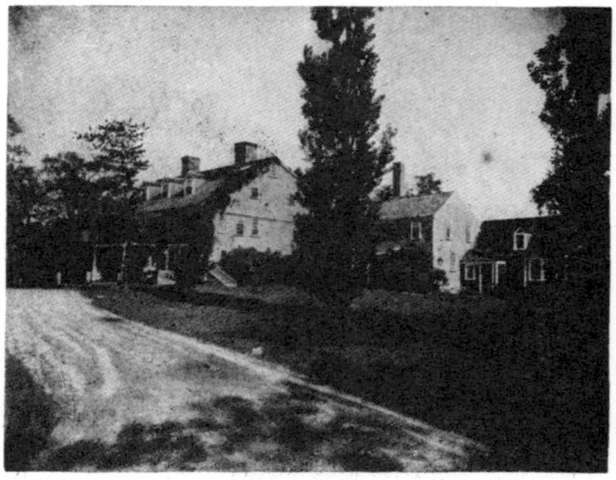

The Wayside's Colonial Dignity Wallace Nutting
A, C and E 648

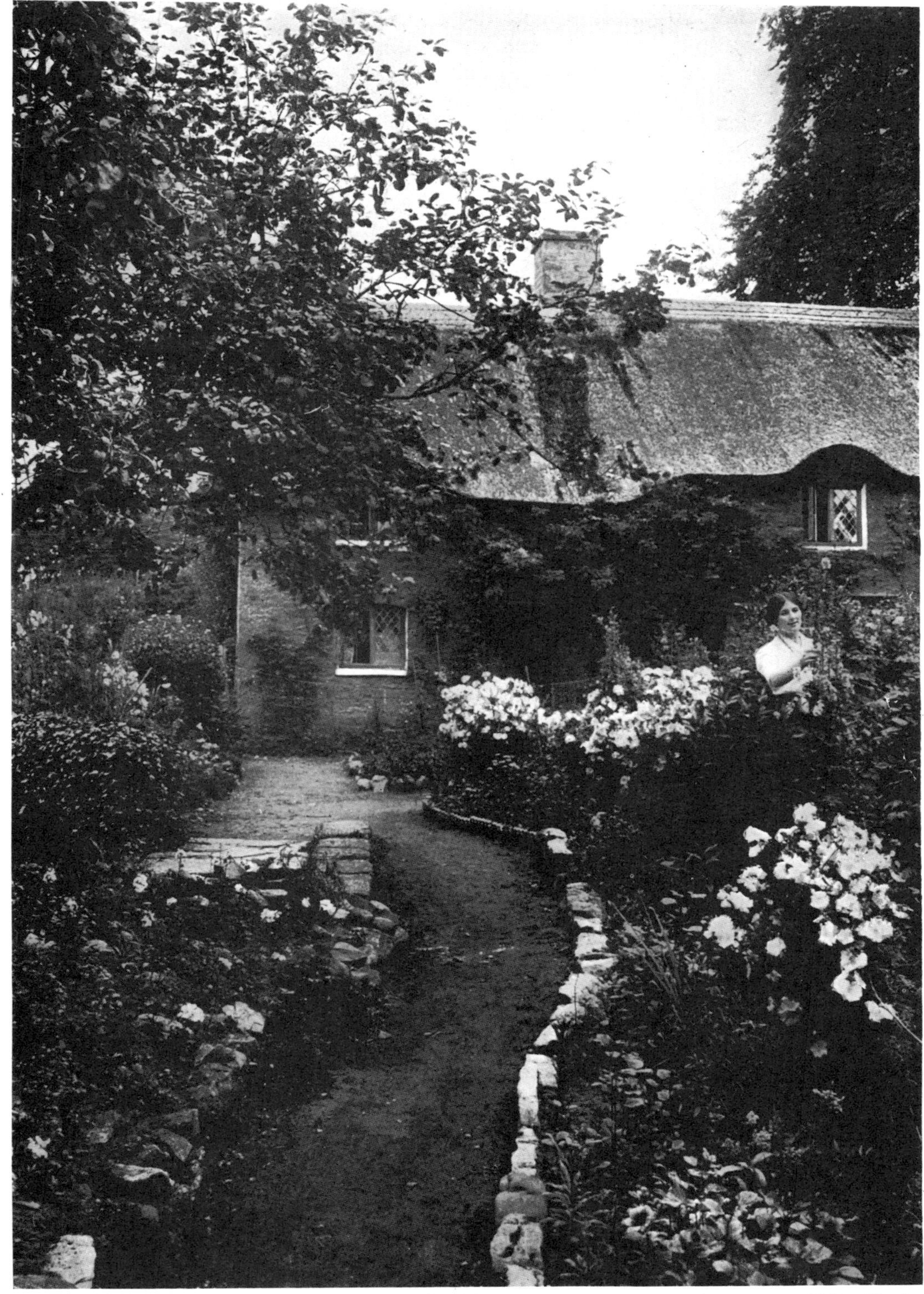

Larkspur | A, C and E 6063 | Wallace Nutting

The above will not make a larger picture

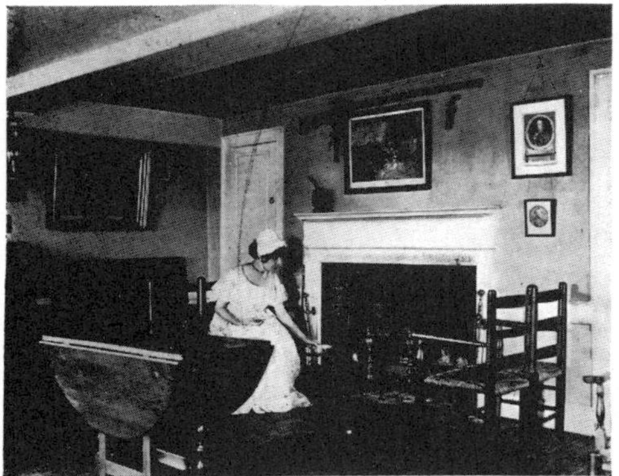

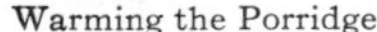

Warming the Porridge C 3522

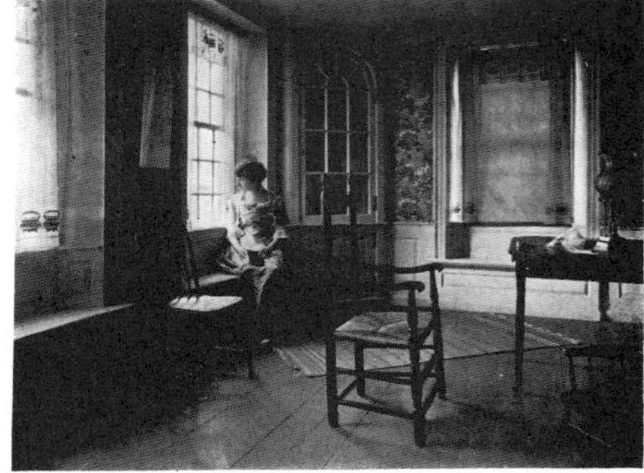

Watchful Waiting C3482

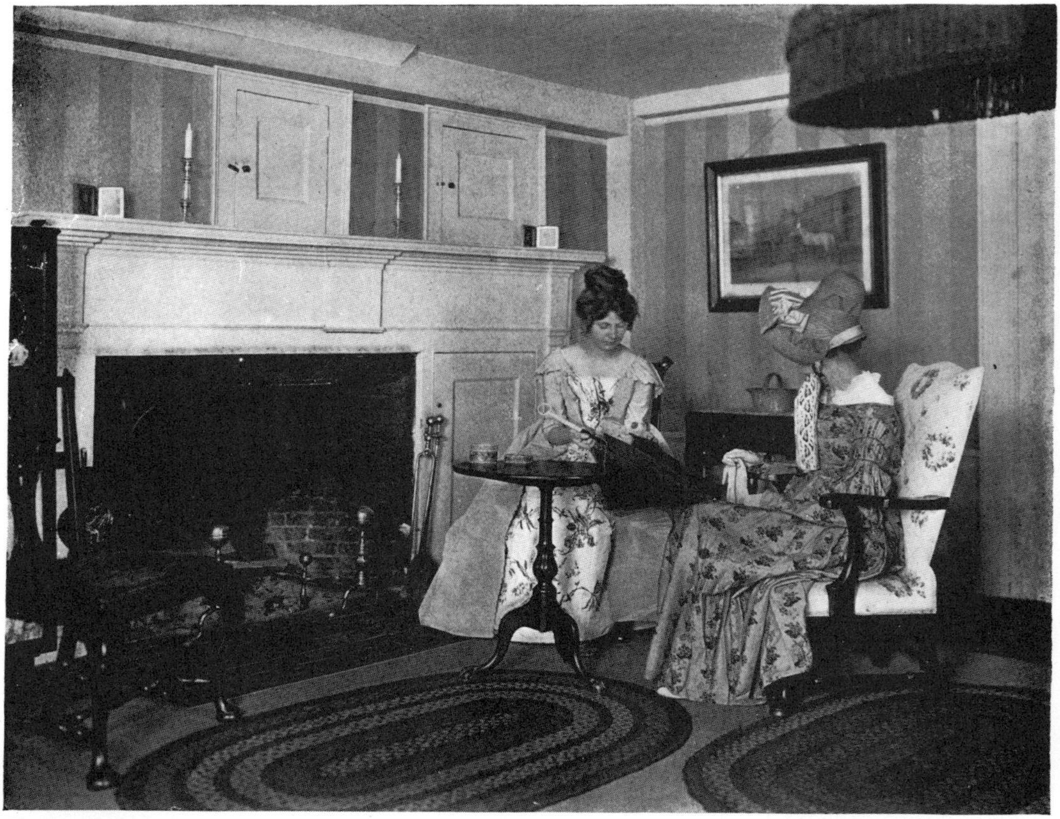

The New Parasol C, E 3650 Wallace Nutting

The room above is very old, and so is all the furniture. "Everything antique but the girls." Mr. Nutting now makes no "Colonial" subjects without insisting that the furniture be absolutely appropriate.

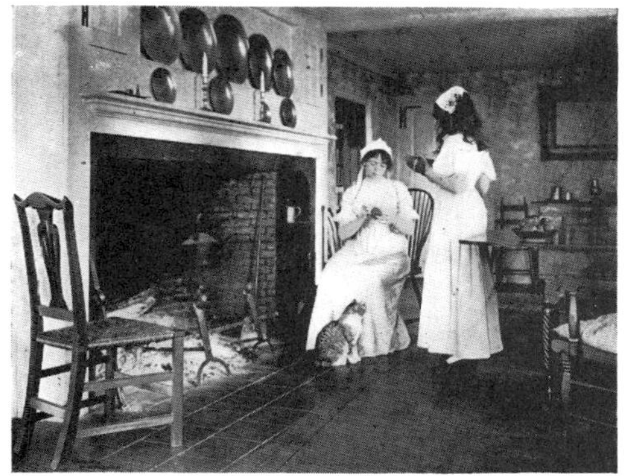

Three Chums A, C, E, F 3082

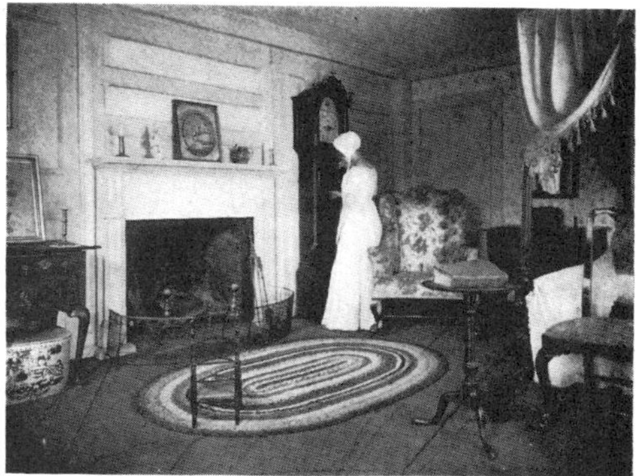

Winding the Old Tall Clock C, P and E 3302

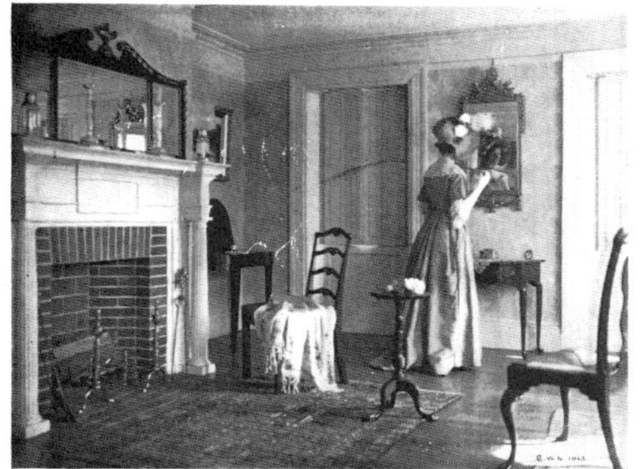

All Smiles C 3004

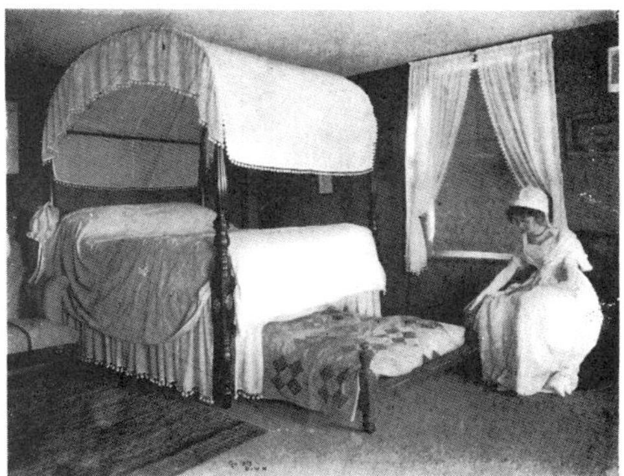

Her Old Trundle Bed C 3126

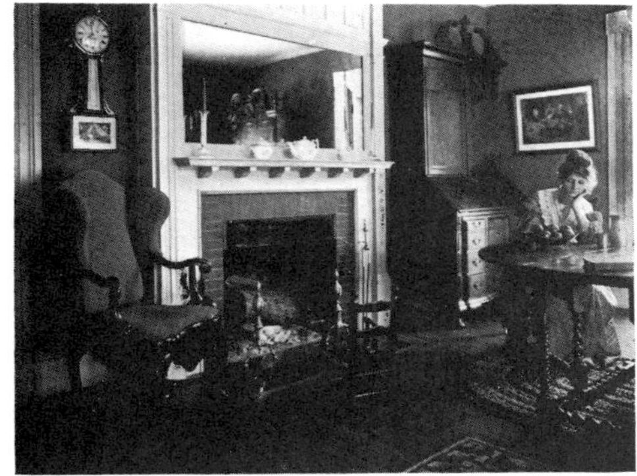

A Fruit Luncheon A, C and E 4010

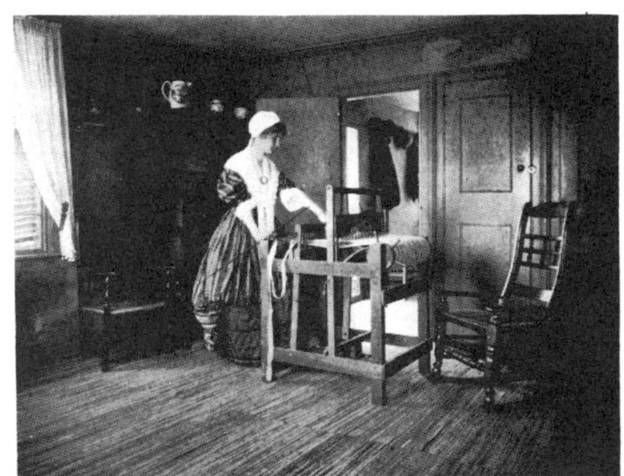

Recreations of our Foremothers C and E 3150

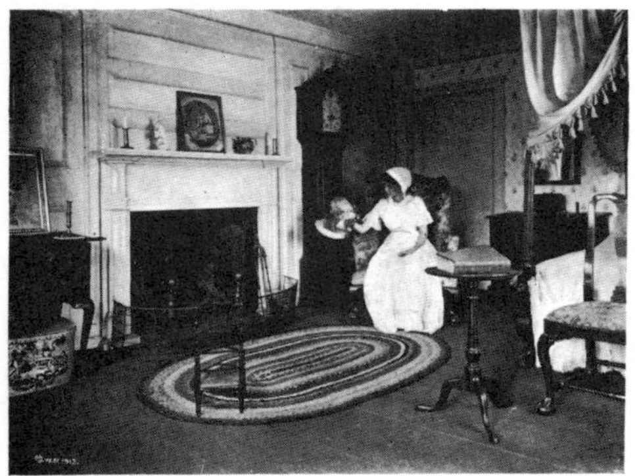
A Discovery A, C, E 3298

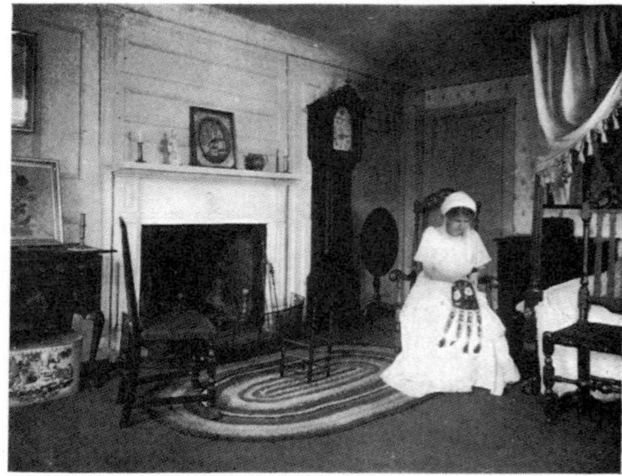
The Treasure Bag A, C, E, G 3304

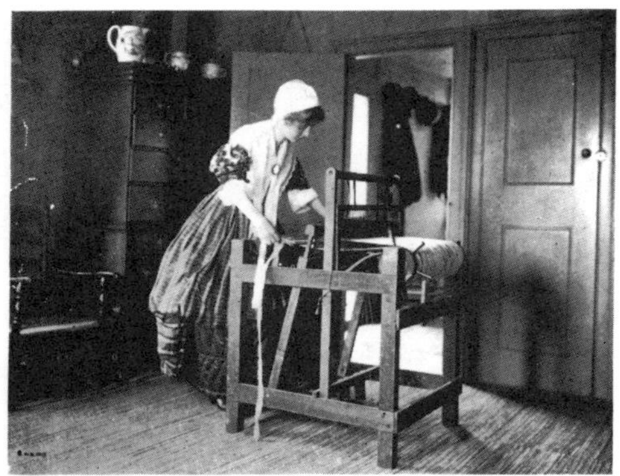
Rag Rug Weaving C 3152
(Recreations of our Foremothers, C, E 3150, similar)

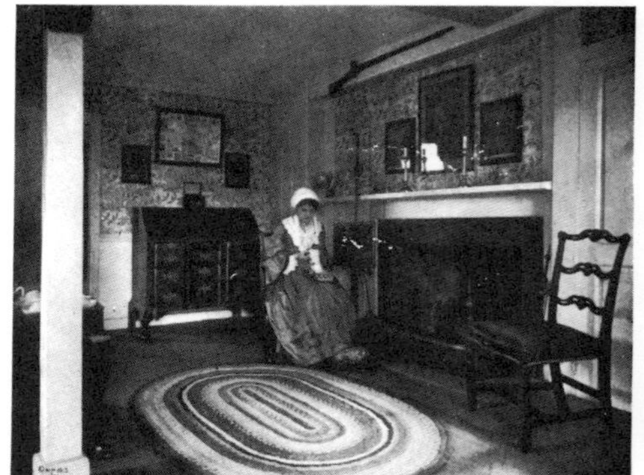
Afternoon Recreation C 3292

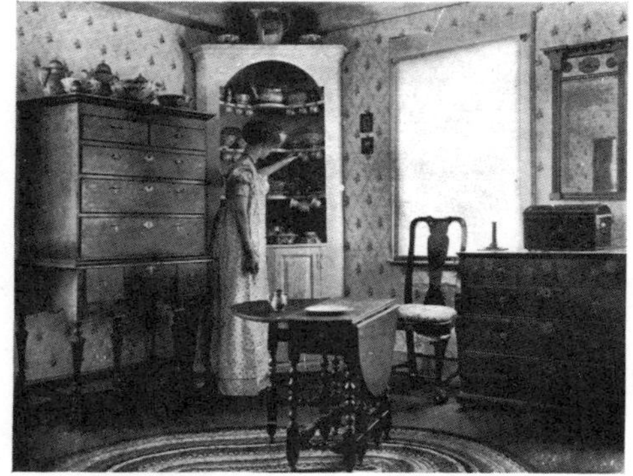
Ancient Treasures A, C 3320

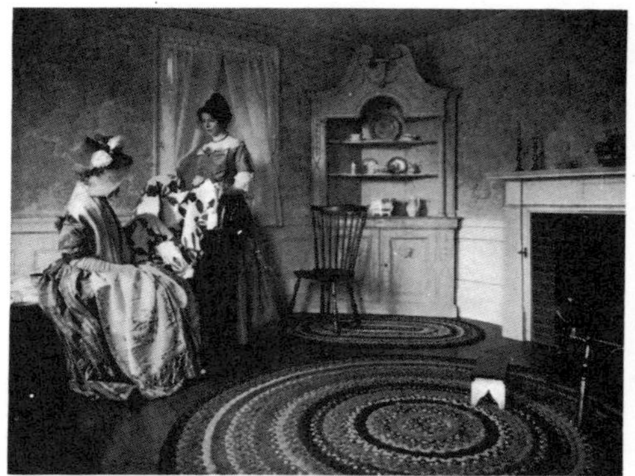
A Family Heirloom C 3030

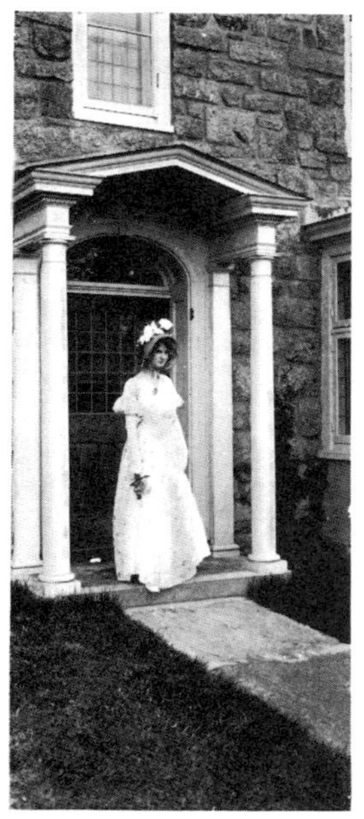

Fair Weather To-day 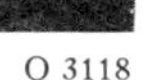 Q 3118

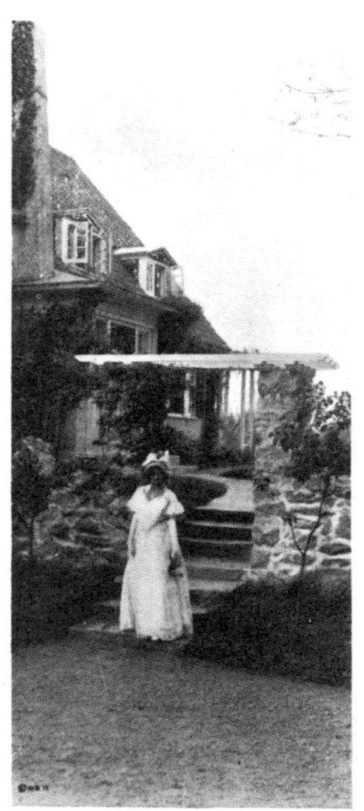

Out of the Garden 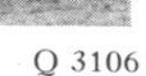 Q 3106

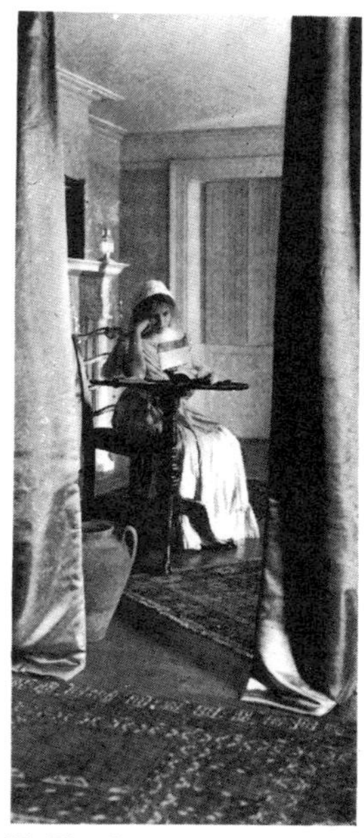

His First Letter Q 3092

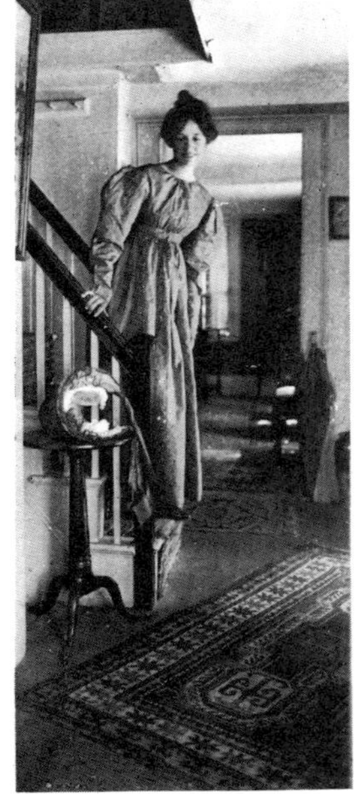

L'Allegro Q and O 3164

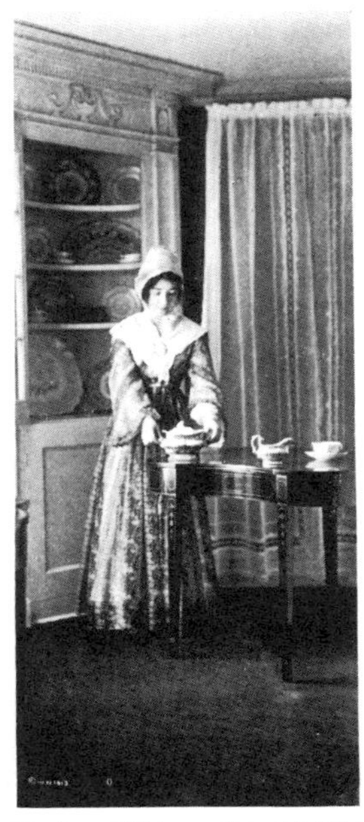

Cupboard China Q and S 3244

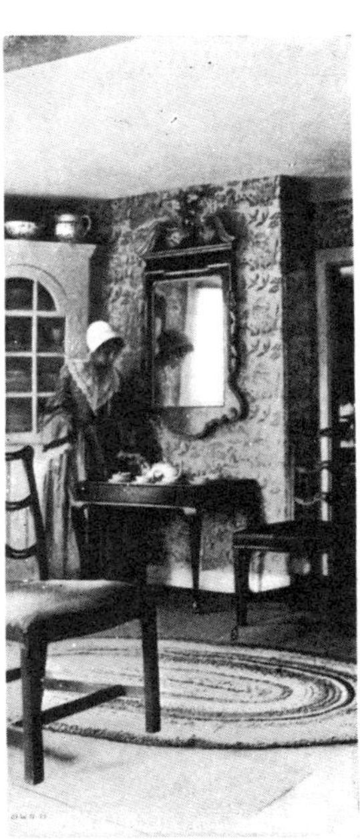

The Tea Table A, Q and C 3314

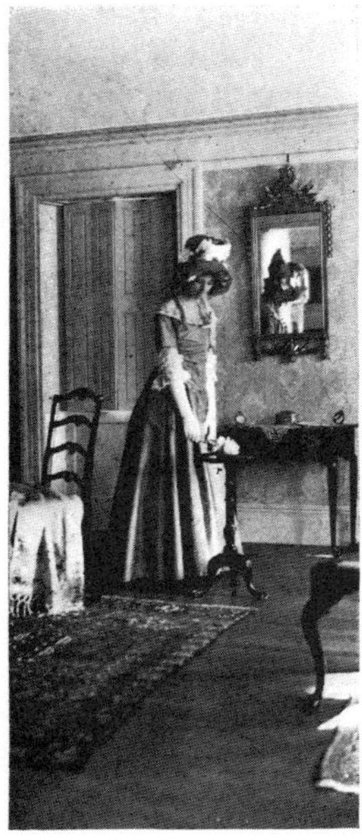

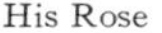

His Rose Q, S. C, P 3016

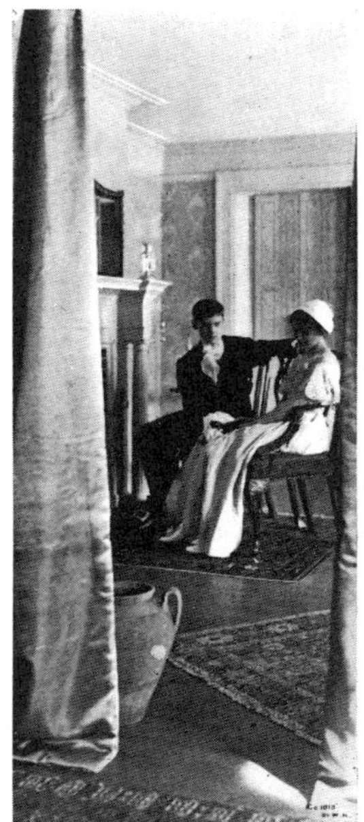

The Old Settle Q 3088

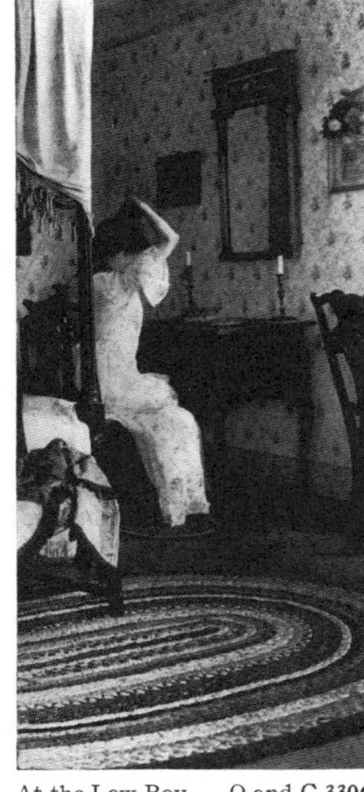

At the Low Boy Q and C **3306**

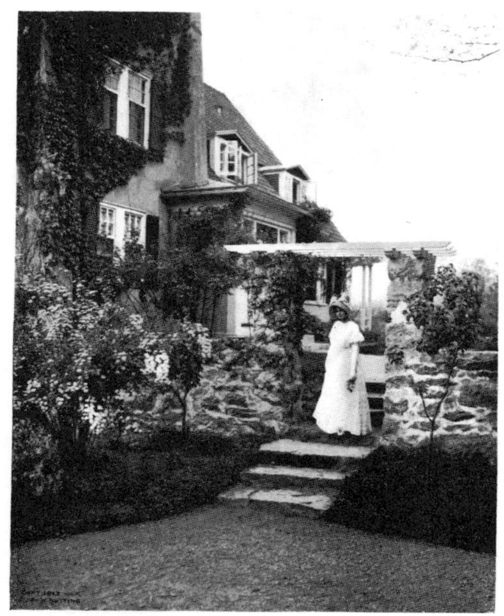

Passing the Portal C 3102

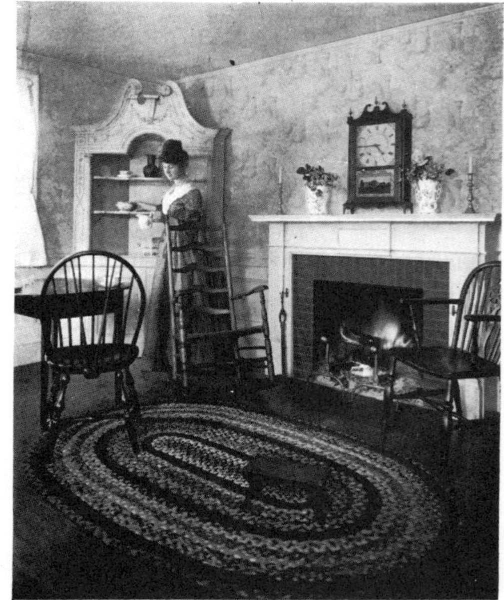

A Windsor Maid Q and C **4006**

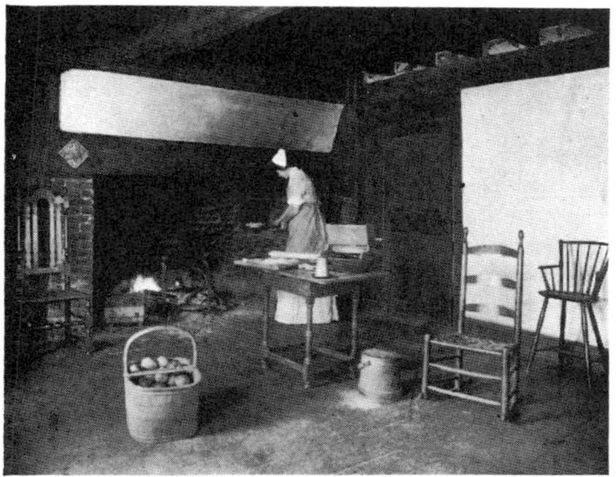

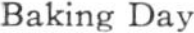
Baking Day A, C, E 3704

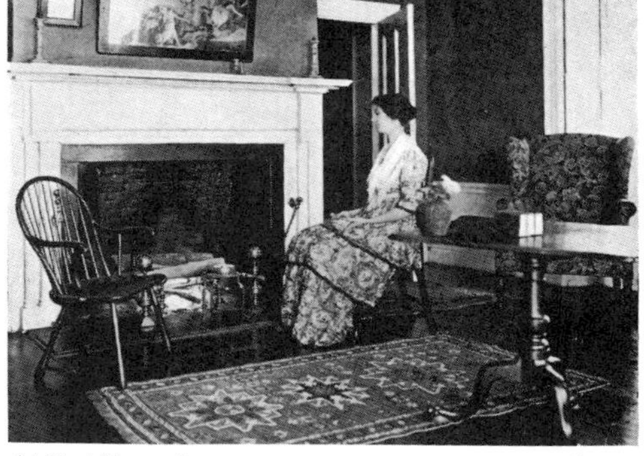

At Paul Revere's C 3586

The vacant chair "At Paul Revere's" was the property of the original Paul Revere. The gown in this picture colors very daintily. The house in which "Making a Rug" was taken is of the 1810 period.

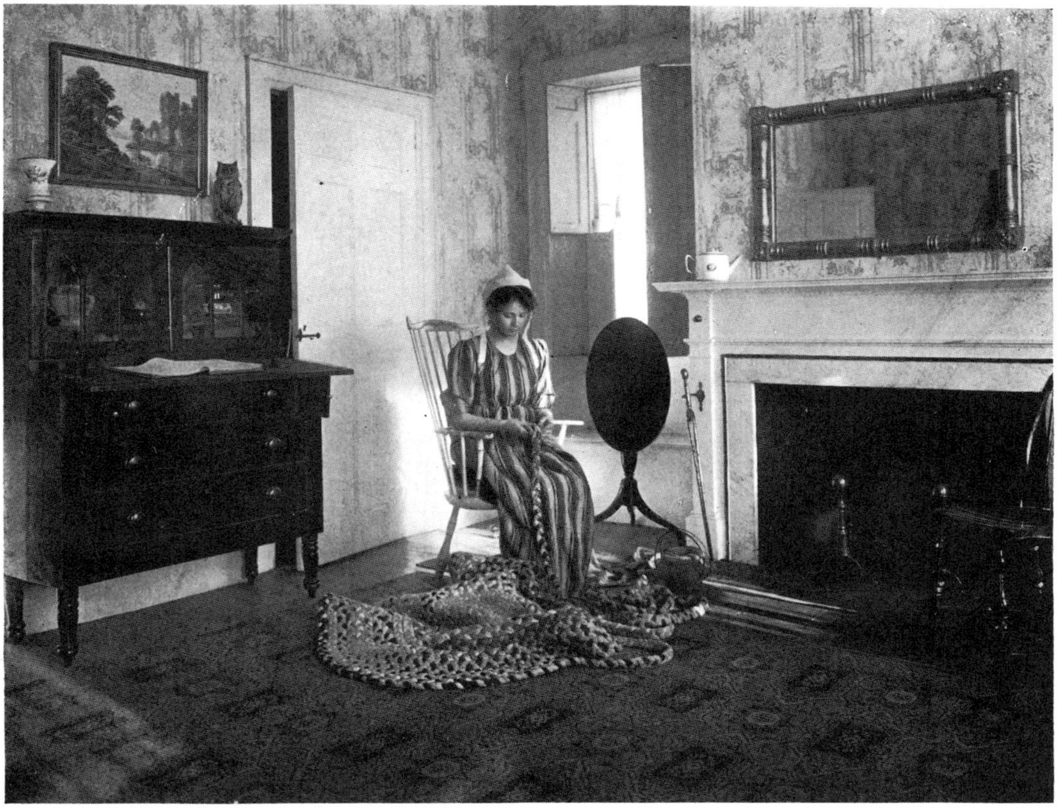

Making a Rug C and E 3716 Wallace Nutting

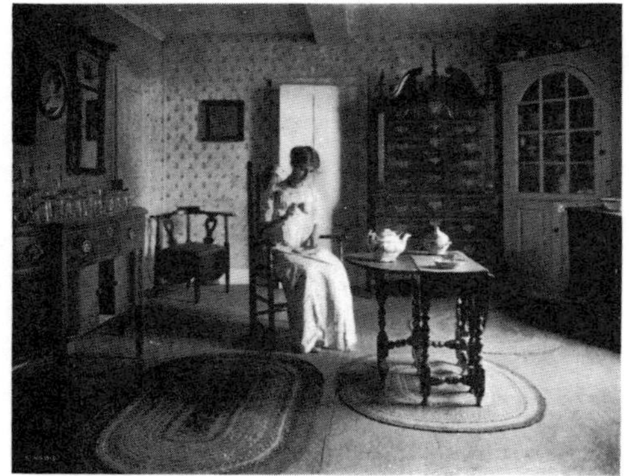

A Divining Cup — A, C, E 3288

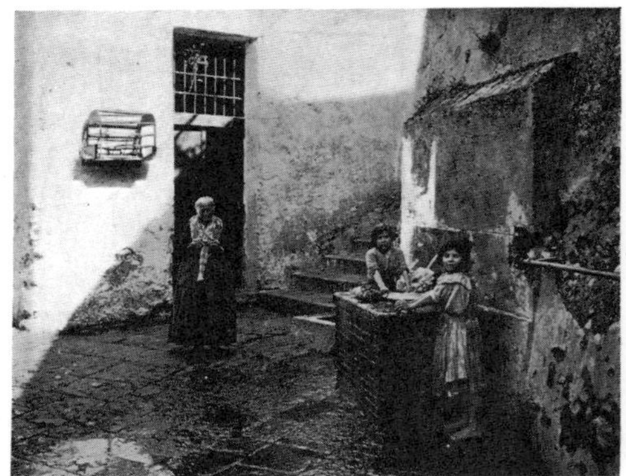

Little Washerwomen, Amalfi — A, C 4065

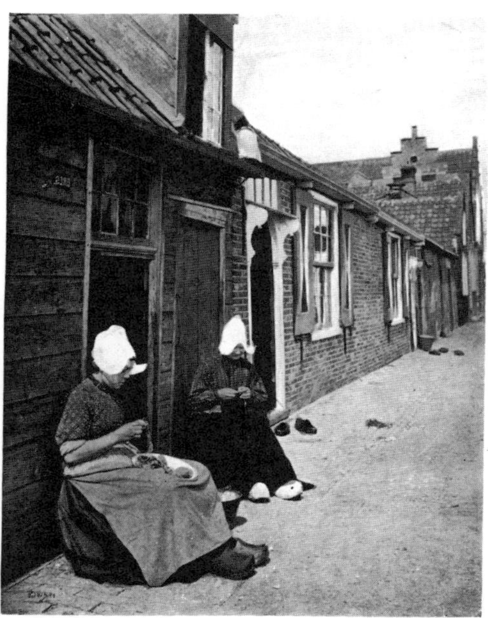

Dutch Maids — A, C 5006

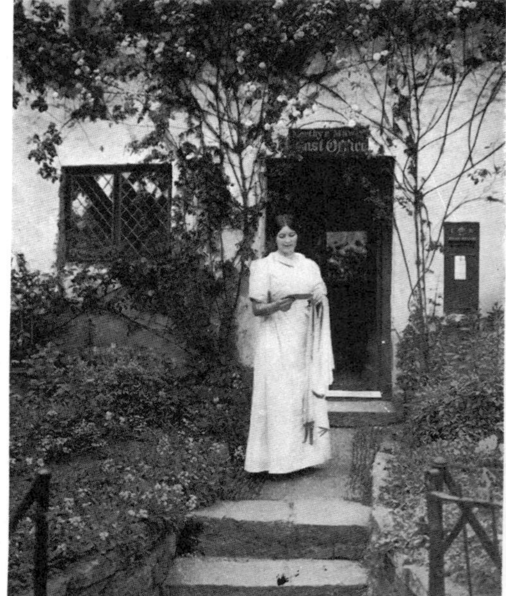

The Expected Letter — A, S, C 6064

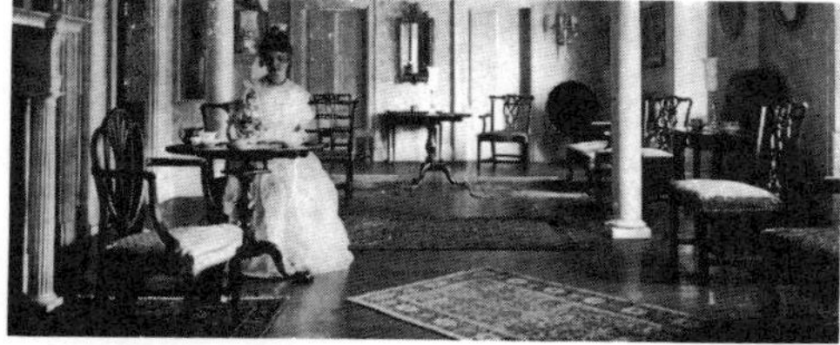

A Double Drawing Room — Q, S 4014

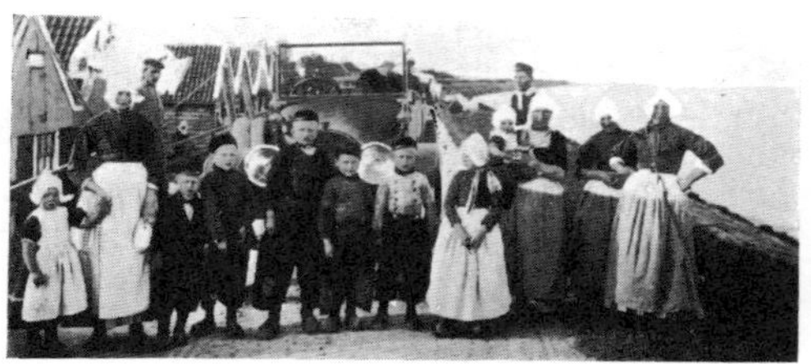

A Yard of Dutchmen — Q 5071

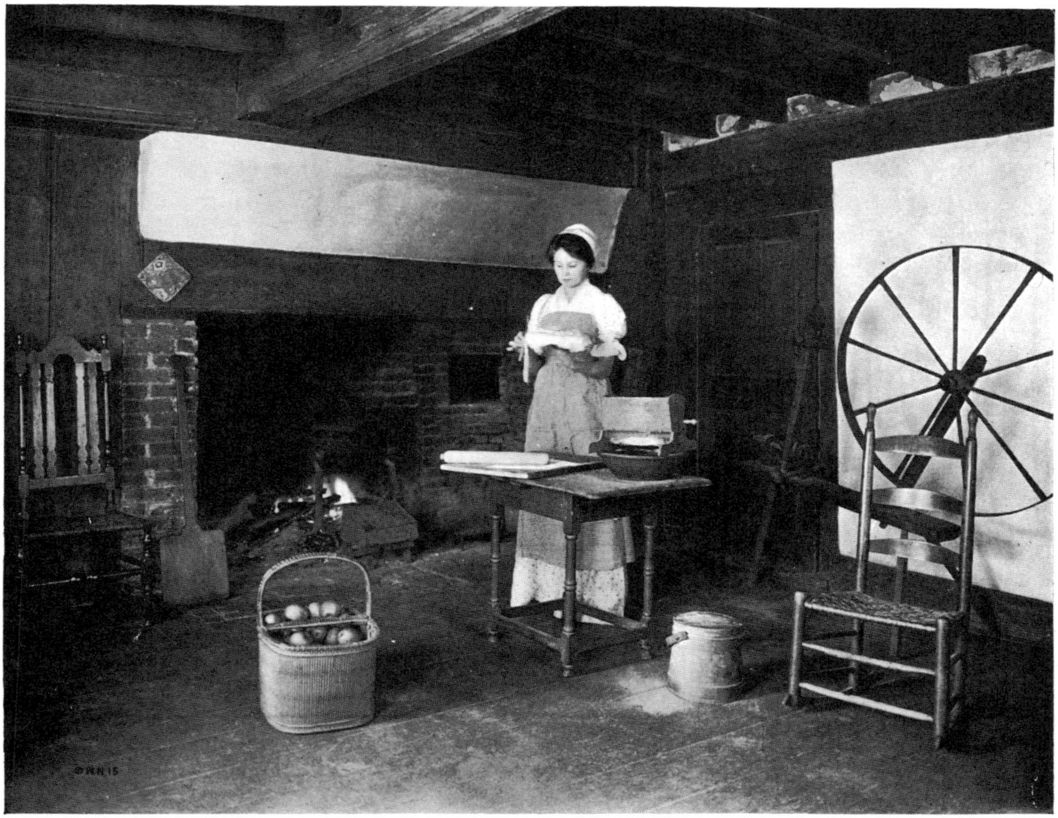

Trimming the Pie Crust A, C and E 3696 Wallace Nutting

For long Mr. Nutting has planned a pie-making picture, only waiting to find a worthy interior. Note the ribbon of dough that is being trimmed from the crust. This house was built in 1658. Note the coped effect above the fireplace. This holds up the hearth on the floor above.

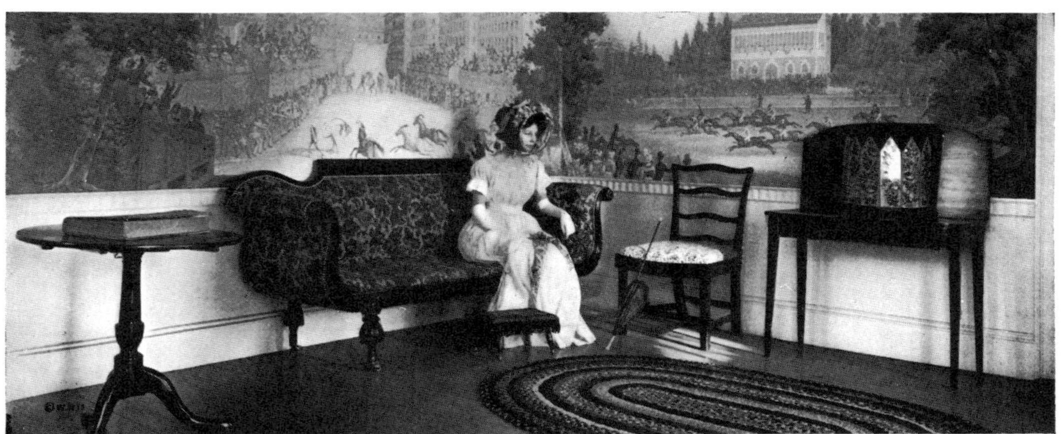

A Newmarket Belle Q, S, O P, E 3734 Wallace Nutting

The name is given because a racing scene appears above on the wall paper. The empire sofa shows an early Victorian room, with the other older furniture retained.

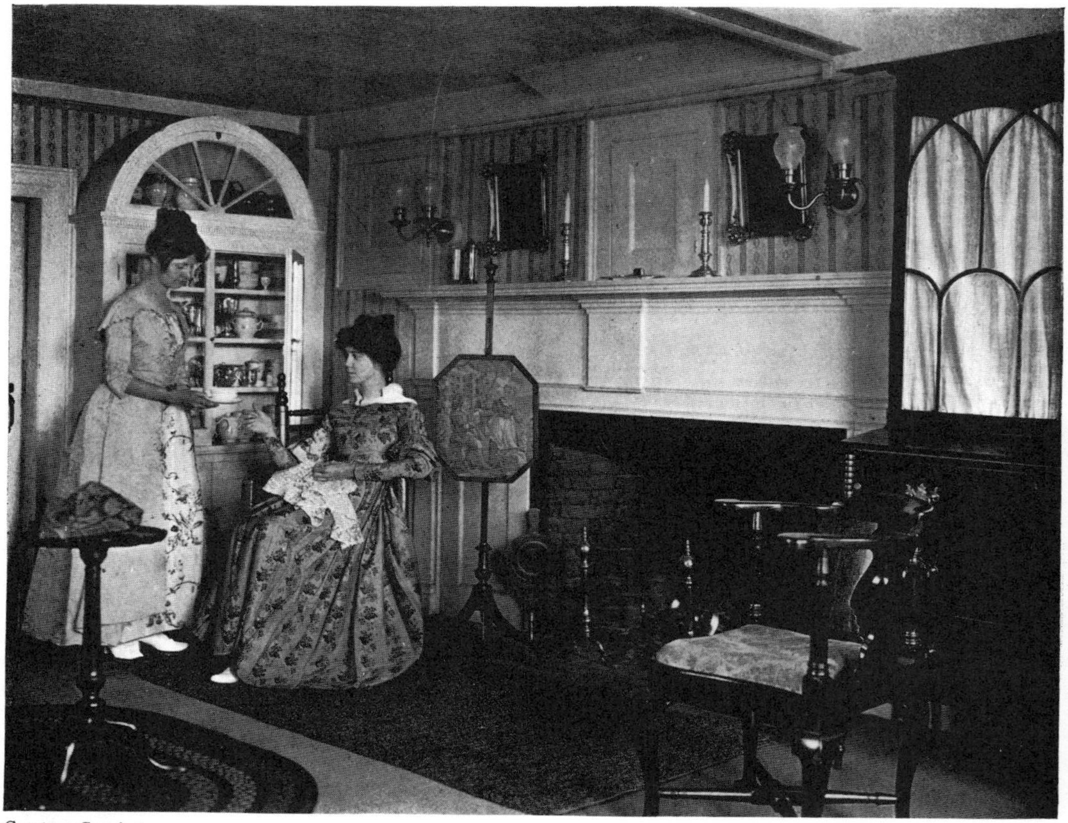

Creature Comforts C, E 3668 Wallace Nutting

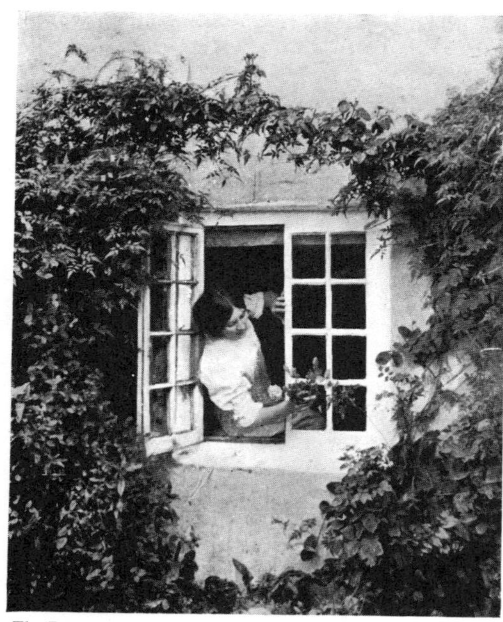

The Rose in Bloom A, C 6455

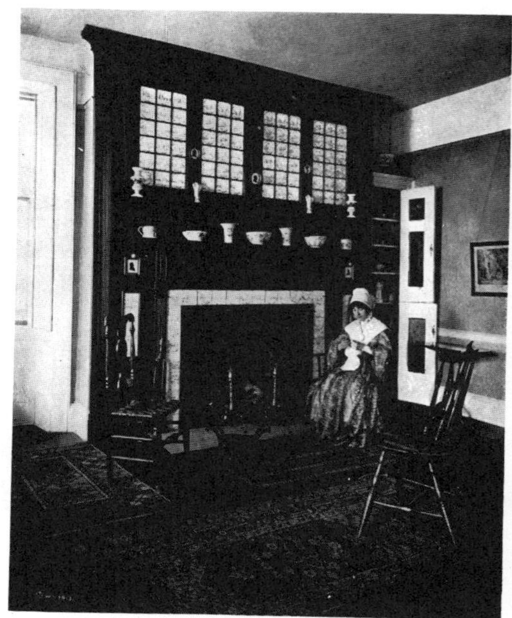

A Knickerbocker Fireplace C 3226

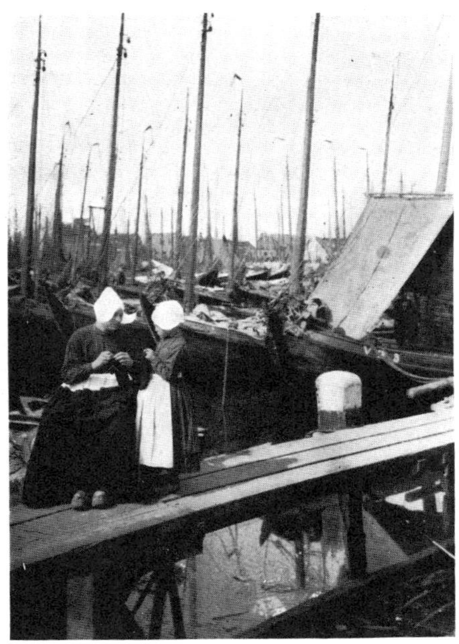

A Cool Spot for Work A, C 5089

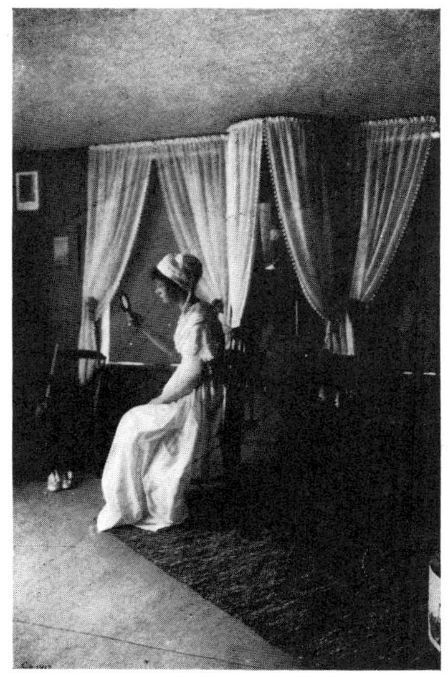

A Classical Maid Q and S and P 3138

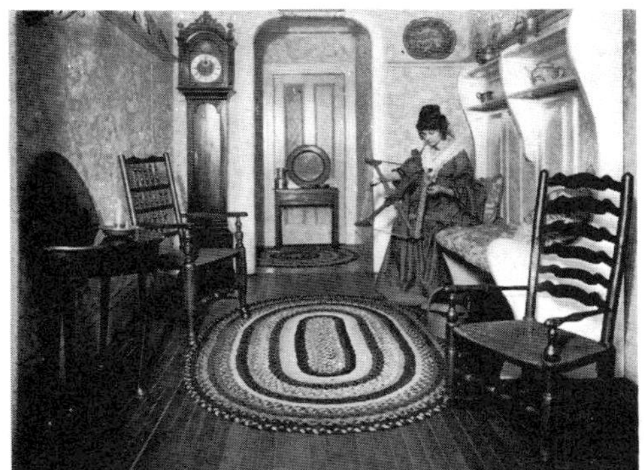

A Virginia Reel C, E 4008

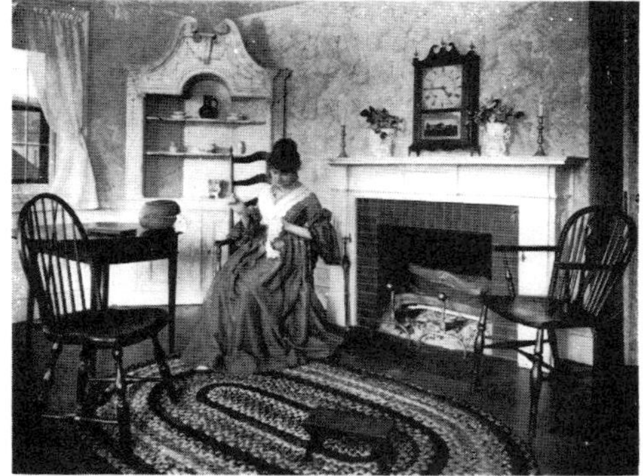

A Stitch in Time A, C, E 4002
(A Delicate Stitch, similar, is A, C, E 1506)

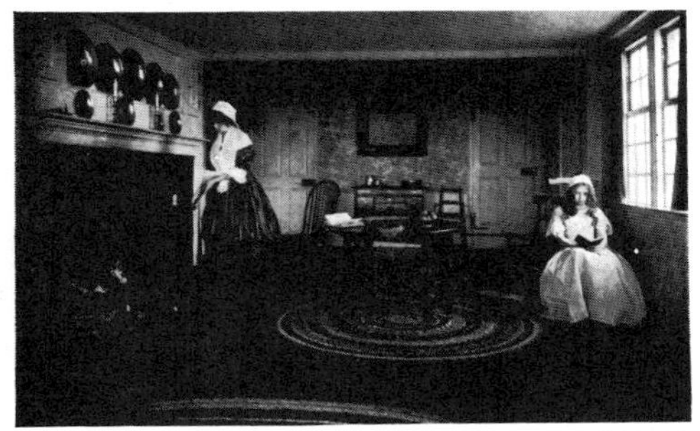

The Old Home Q, S, O and P 3072

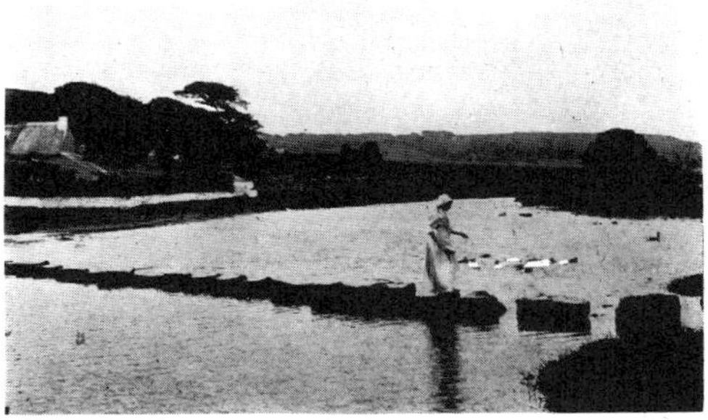

Breakfast Time A, S 6385

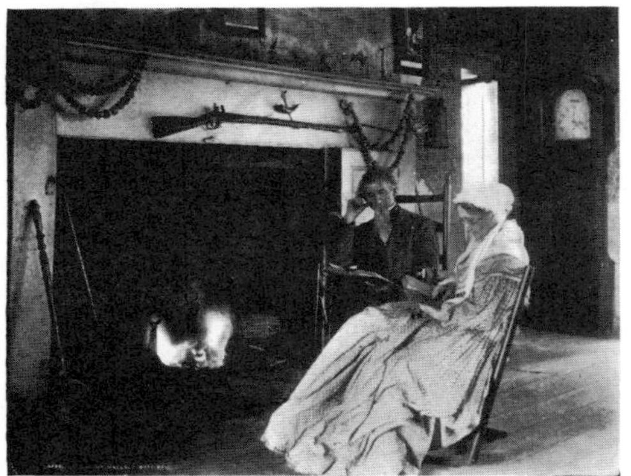

Sunday Afternoon in the Old Home C 1816

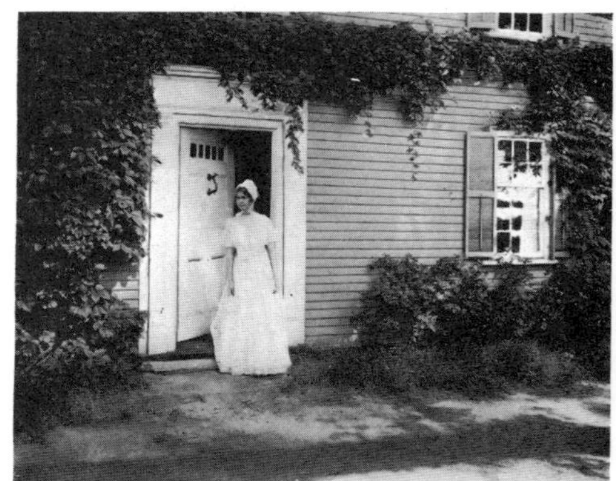

Rose Standish C 3518
(Doorway Welcome, C 3516, similar)

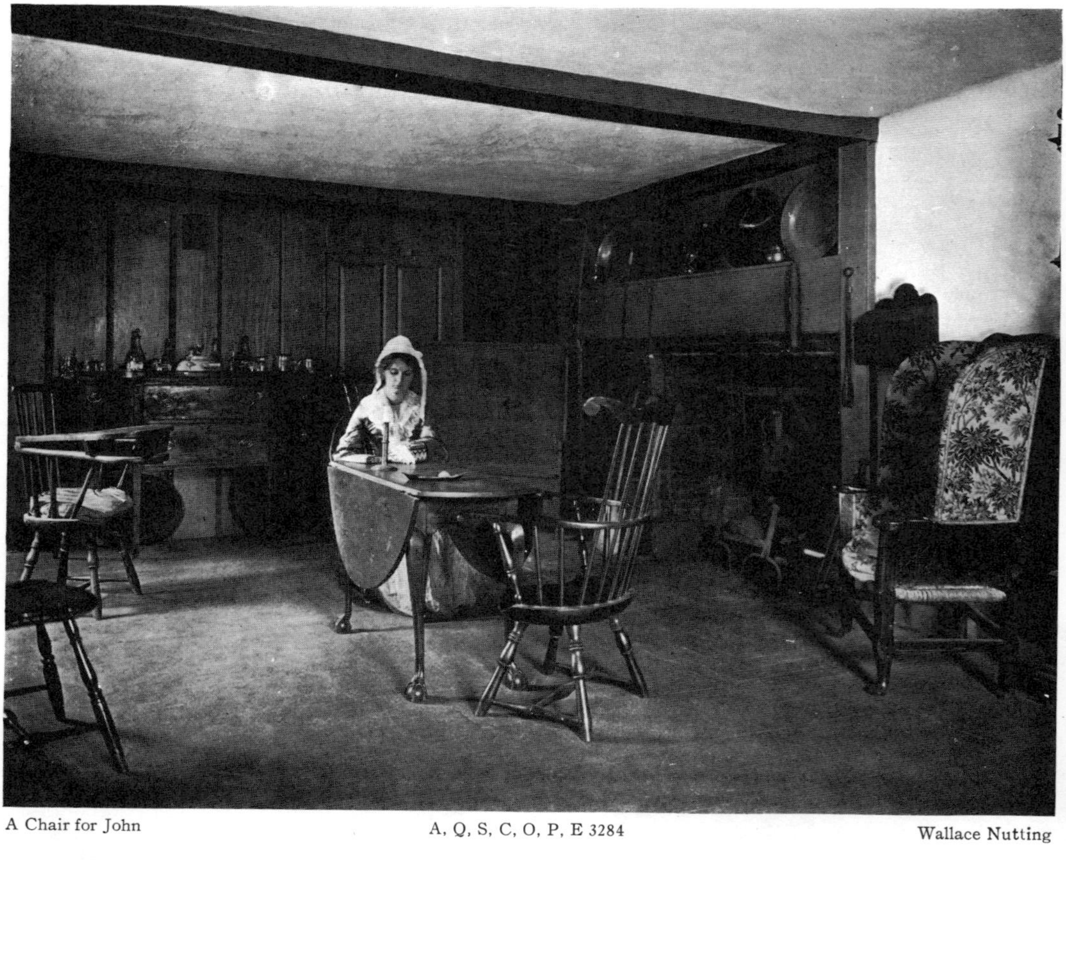

A Chair for John A, Q, S, C, O, P, E 3284 Wallace Nutting

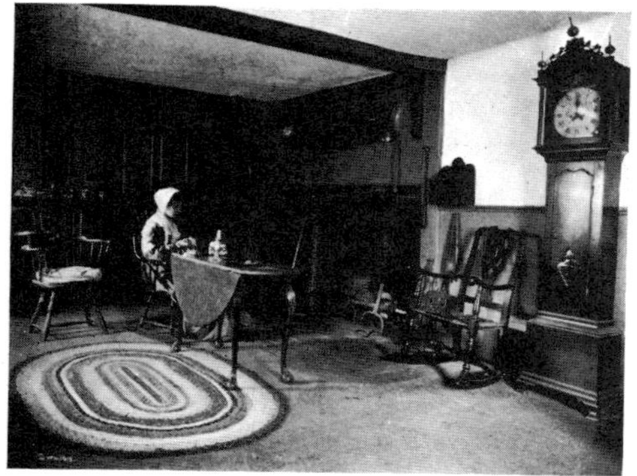

A Colonial Kitchen C, E, G 3282
(An Old Colony Home Room, C 3280, similar)

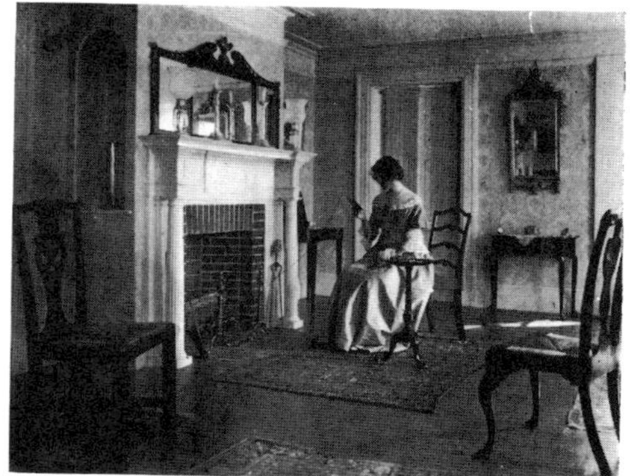

The Daguerreotype C 3002

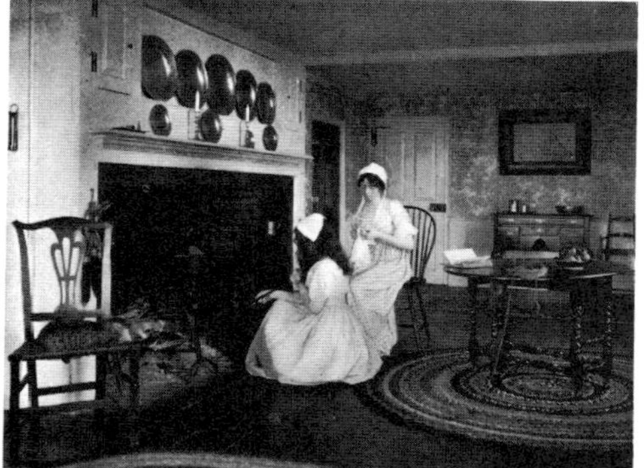

The Charms of Home C and E 3068

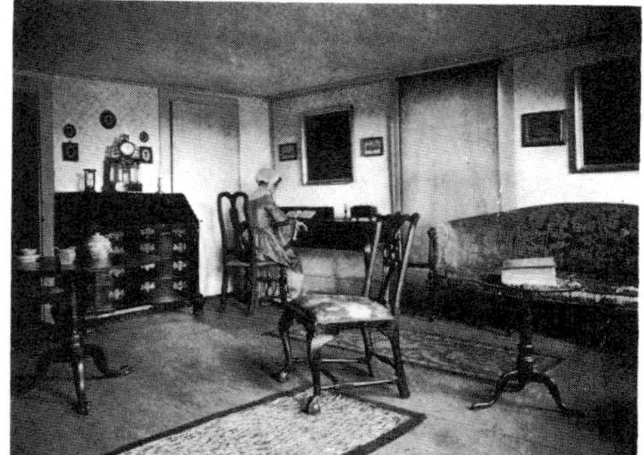

An Old Colony Parlor C and E 3290

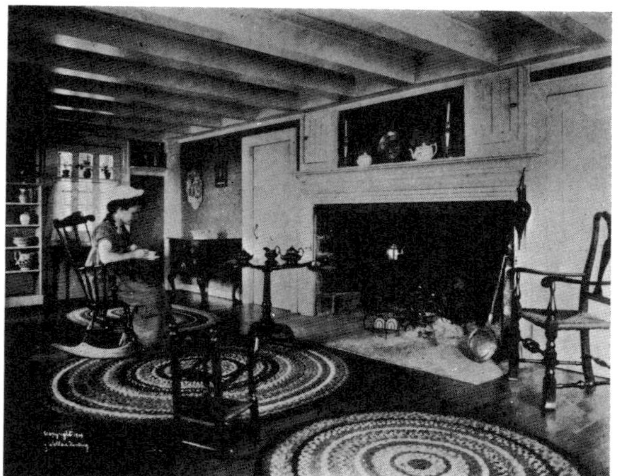

The Home Room C or E 745

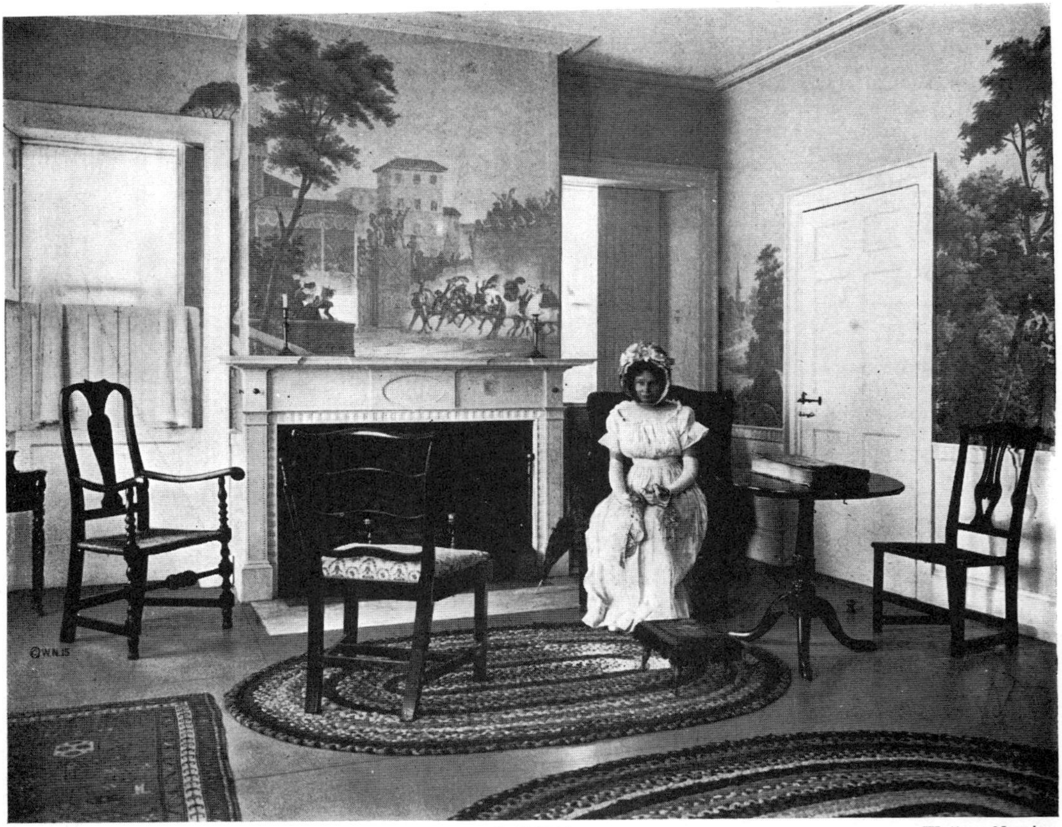

The Formal Call C, E 3744 Wallace Nutting

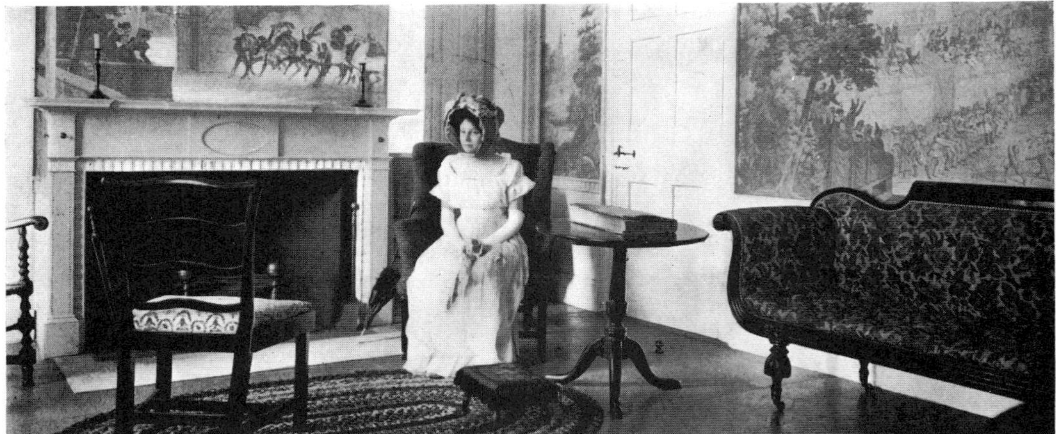

A Colonial Belle Q 3736 Wallace Nutting

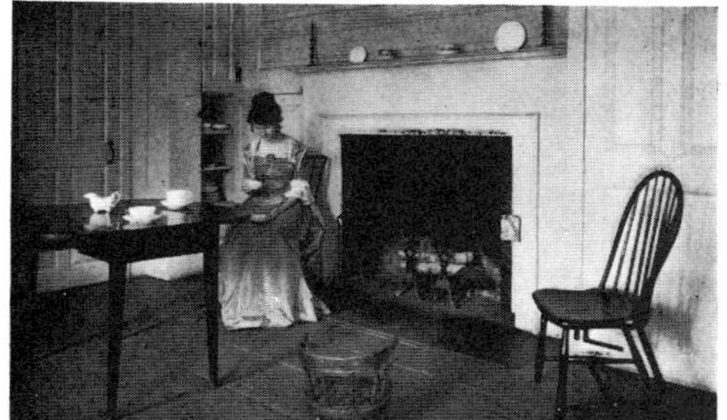

The Long One or the Short One ? S. C 3470

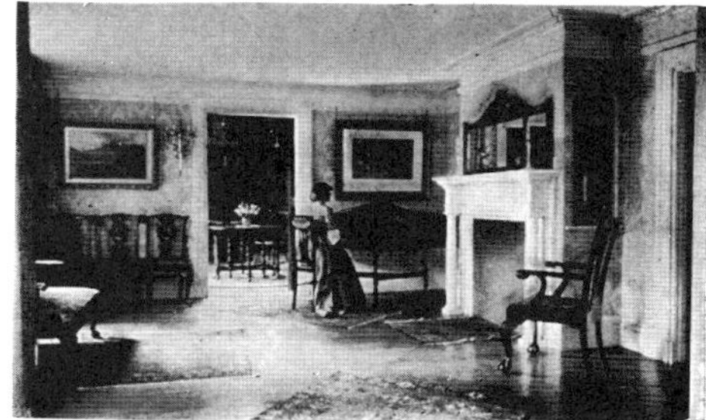

Sunshine and Music Q, S, C 1340

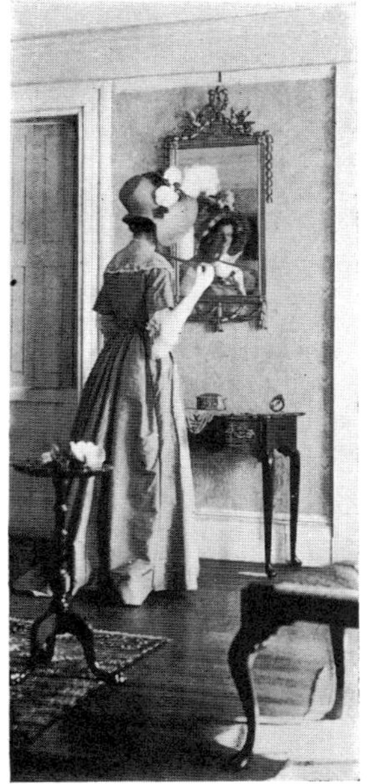

All Smiles Q 3692

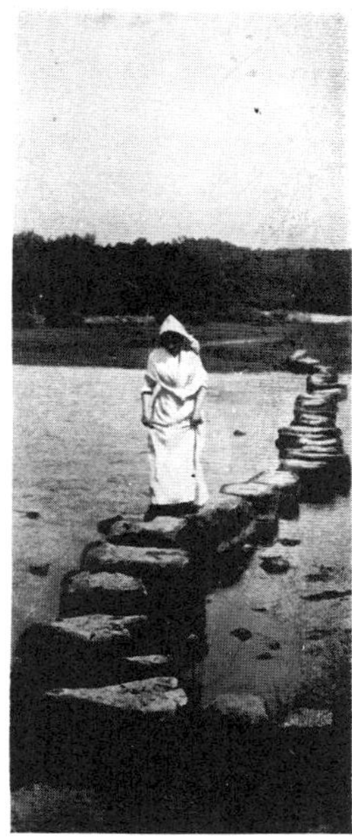

Ancient Stepping Stones
Q, O 6108

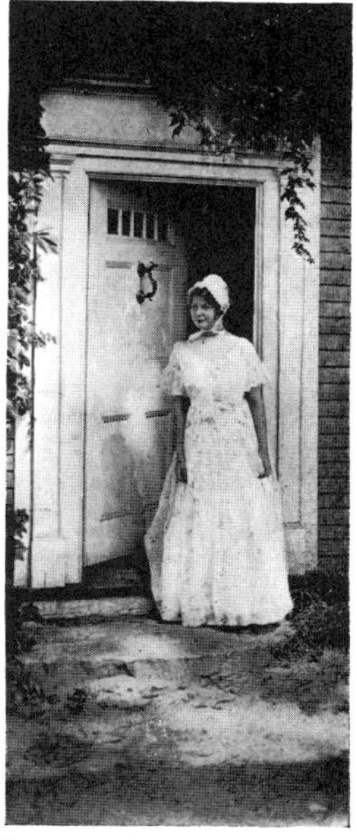

Rose Standish Q 3694

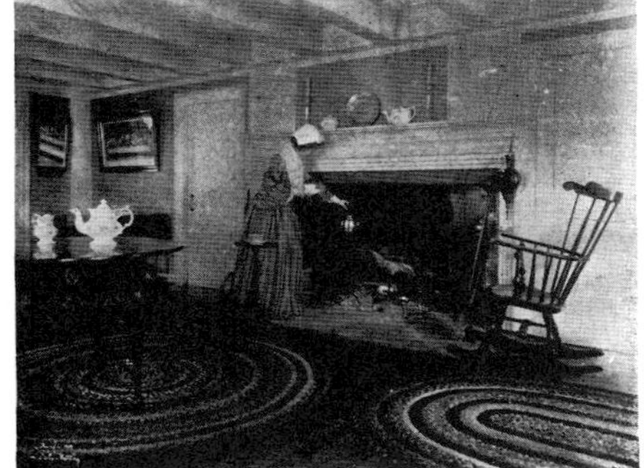

Prudence Drawing Tea C or E 707

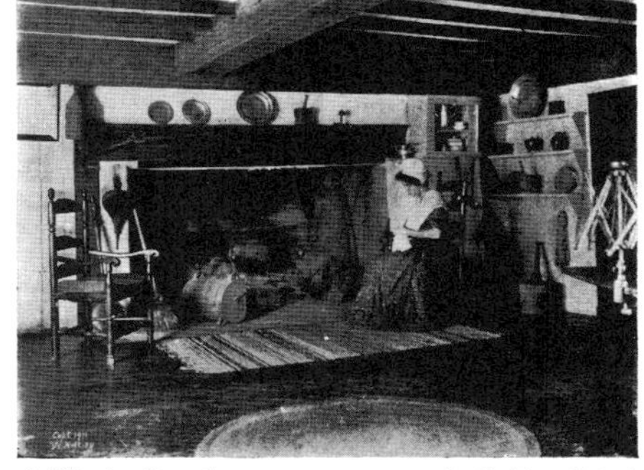

A Pilgrim Daughter A, C, E or G 988

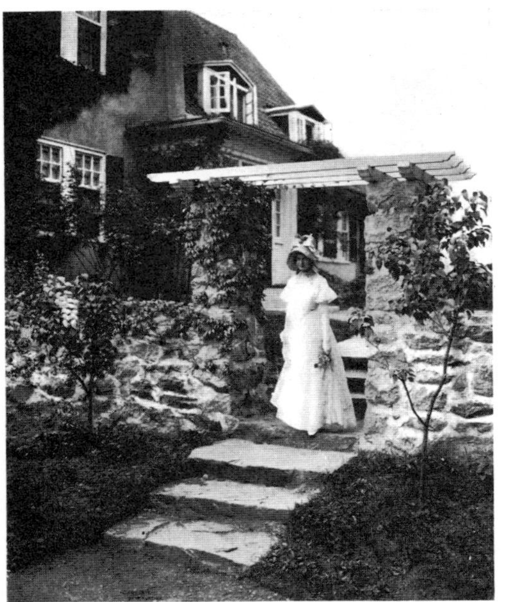

All in a Garden Fair C, S, P, E 3108

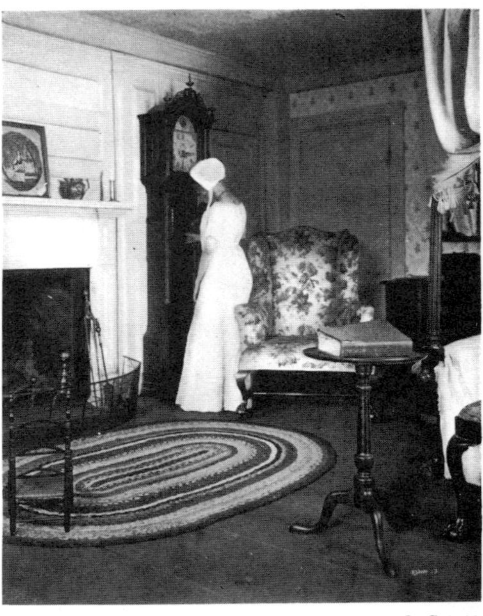

Grandfather's Clock Q, C 3602

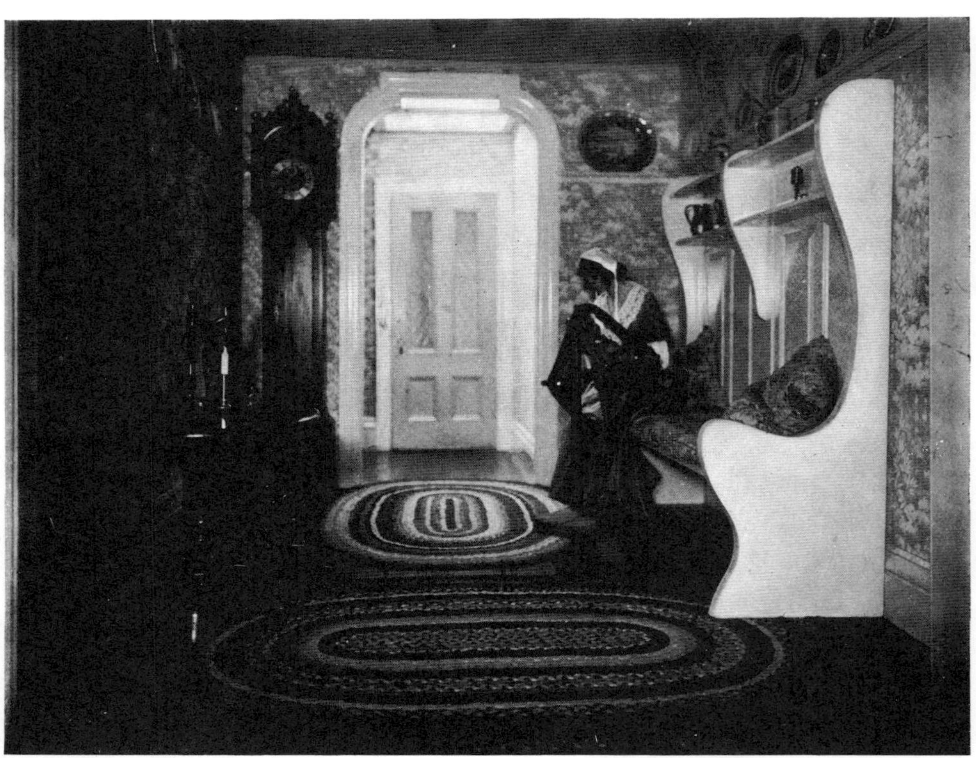

The Settle Nook A and C 1511 Wallace Nutting

The Settleback is 242 years old

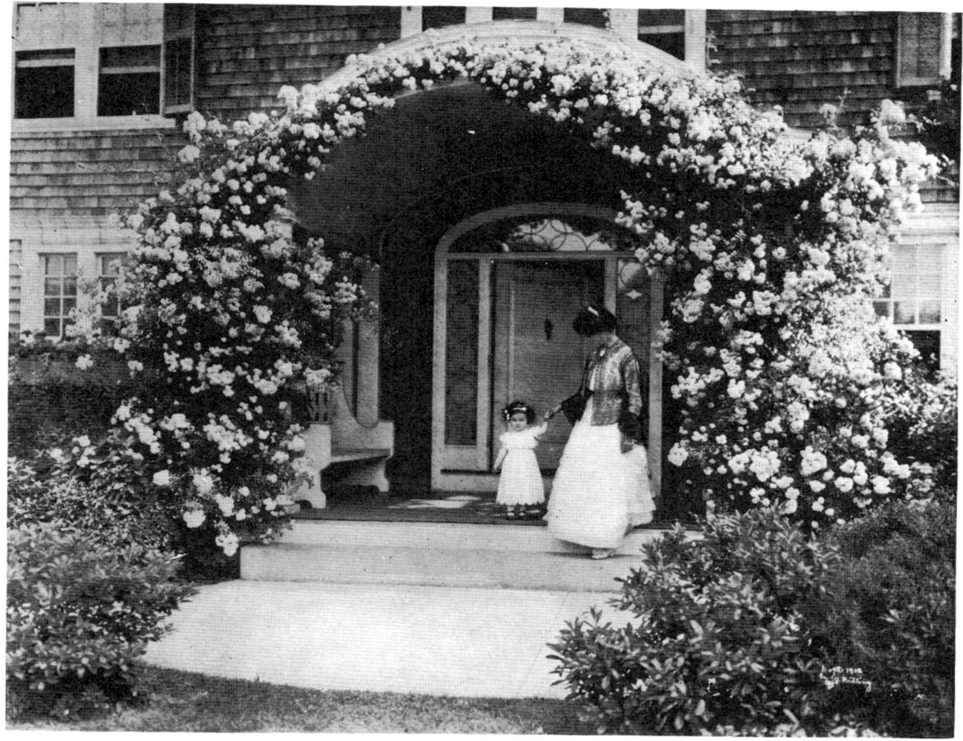

The Coming Out of Rosa A, C, E or F 2530 Wallace Nutting

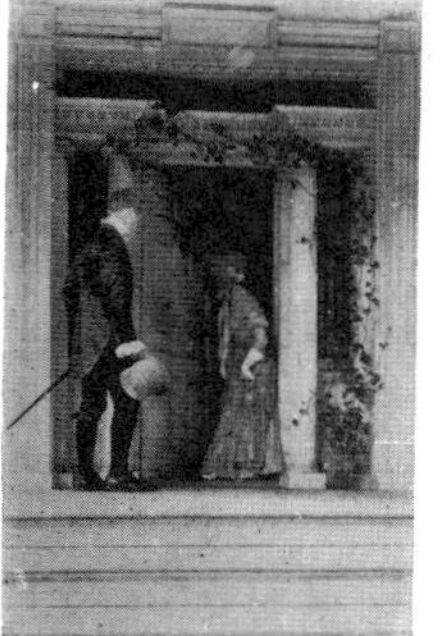

In Grandpa's Day S 212

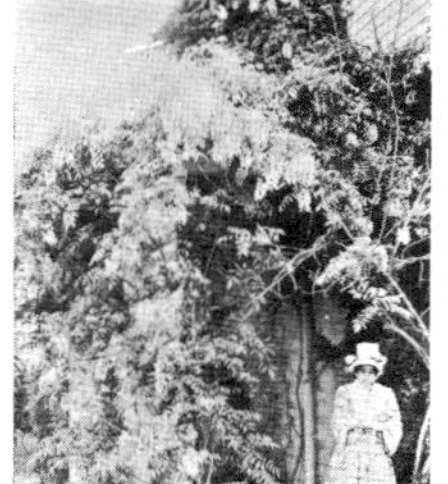

Easter Morning S 2188

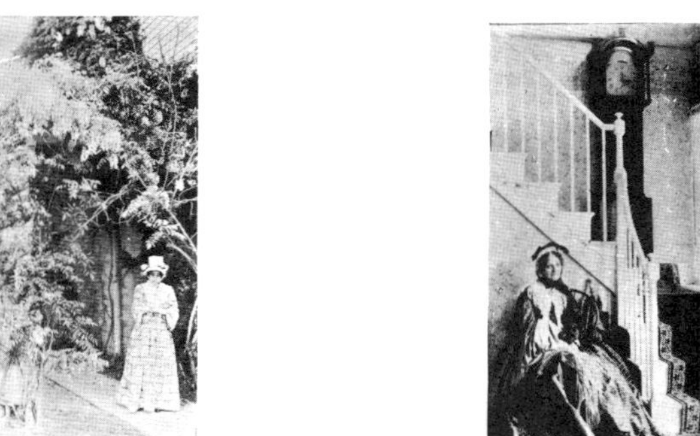

Waiting for Jacob
Q or S 444

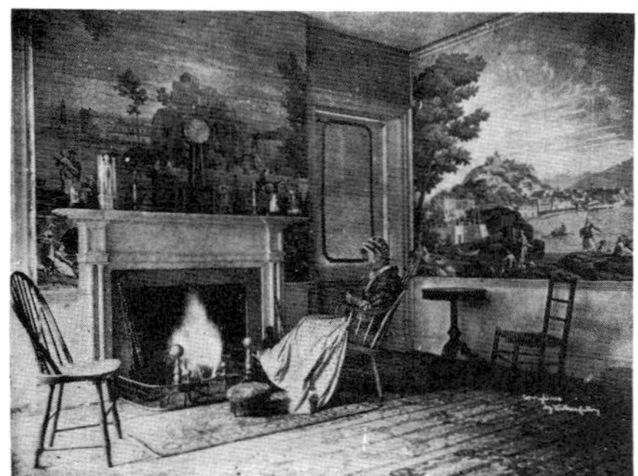

At the Fender C or E 136

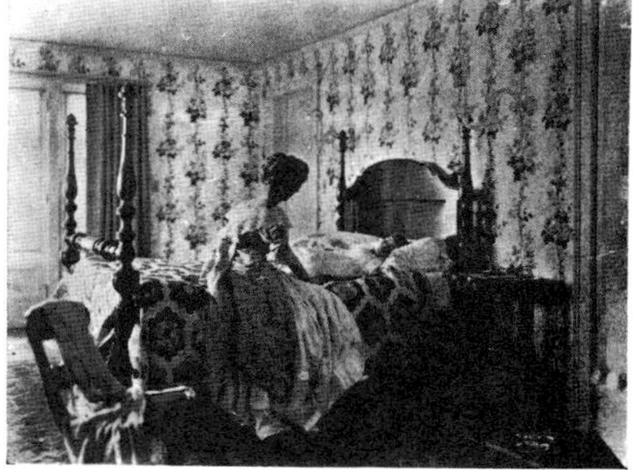

A Patchwork Siesta C or E 2293

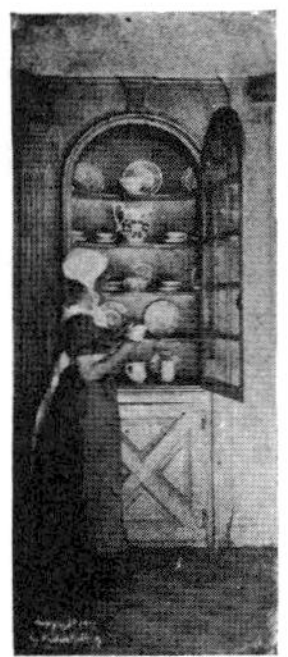

The Connoisseur
Q 841

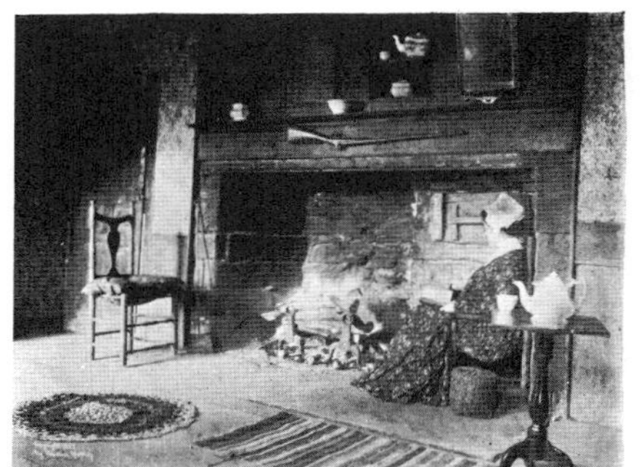

The Chimney Corner C 500

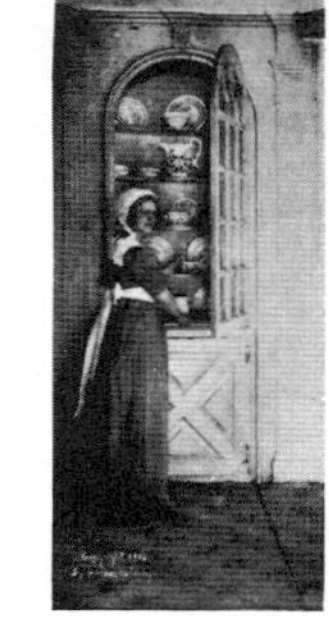

The Corner Cupboard
Q or P 873

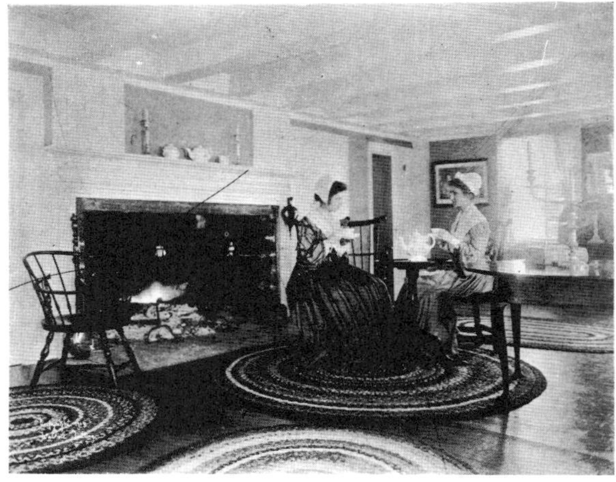

Confidences Q, C, E or F 704

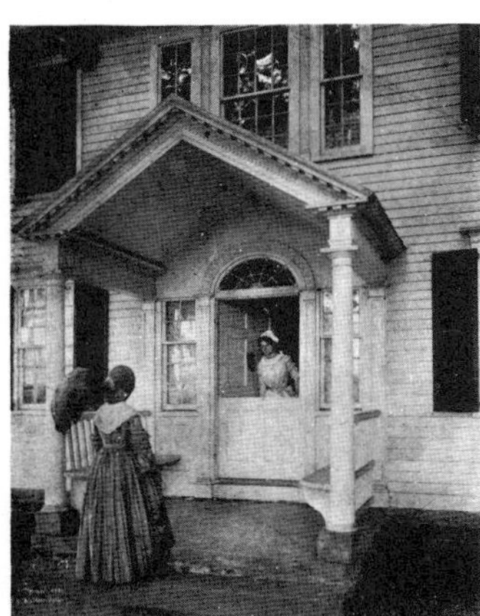

The Admiral's Door E 394

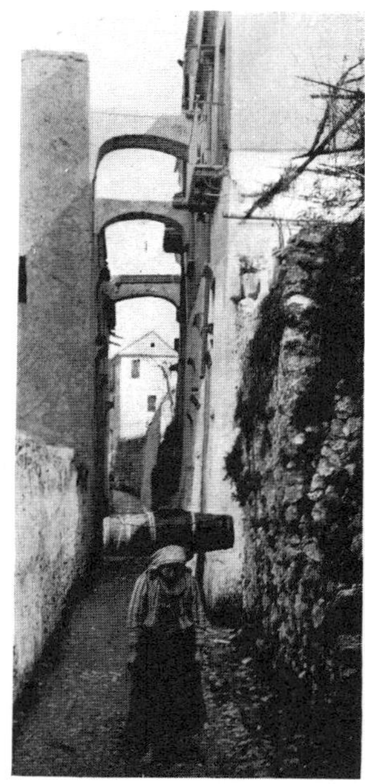

Wine Carrier, Ravello Q 4048

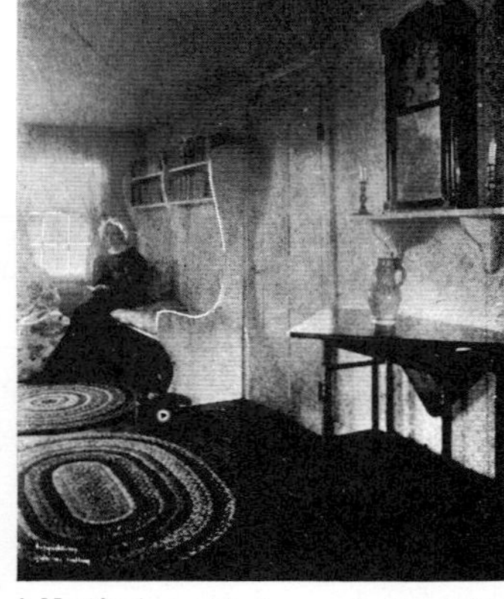

A Nuttinghame Nook Q, C or E 748

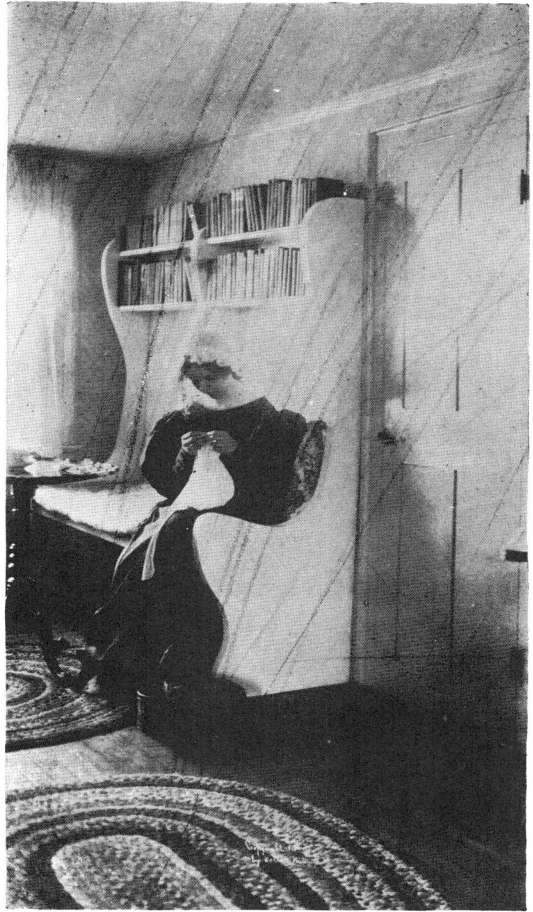

The Book Settle Q, O or P 750 Wallace Nutting

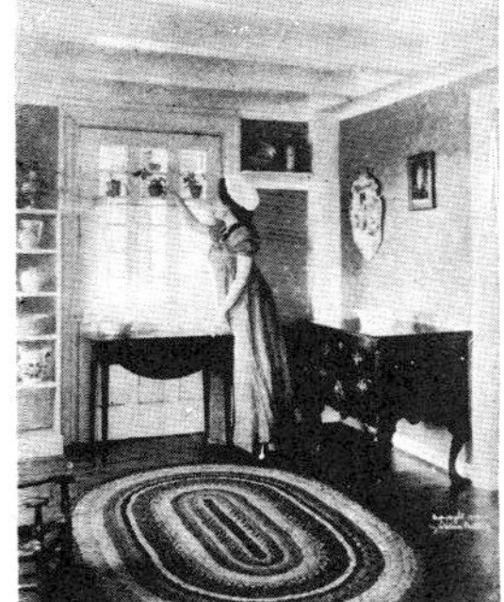

The Window Garden
C 771

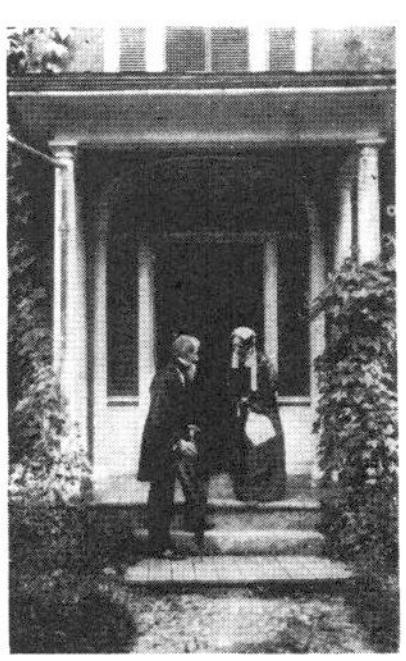

Uncle Sam Taking Leave
S or C 294

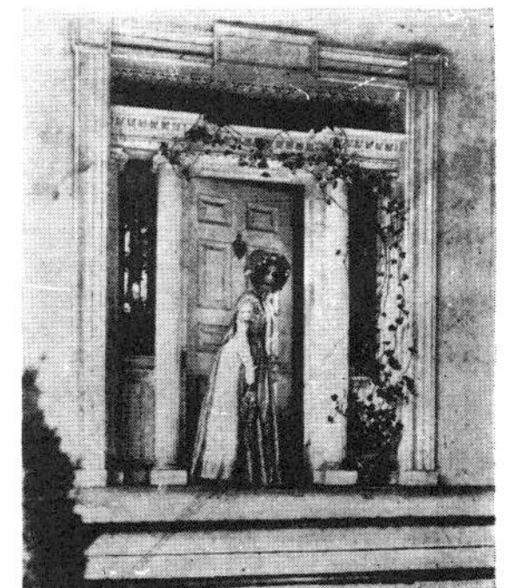

The Sallying of Sally
C 118

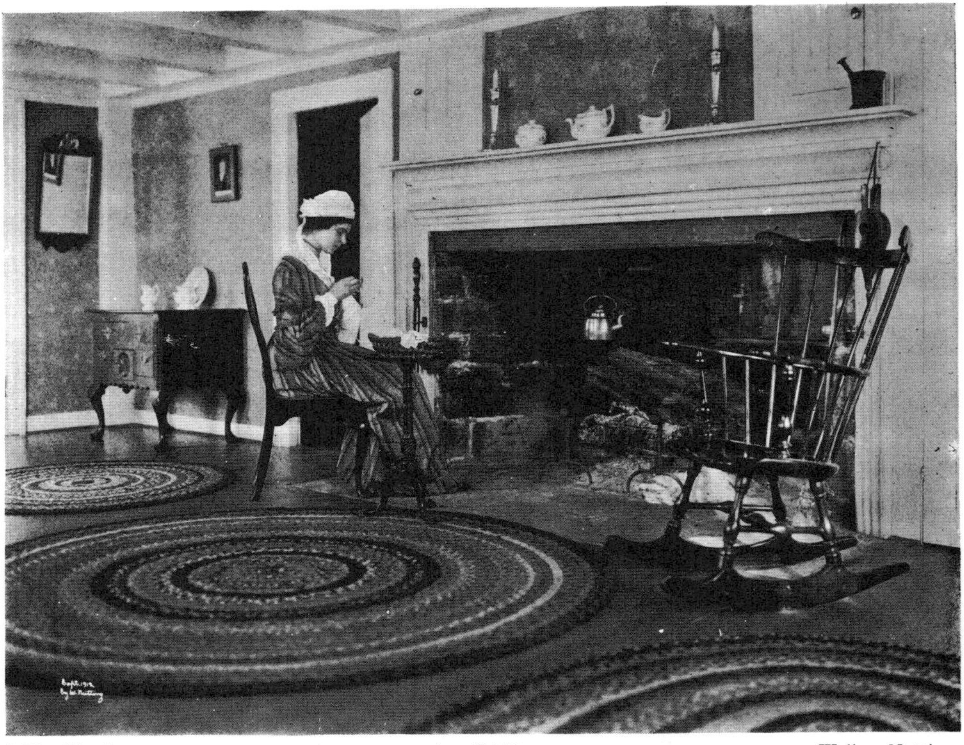

A Bit of Sewing	A or C 173	Wallace Nutting

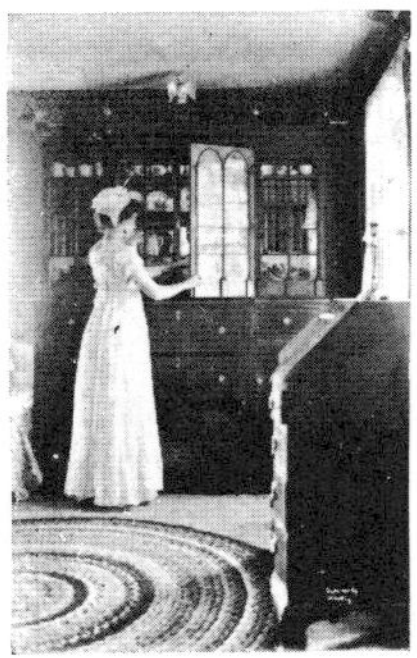

An Ancient Secretary
S 966

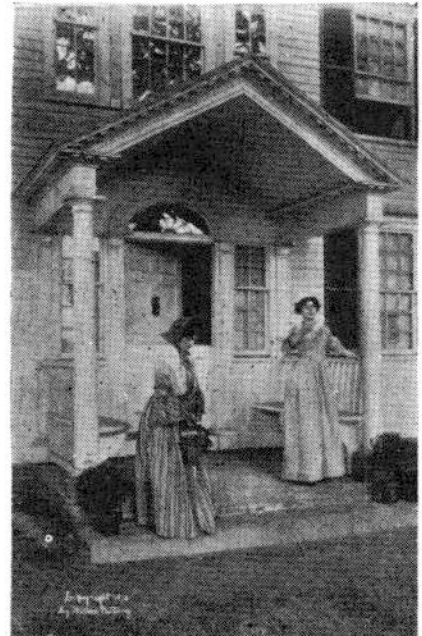

A Threatened Shower
C or S 495

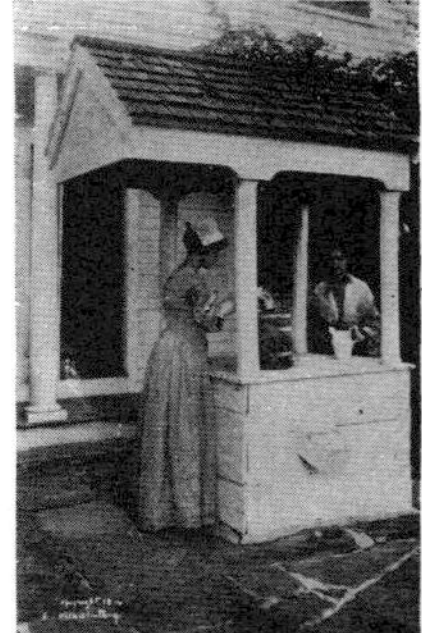

From the Old Bucket
S or C 942

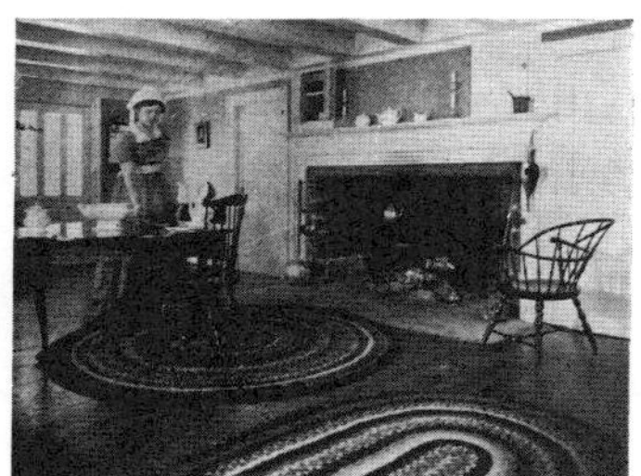

A Plate of Cookies	C 67

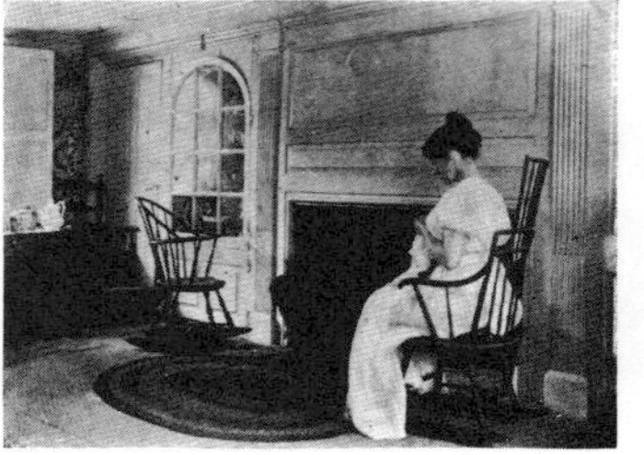

A Chair to be Filled	C 1301

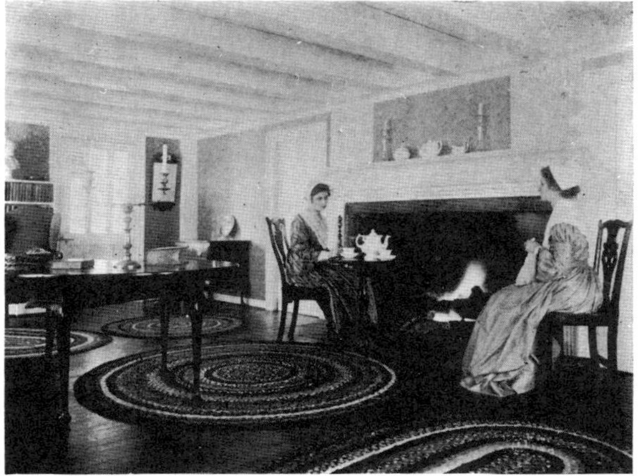

An Afternoon Tea C, E or G 703

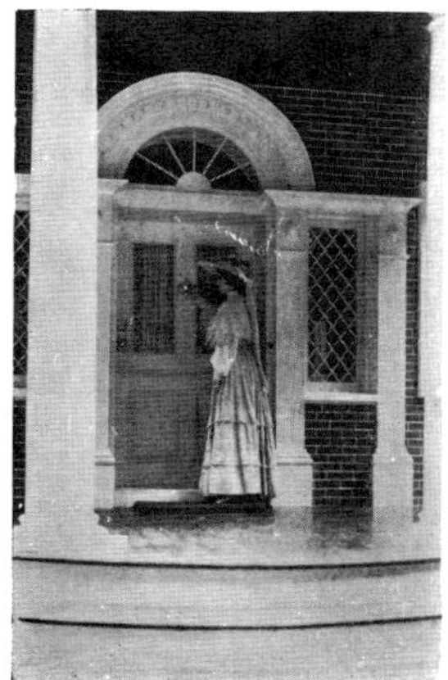

The Lady in Green S 141

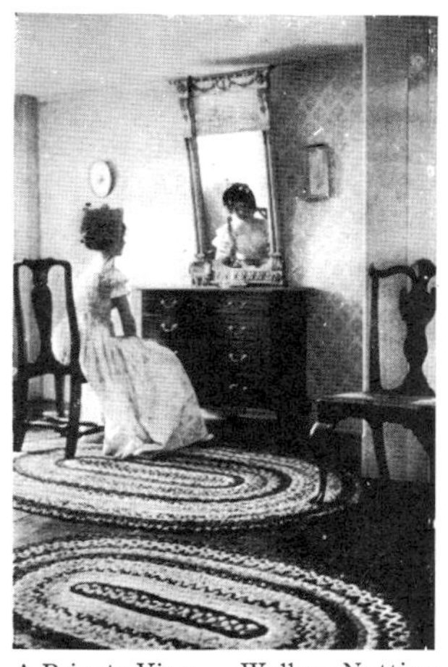

A Private View Wallace Nutting
A, Q, S, O, P 209

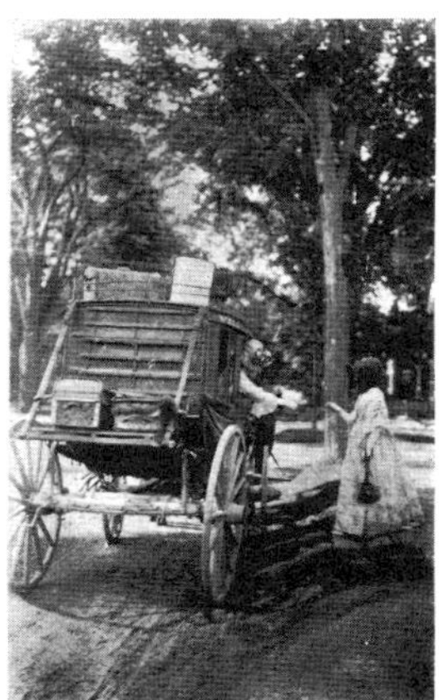

Bag and Baggage S 106

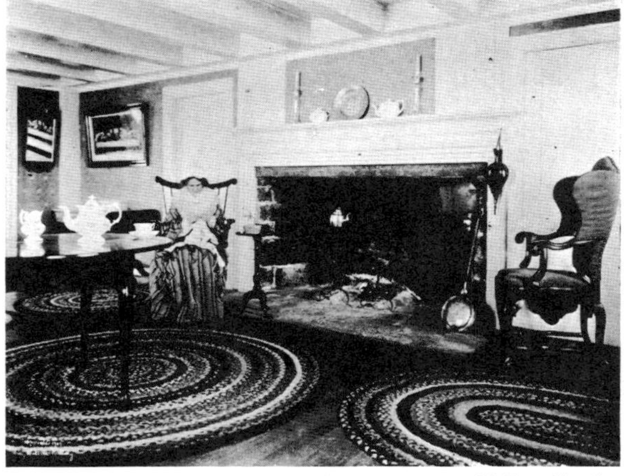

Mending C, E or G 677 Wallace Nutting

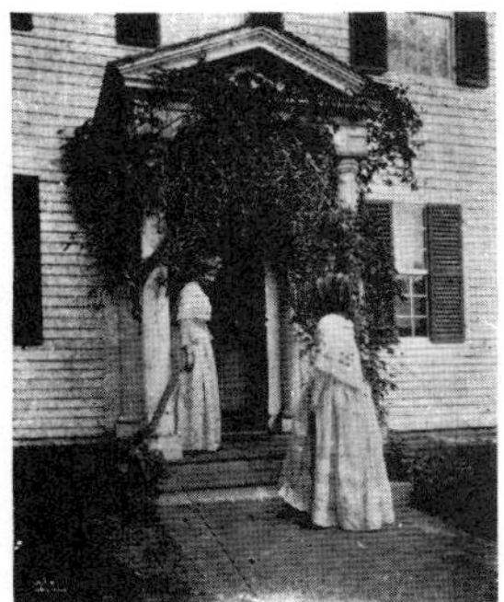
A Call in State C 140

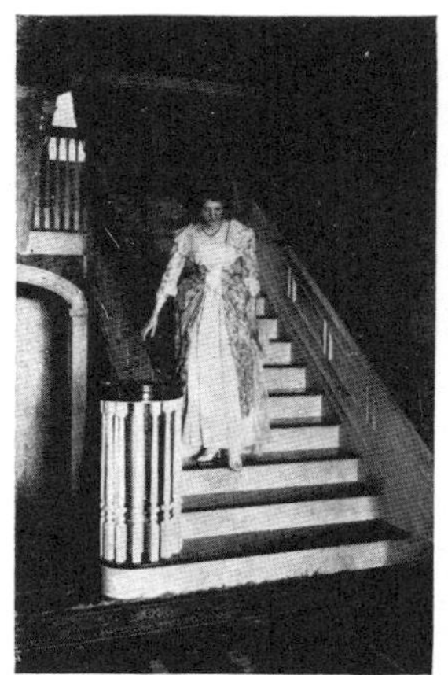
What Shall I Answer? S or P 2472

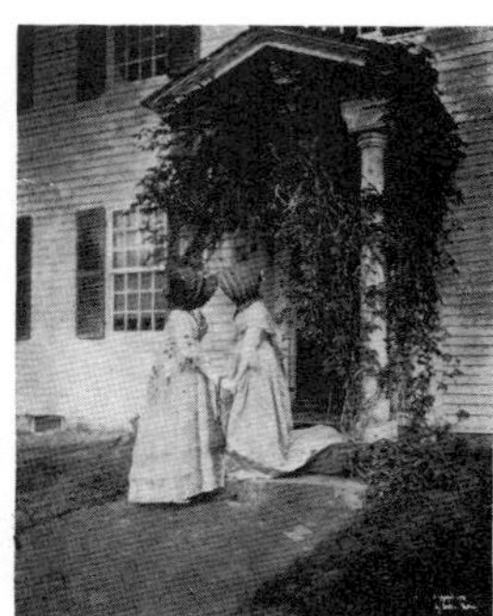
An Affectionate Greeting C 113

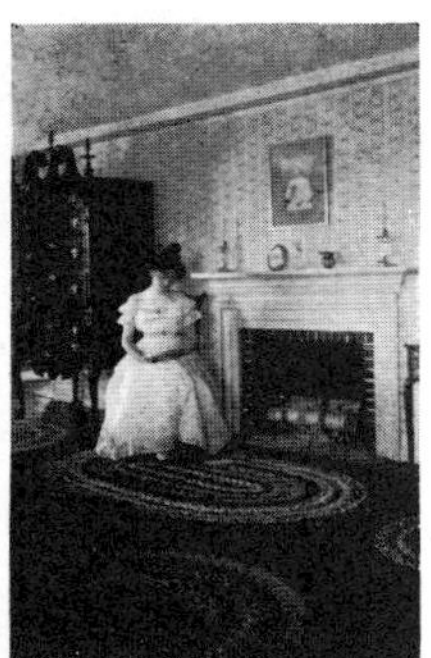
From a Friend S 159

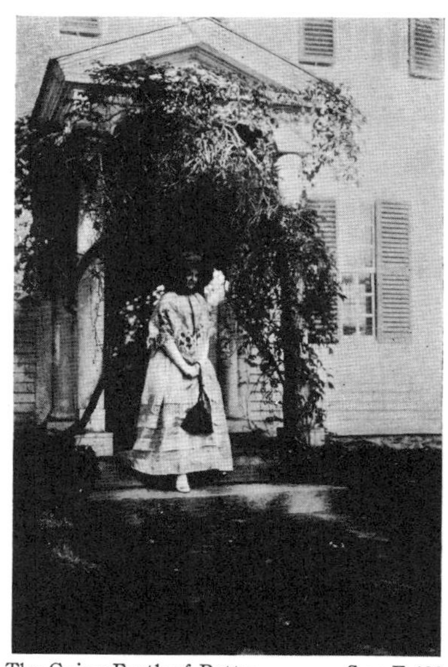
The Going Forth of Betty S or E 420

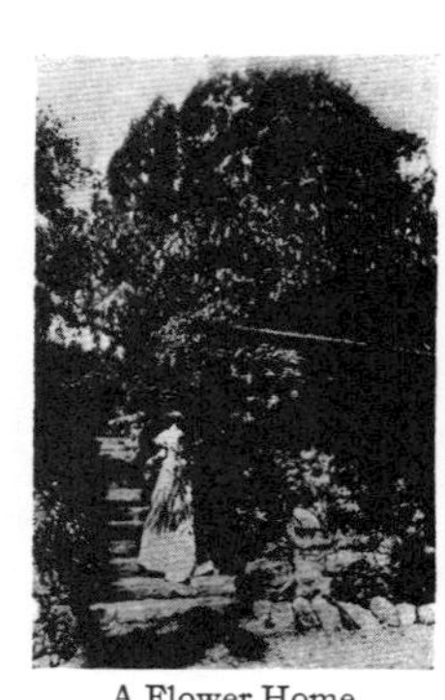
A Flower Home
Q or S 2235

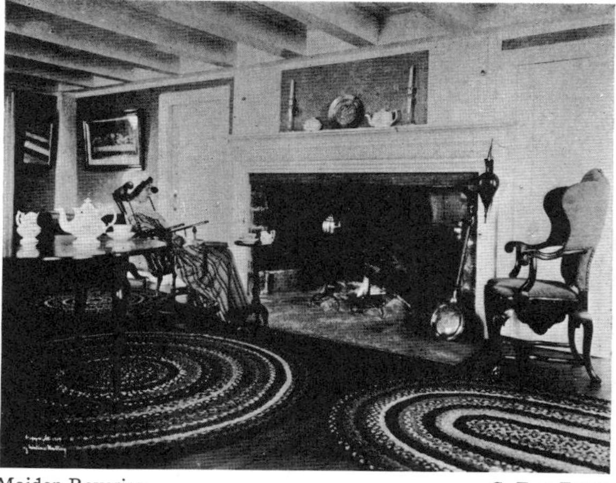
Maiden Reveries C, E or F 681

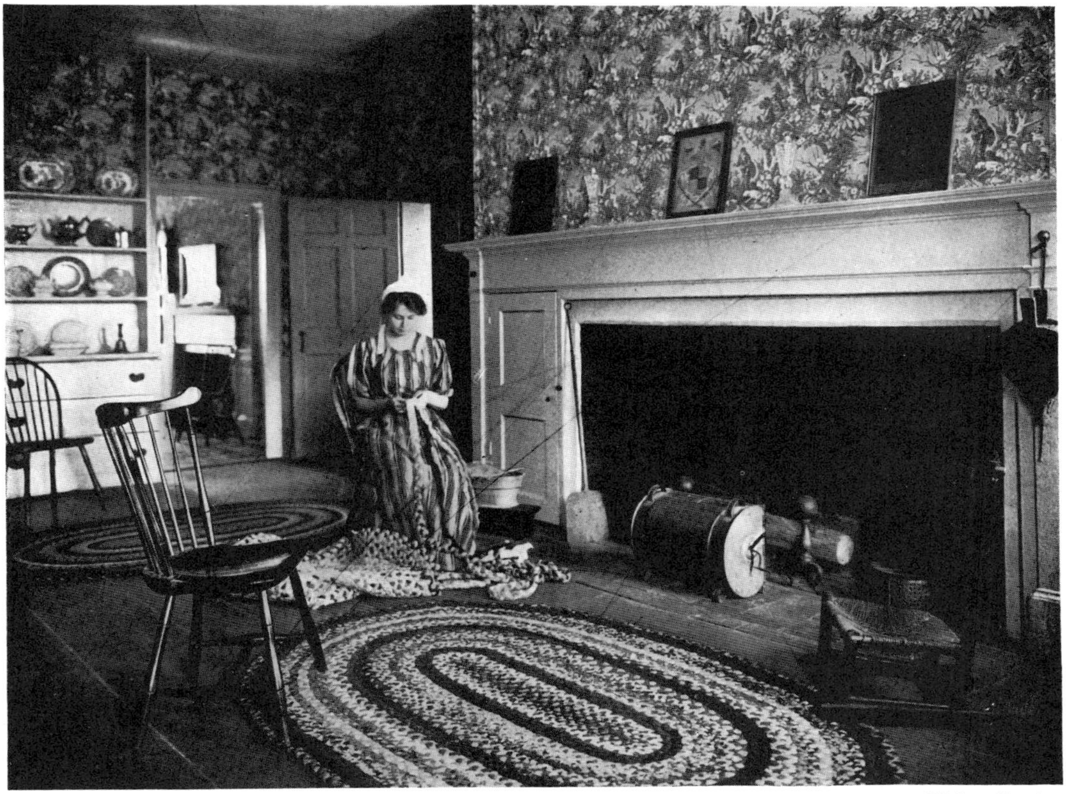

Braiding a Rag Rug A, C and E 3728 Wallace Nutting

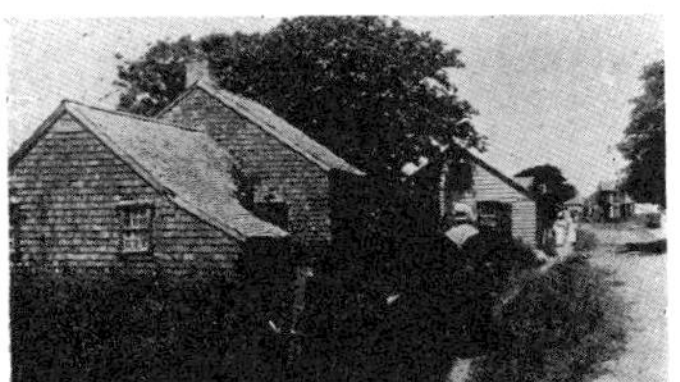
Afternoon in Nantucket S or C 1026

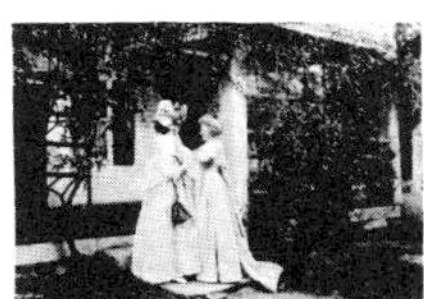
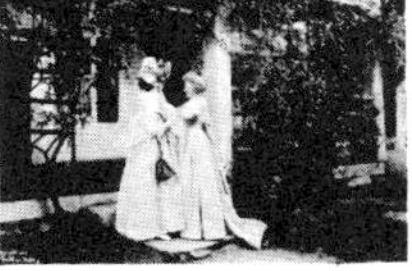
Primping A 135

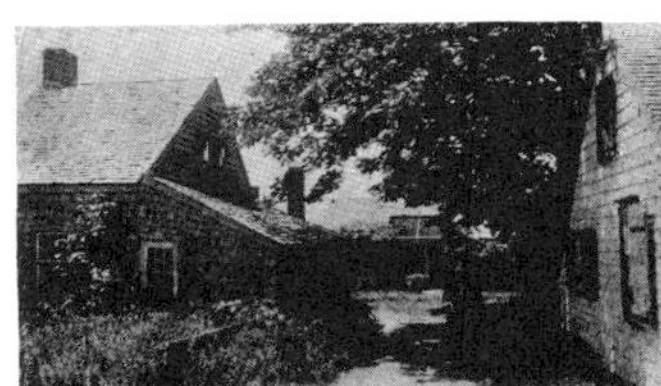
Fashionable 'Sconset S or C 1022

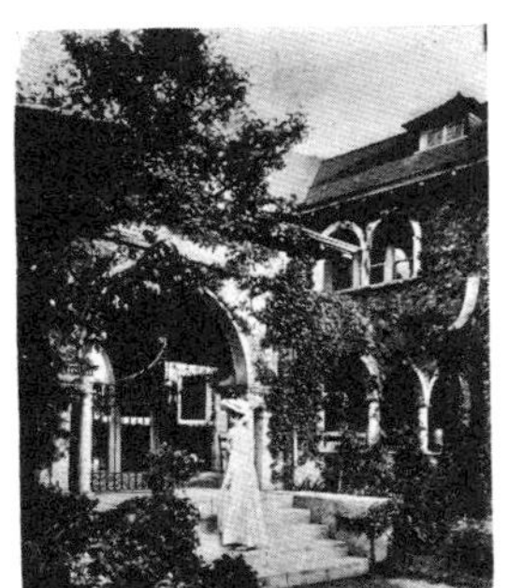
The Judge's Daughter
S or C 2181

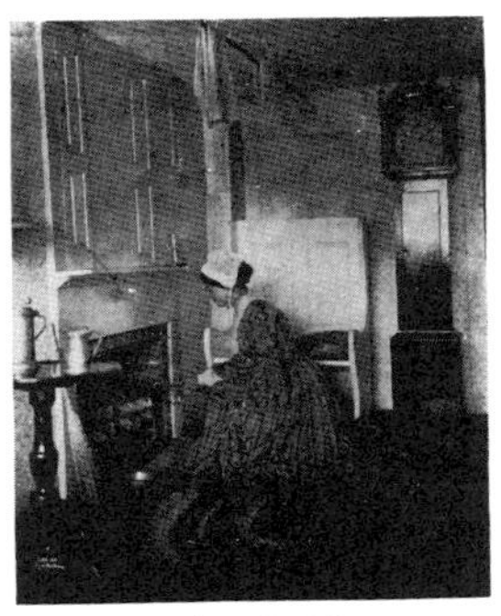
Laying the Fire
S or C 17

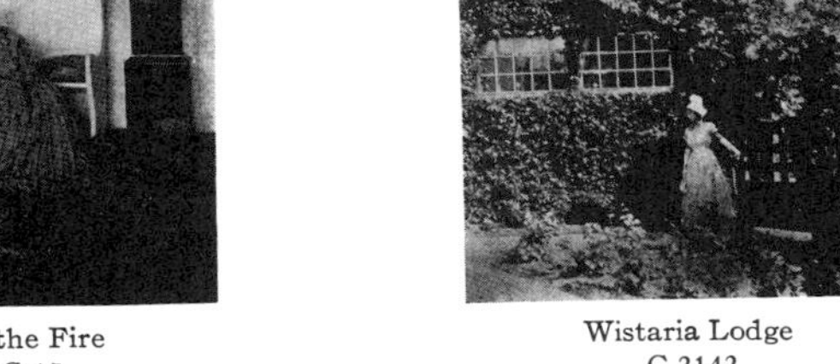
Wistaria Lodge
C 2142

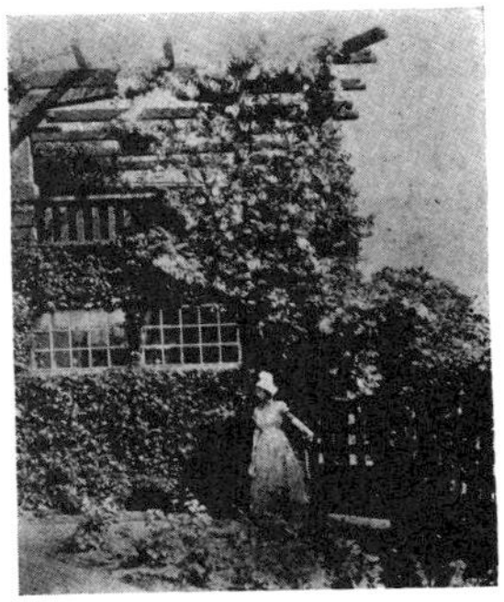

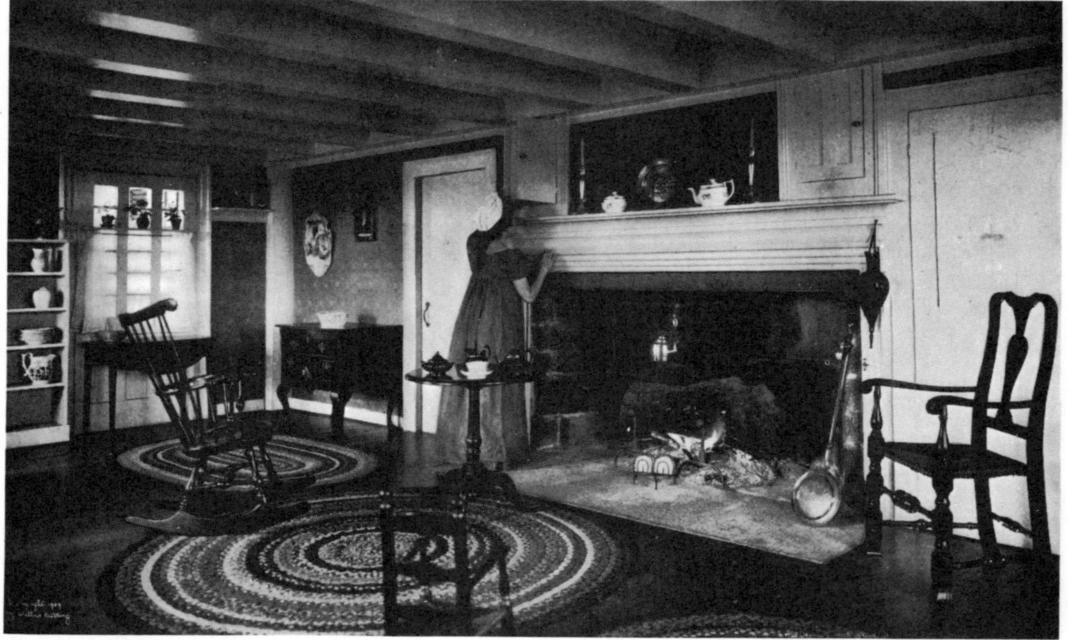
The Maple Sugar Cupboard C, P, E, G 734 Wallace Nutting

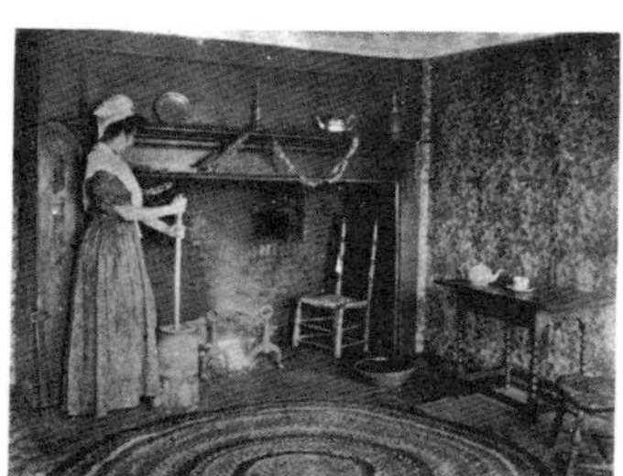
Warming the Cream C 963

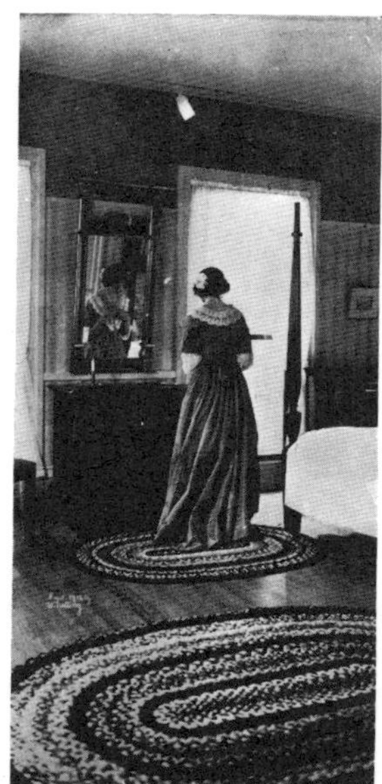
Pinning the Lace Q, S, O, P 1393

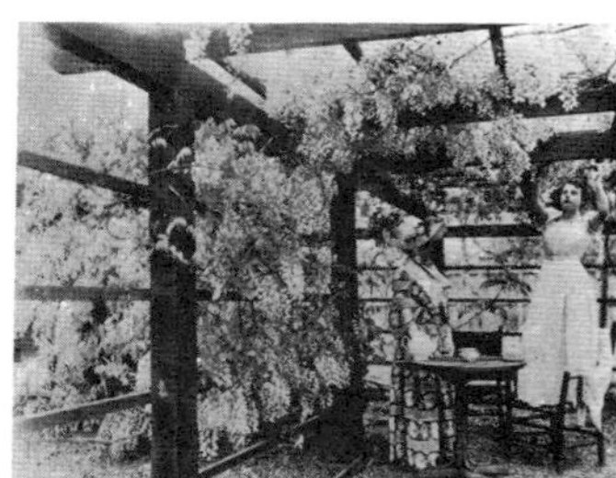
A Lavender Canopy C 2180

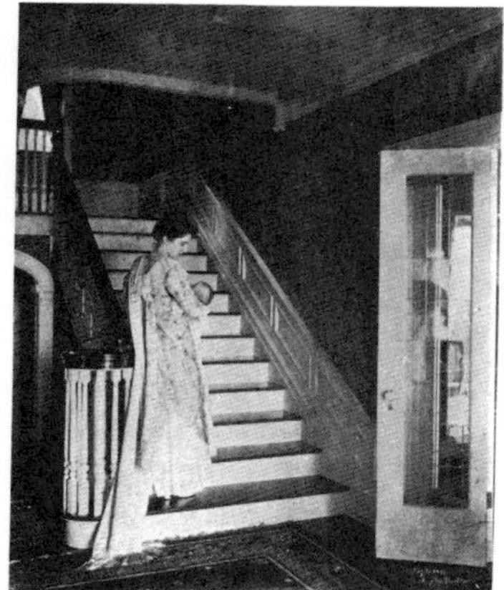
To Slumberland A, C or E 2292

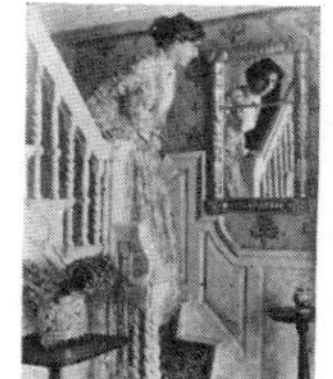
Who's in the Parlor ? A 59

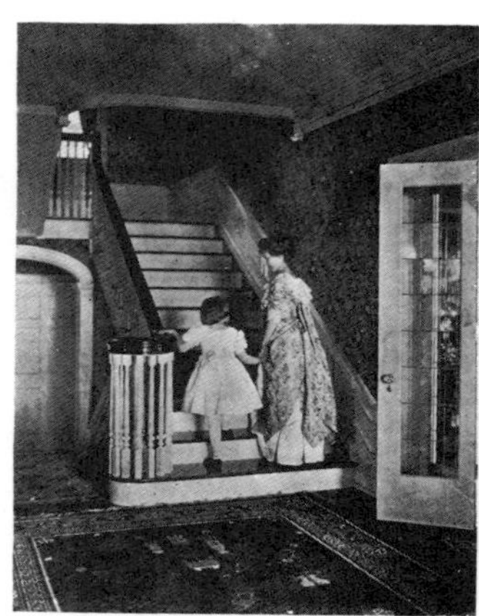
After the Party C or E 2295

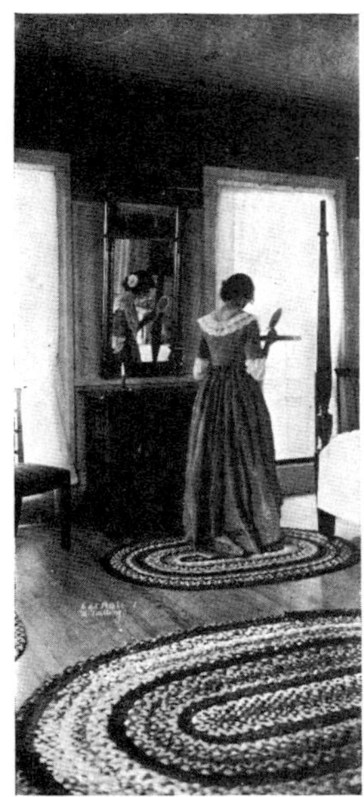

A Maid and a Mirror Q, S 1394

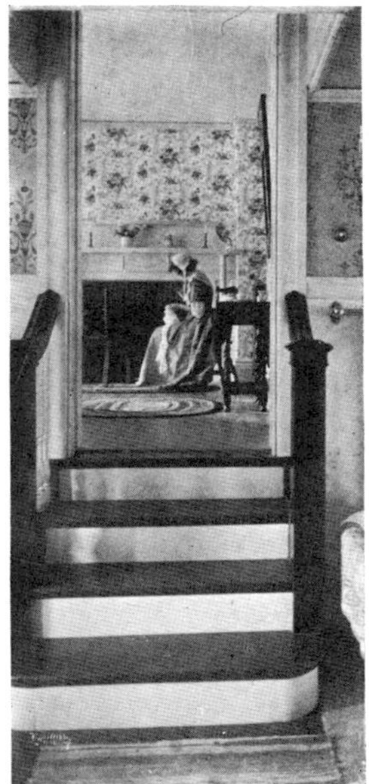

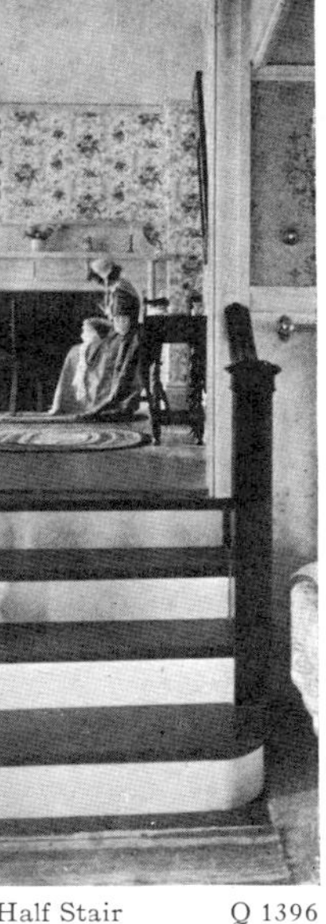

Up the Half Stair Q 1396

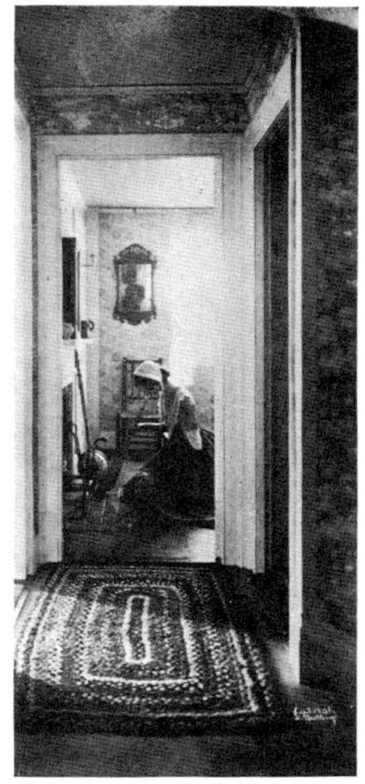

The Last Touches
Q, S, O, P 1498

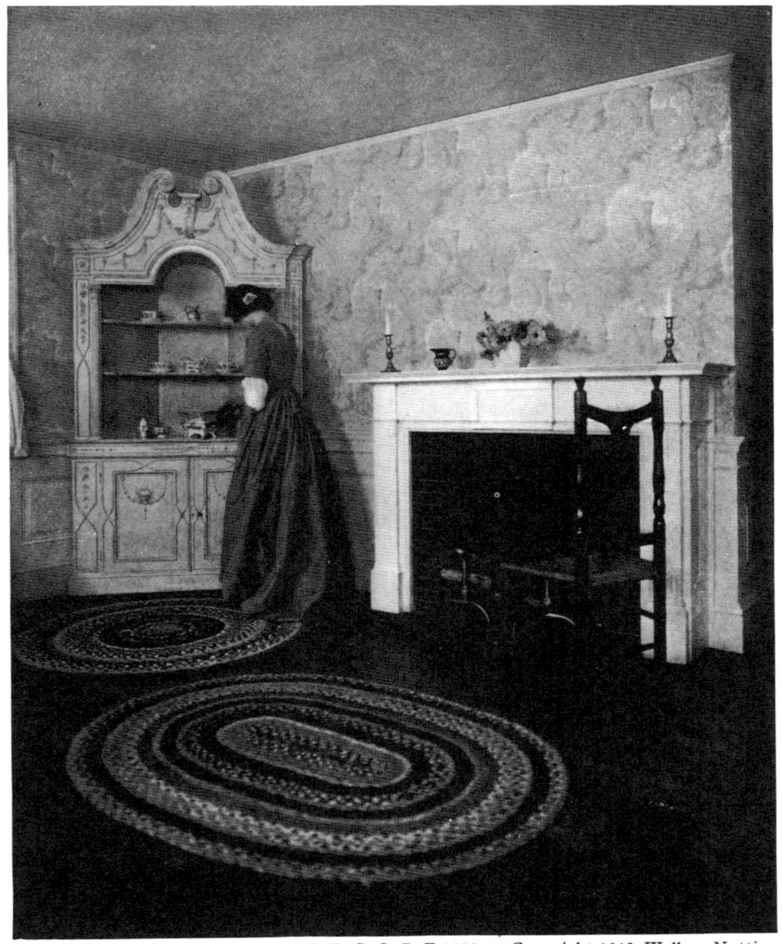

Dainty China A, Q, S, C, O, P, E 1499 Copyright 1912, Wallace Nutting

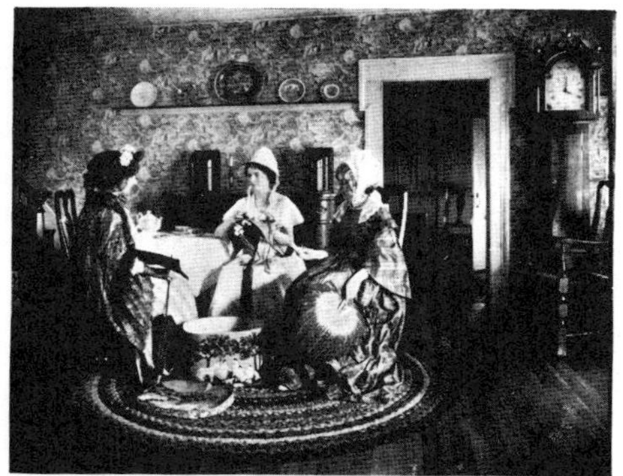

Admiration — Wallace Nutting
C 454

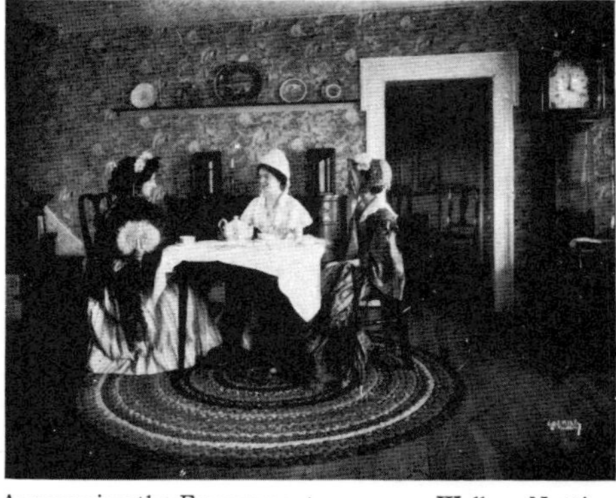

Announcing the Engagement — Wallace Nutting
A, C and E 403

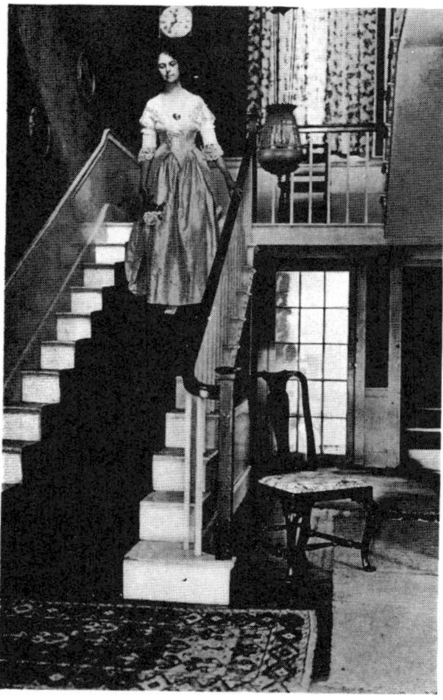

The Reception — S 3588

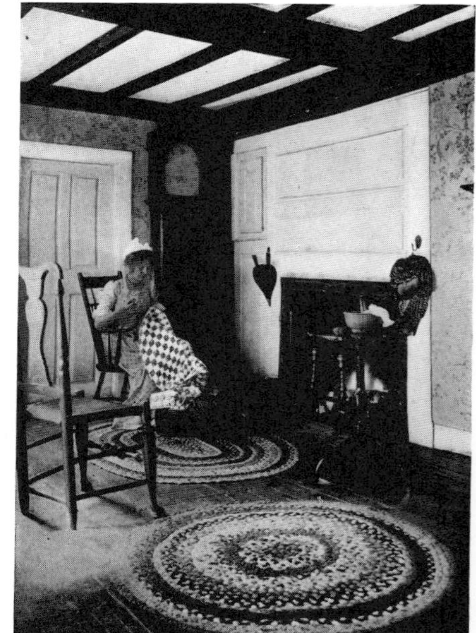

Mending the Quilt — A 3625

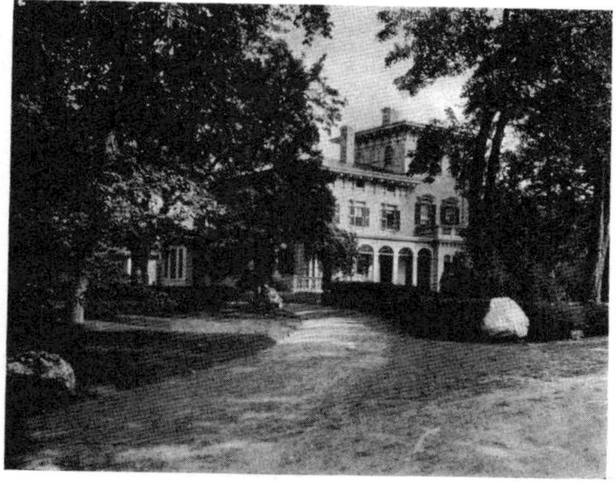

Nuttingholm at Framingham
(Not an art subject)

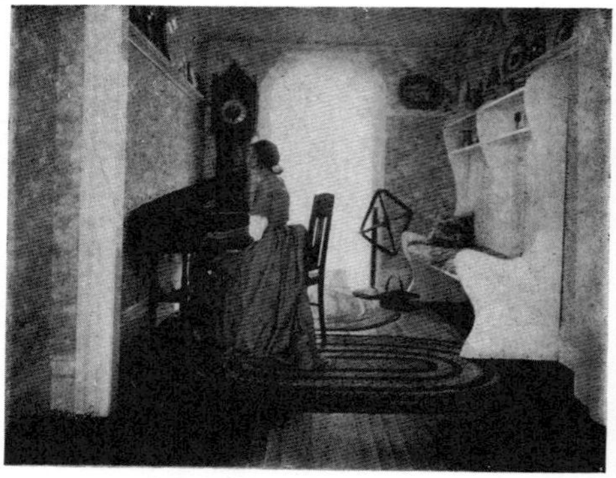

A Musical Reverie — Wallace Nutting
C 1509 — A Dreamy Poetic Theme

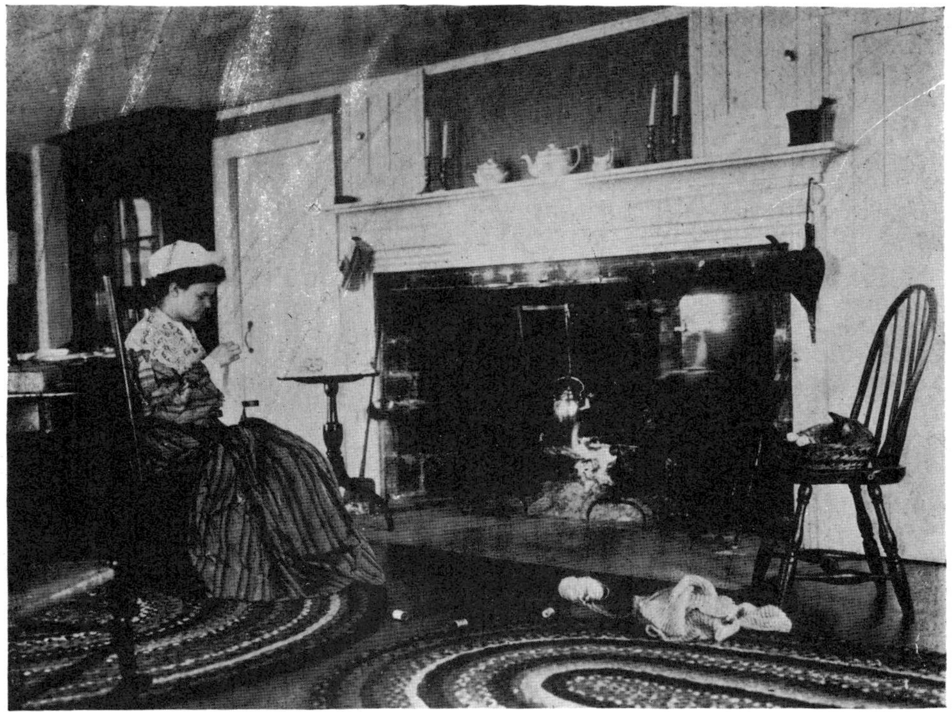

Comfort and a Cat C 545 Wallace Nutting

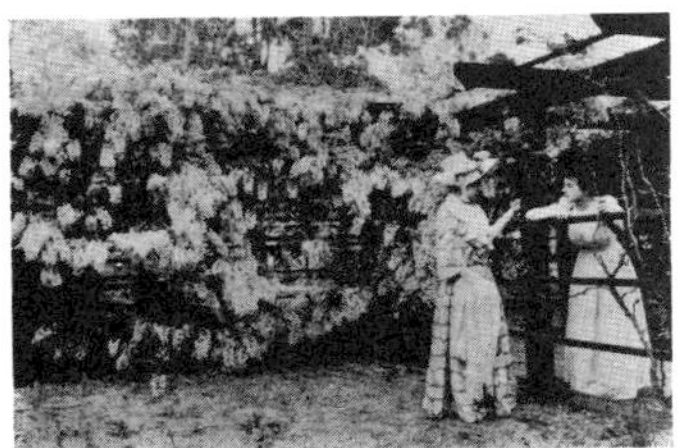

Garden Gossip A or S 2250

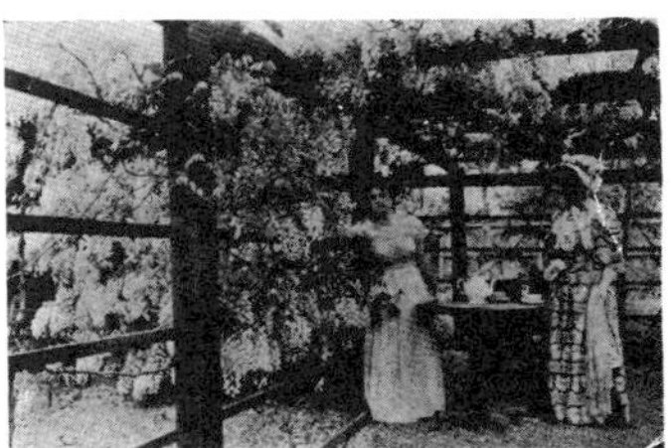

After Tea A or C 2249

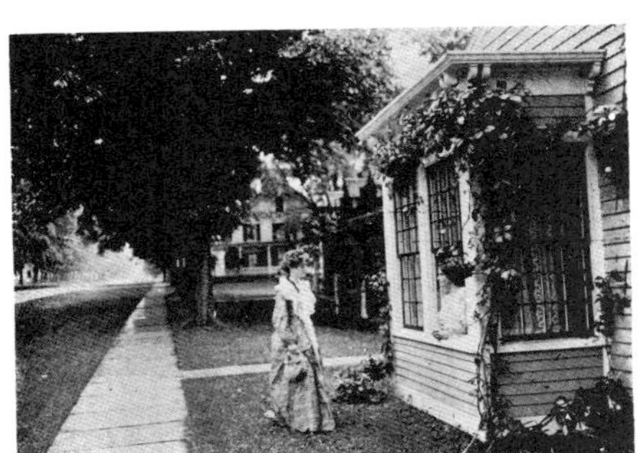

A Chat at the Window C or E 915

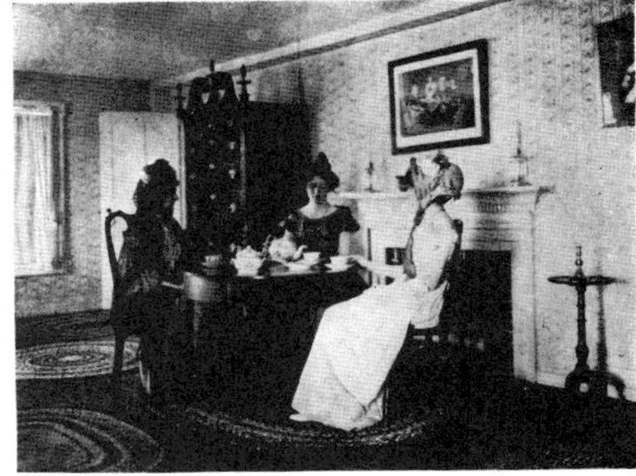

The News in Brief A, C and E 254 Wallace Nutting

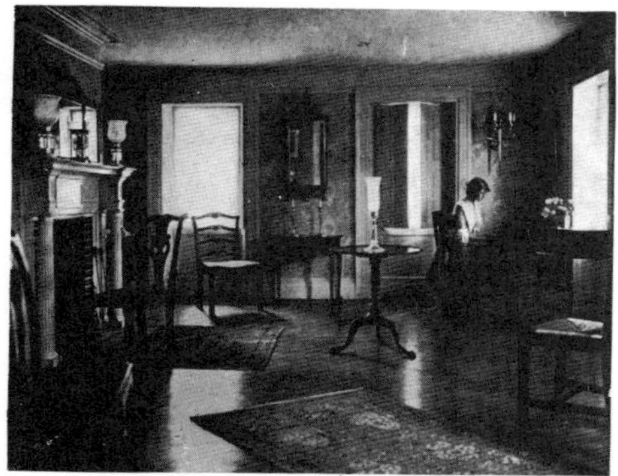

An Old Drawing Room C 1388 Wallace Nutting

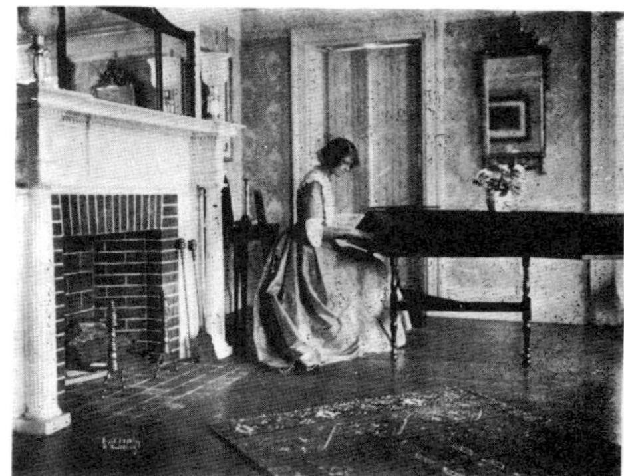

The Spinet Corner A, C, E 1389 Wallace Nutting

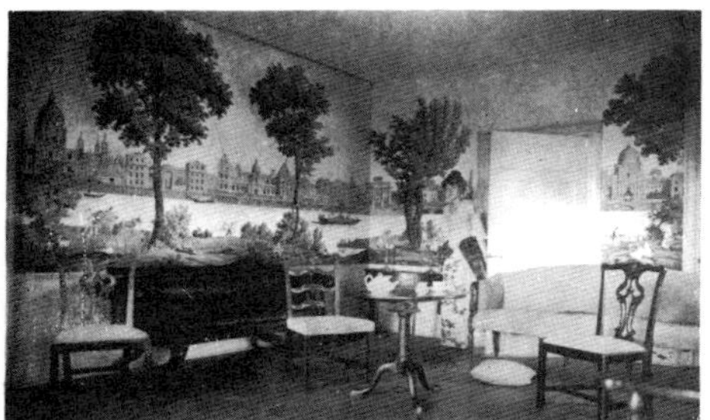

City of Paris Paper A, S and P 779 Wallace Nutting

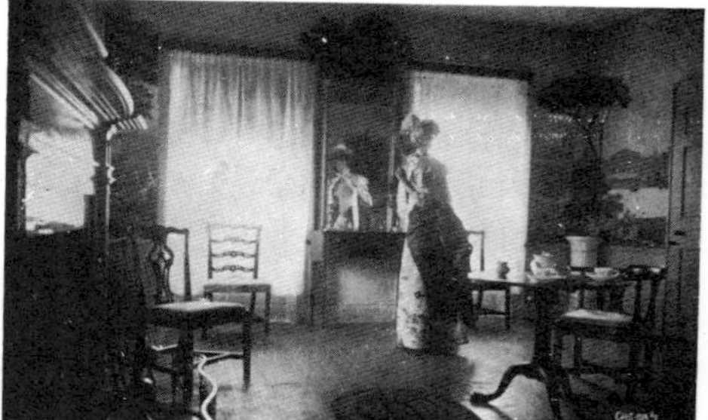

Panniers of the Past S 1339 Wallace Nutting

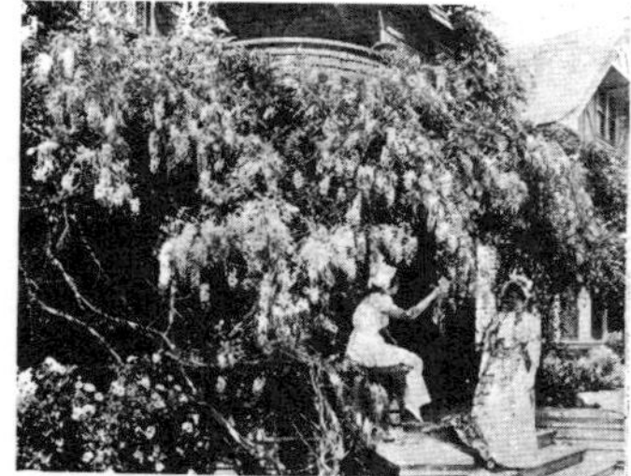

Under the Wistaria C 2177

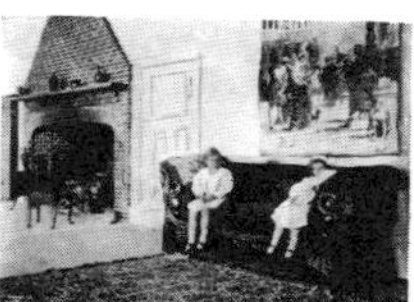

Her First "At Home"
A, G 320

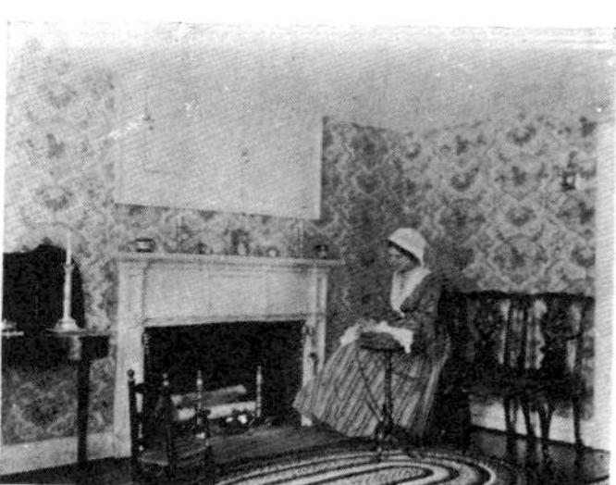

While I Was Musing Q, C 283

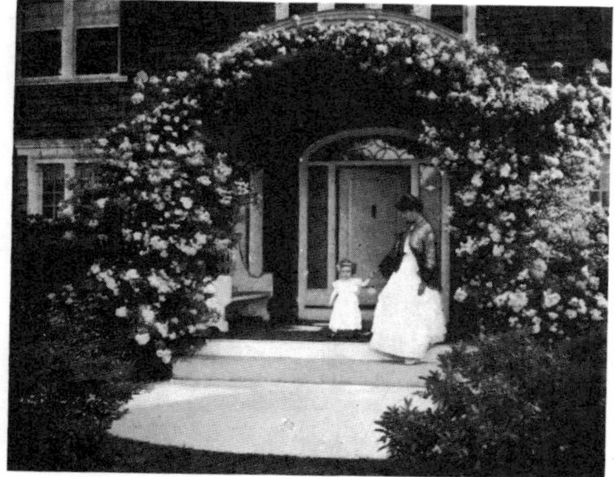

Wavering Footsteps C 2531

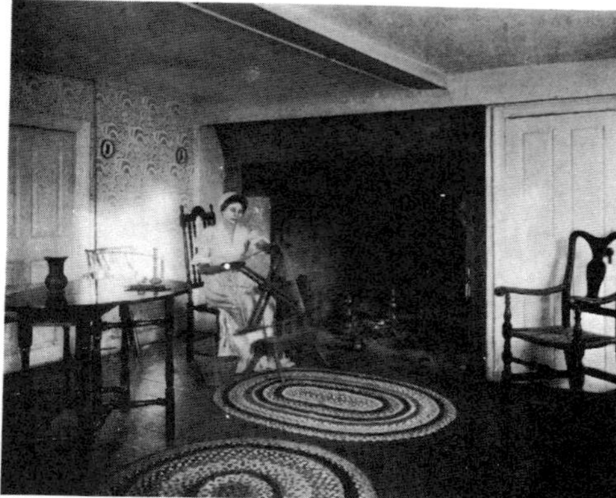

A Sunny Corner A, C 3702

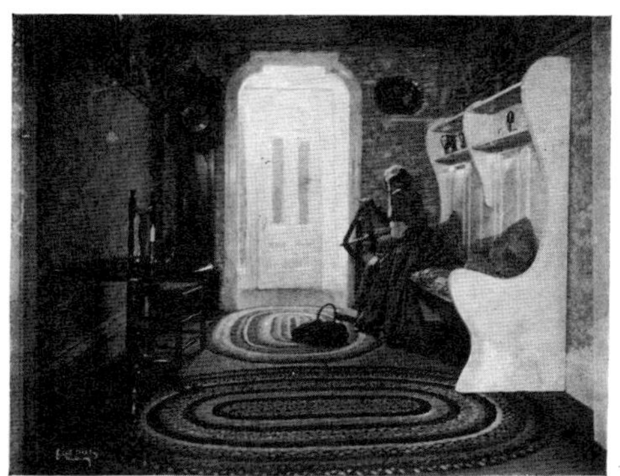

The Tangled Skein C 1510 Wallace Nutting

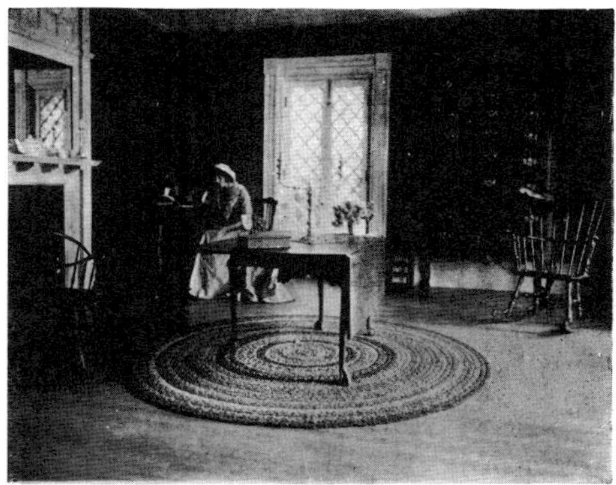

The Morning Mail C 1507 Wallace Nutting

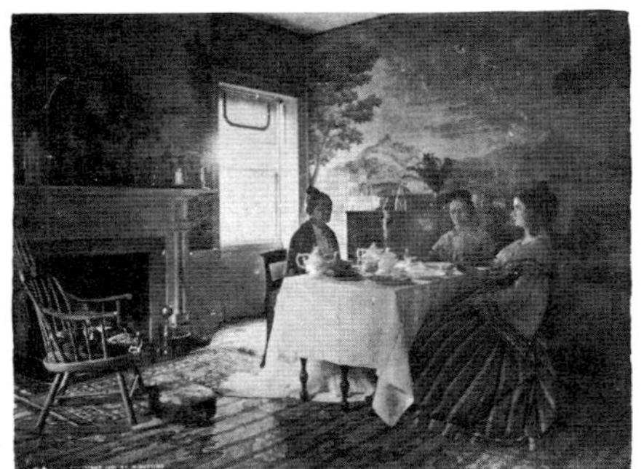

Colonial Dames at Tea C 298

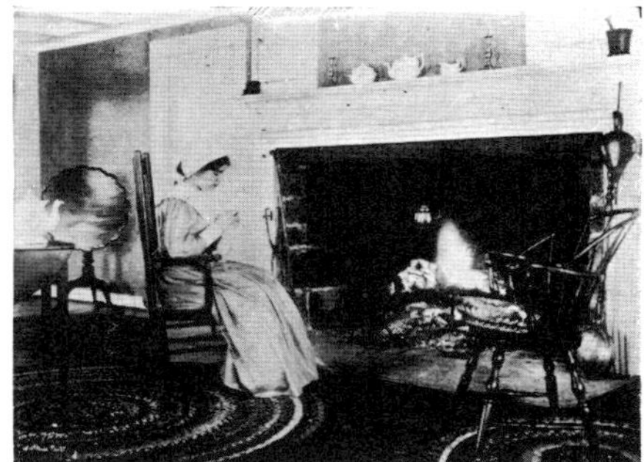

17th Century A, C or E 10

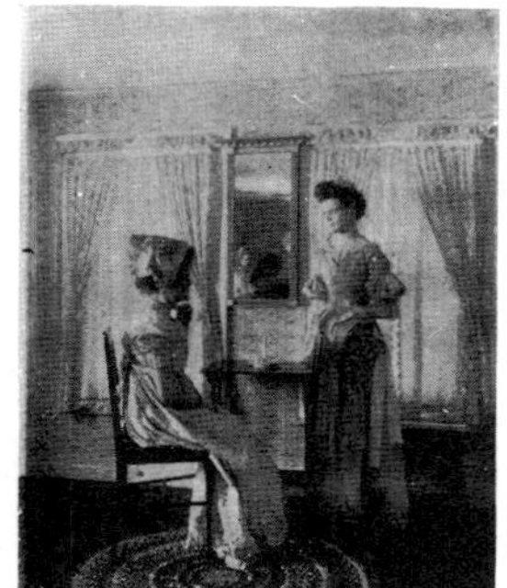

Sisterly Criticism C 804

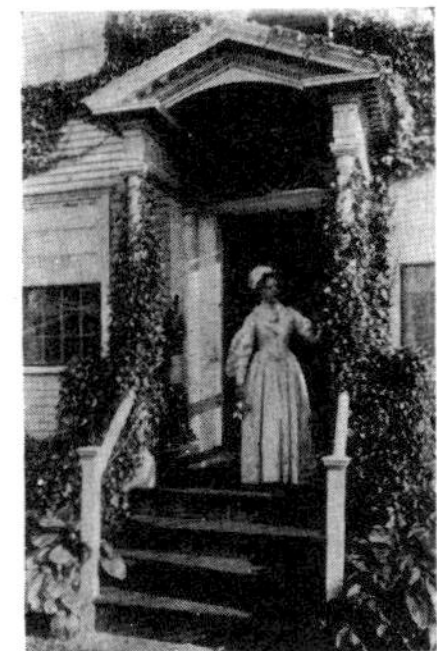

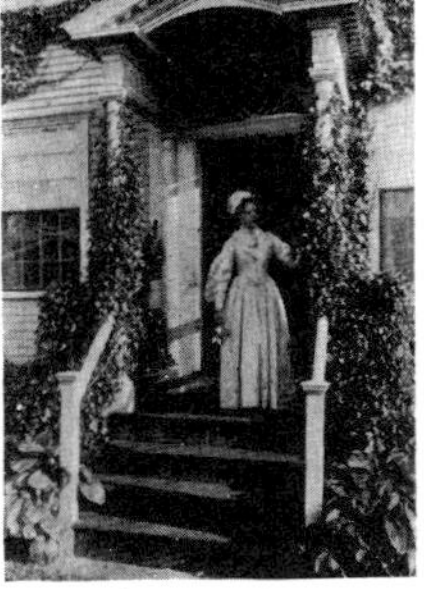

Ivy Pruning S 1024

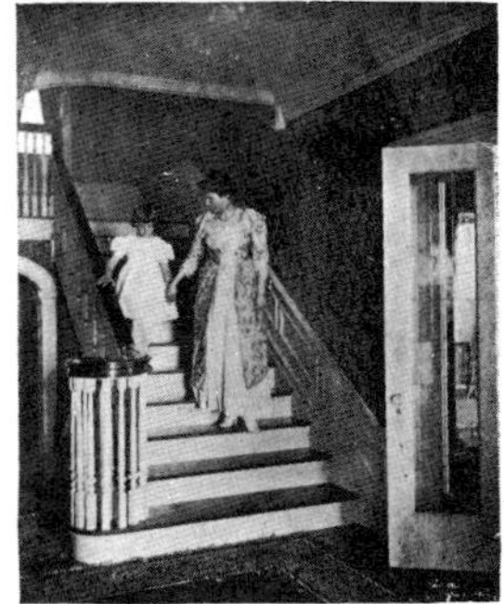

Shy Before Guests C 2291

In order to guarantee the appropriateness of our old-fashioned subjects, Mr. Nutting has for years made a special study of old furniture and Colonial architecture, and has at last even written a book on the subject illustrated in color with his pictures.

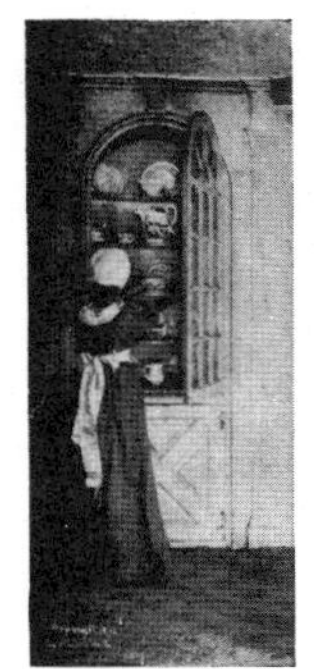

For the Honored Guest
Q 889

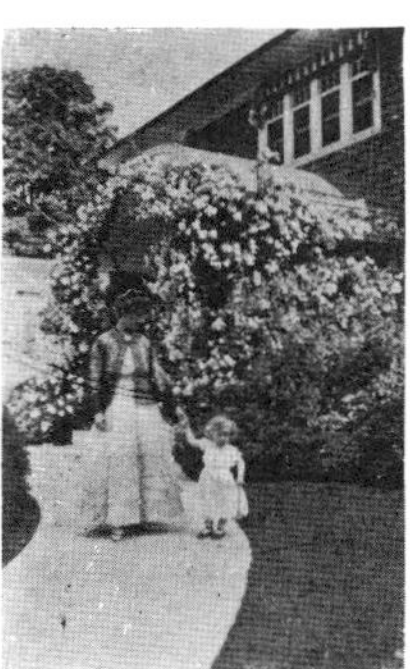

Watching for Papa
S 2532

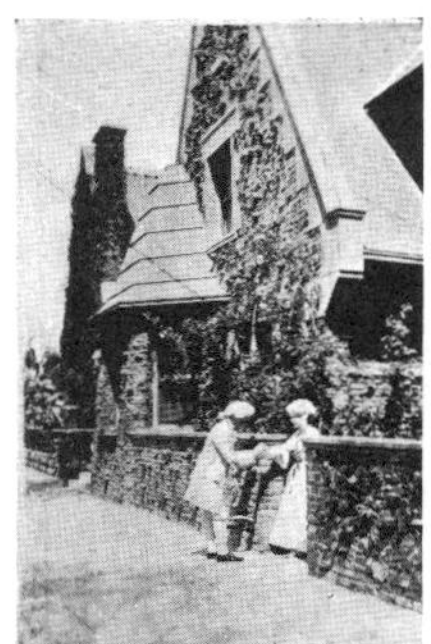

Parting at the Gate
S 2133

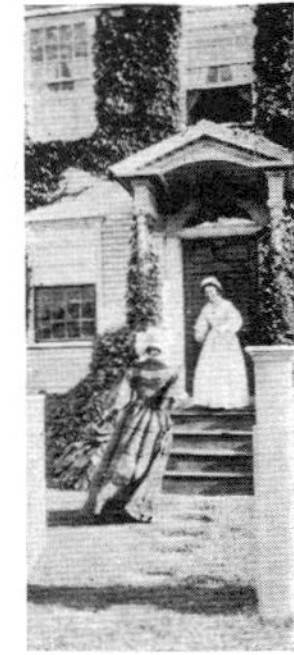

A Breezy Call
Q 1018

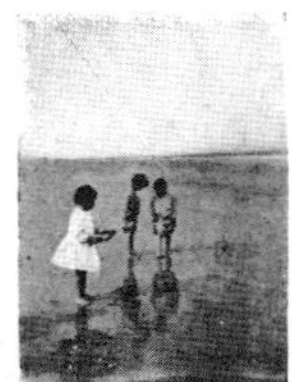

The Sand Mirror
A 2074

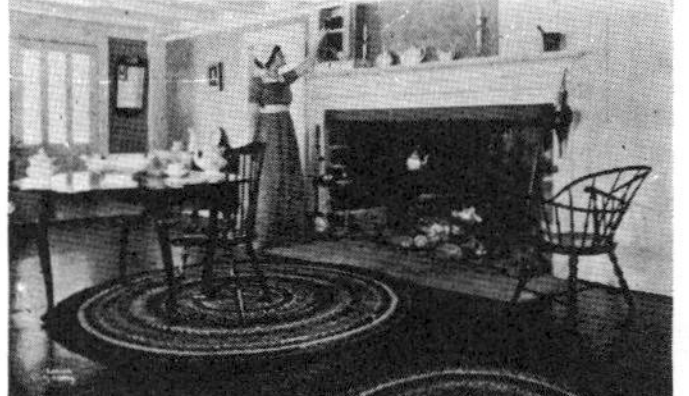
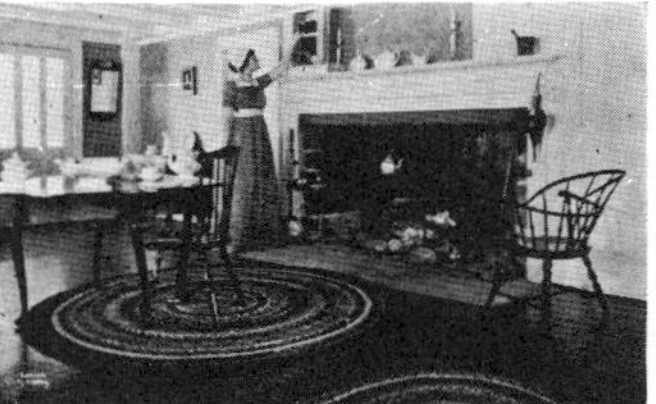

Christmas Jelly S 52

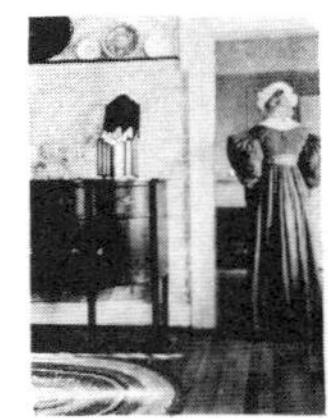

Summoned to the Parlor
A 2589

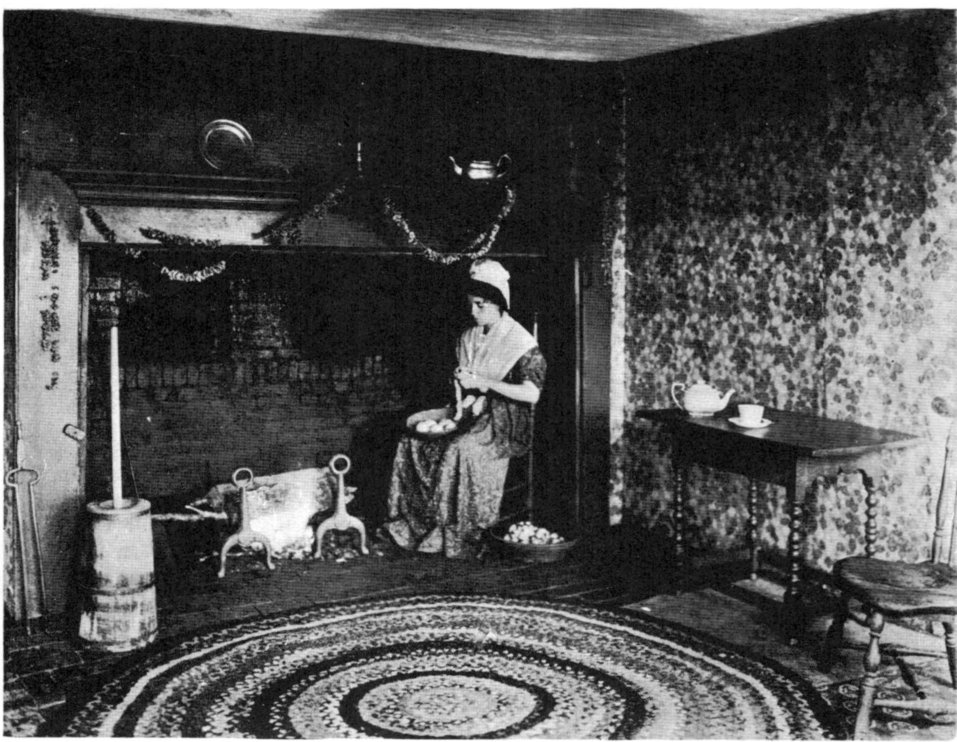

A Cold Day A, C or E 962 Wallace Nutting

A very ancient North Shore fireplace made in the days of double ovens back of the hearth itself.

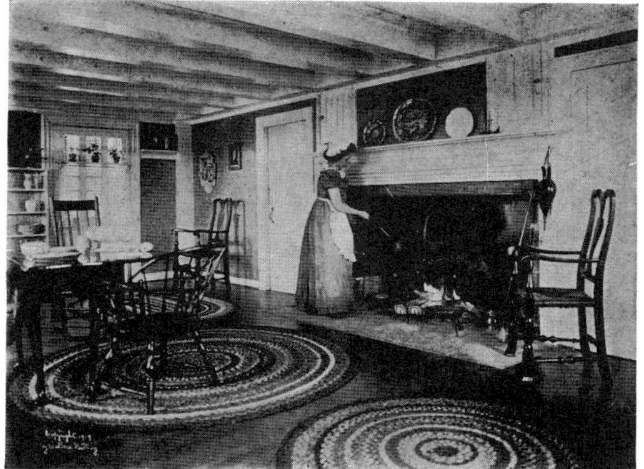

An Elaborate Dinner C, E, F or J 746

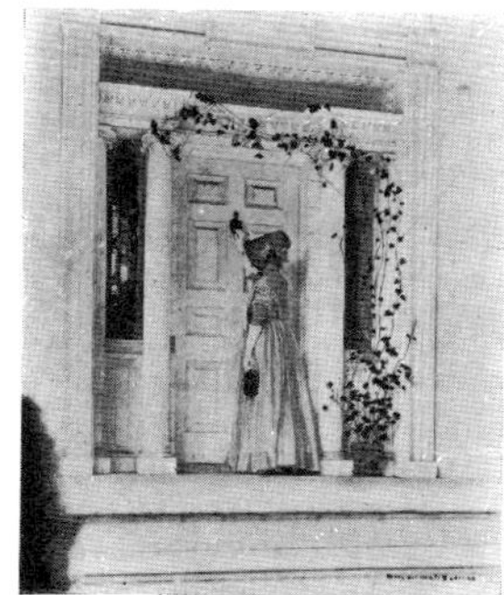

A Tap at the Squire's Door
C 119

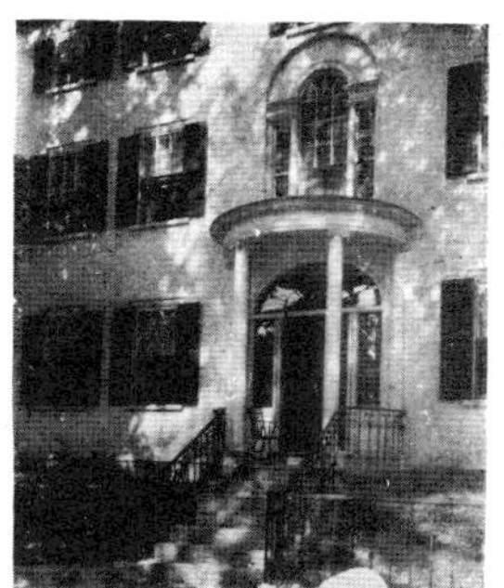

The Marvin Door
Q, S or C 918

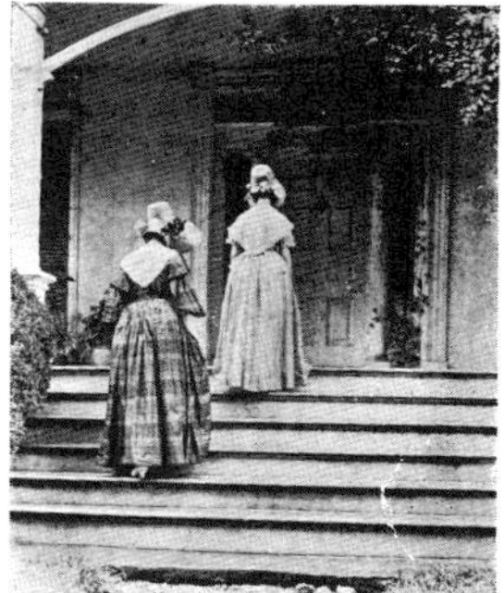

Callers at the Squire's
C 124

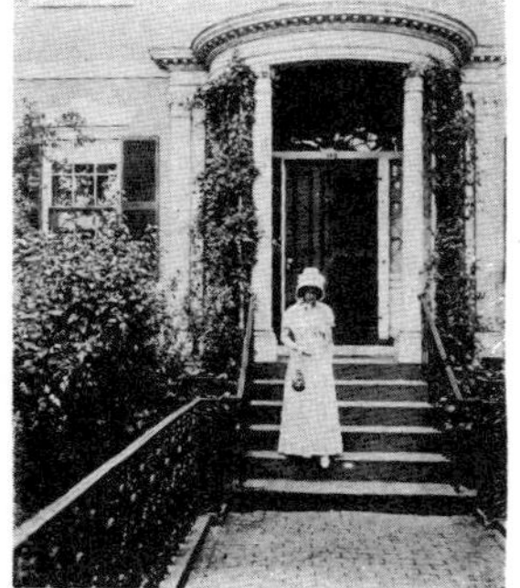

Salem Beautiful C 994

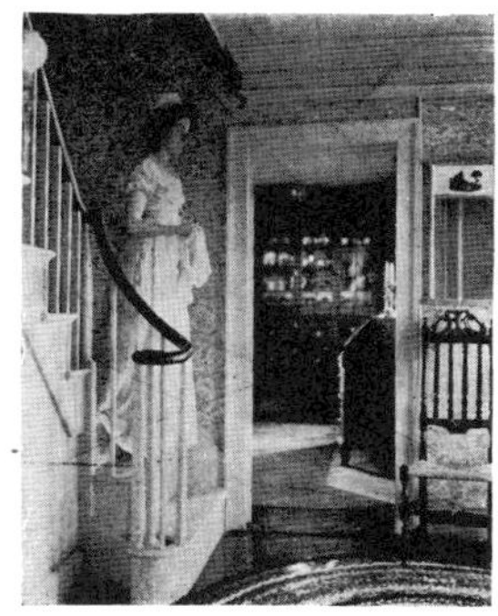

Beth C 999

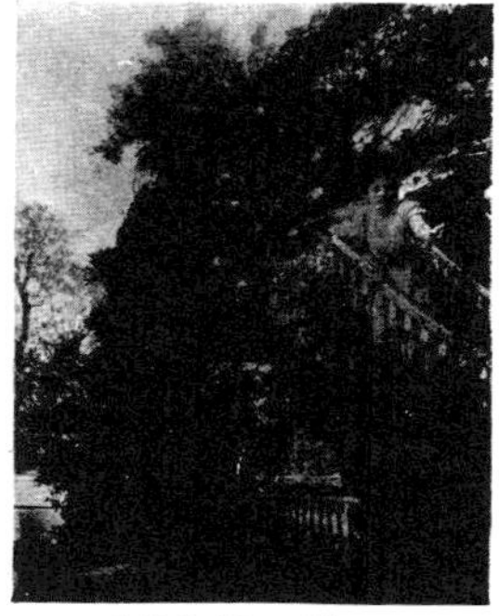

A Rebellious Vine
Q, S or C 2165

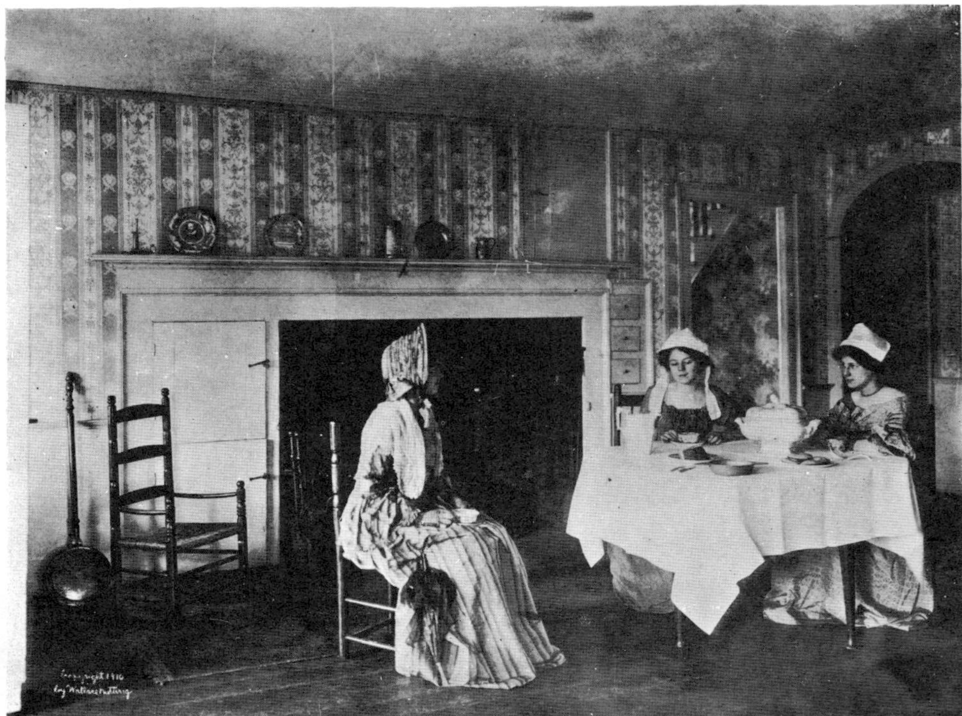

All the News—and More C, E, F and G 396 Wallace Nutting

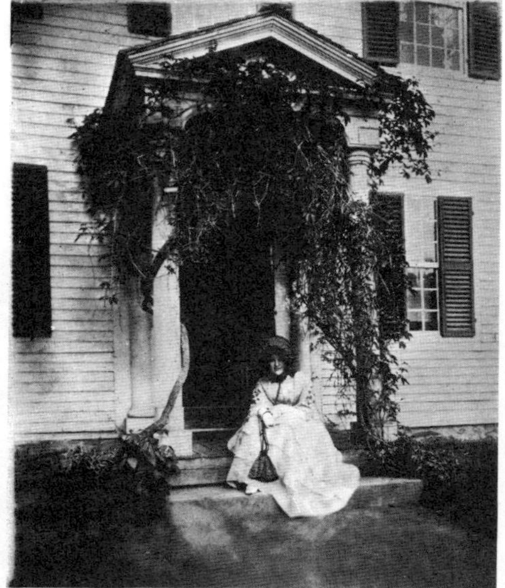

Resting at the Old Stoop A, C or E 416

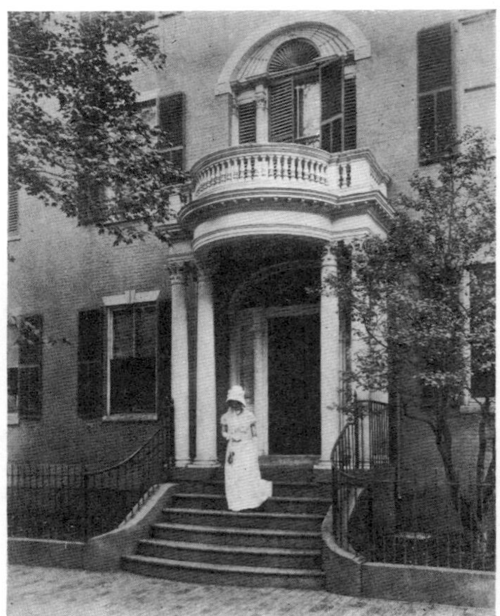

The Sea Cap'n's Daughter Q, S or C 995

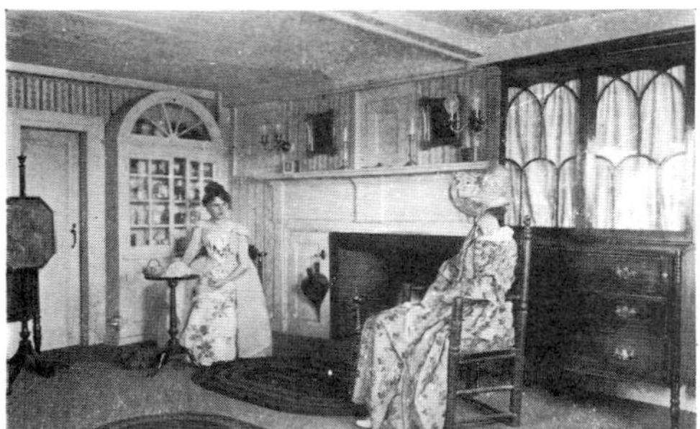

In John Hancock's Chair S, P 3670

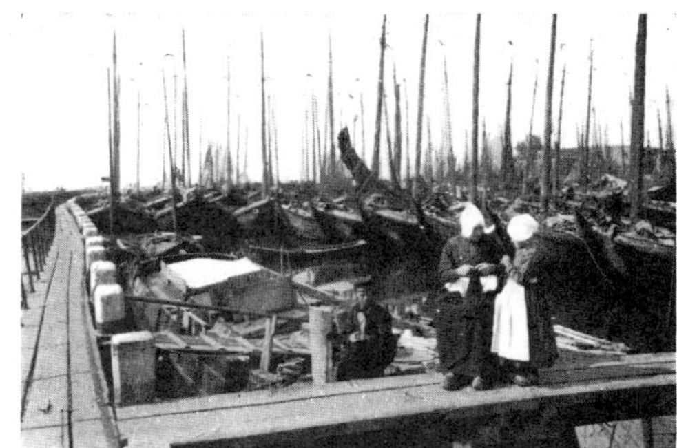

A Dutch Knitting Lesson A, S, C, E 5066

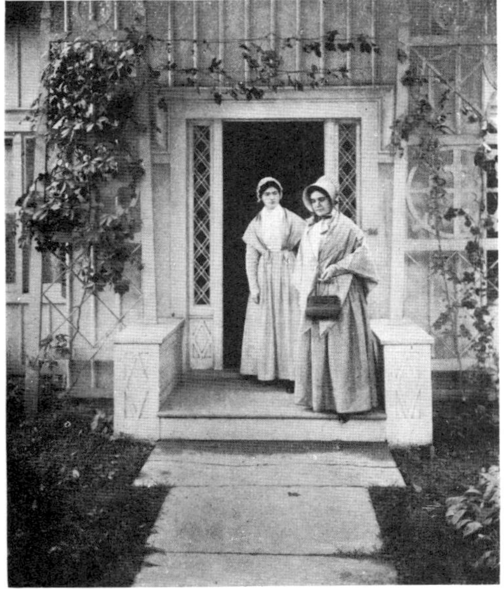

A Friend's Farewell A and C 1356 Wallace Nutting

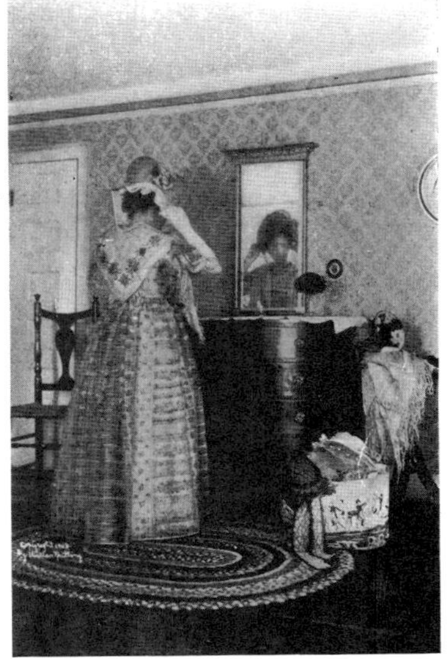

Almost Ready S, C, E or G 641

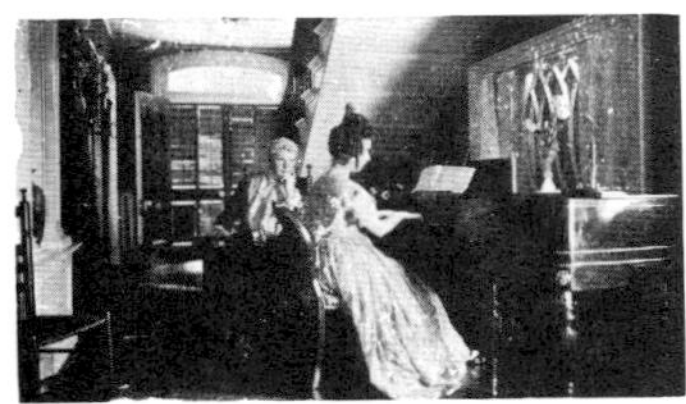

An Old Tune Revived S or C 261

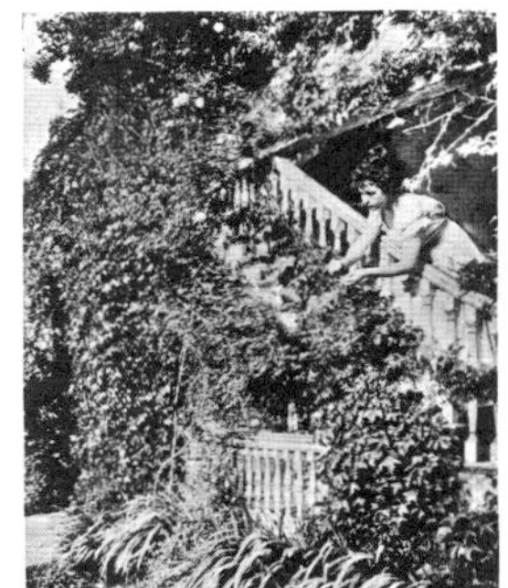

A Wayward Branch C 2182

Children of The Sea A or S 2071

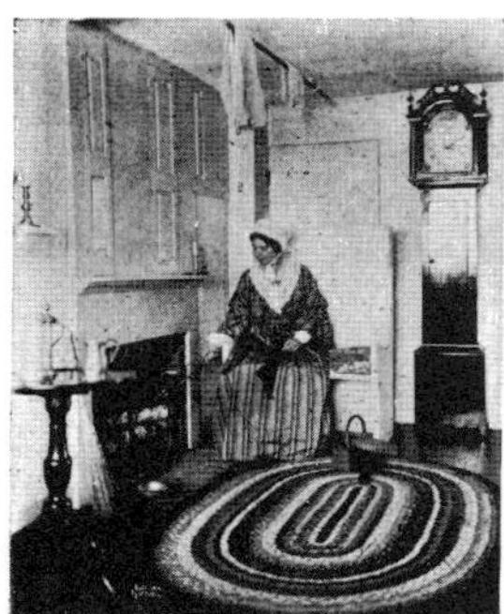

Nursing the Fire A, Q, S or C 7

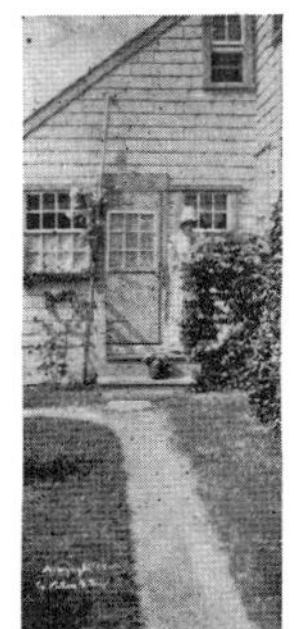

Gathering a Bouquet
Q 1033

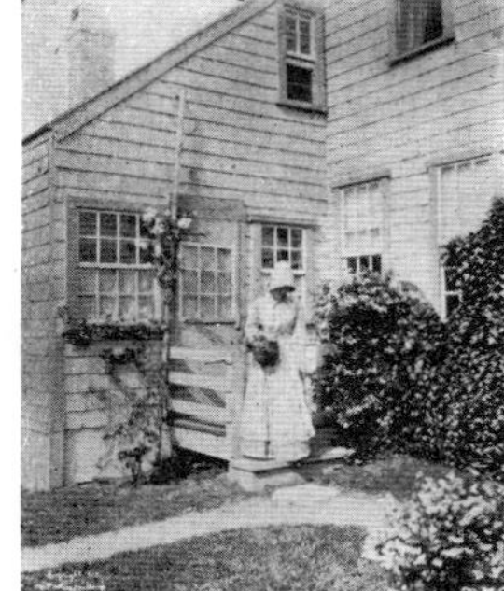

The Flower Missionary
Q or C 1029

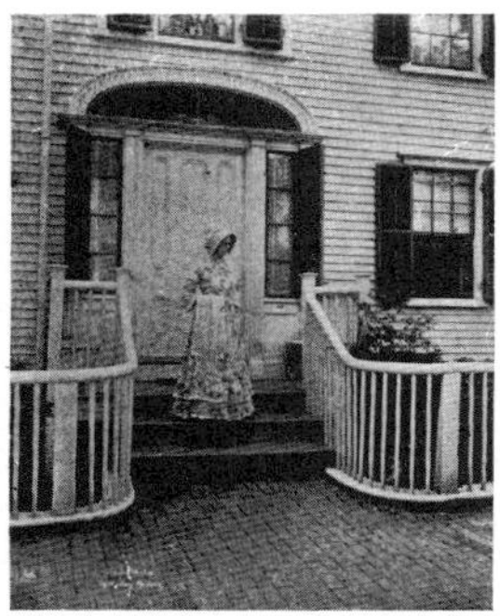

Jane A, Q or C 1031

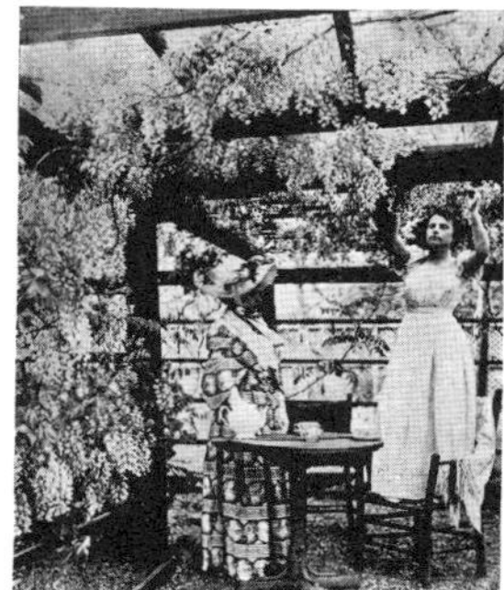

Gathering Blossoms C 2613

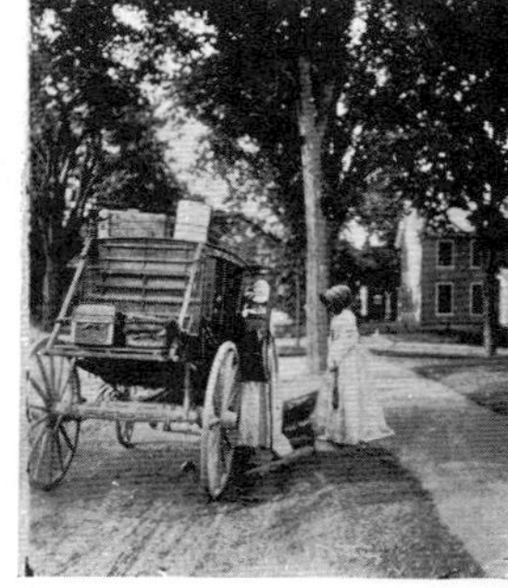

An Eventful Journey C 101

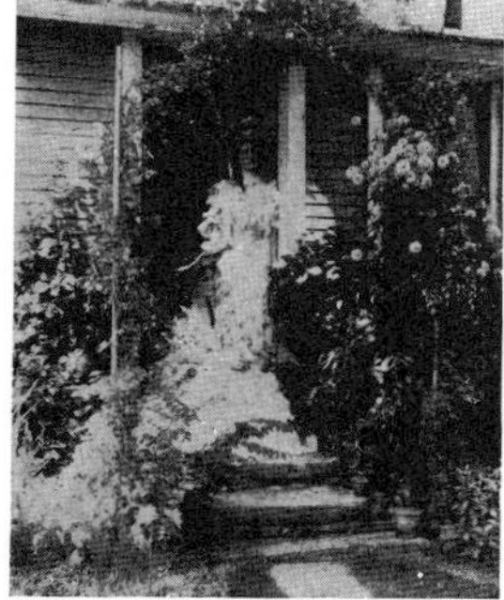

At the Side Door C 175

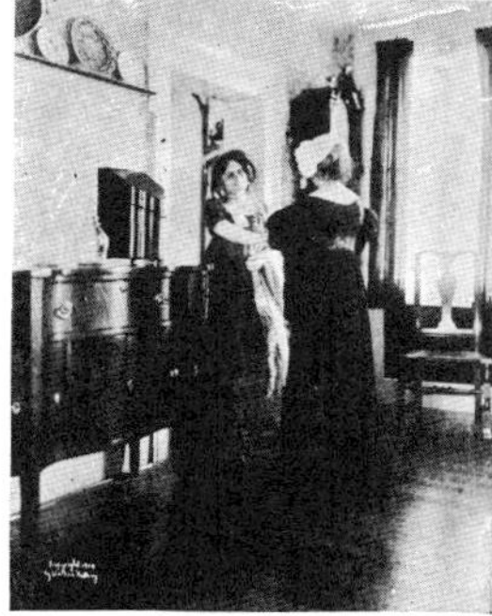

A Hearty Welcome C 747

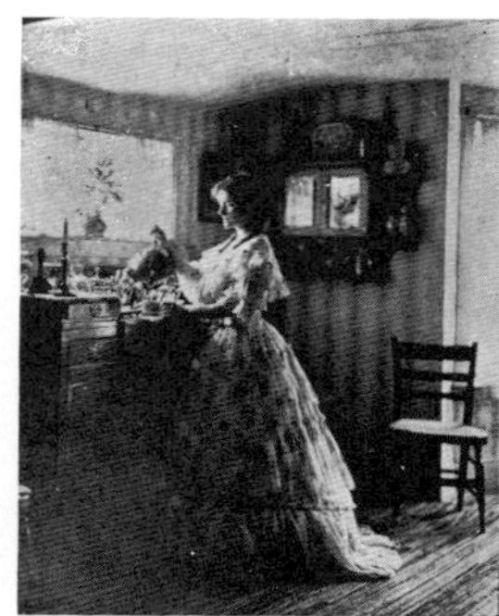

A Cranford Tea Pouring
C 914

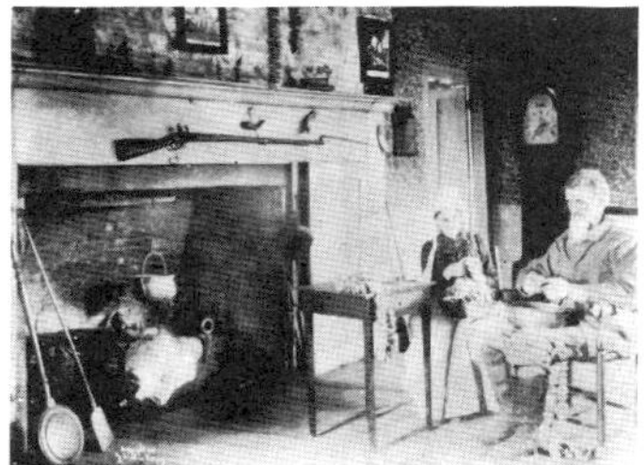

Drying Apples C 429

Is the Fire Ready? C 222

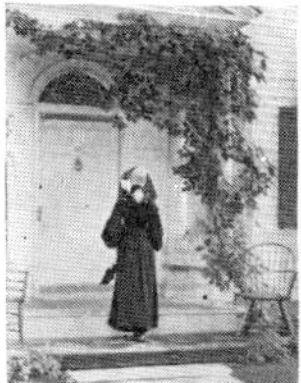

In Grandma's Day
A 401

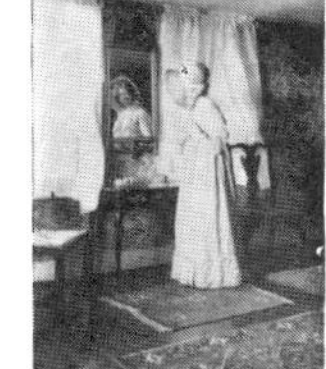

A Peep in the Mirror
A 448

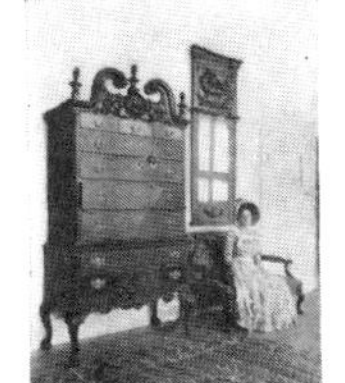

Patience on a Chippendale
A 349

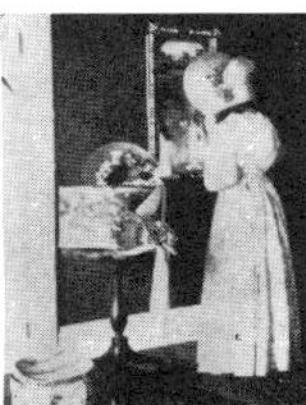

A True D. A. R.
A or S 232

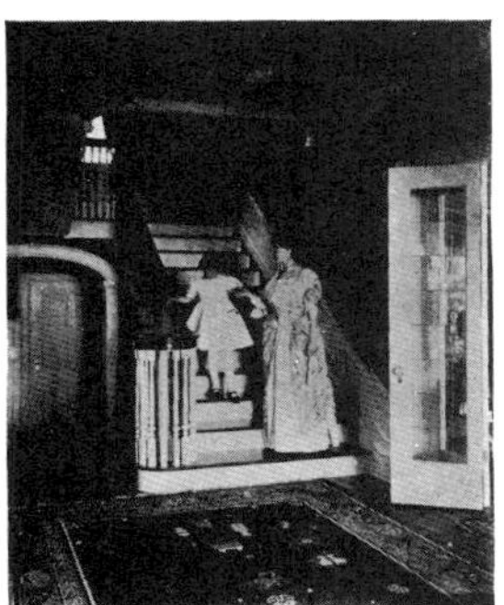

To Meet the Rector C 2499

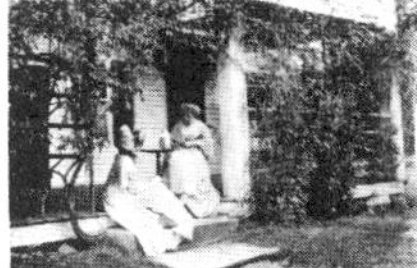

Maidenly Pleasures
A 156

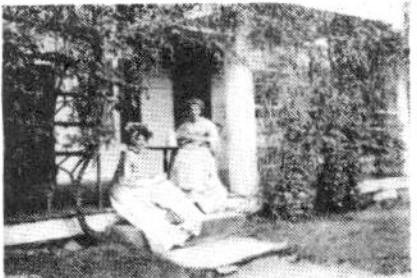

A Friendly Reception
A or C 142

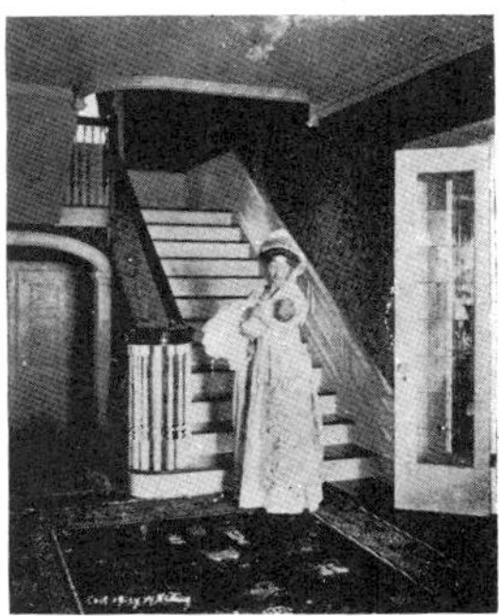

To Meet Papa C 2296

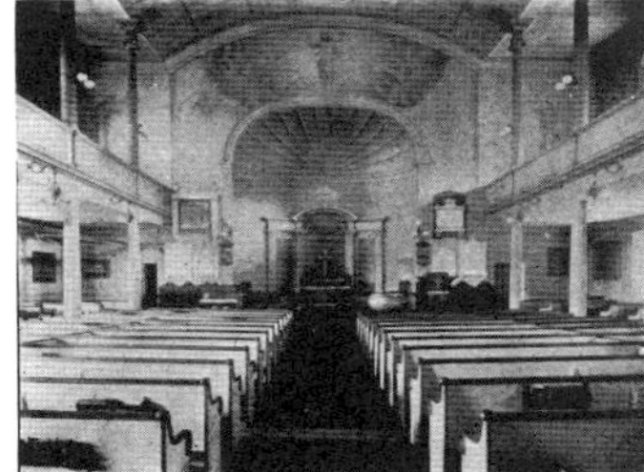

St. John's Church, Portsmouth, N. H.
C 568

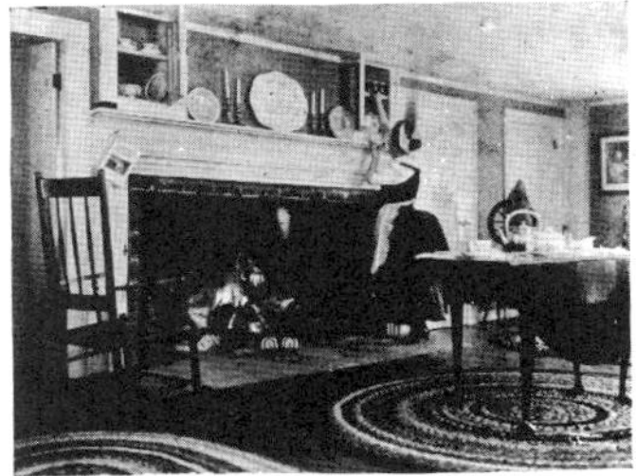

Thanksgiving Goodies C 595

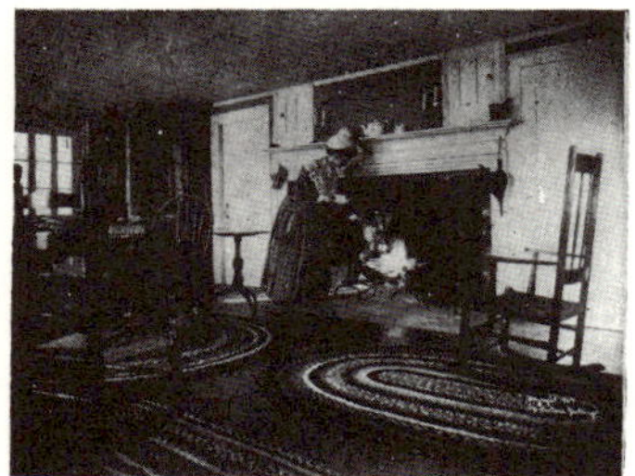
A Sip of Tea C 551

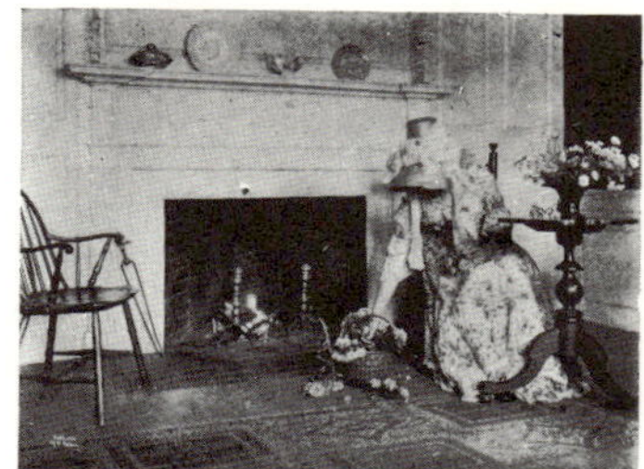
Morning Duties A or C 66

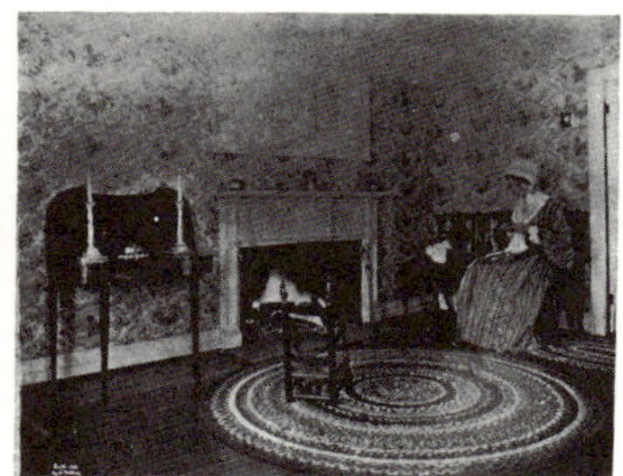
Diligence C 259

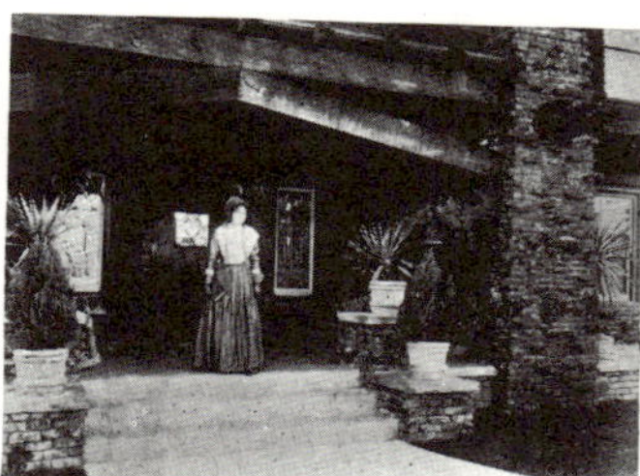
A Southern Puritan C 2122

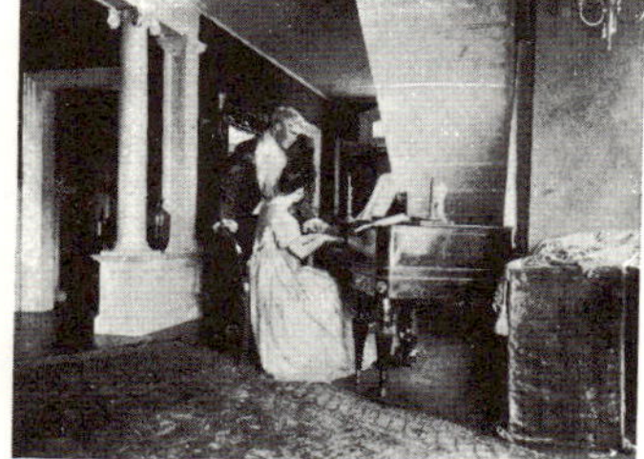
The Way it Begins C 214

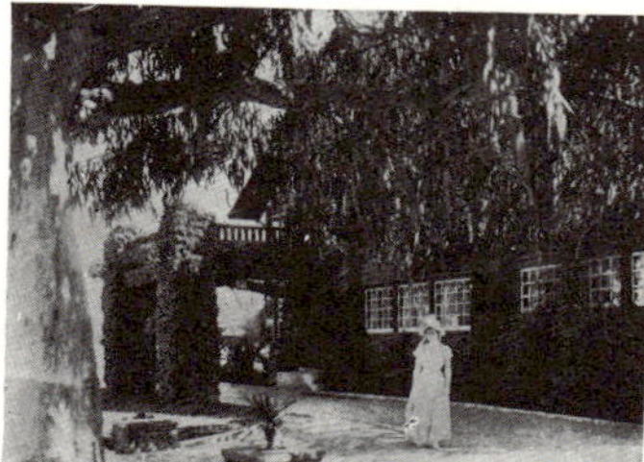
A Morning Errand C 2143

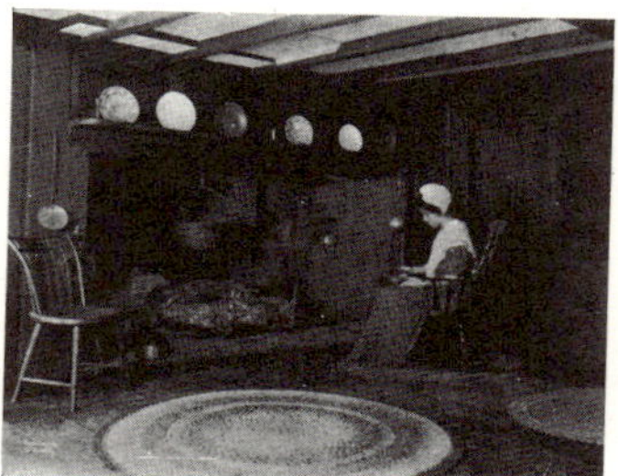
The Chopping Bowl C 960

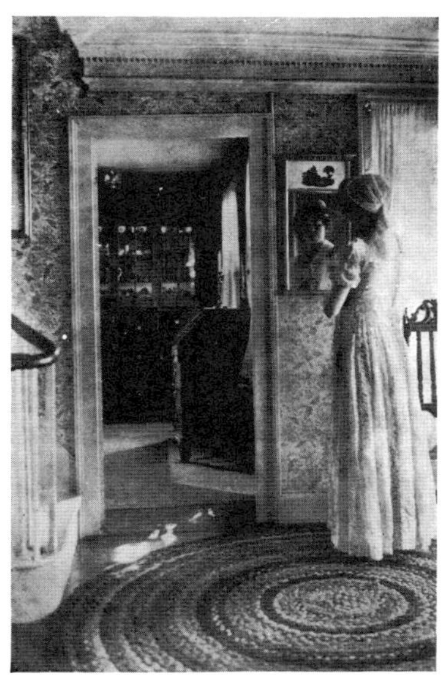
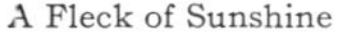
A Fleck of Sunshine S, P or T 985

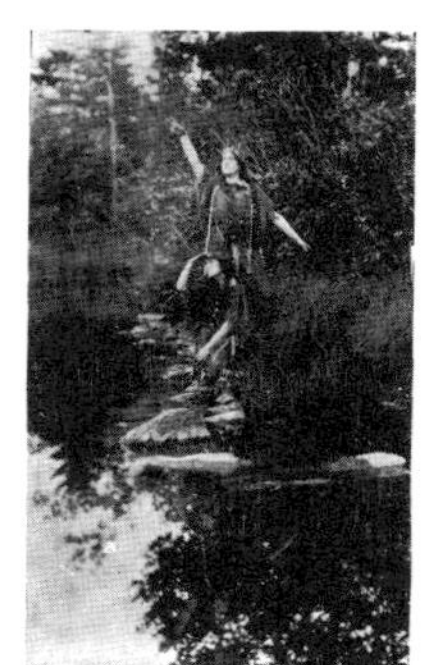
Indian Maidens S 533

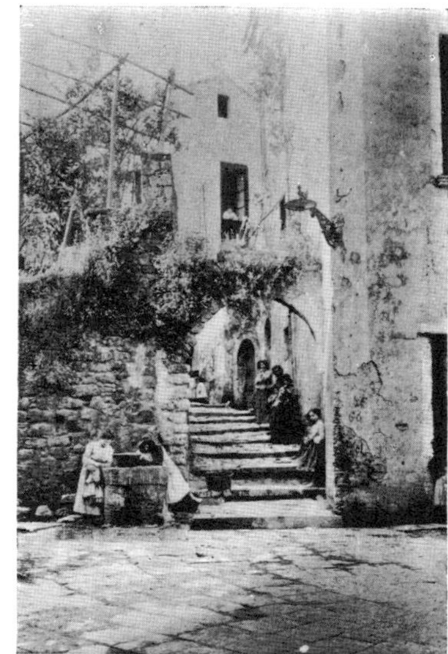
At the Well, Sorrento Q, S or P 433

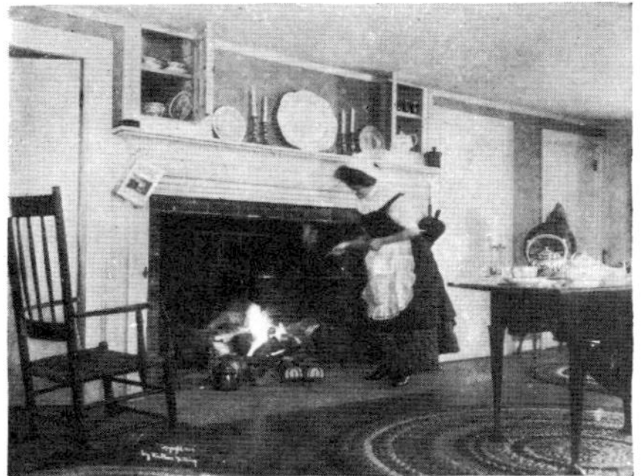
Bean Porridge Hot C 591

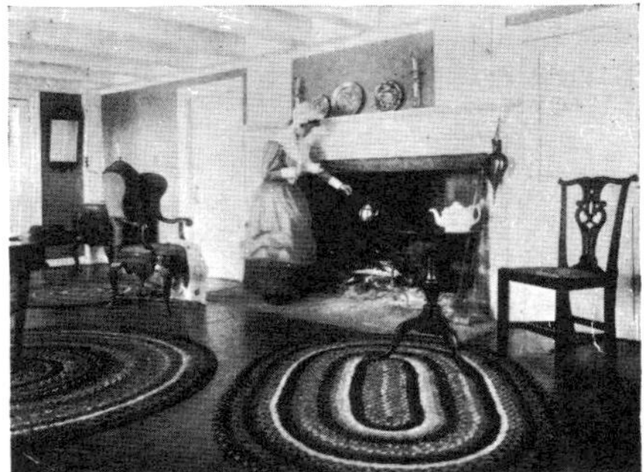
The Cup that Cheers A or C 72

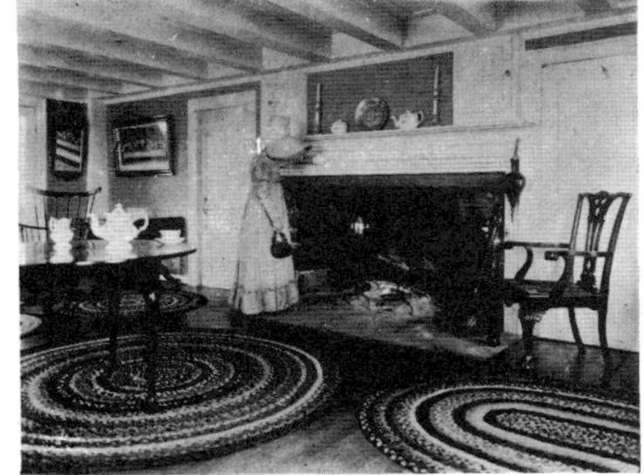
A Dilatory Escort C or E 772

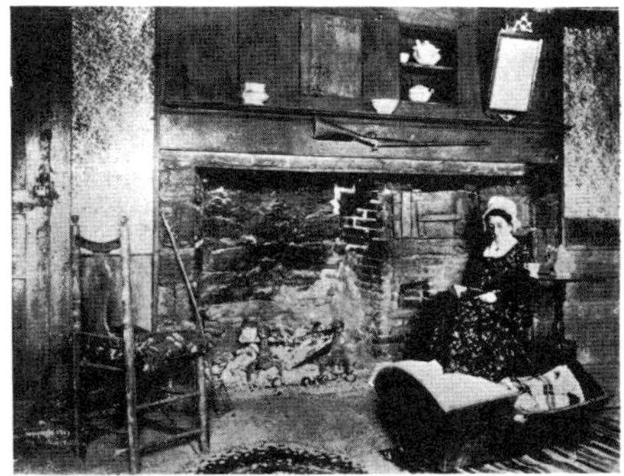
A Mother of the Revolution A, C or E 485

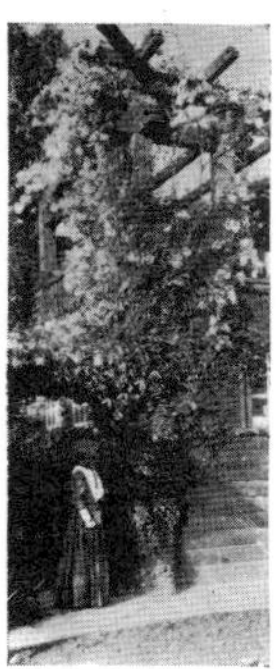
Wistaria Gate
Q 2117

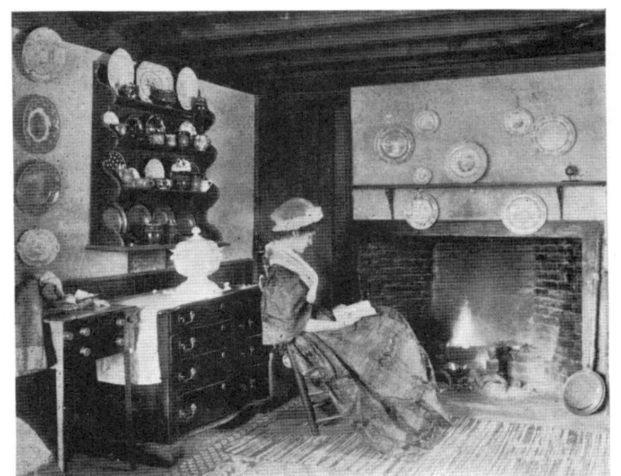

A Corner in China A, C or E 1021

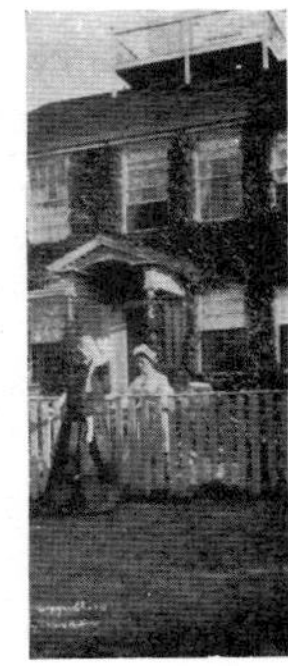
The Last Word
Q 1023

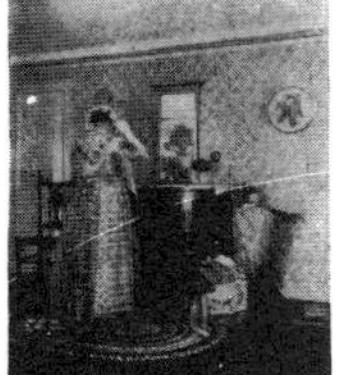
A Daughter of Eve
C 631

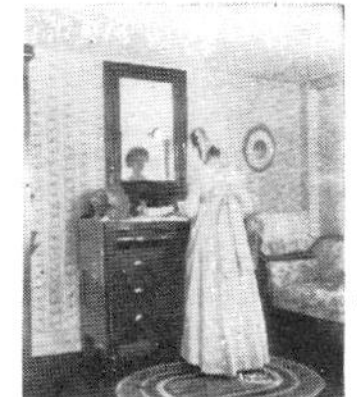
The New Cap
C 613

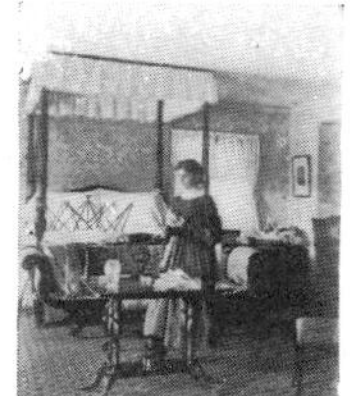
The Swift C 687

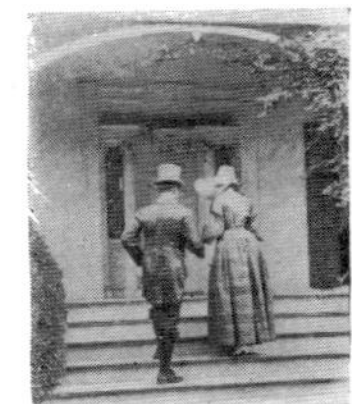
An Old Time Gallant
C 208

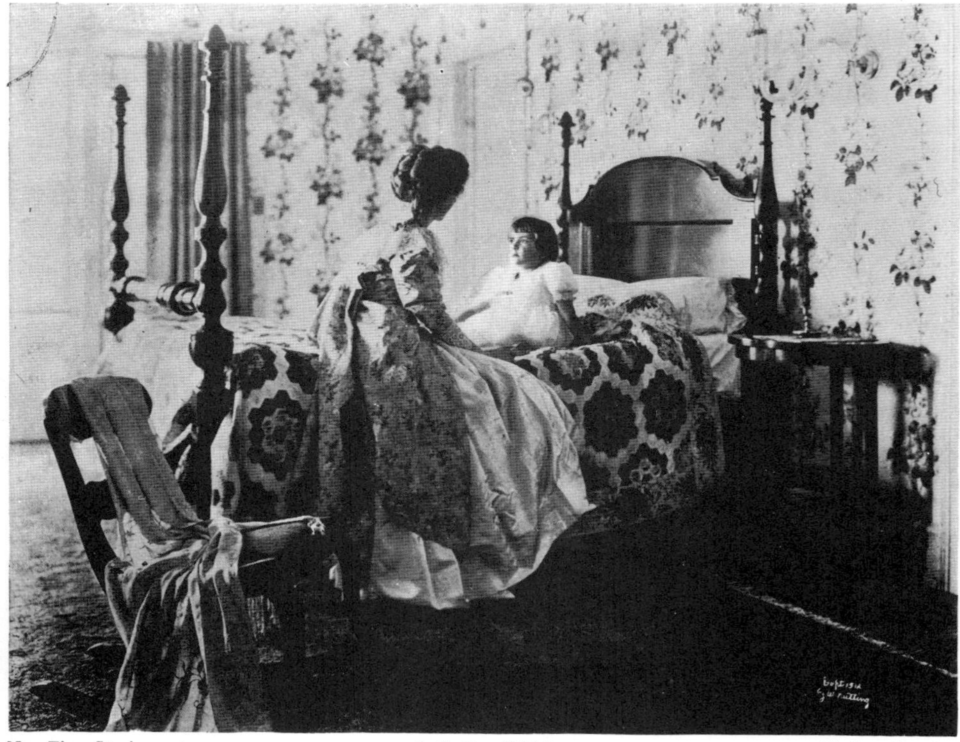
Nap Time Stories A, C, E or F 2511 Wallace Nutting

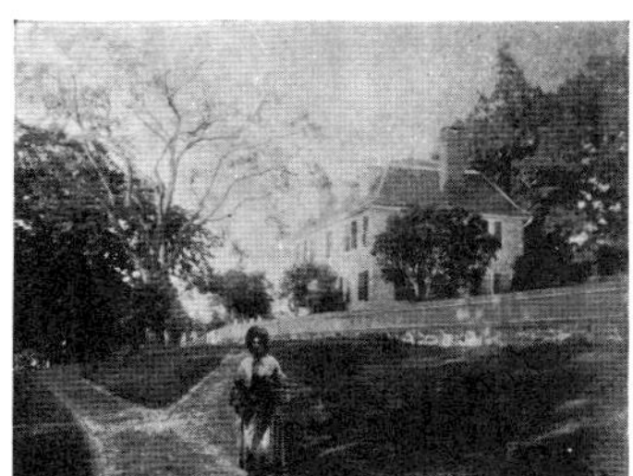

Betty and her Basket C 227

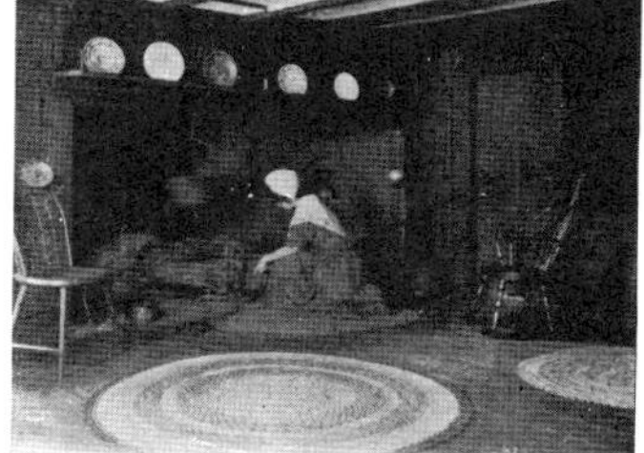

A Slow Fire C 961

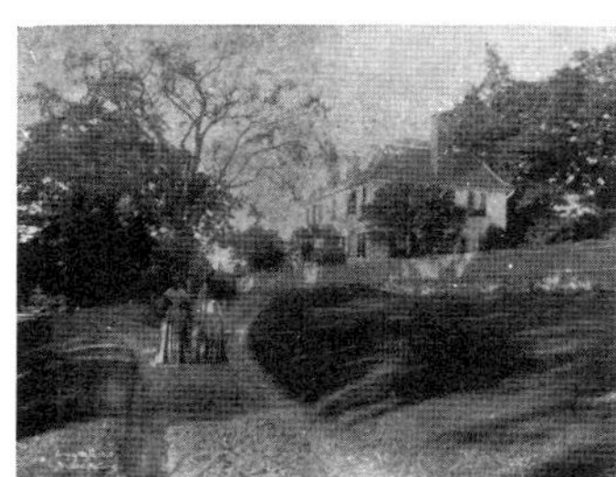

Afternoon Shadows C 486

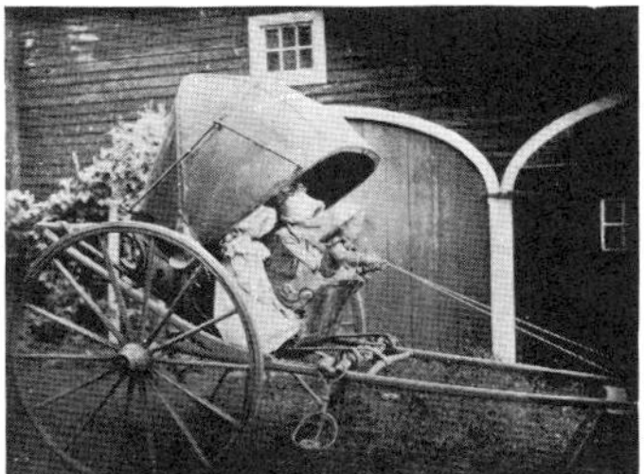

Going for the Doctor C 279

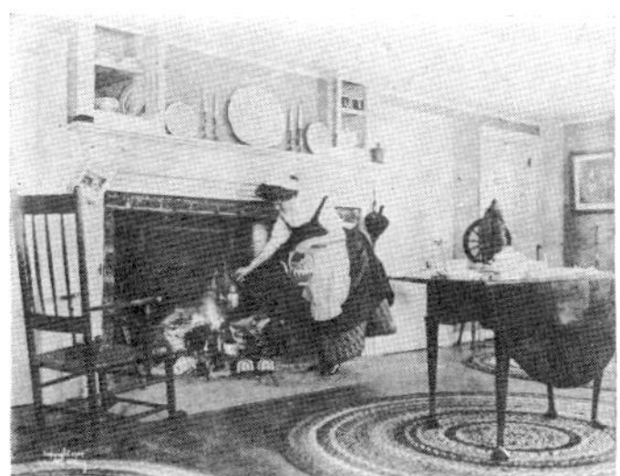

The Tea Maid C 602

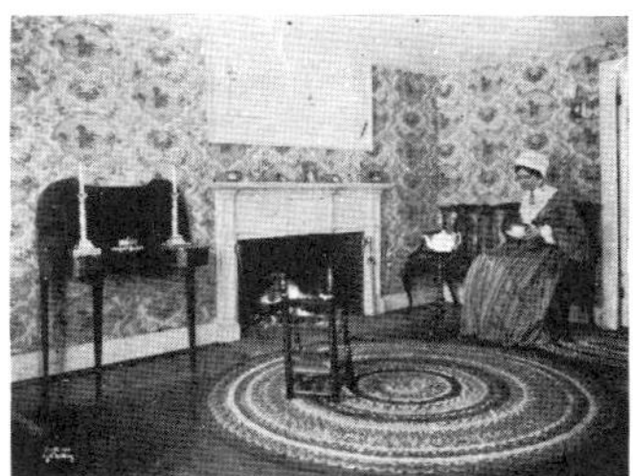

Light Refreshments C 329

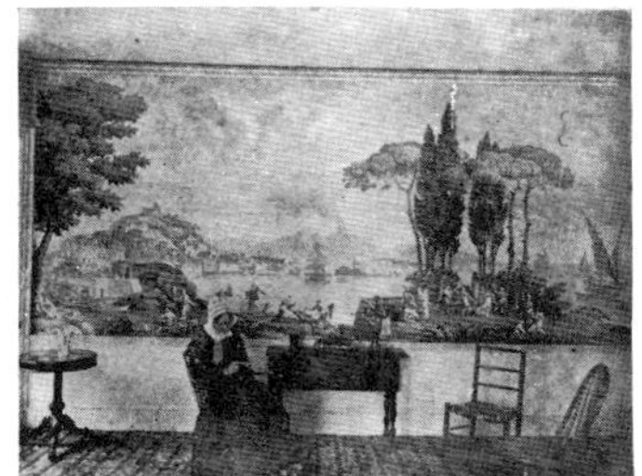

Picture Paper C 302

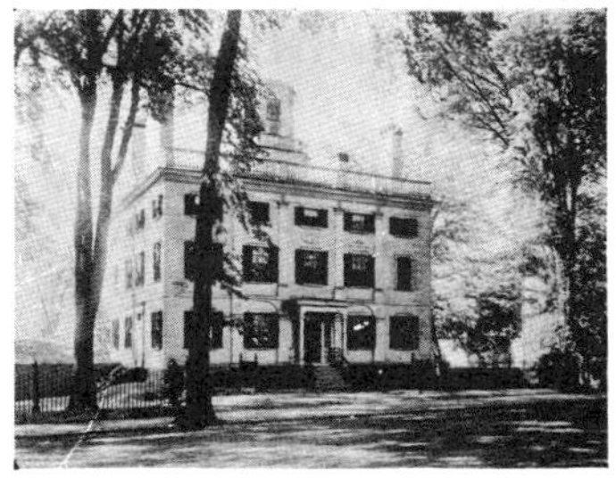

A Colonial Three Decker C 636

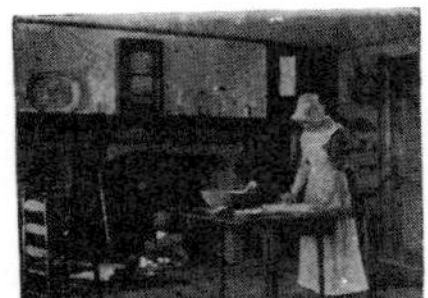
Cutting Biscuit
C 226

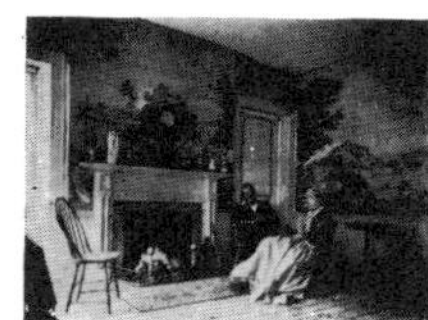
An Old Parlor Idyl
C 127

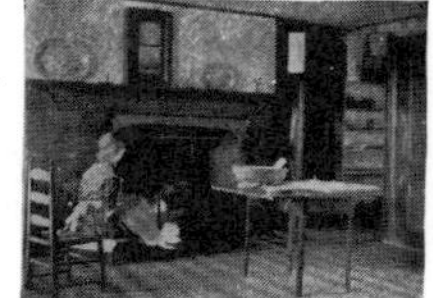
A Watched Pot
C 223

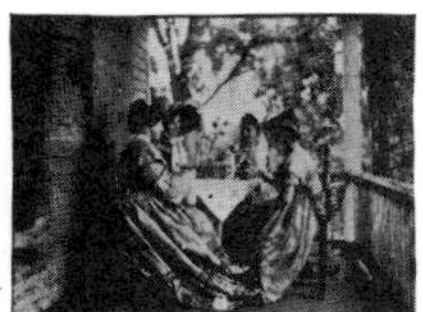
A Porch Tea
C 2721

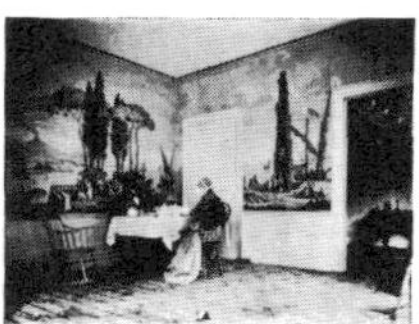
Tea at Uncle Jonathan's
C 129

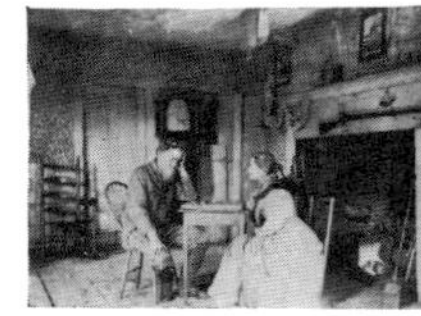
His Move
C 236

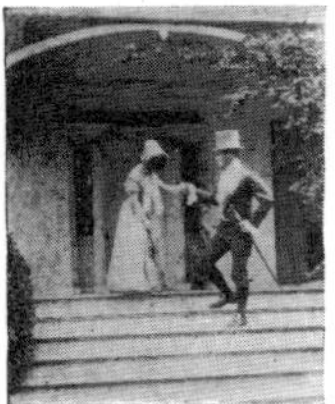
Hesitancy
C 231

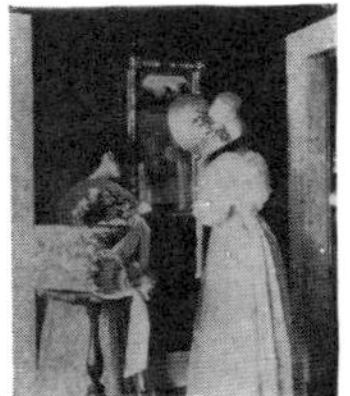
Choosing a Bonnet
C 2627

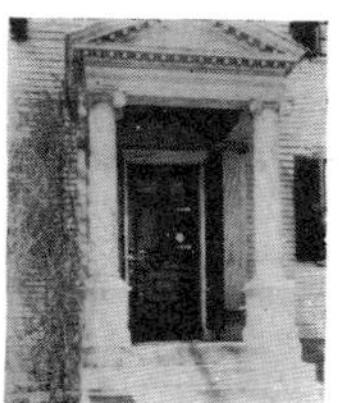
Front Door with
Hinged Panel
C 2653

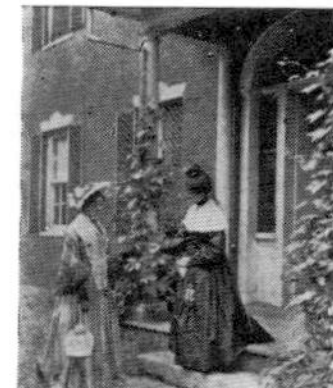
There's Rosemary
C 309

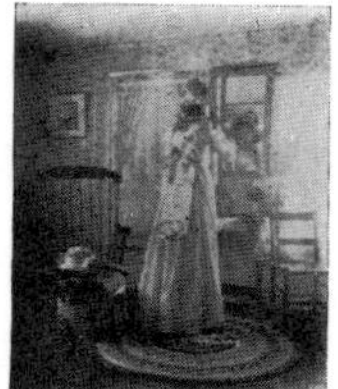
The Selection
C 614

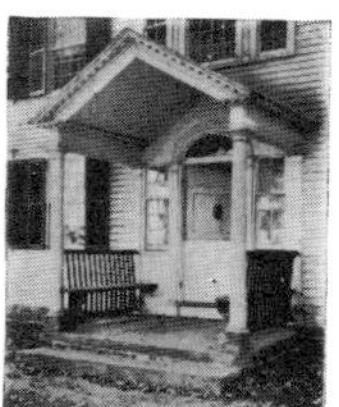
Southbury Porch
C 195

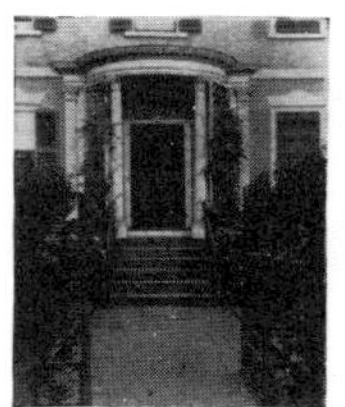
A Salem Door
C 180

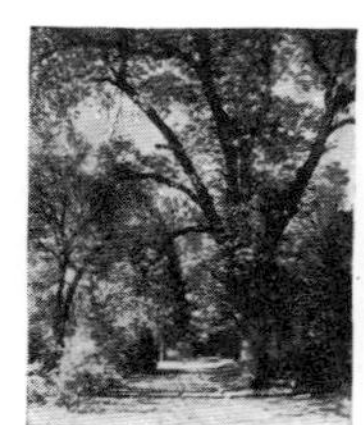
Winding Among
Yosemite Oaks
C 877

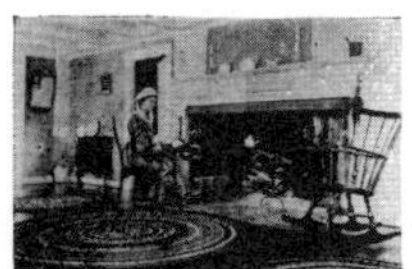
The Work Basket
A 2736

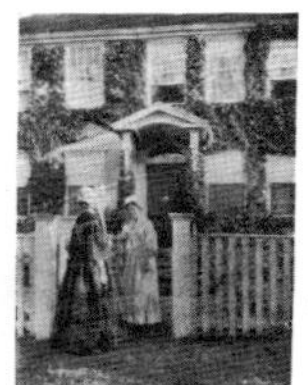
The Parson's Gate
A 96

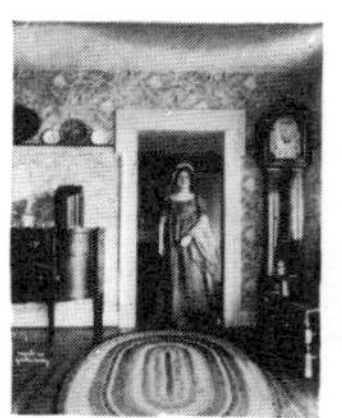
Pride
C 744

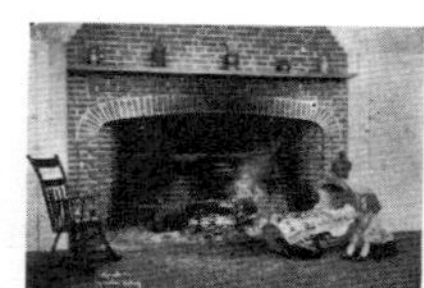
Early Mother Instinct
A 623

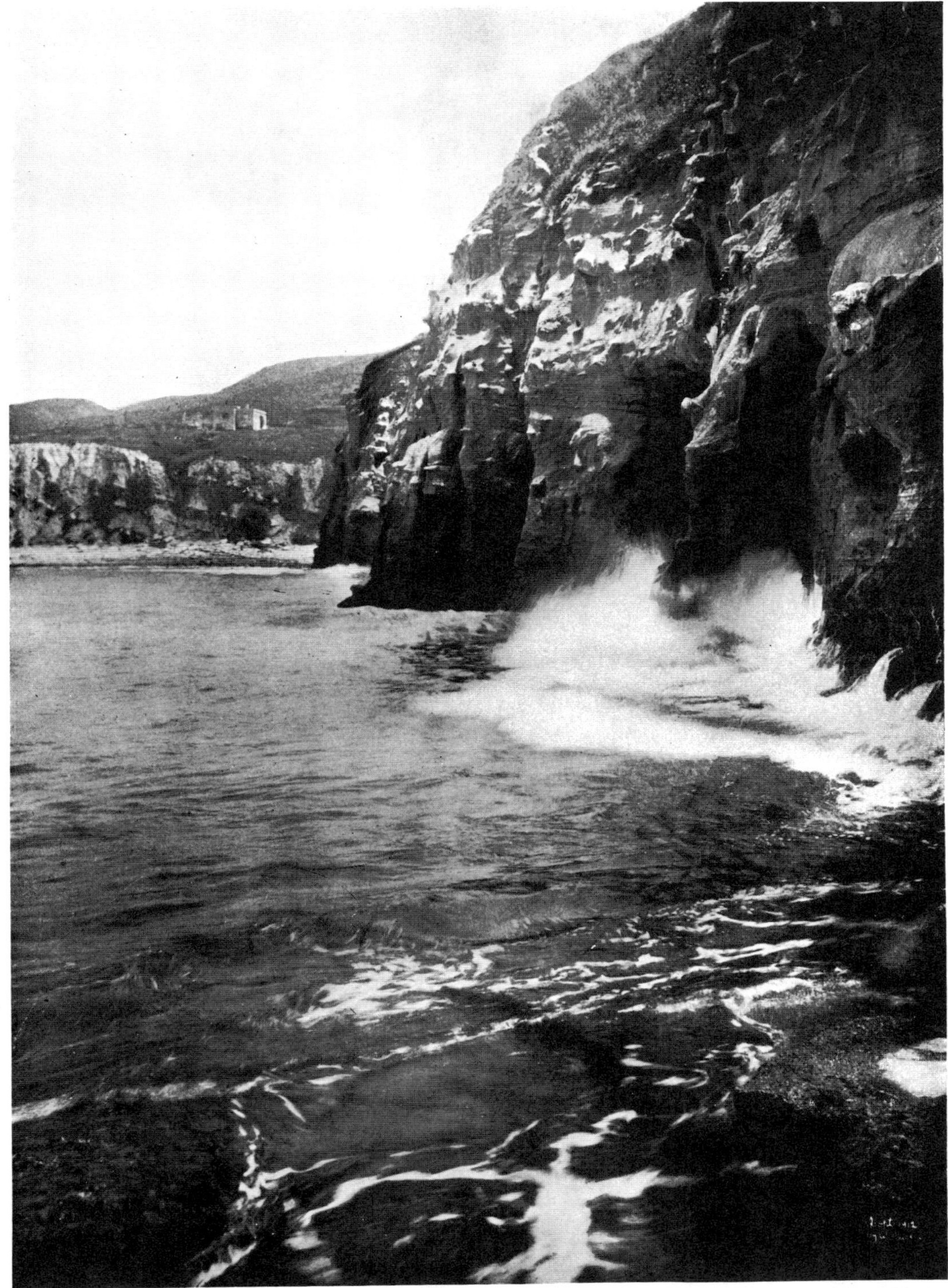

La Jolla | Q, S, C, O, P, E, T, G 2240 | Wallace Nutting

The picture above shows the finest cliffs on the American coast. There are caves behind the great breakers. The cliff being hundreds of feet in height the waves are really high also. This beautiful marine is attractive especially when well understood.

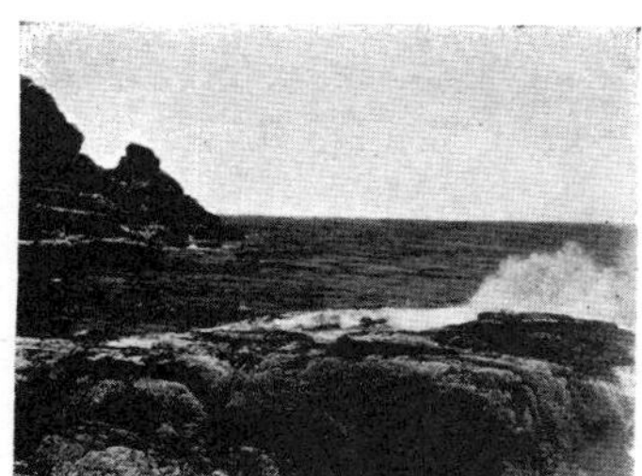
The Restless Deep Q or C 660

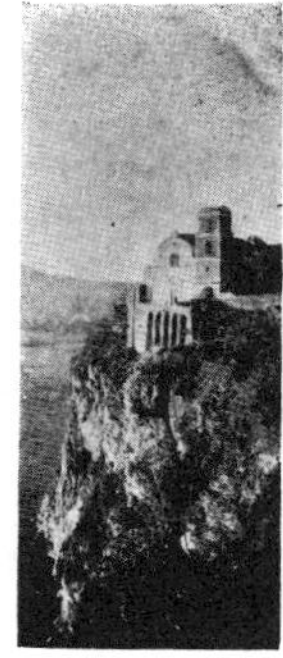
On the Heights
Q, S or C 65

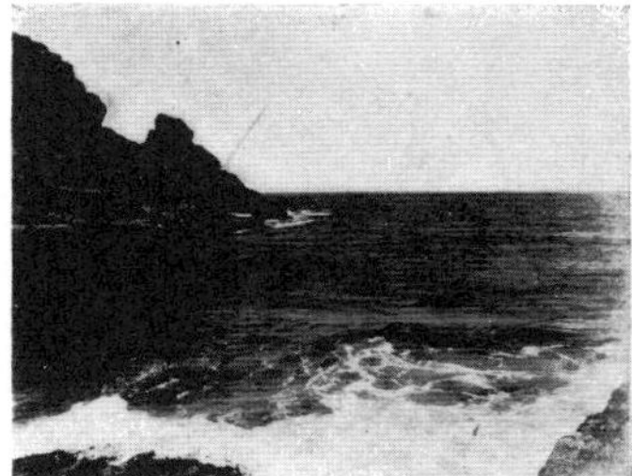
A Stone Churn C 412

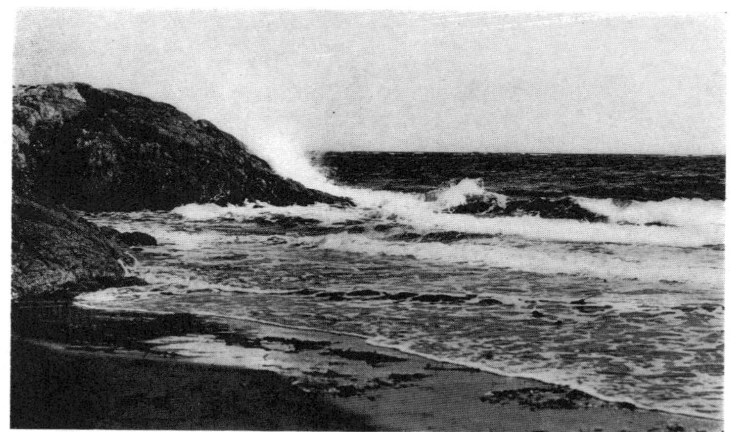
Sea Ledges Q, S, C, O, P, T, G, H 240 Wallace Nutting

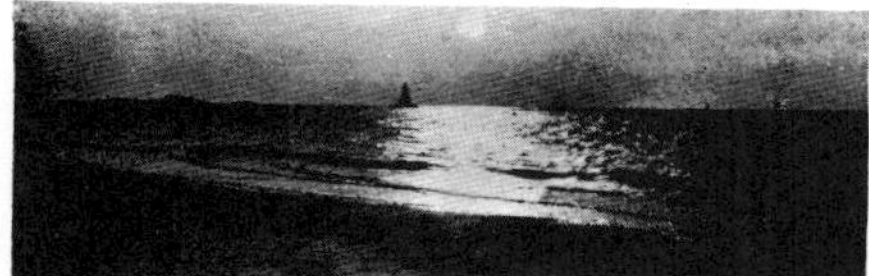
The Rhode Island Coast O 300

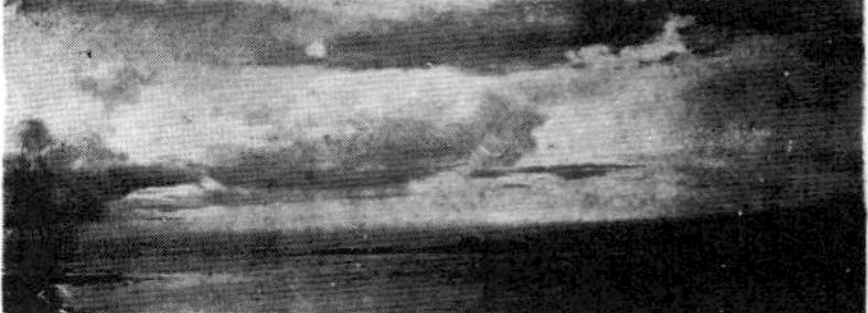
Hunter's Island O or P 206

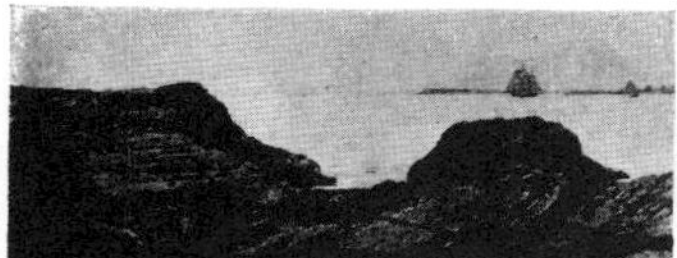
Off Shore Q 425

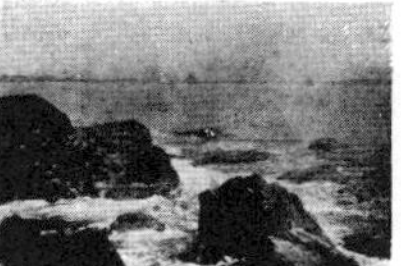
Rocks off Portland, Me.
A 297

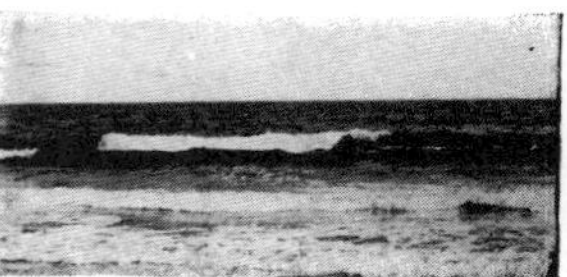
Sea Foam P 28

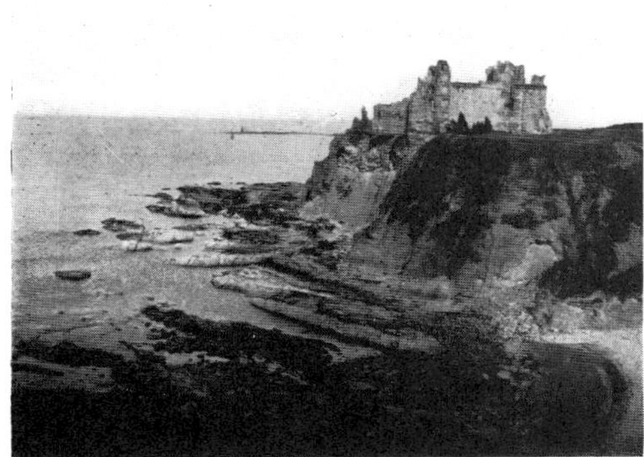

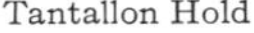

Tantallon Hold A, C 5820

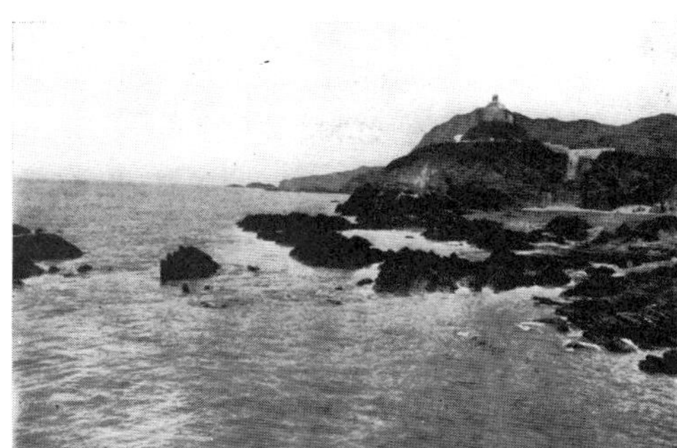

Ilfracombe S 5664

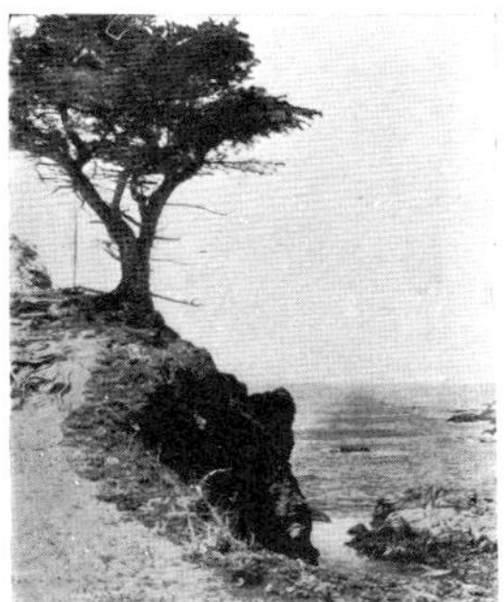

A Cypress by the Sea C 2280

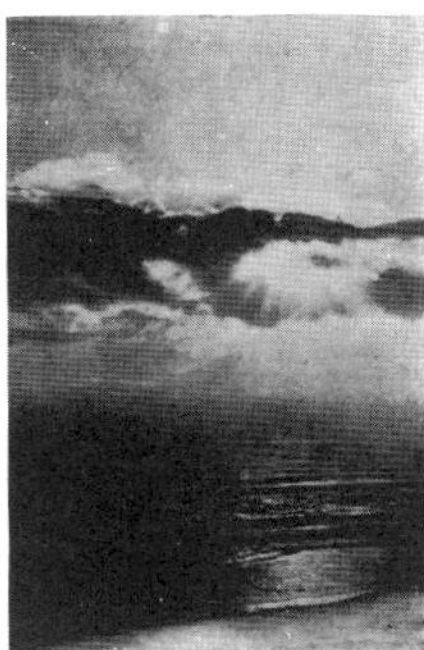

A Florida Sunrise
A, Q or S 1119

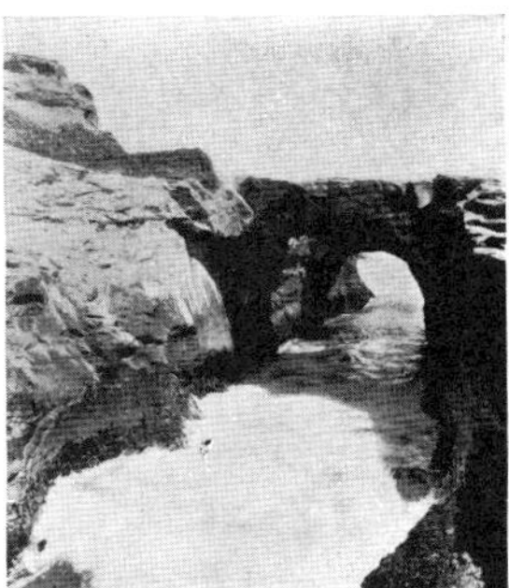

The Way of the Sea C 2303

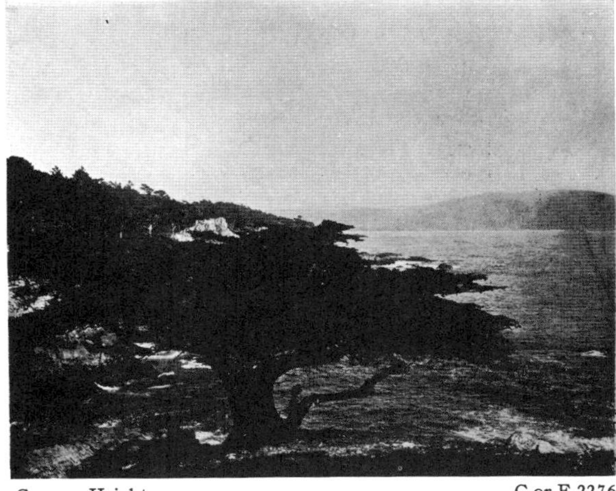

Cypress Heights C or E 2276

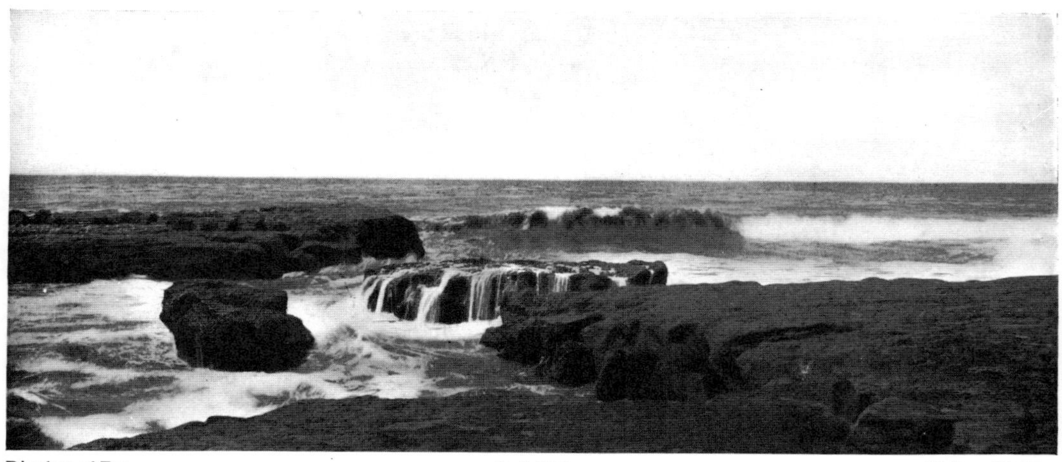

Rivulets of Foam Q, S 2257 Wallace Nutting

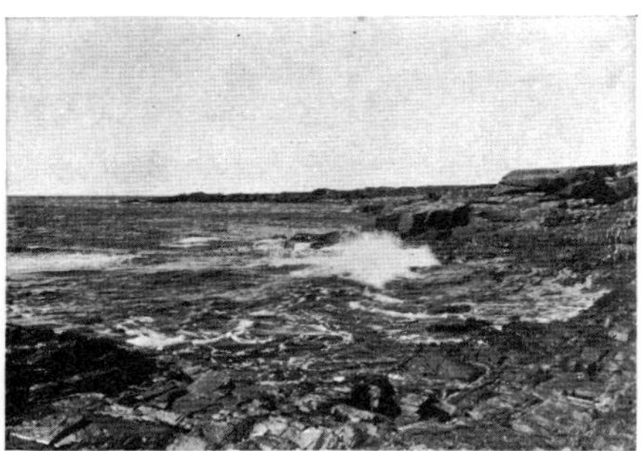

Ocean Eddies O, P or E 385

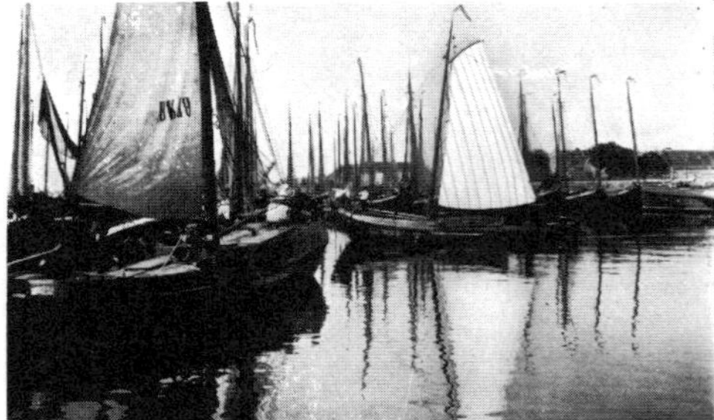

Dutch Fishing Boats A, S 6514

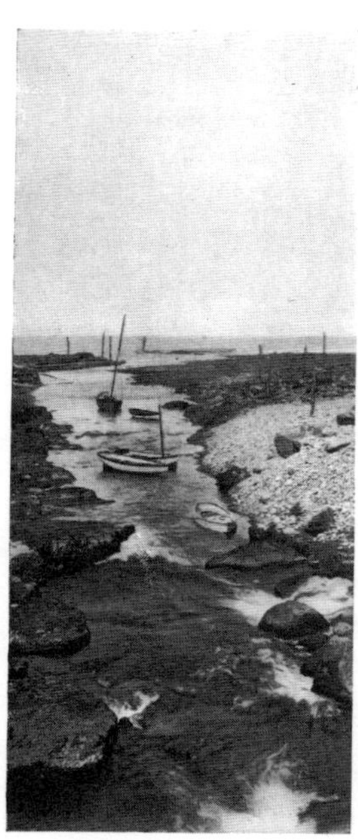

The Brook's Mouth
A, Q, S, O, P 5677

A supplement to the Marines will be issued in the course of the spring of 1915, showing various additional surf scenes. Buyers who require such scenes are safe to order them for spring delivery. The picture on this page called "The Brook's Mouth" is on the North Devon coast, and is very attractive in wider forms also. Under the title "A Little Haven," somewhat different, it is supplied in the C and E sizes long vertically.

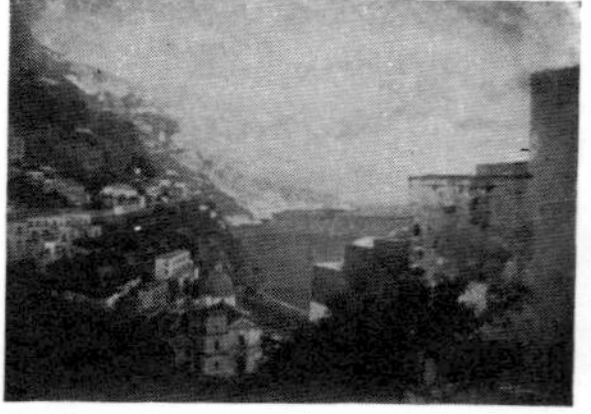

Positano E 13

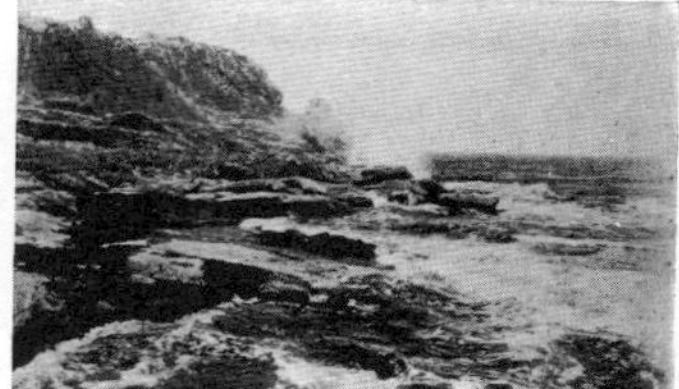

The Endless Battle S 407

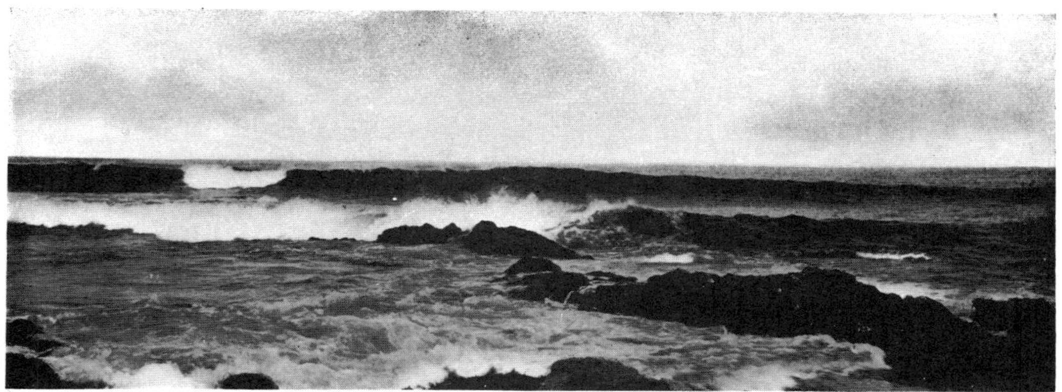

Maine Surf O and W 3 Wallace Nutting

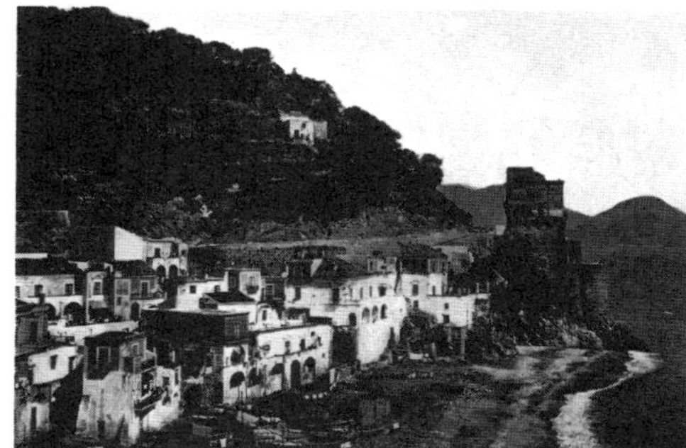

Cetara C 4071

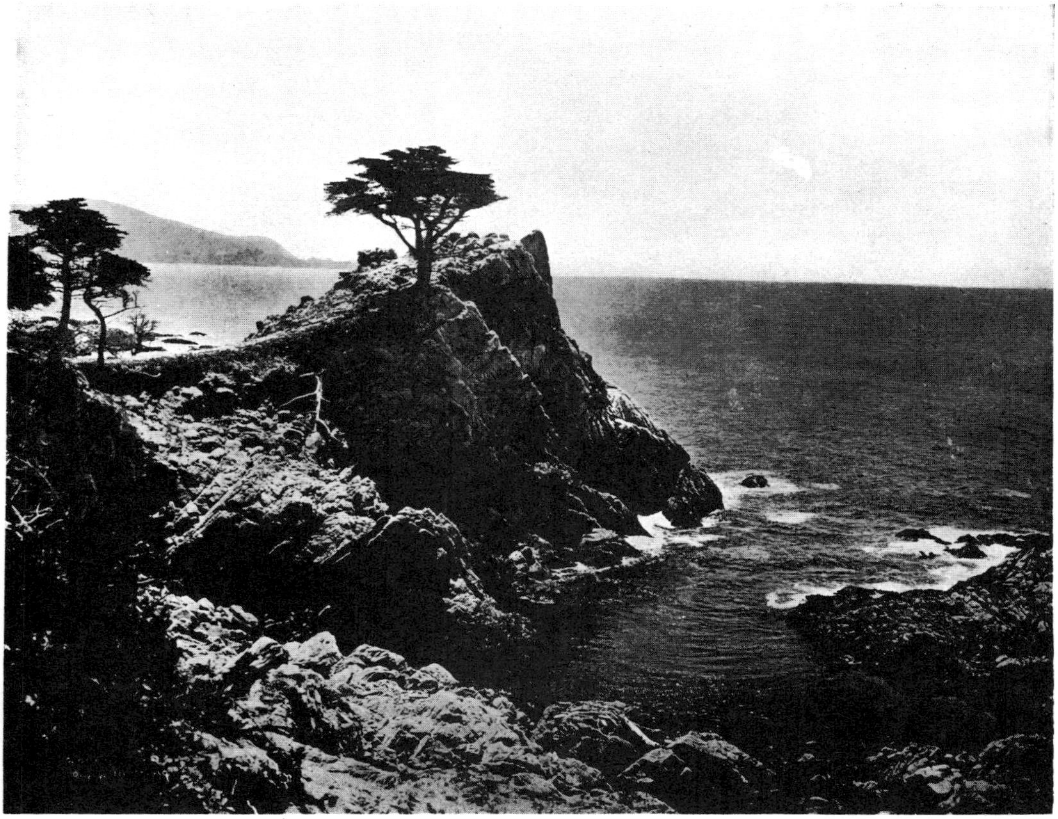

Cypress Rocks C and E 2253 Wallace Nutting

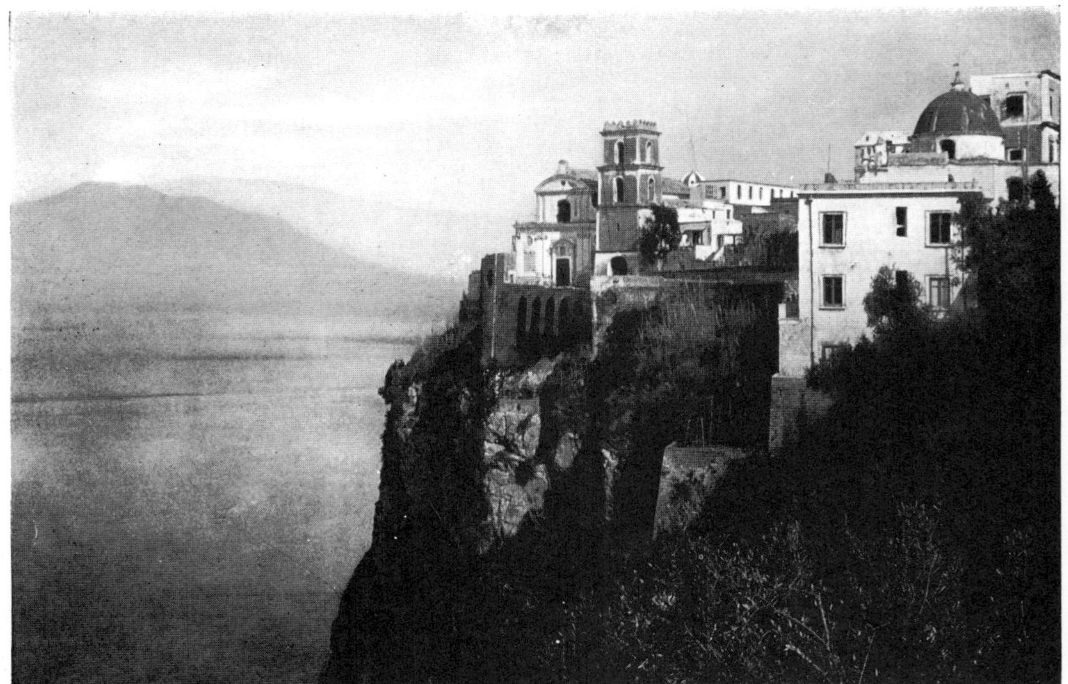

Vico Equesne S 4007 Wallace Nutting

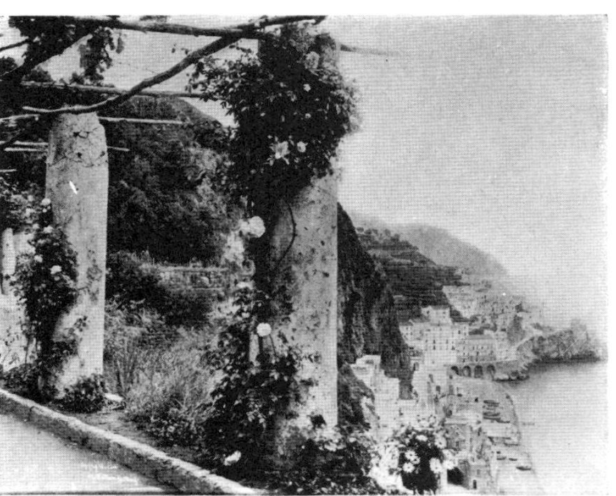

The Pergola, Amalfi A, C, E or F 480 Wallace Nutting

The Pergola at Amalfi is perhaps the best known Italian picture. It has been made by a multitude of artists, who usually have a person pose as a monk in the foreground. Mr. Nutting paid him to remove himself, because he is no real monk and the scene requires dignity without personality. It has been, and still is, one of the most popular subjects. "Vico Equesne," at the top of the page, shows the streamers of smoke from Vesuvius. It is on the south side of the Bay of Naples near Sorrento.

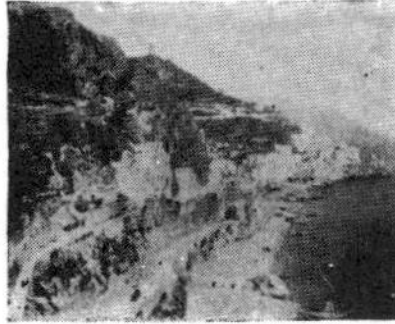

Amalfi C or E 47

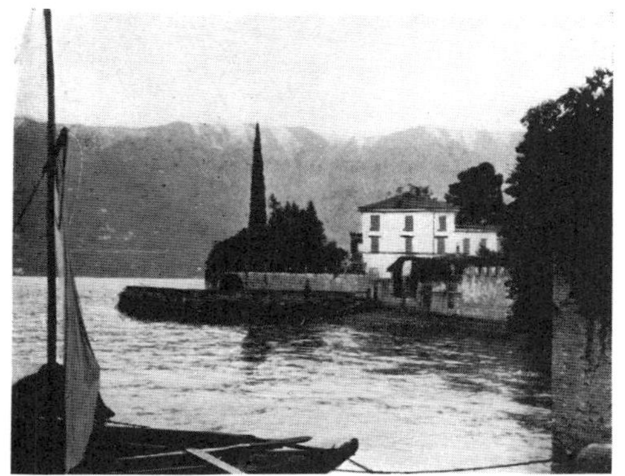

A Lakeside Belvidere A, C 4483

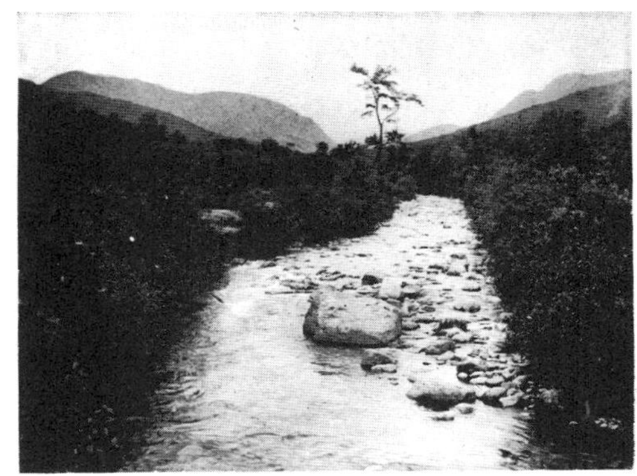

A New Hampshire Stream A, C 3469

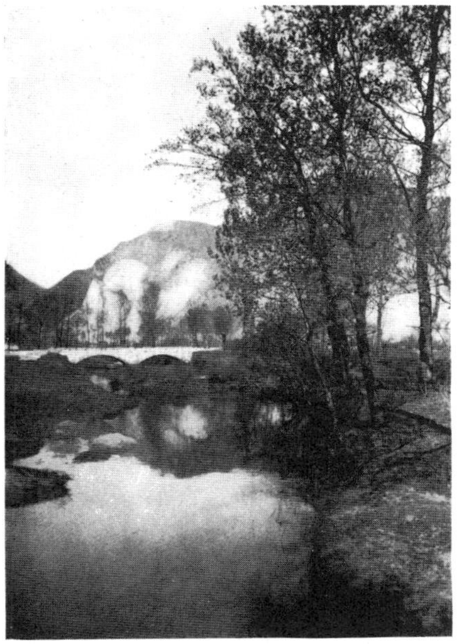

Spring in the Mountains A, C, E 4479

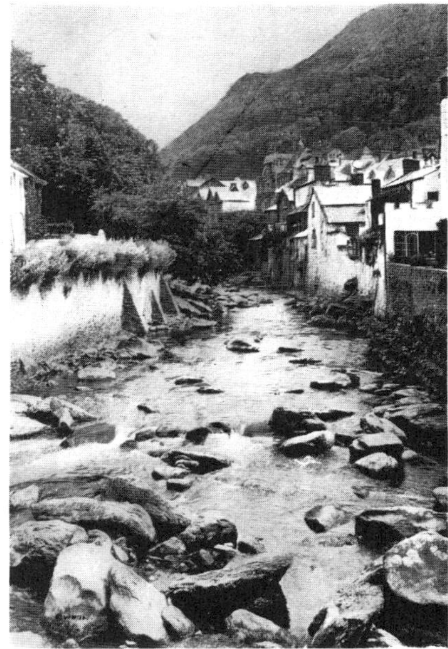

A Nestling Village A, C 5680

MOUNTAINS

The scene above, "Spring in the Mountains," in this shape, and as a horizontal on page 653, is a charming combination of stream, bridge, foliage and mountain. It is made in North Italy near Lake Maggiori. "A New Hampshire Stream" shows the White Mountains in the distance and ought to be very popular with people who like the New England hills. "The Nestling Village" is in Lynmouth, on the north shore of Devon.

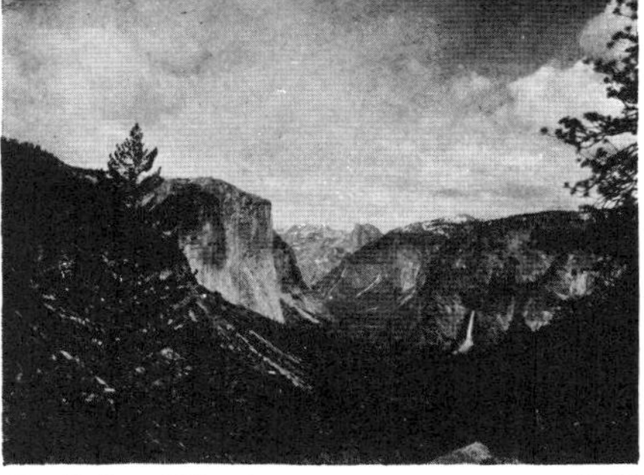

The Valley of Wonder C 680

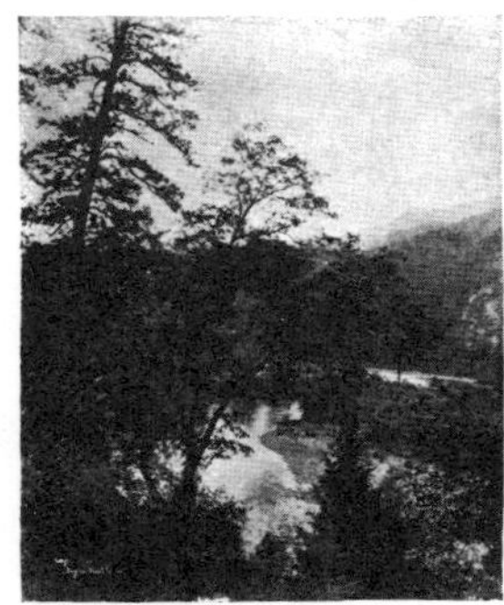
A Cañon Stream C 2468

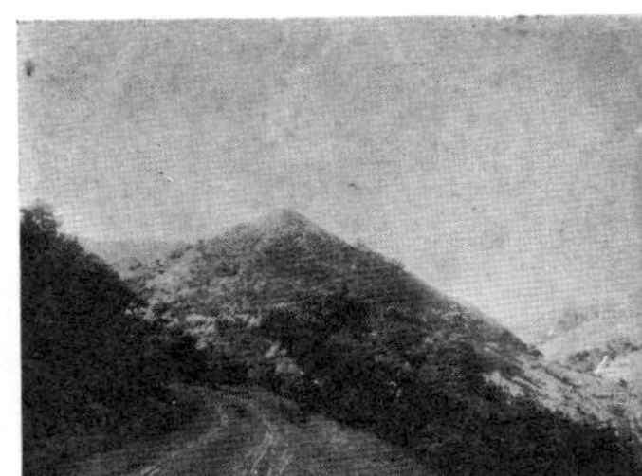
California Hill Tops C 866

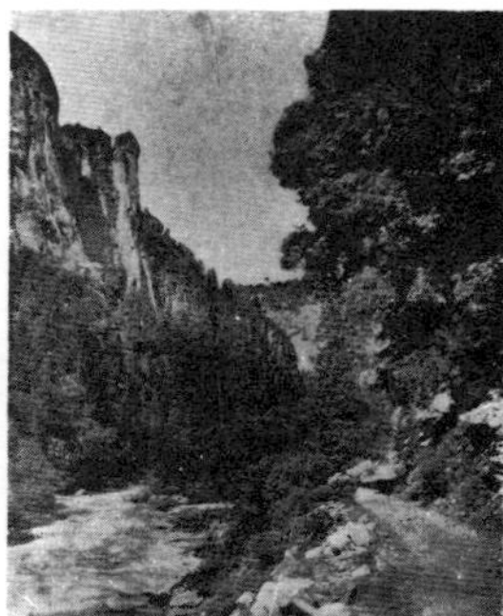
The Strength of the Hills C 787

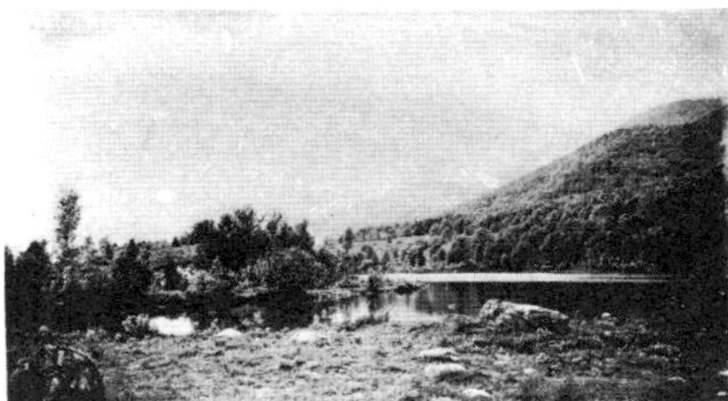
Equinox Pond P 2621

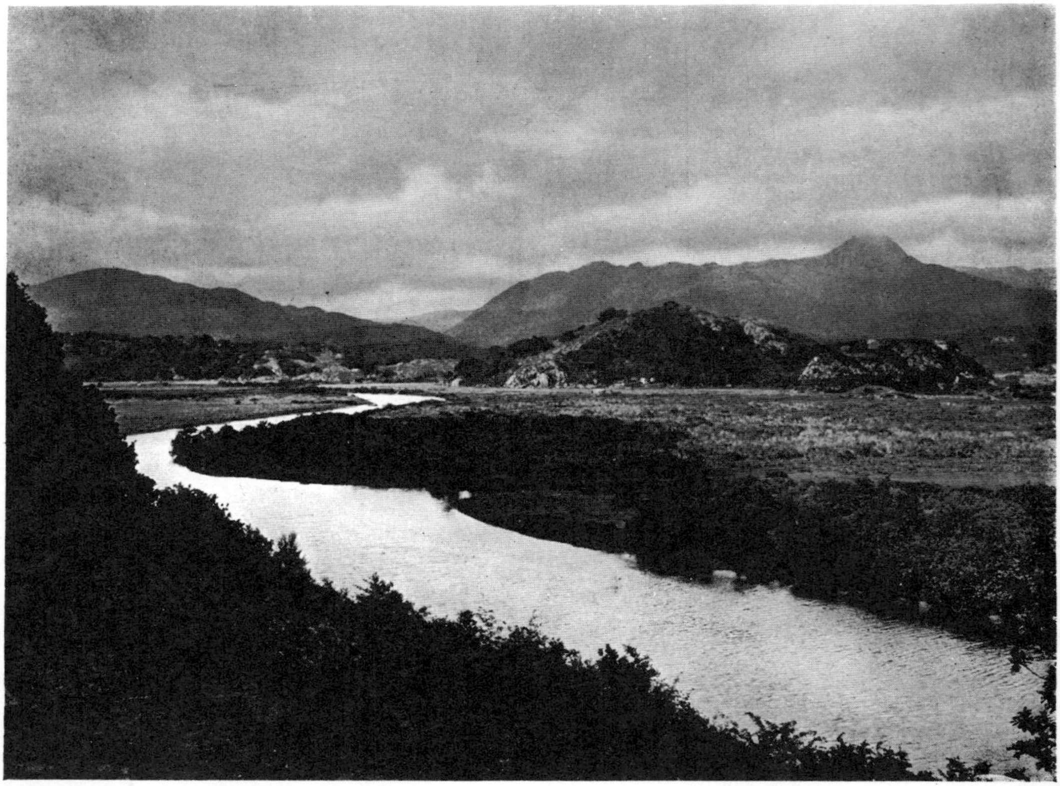

Fair Vale A, S, C, P, E **6123**

(Midsummer Vale, A, C, E, G 6114, similar and better)

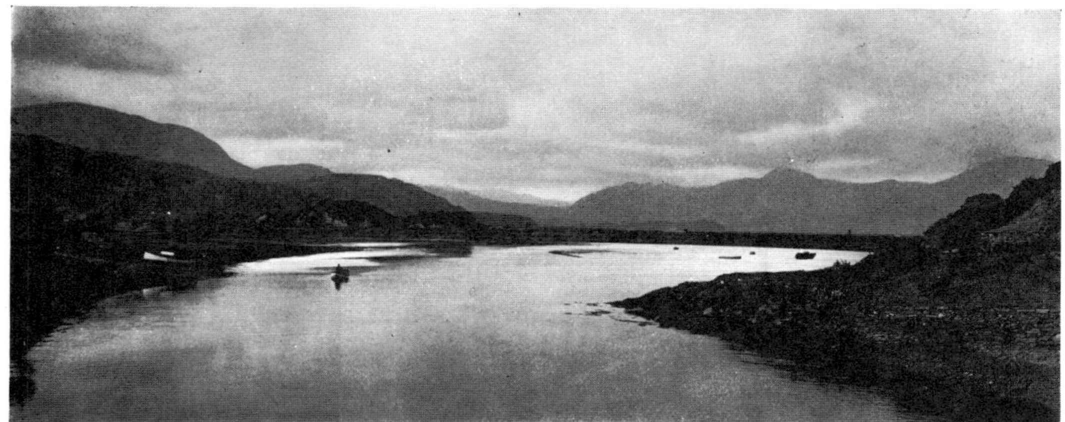

The Tranquil Vale A, Q, S, O, P 6134

The picture above is a wonderfully charming combination of stream and mountain, the boat in the mid-distance enhances the attraction. The peak in the central distance is Snowdon. The stream is the Glasslyn in South Wales, near the Vale of Festiniog. Wales is by all odds the most picturesque portion of Britain and Britain is the best of Europe. We have no less than 400 subjects made in Wales.

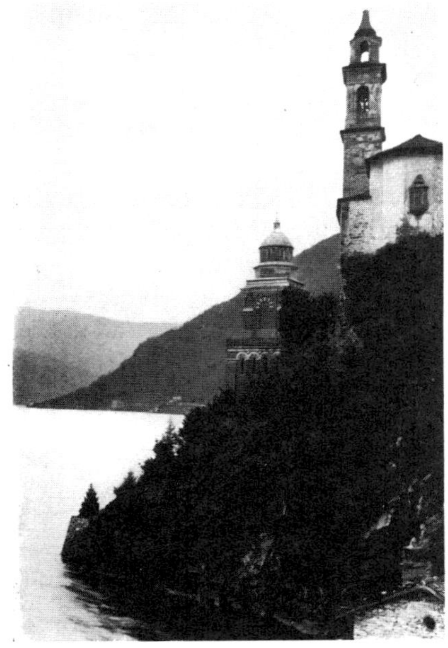

A Como Promontory A, S, C 4461

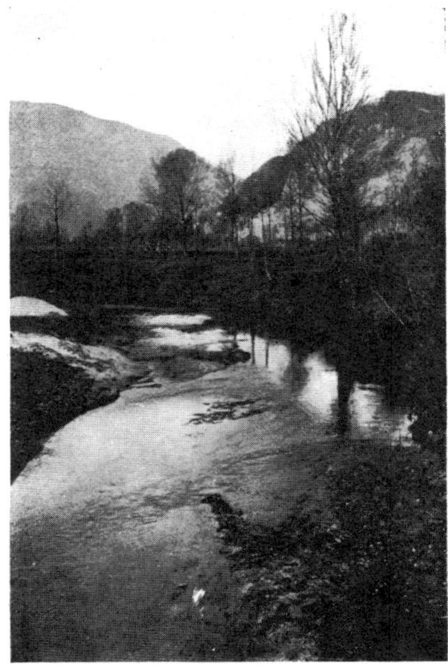

Spring Brookside S 4484

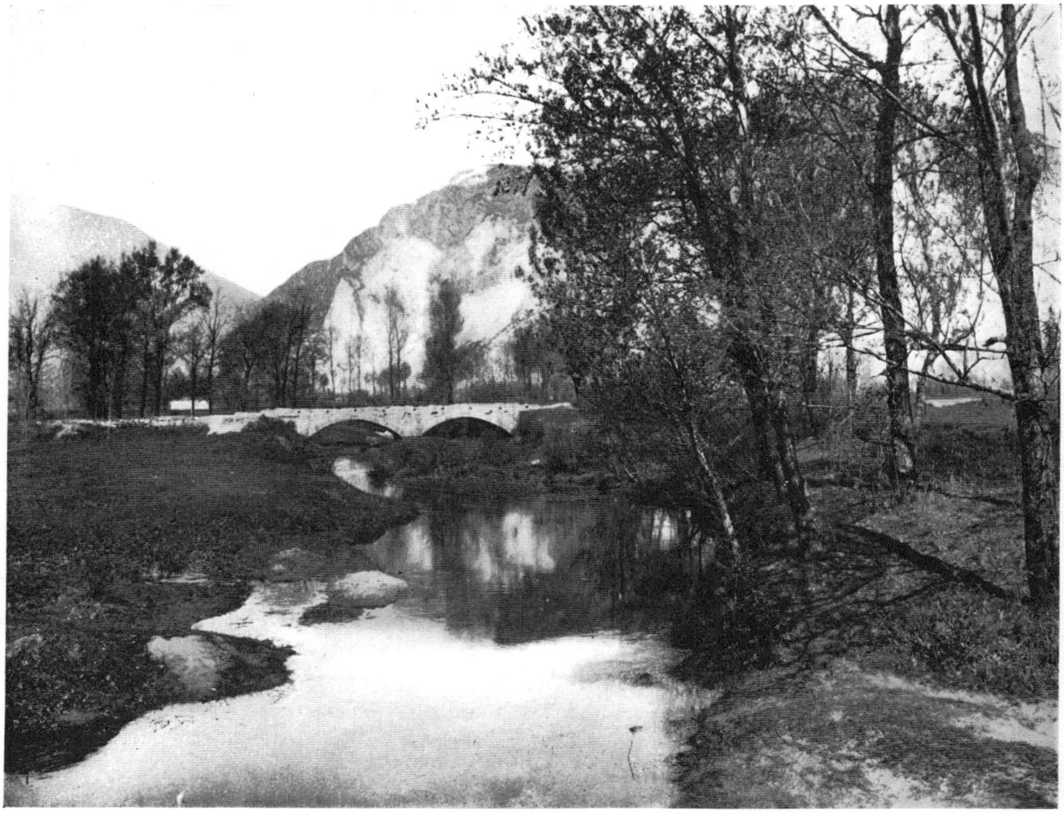

Spring's First Green A, C, E, G 4463 Wallace Nutting

MOUNTAIN SCENERIES

Men buy very few pictures. They usually leave this attractive pastime to their wives, who do not care so much for mountains as for blossoms and figures. Nevertheless, year in and year out, a mountain view is reposeful and inspiring and perhaps wears better than almost anything else. We lift up our eyes to the hills and get help.

"Skirting Lake Como" shows a section of the highway just before entering a tunnel. It is a soft golden-orange day.

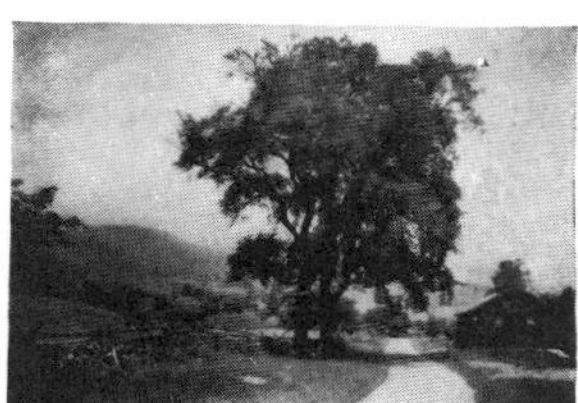

The Old Red Schoolhouse E 162

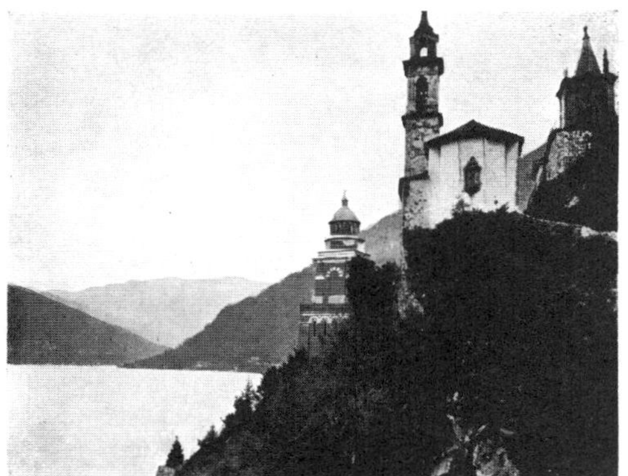

A Como Crest A, C 4459

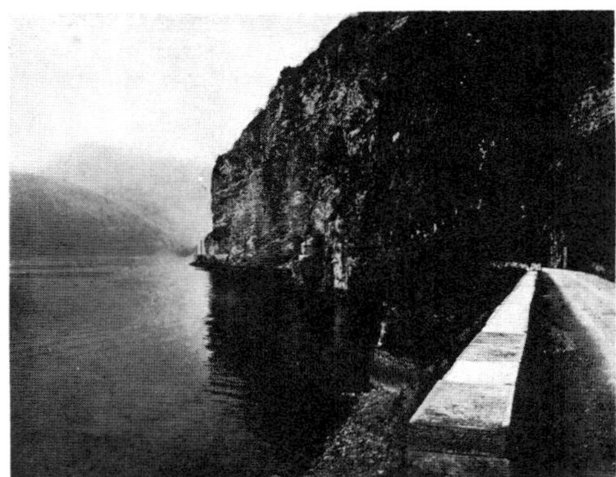

Skirting Lake Como A, C 4370

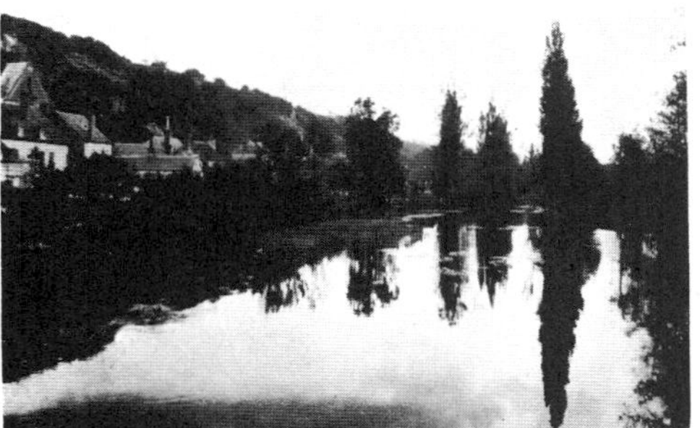

A Twilight River A, S 4745

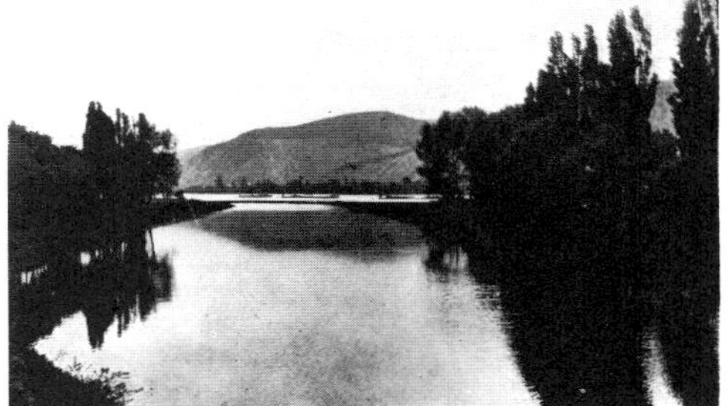

The Rhine at Drechenfels A, S 4875

On the next page appears a most attractive view of Derwentwater. The reeds in the foreground with a ripple running through them and the soft clouds on the mountains, together with breadth of effect, can scarcely be surpassed as a mountain scene. We recommend this very highly, especially in the Q and S sizes.

On pages 655 and 656 appear the same subject, one made in the morning and one in the evening. The evening print gives rich golden twilight lights. " The Long Look " on page 656 is a magnificent sweep of a Vermont river without the natural clouds. If you wish to get natural clouds it is easy to do so, but when the sky is clear we paint in clouds as the scene seems to require.

We do not show many scenes in the Yosemite, although we have more than seventy; especially there is one called " The Valley of Wonder " from Inspiration Point, in various sizes, which cannot fail to please. It is not illustrated here. There is also a view of the Yosemite Falls against Mercia showing a reflection of the fall in the river and the fine natural clouds.

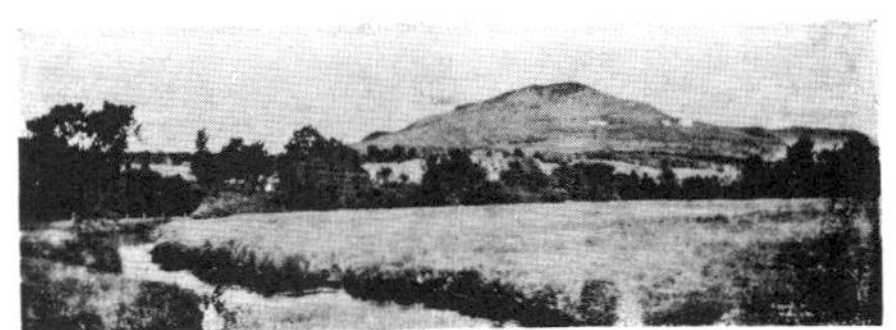

The Meandering Battenkill O or E 216

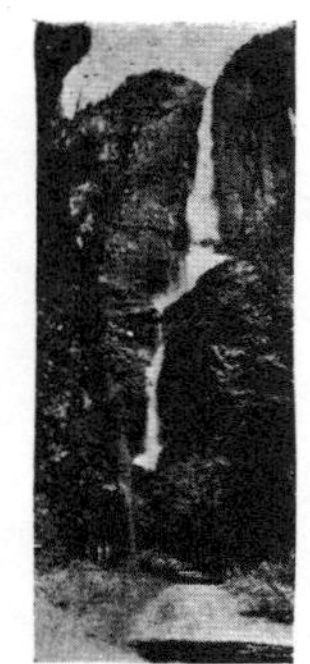

Beneath the Yosemite
Q 740

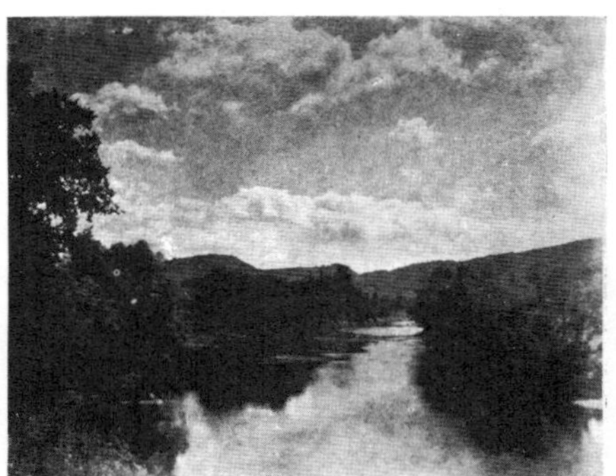
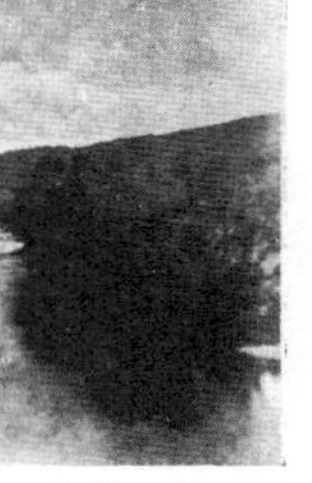

The Long Look A, C or E 2570

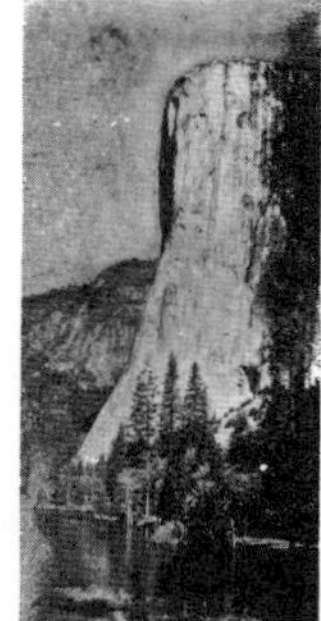

El Capitan
Q or C 725

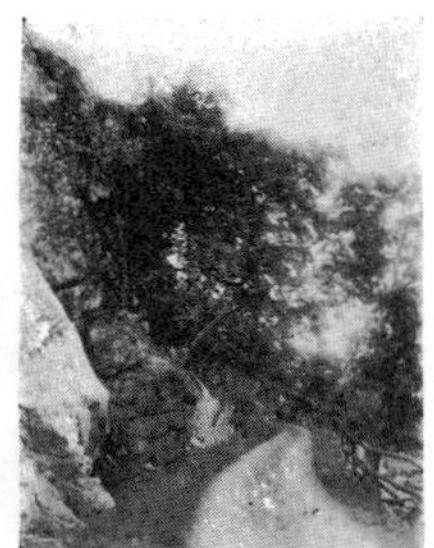

The Windings of Undercliff
E 79

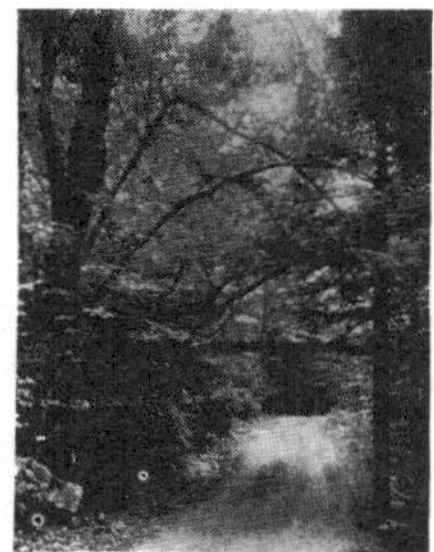

A Forest Portcullis
E 2685

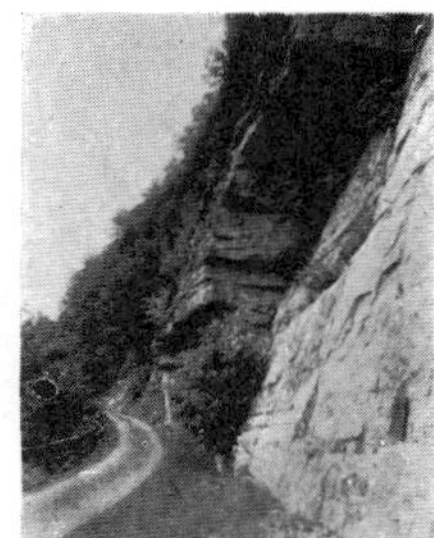

Undercliff Drive E 76

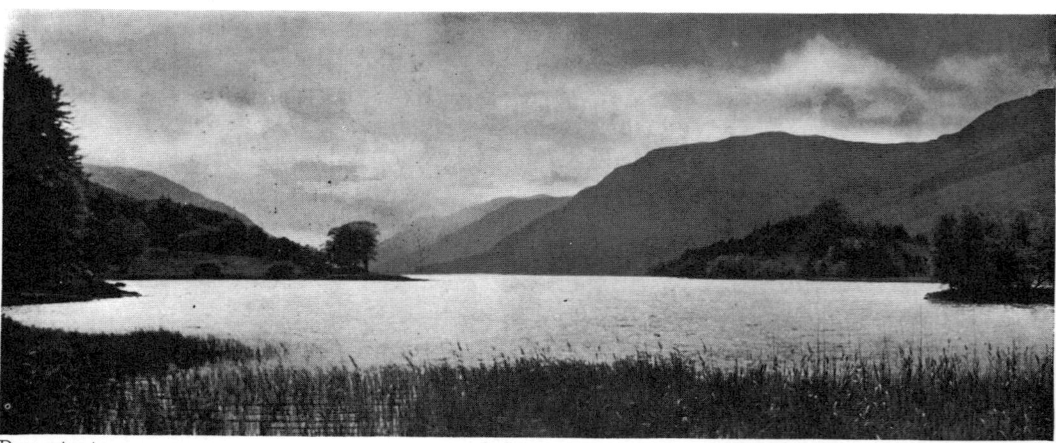

Derwentwater Q, S, P 5949 Wallace Nutting

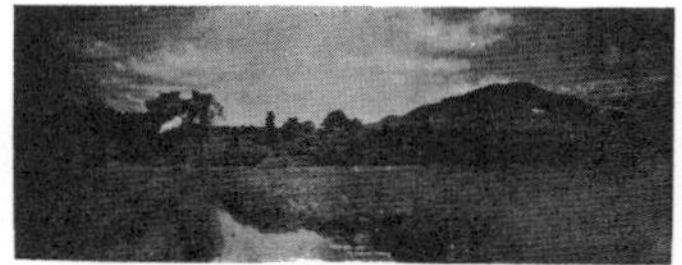

Across the Meadows Q 529

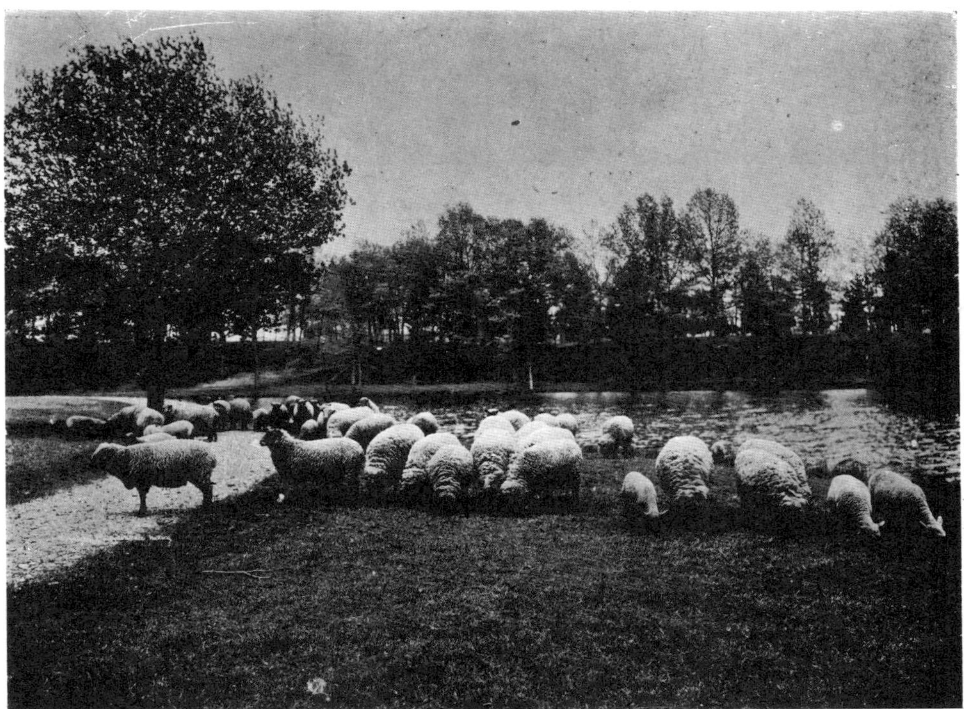

A Warm Spring Day Q S, O, P, E, T 323 Wallace Nutting

By far the most popular sheep picture ever made. It has been pirated and one pirate has even signed his name to it. Yet it continues to hold its place at the head.

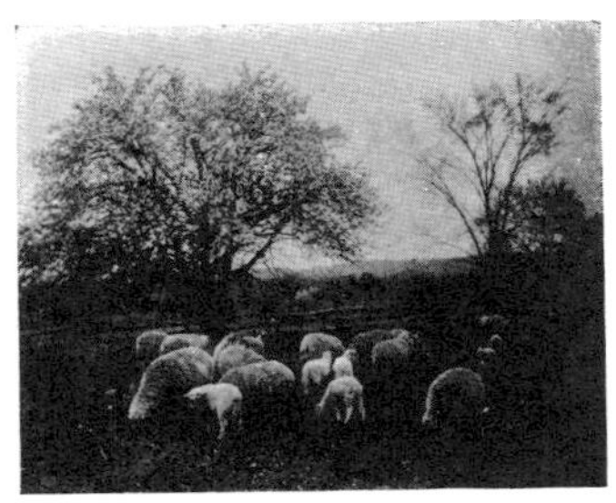

Under the Blossoms C 6

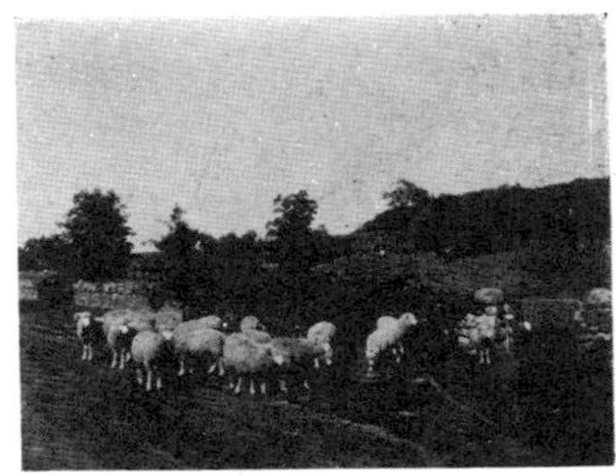

Tranquility Farm S or C 860

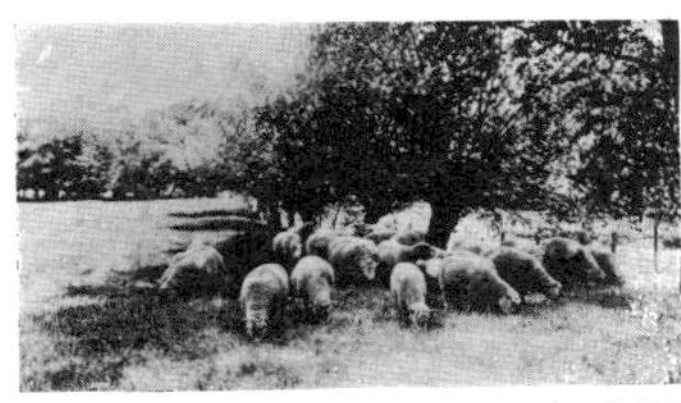

A Willow Pastoral S 732

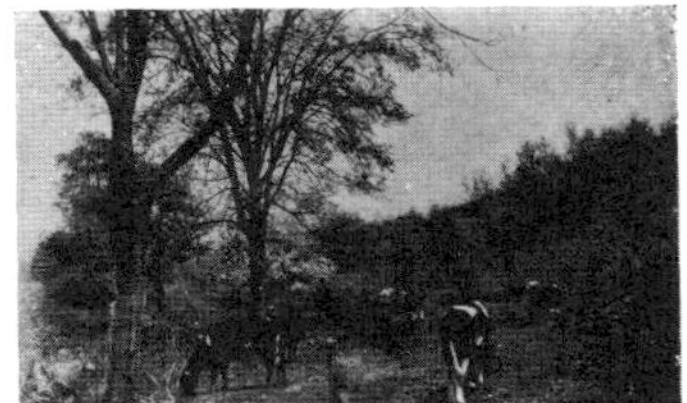

Pasture Dell S 257

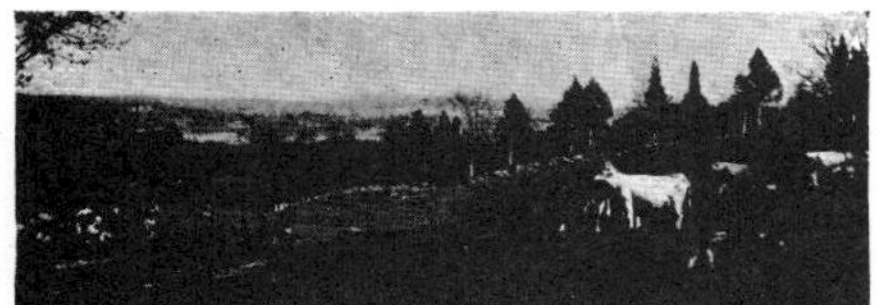

Arlington Hills O 192

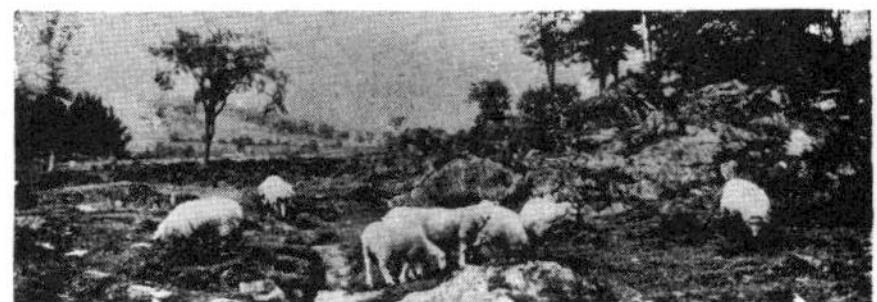

Among the Rocks O 98

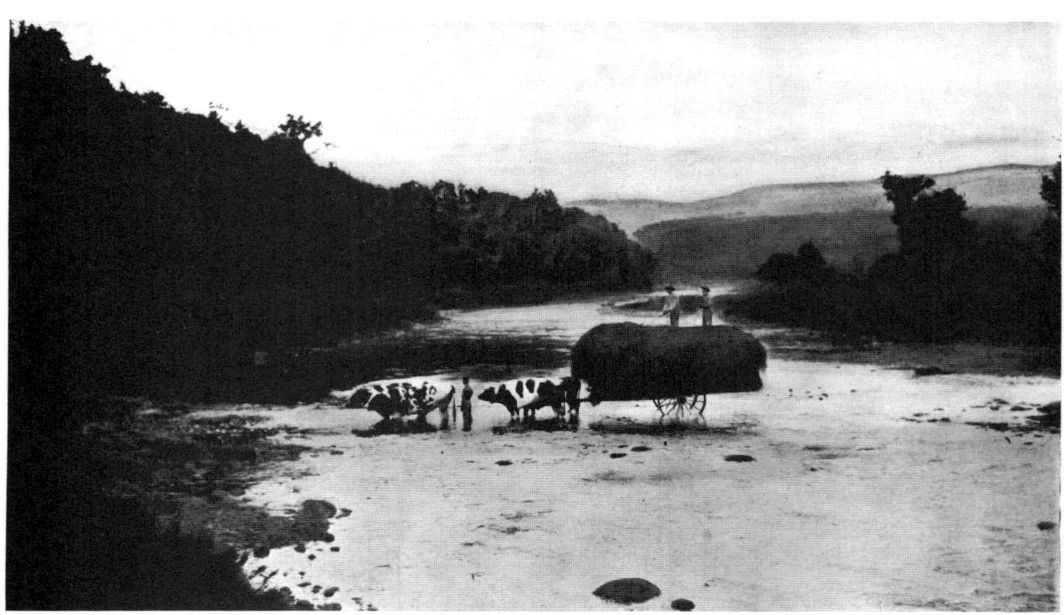

Fording the Connecticut Q, S, O, P, T 3027 Wallace Nutting

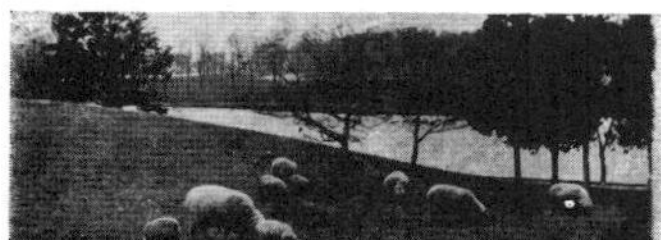

The Breakfast Hour Q or S 237

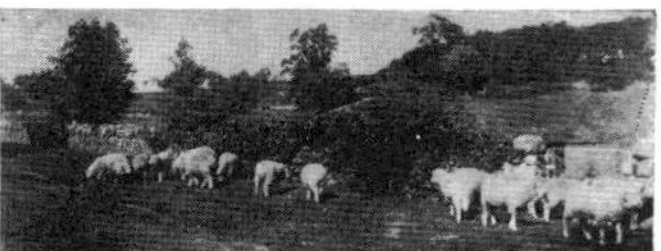

By the Wayside Q 859

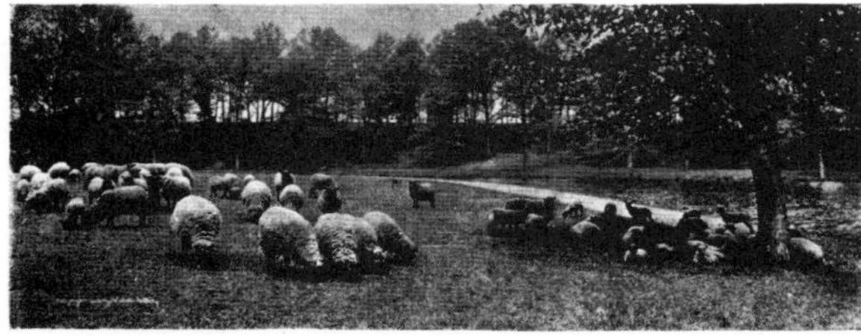

The Life of the Golden Age S, O, P, T 321

Under Cathedrals on page 359 will be found a beautiful aspect of Bolton Abbey, appearing in several sizes, with cows in the stream. Also on the same page is St. David's Palace, taken in a pasture, with sheep.

The following are not illustrated: C and E 8055, "Salting the Sheep"—a fine merino subject. "Feminine Curiosity" (C and E 8009), a spirited picture of Jerseys. "Merinos" (Q 8759) shows a line of Merino bucks.

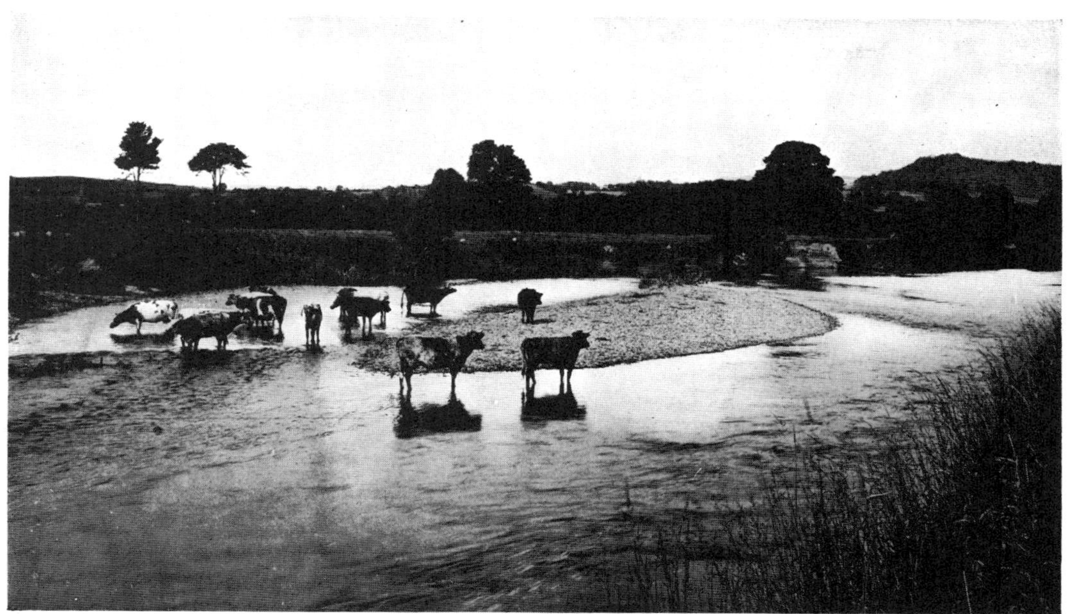

A Genial Stream A, Q, S ,O, P 6283 Wallace Nutting

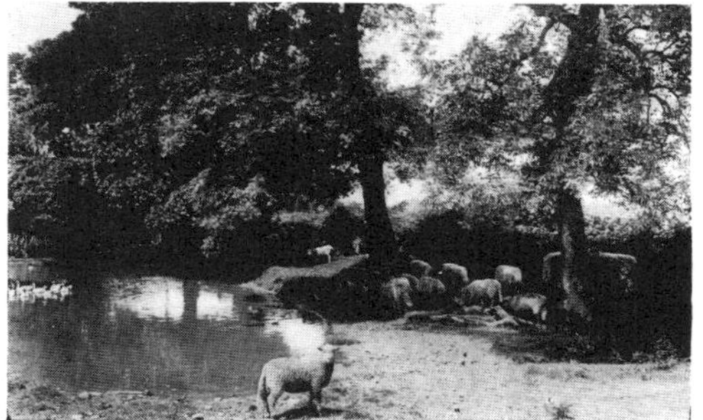

Seeking the Shade A, S 6227

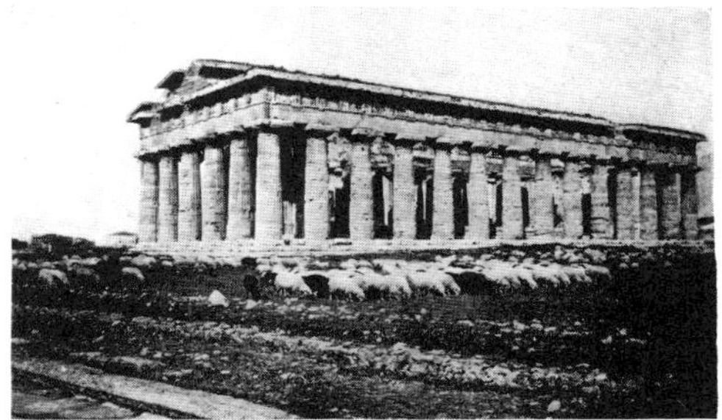

Sheep at the Temple, Pæstum A, S, T, G 4079

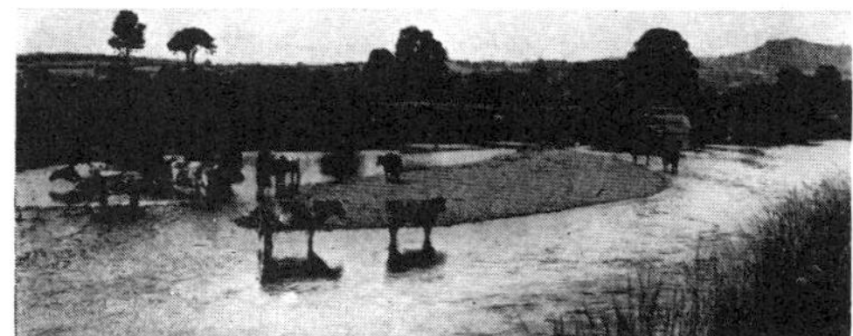

The Herd in the Stream A, Q, O 6205

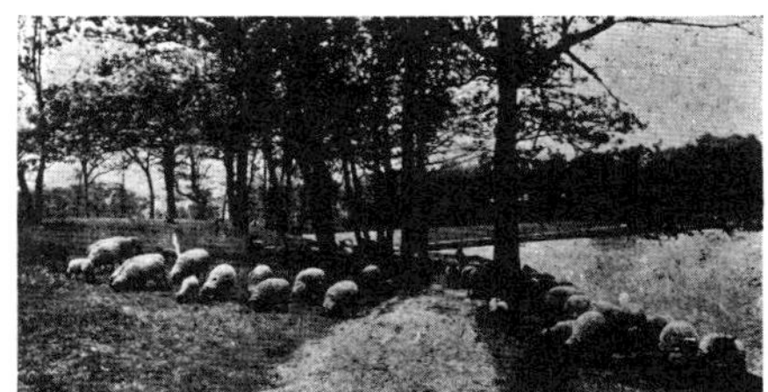

On the Slope S or P 312

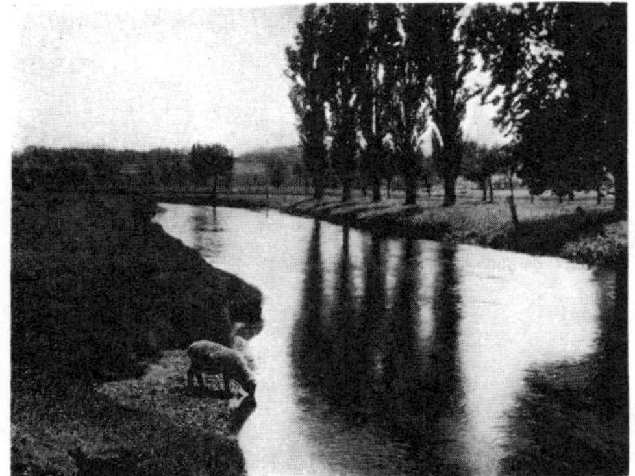

Mary's Little Lamb A, C 5561

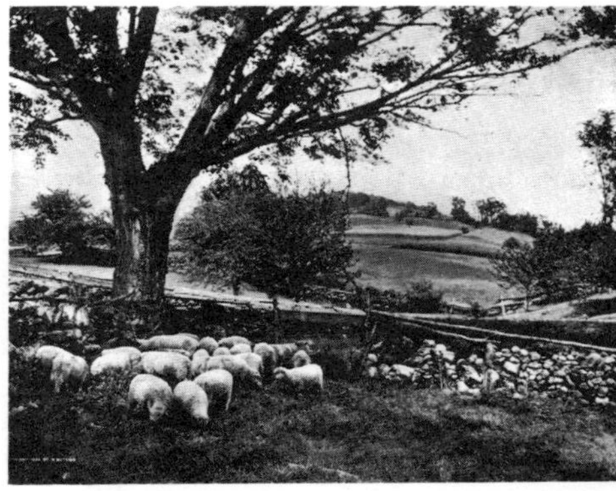

A Favorite Corner A, C and E 8005

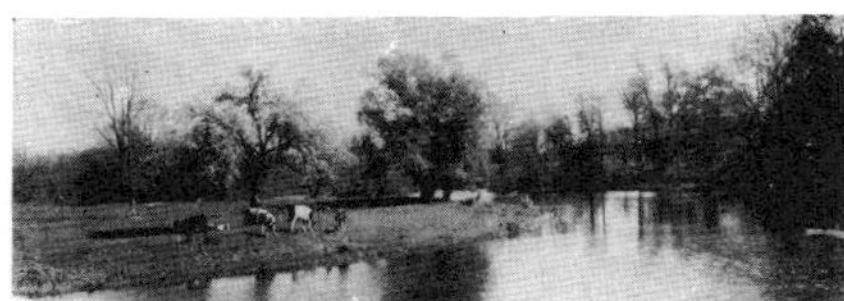

Blossom Pasture O 46

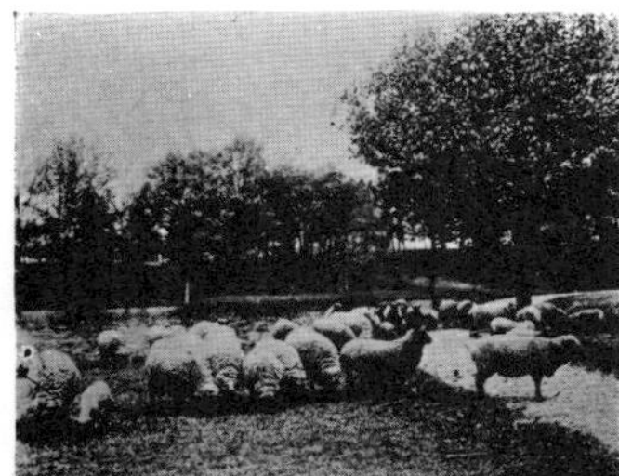

Not One of the Four Hundred C 2604

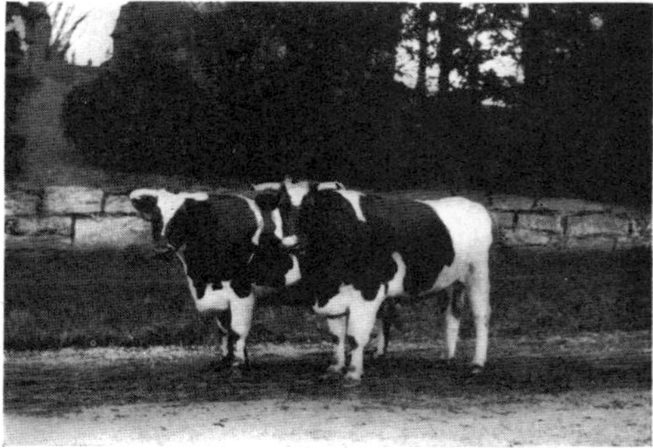

Noblesse Oblige C 1857

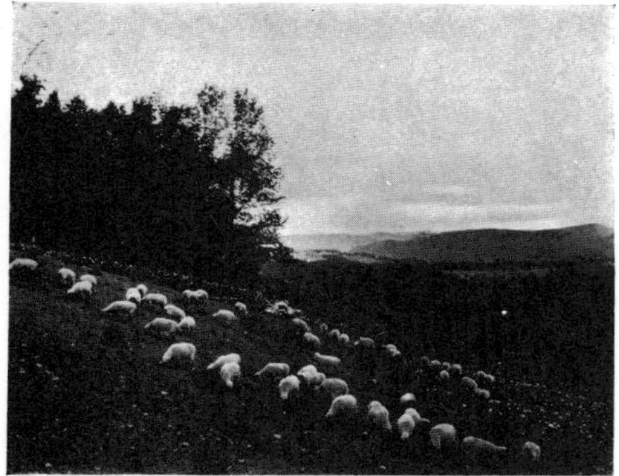

Wilburton Slopes C 3568

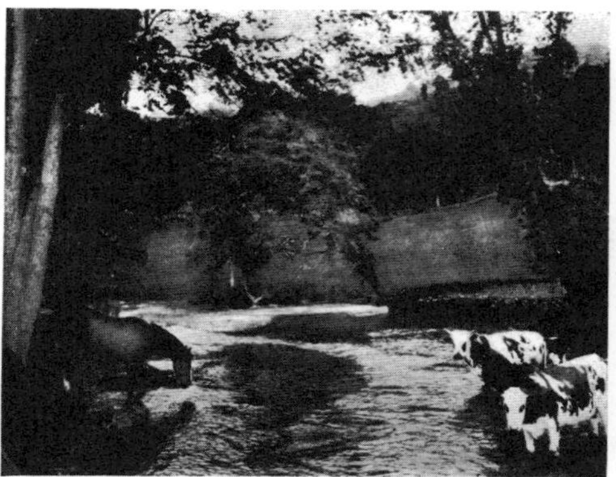

The Meeting Place C, E and G 916

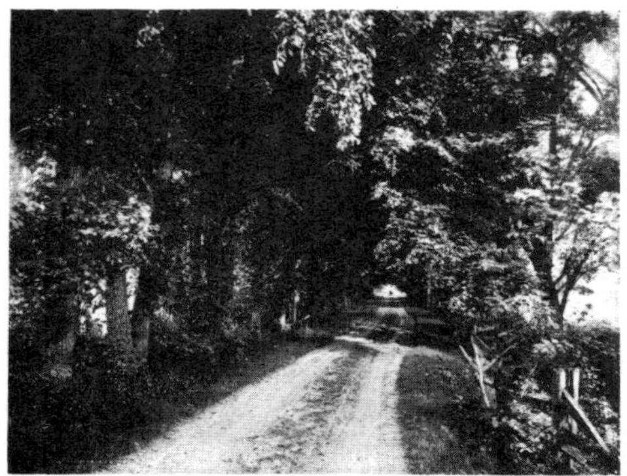

Seven Bridge Road C and E 8033

The Arched Lane C 1726 Wallace Nutting

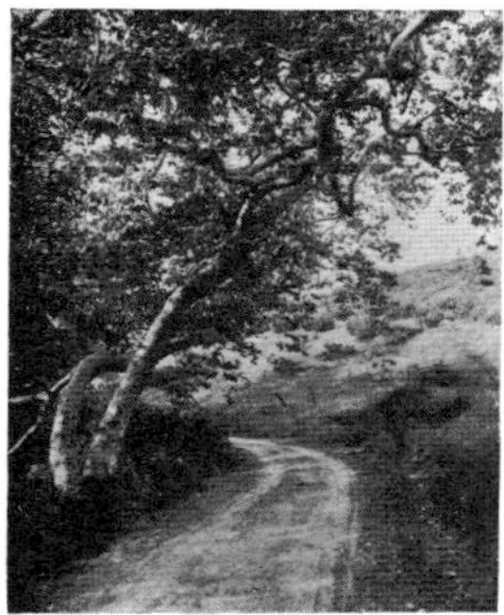

Under the Sycamore Bough
C 2308

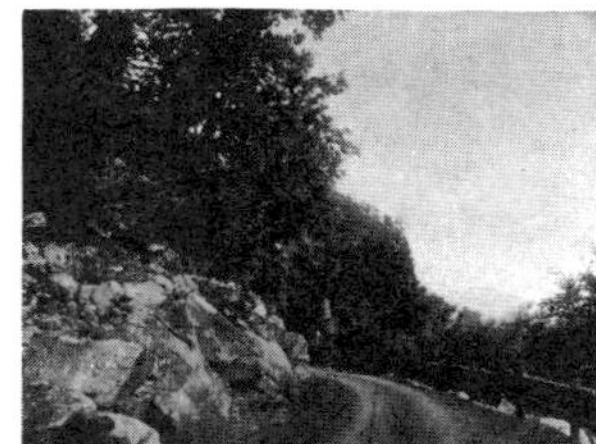

The Mystery of Curves
E 71

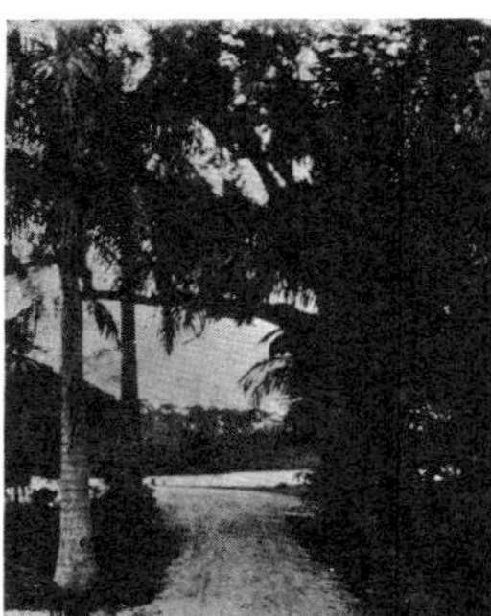

Royal Palm and Oak
A, S or C 1117

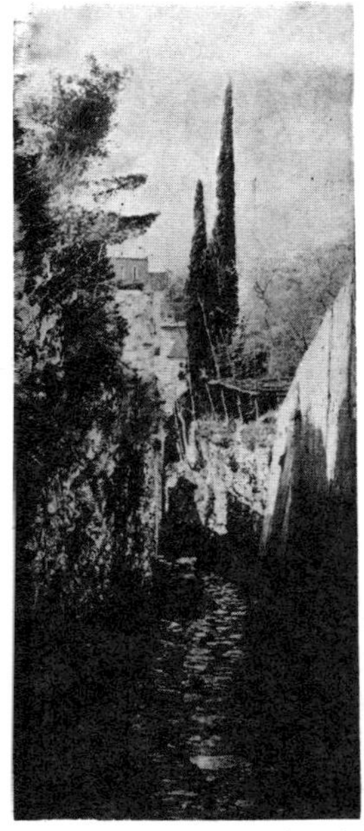

Cedar Lane, Ravello Q 4107

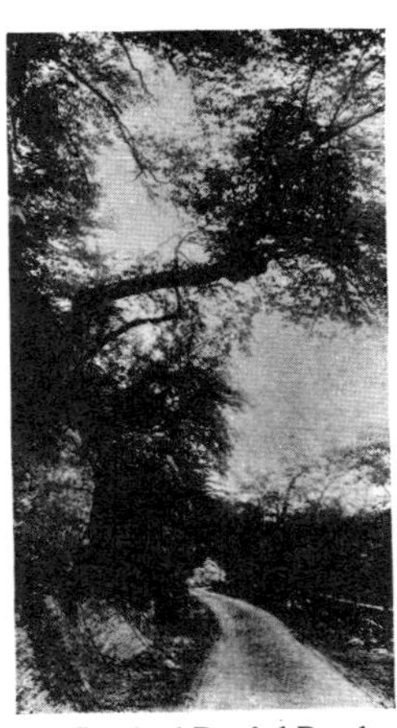

A Gambrel Roofed Road
P 80

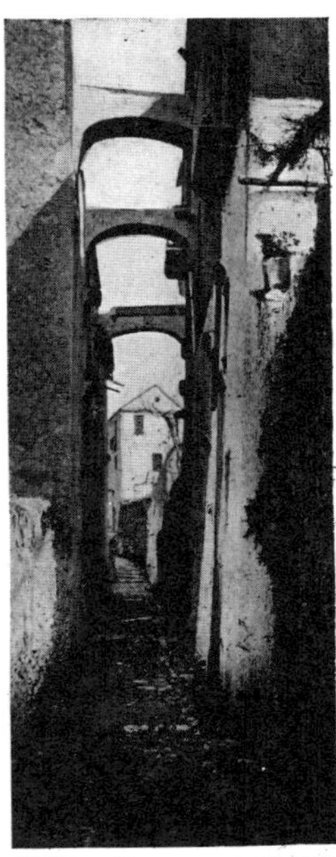

Old Ravello Q 4034

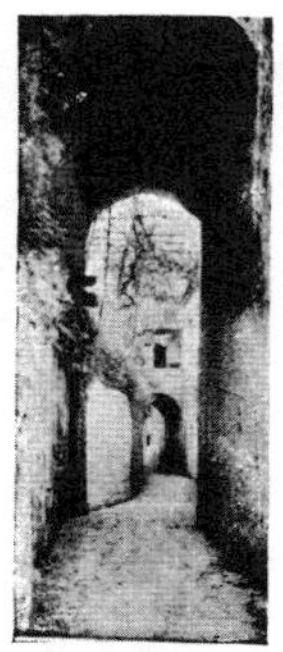

A Sorrento Lane
Q 32

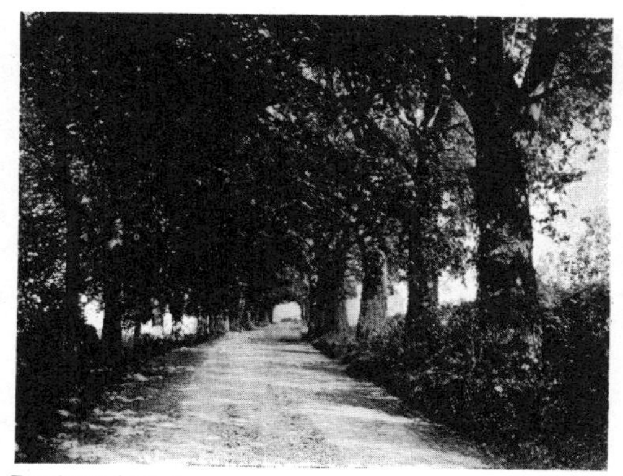

Roadway Arches A, C 4748

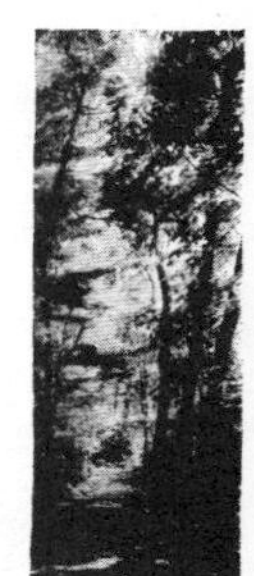

A Woodland Drive
O 51

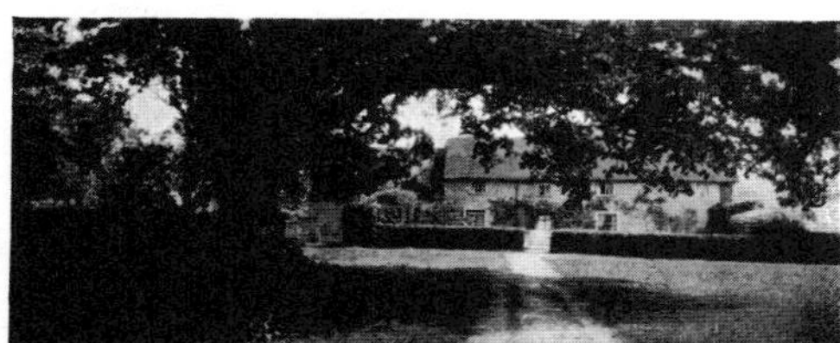

The Village Manor S, P, T 5610

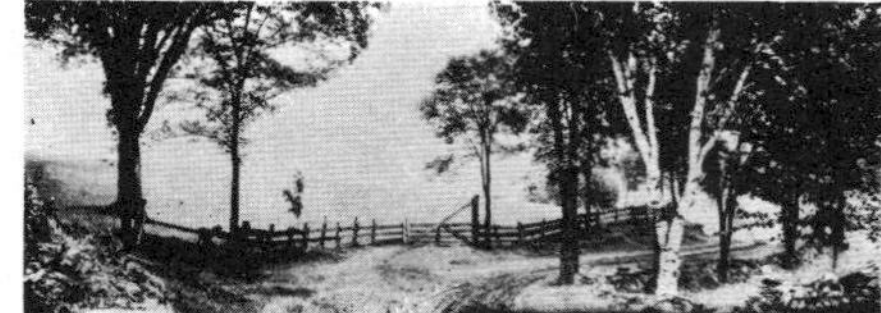

The Curve Q, O 2706

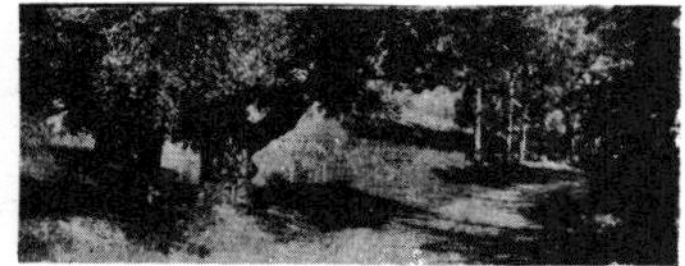

Friendly Oak Arms Q 865

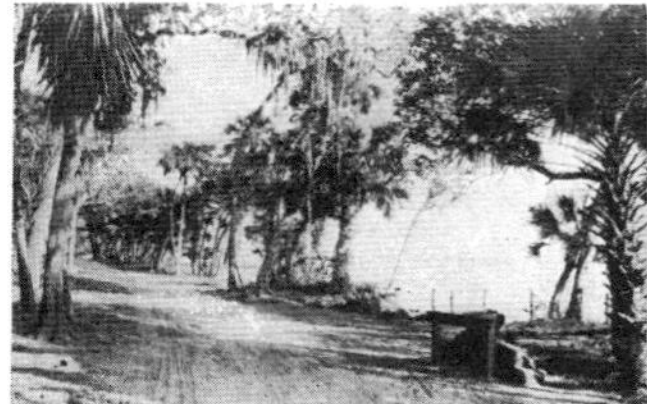

A Southern " Watering Place "
A or S 2034

In Mr. Nutting's early picture making, roads were the principal subjects; but in process of time it appeared that roads with blossoms, or birches, or cottages absorbed the greater part of this classification. The roads here shown, therefore, are for the most part only such as have none of those features. They consist largely of elms, or oaks, or evergreens, and were made in many states of the Union. They include scenes all along the Atlantic and Pacific Coasts.

The Seven Bridge Road on page 751 is the finest elm road to be found. It can no longer be photographed satisfactorily, as it has been straightened and trimmed until it has lost all artistic quality. " The Southern Moss " shown on pages 756 and 757, is very attractive. There are also live oaks and western forest scenes. For pure art we recommend " Cedar Lane " on page 751. It would not, however, be so popular as the " New England Road in May " on page 754.

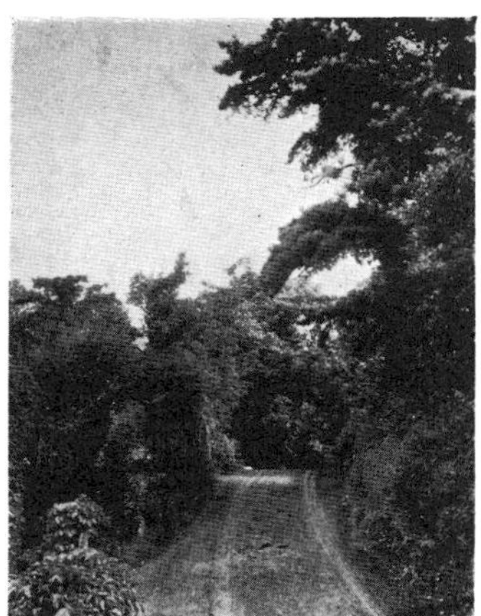

The Pine by the Cleft E 56

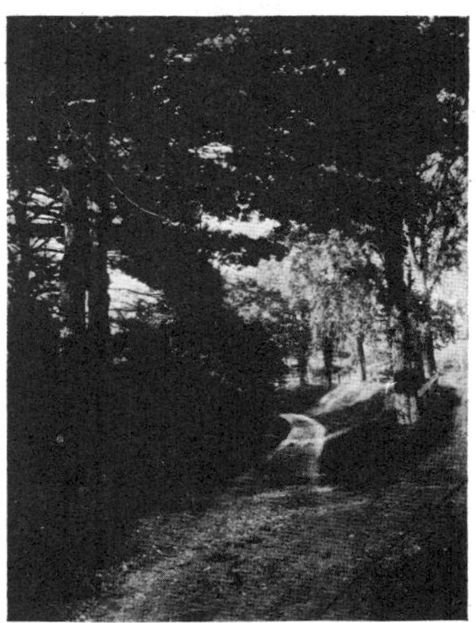

The Dell Road Wallace Nutting
S 762

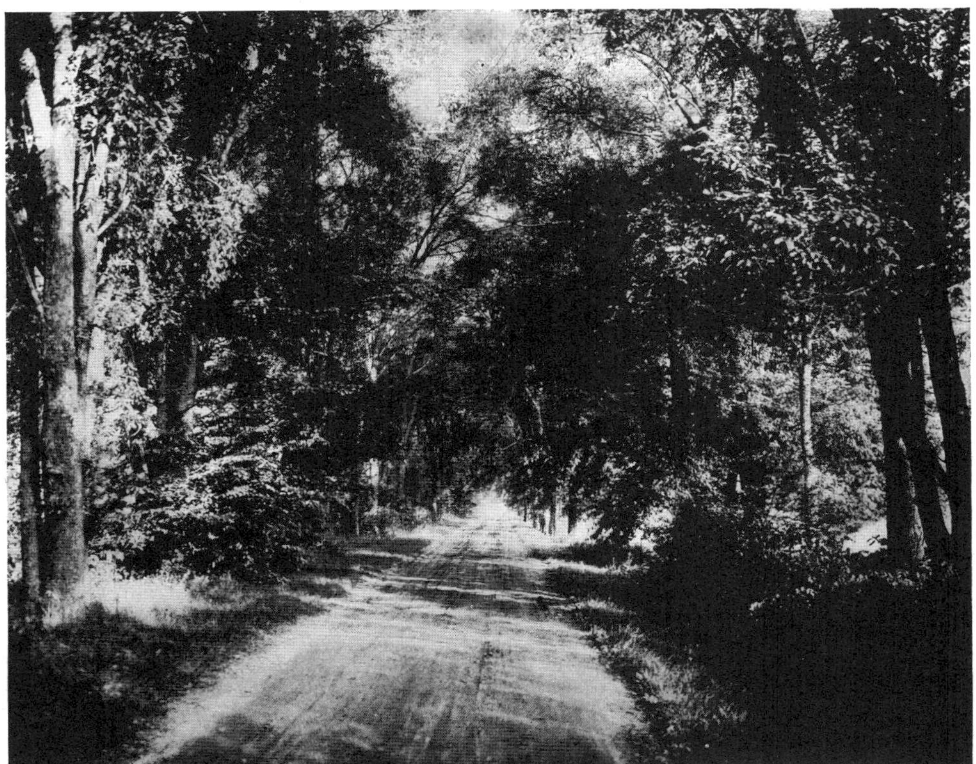

Meadow Arches A, S, C, P, E, F, T, G 1328 Wallace Nutting

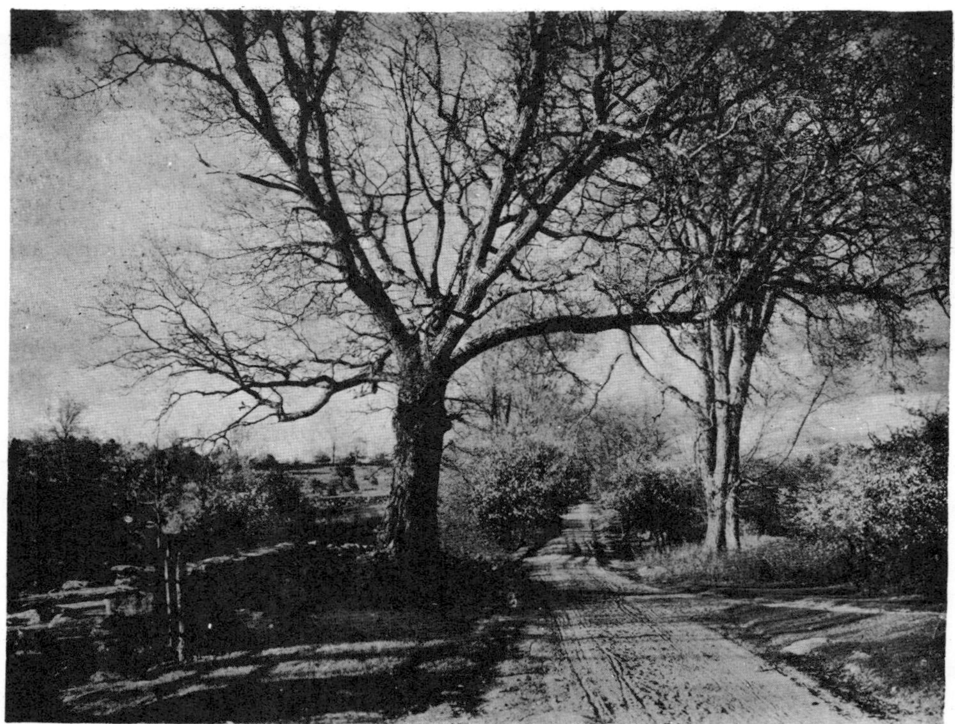

A New England Road in May E 134 Wallace Nutting

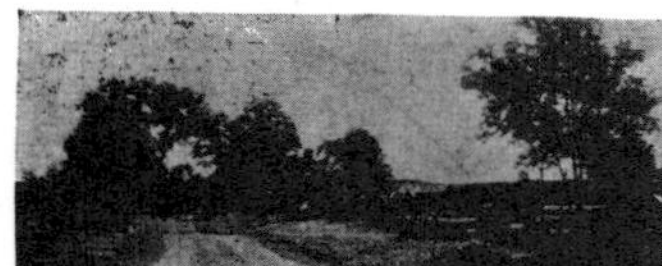

A Connecticut Roadside Q 973

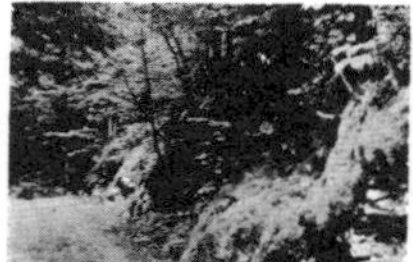

A Mossy Drive A 82

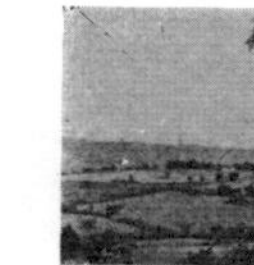

Over the Valley Q 343

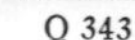

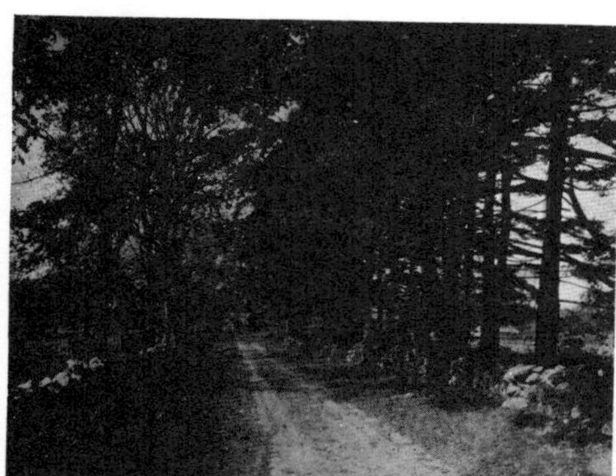

The Home Lane Wallace Nutting
C 1432

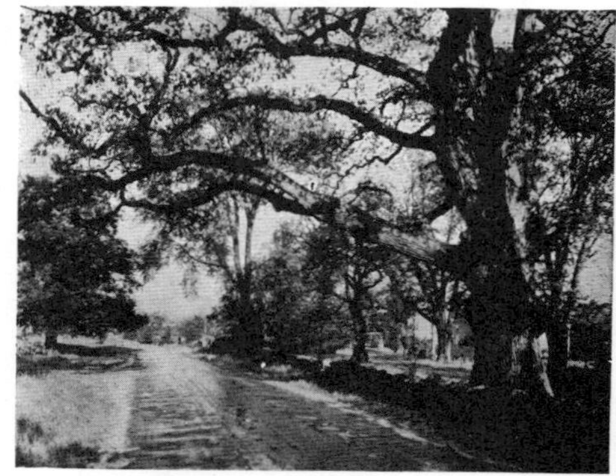

A Great Wayside Oak Wallace Nutting
A, C, E and F 608

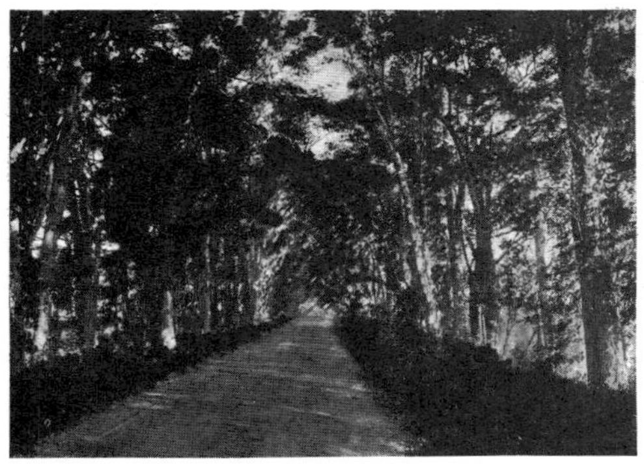
A Sunkissed Way A, S, C, P, E, F, G, H and J 964

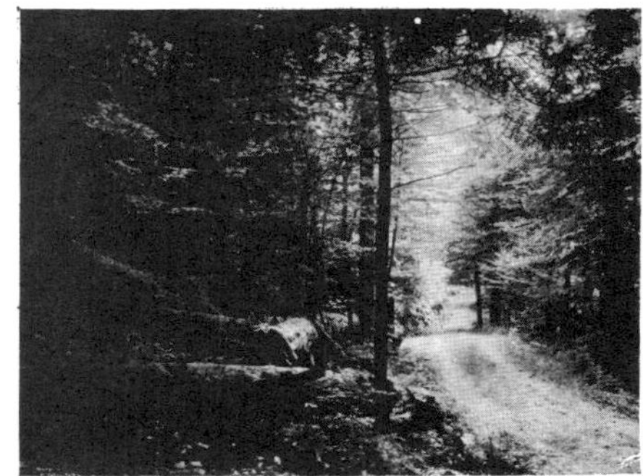
Mossy Logs E 83

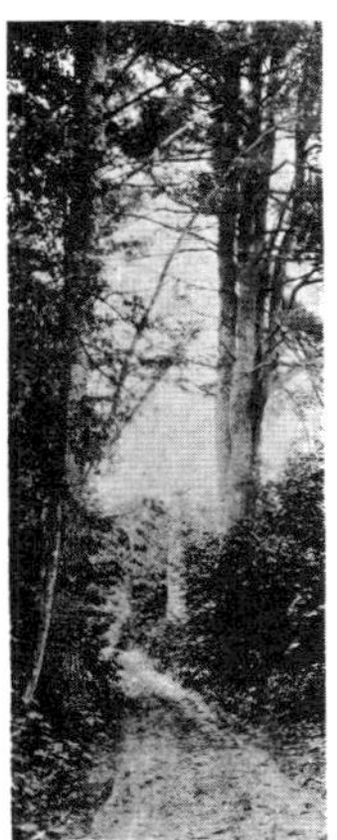
A Forest Drive
O 102

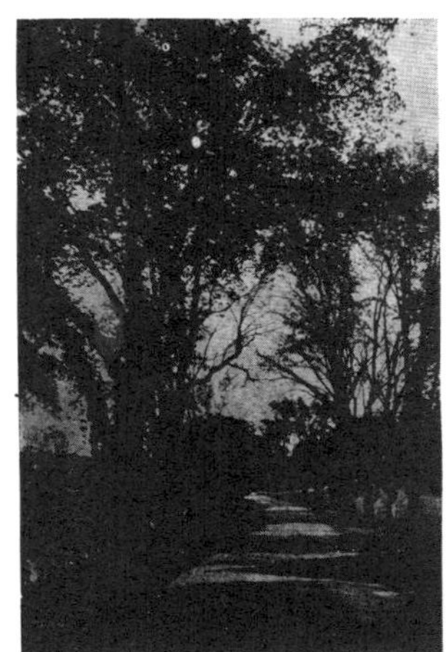
A Sherborn October S 1730

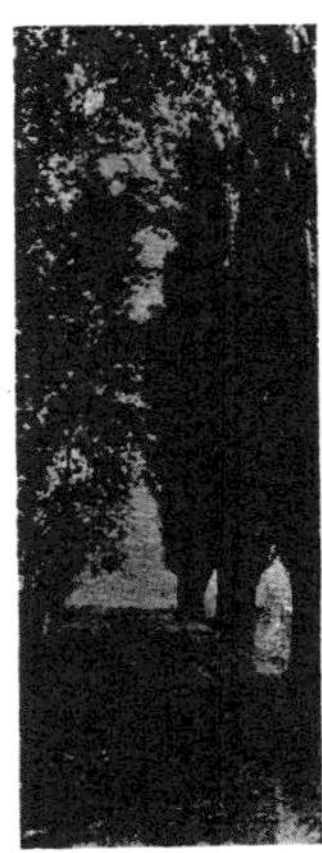
Poplar Lane
O 215

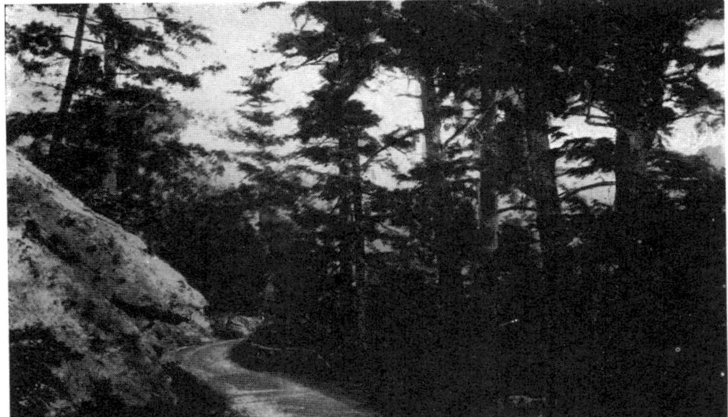
Eagle Cliff Drive E and H 1 Wallace Nutting

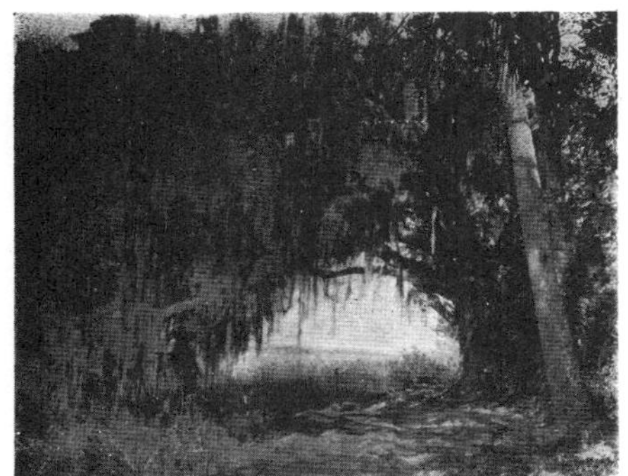

A Disappearing Curve A, C or E 887

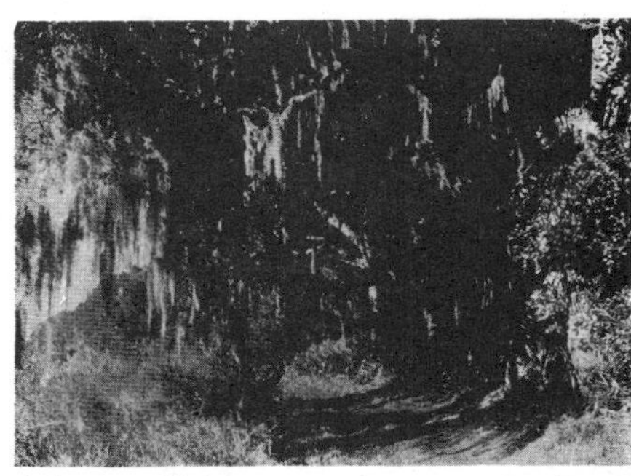

A Southern Highway C or E 1057

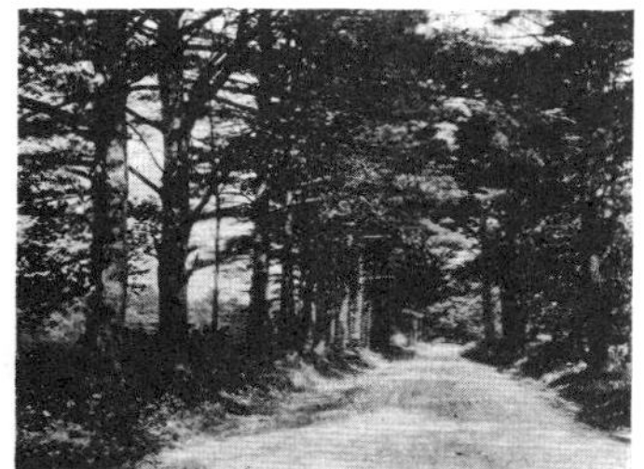

Evergreen Shadows C 430

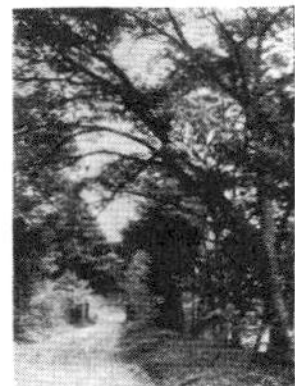

A Woodland Way
A 901

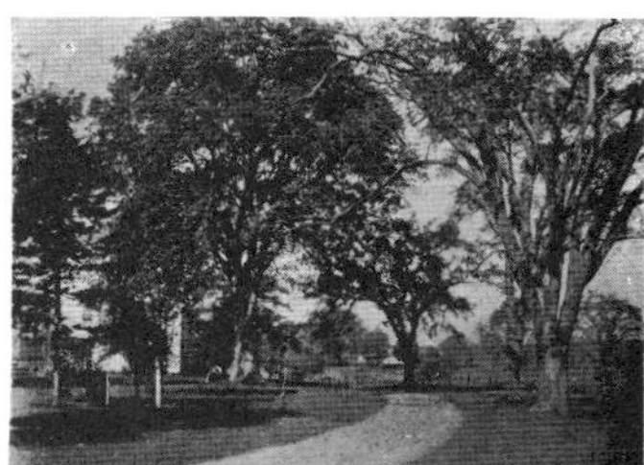

The Sweep Under the Elms C 705

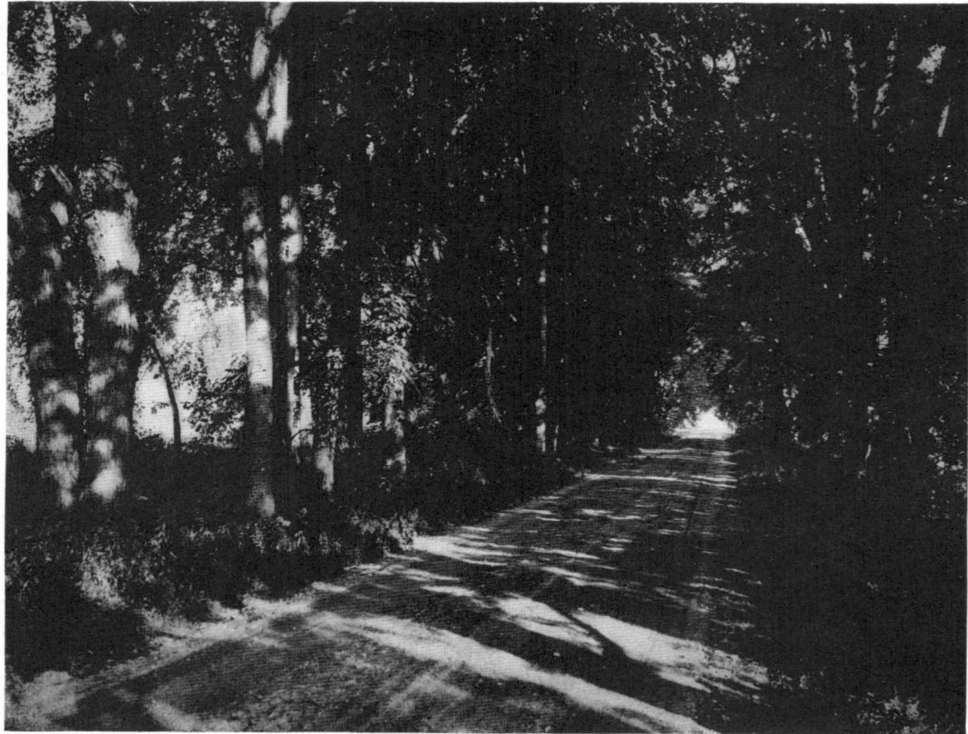

Shadows Athwart A, S, C, P, E, F, J, W 950 Wallace Nutting

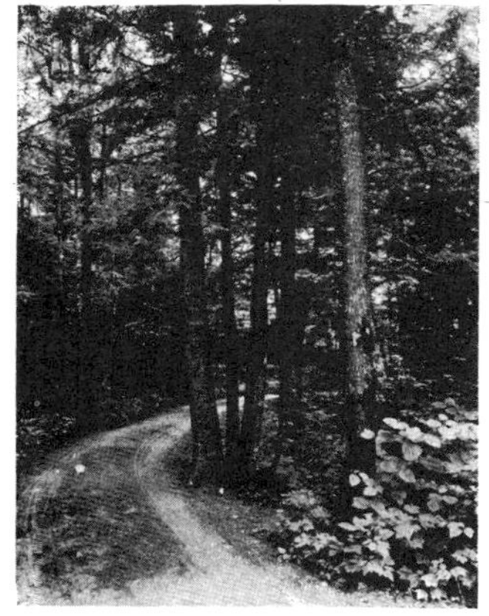

A Minnewaska Road E 86

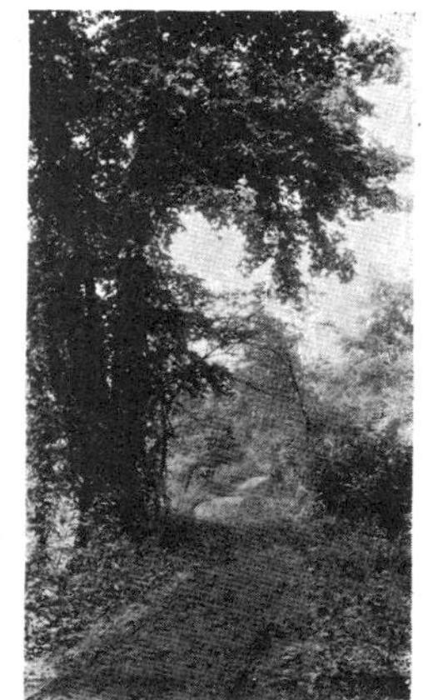

Elm Drapery S, P or J 197

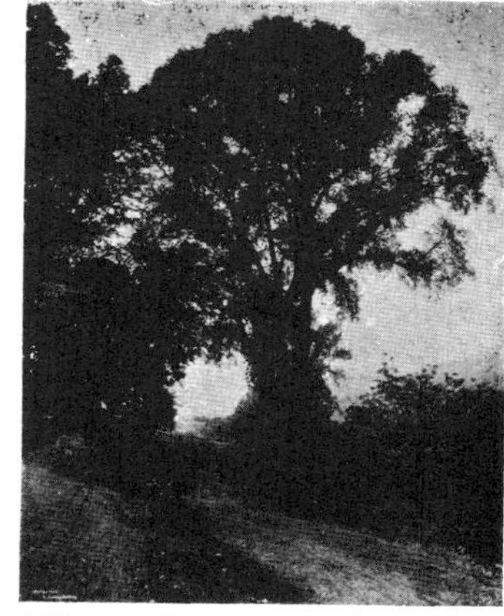

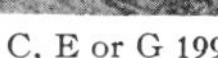

A Vermont Road C, E or G 199

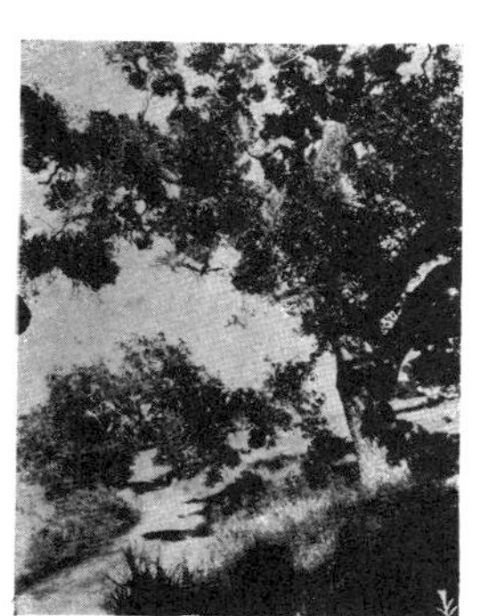

The Hill Road Oak C 2274

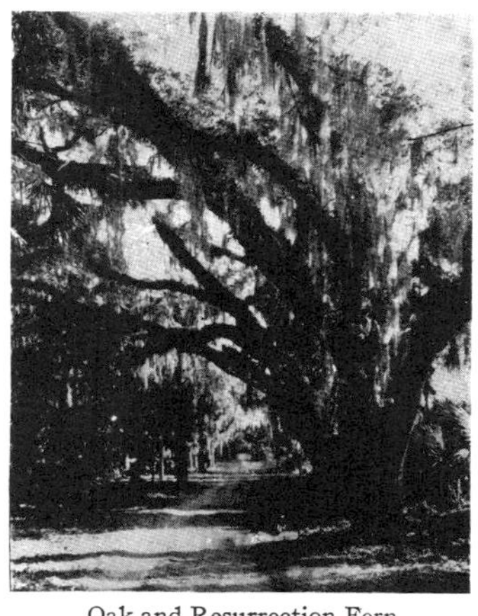

Oak and Resurrection Fern
A, C or E 1123

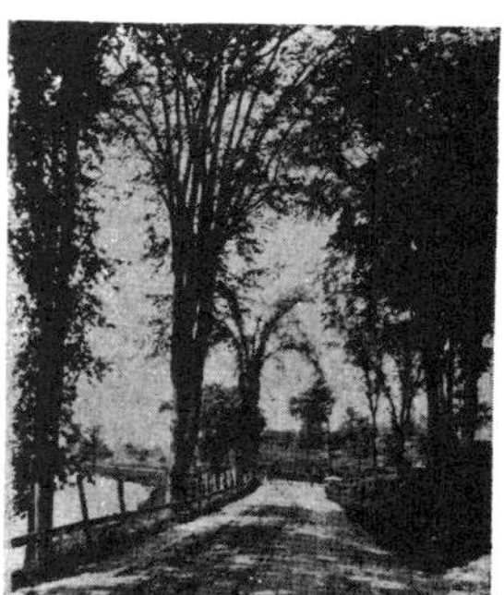

A Bridgewater Road C 858

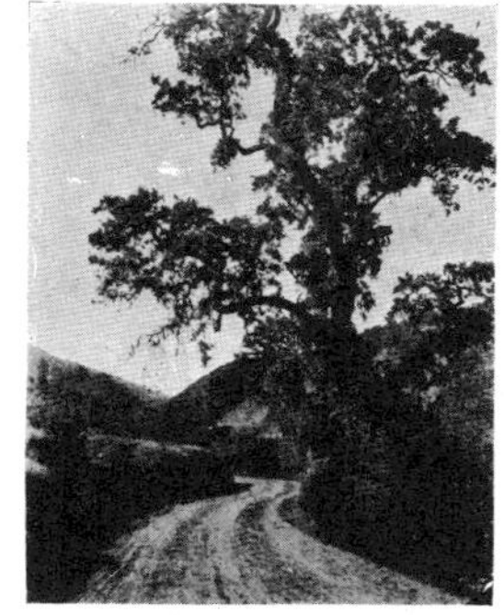

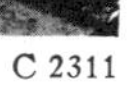

A Mountain Oak C 2311

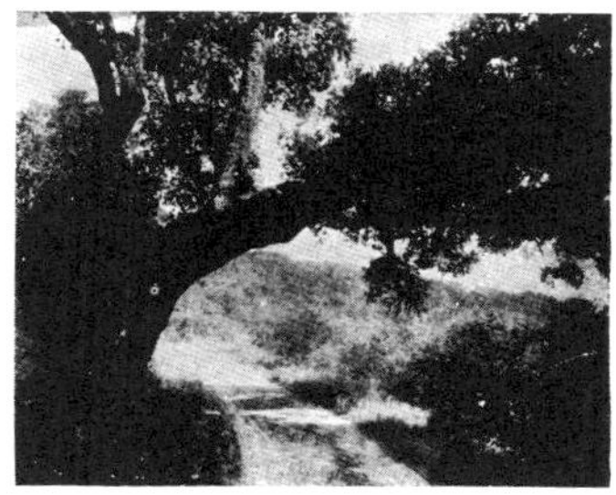

A California Oak C 2212

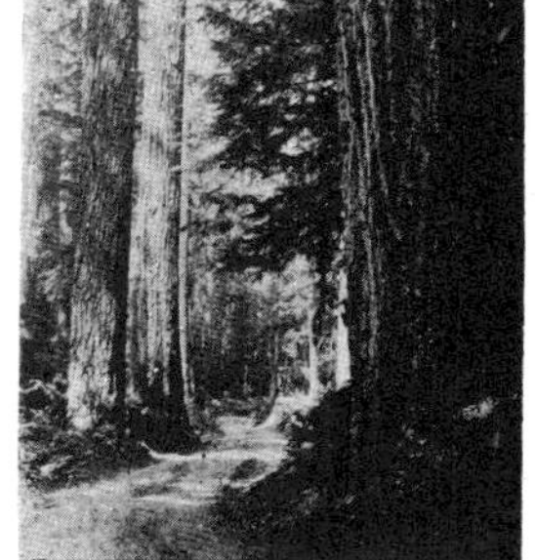

In the Big Timber C or J **2464**

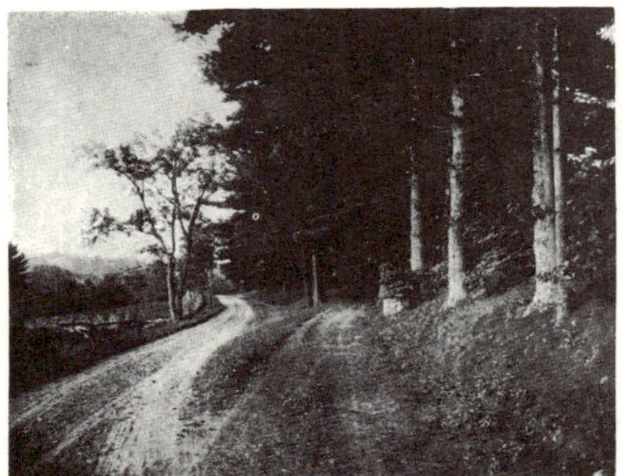

The Meeting of the Ways Wallace Nutting
A and C 475

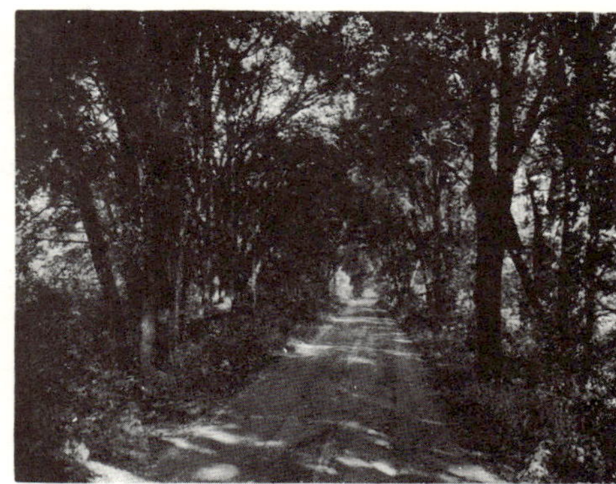

Soft Summer Shadows Wallace Nutting
A, C and E 1725

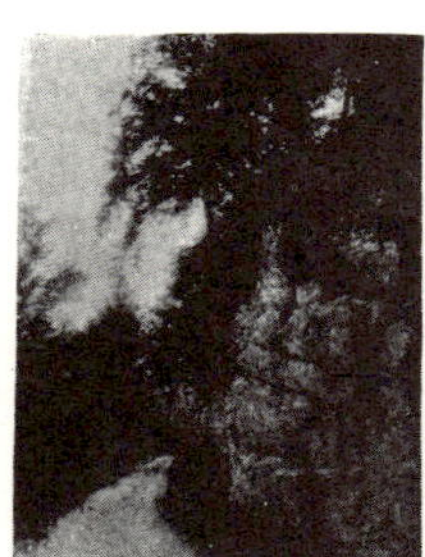

A Mohonk Drive
O or E 75

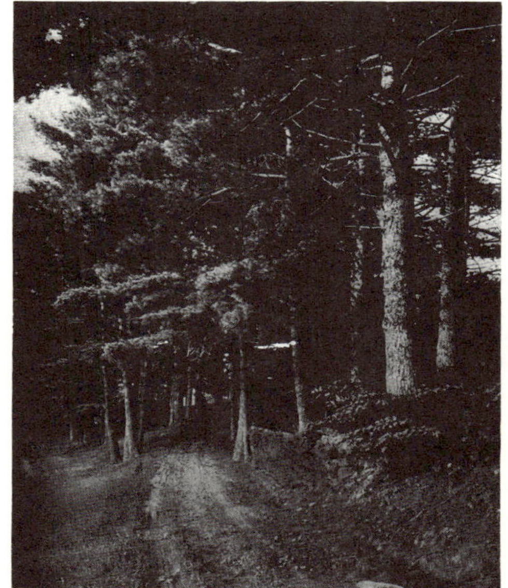

The Turn Homeward C and E 406 Wallace Nutting

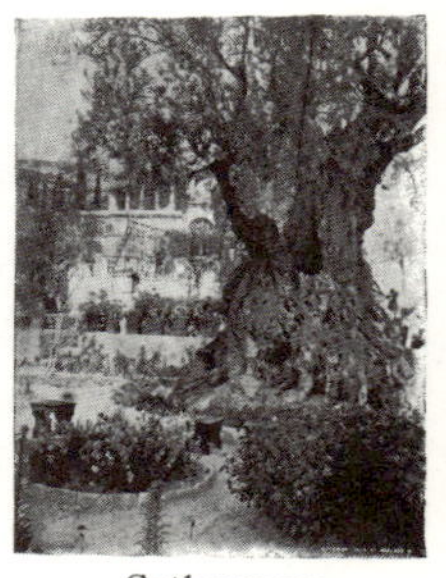

Gethsemane
C or E 44

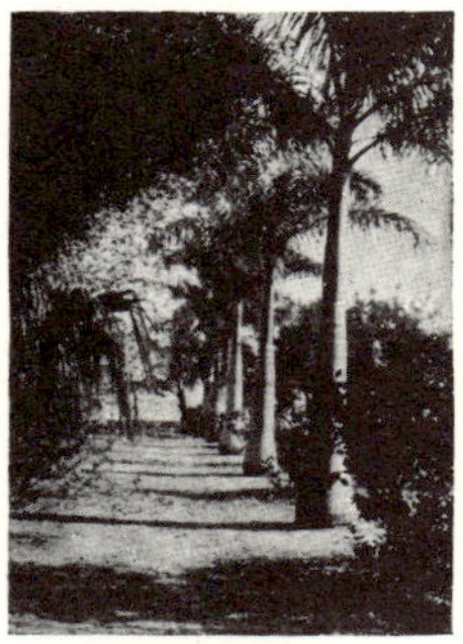

Royal Palm Border
A or C 632

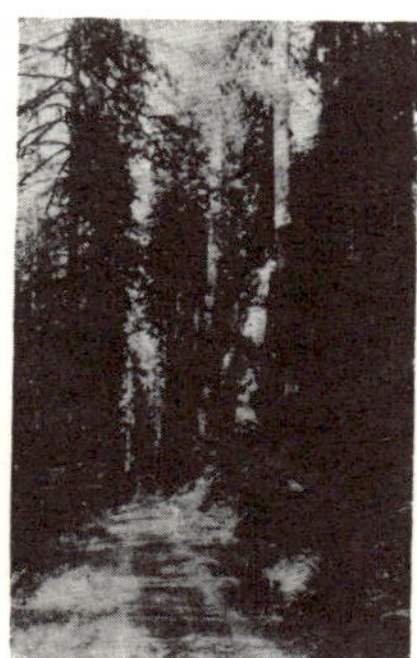

A Cedar Forest
S or W 2463

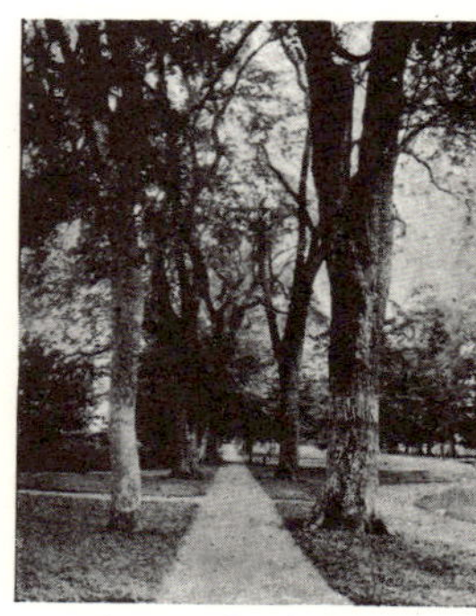

Autumn in Litchfield
C 853

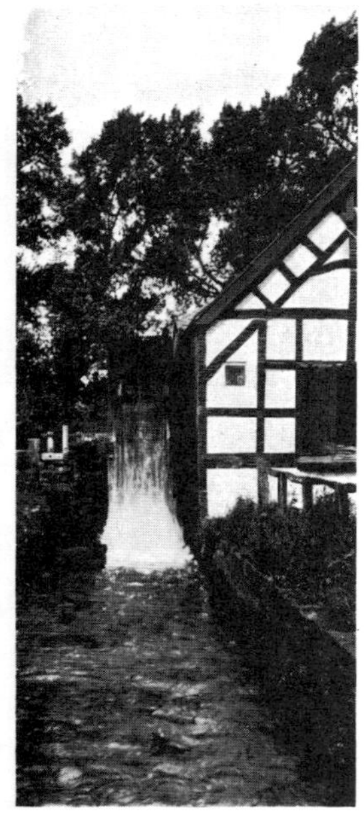

Millside Q 6428

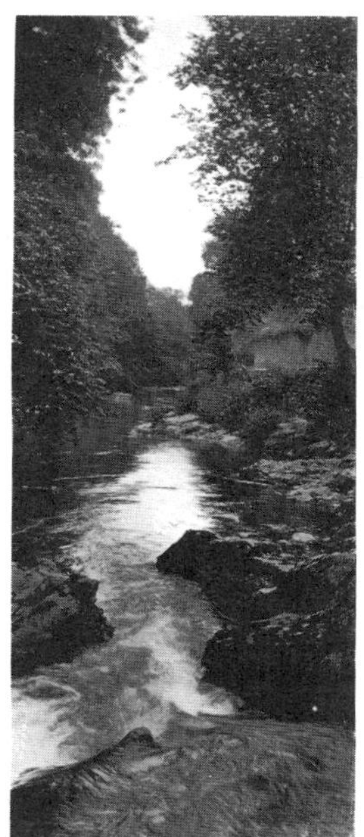
From the Mountain Q 5681

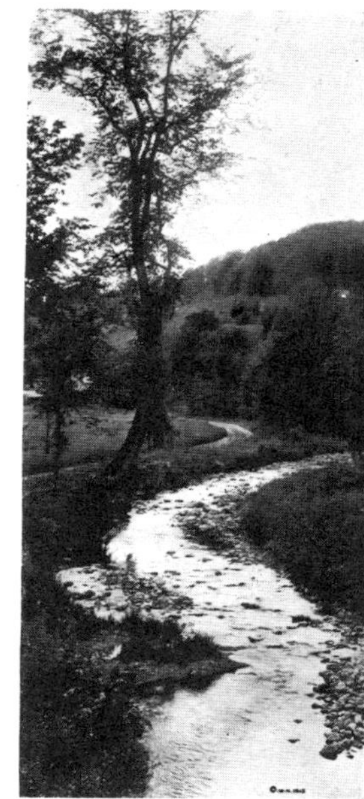
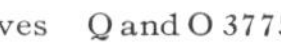
Plymouth Curves Q and O 3775

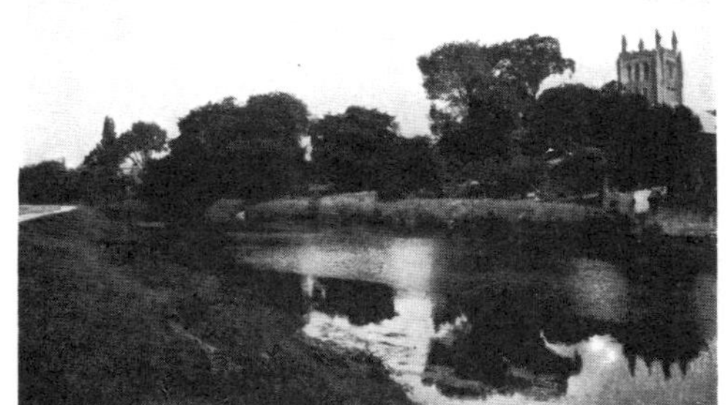
Hereford S 5838

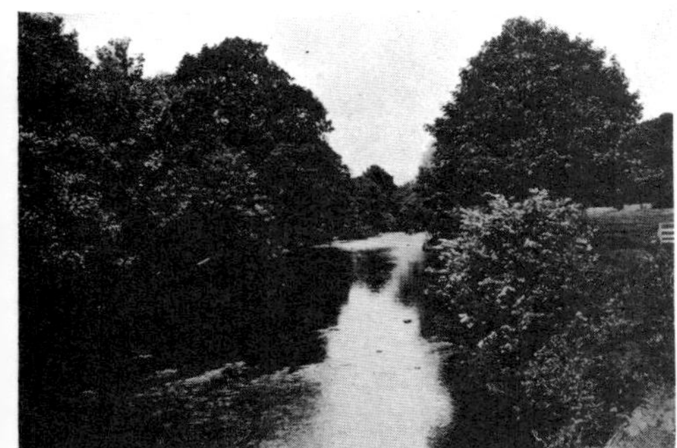
Long River Lights A 5732

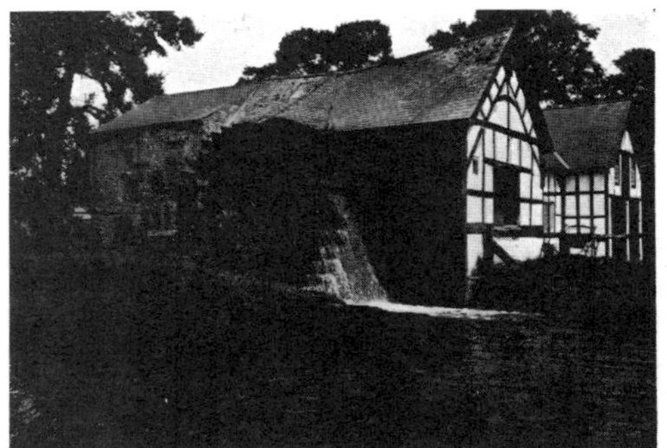
The Old Breast Wheel A, C 6426

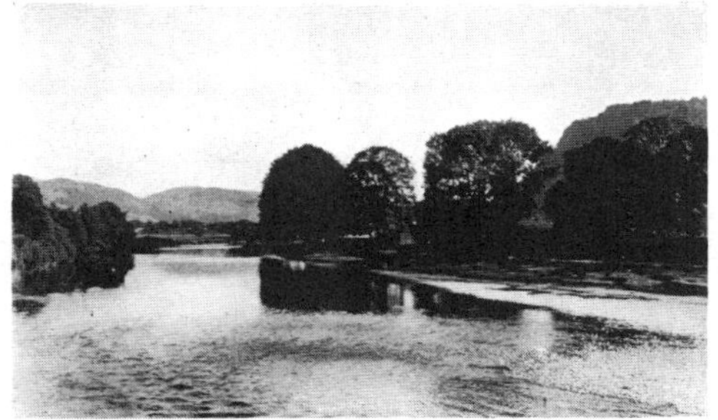

The Calm of Twilight — A, Q, S, C 6115

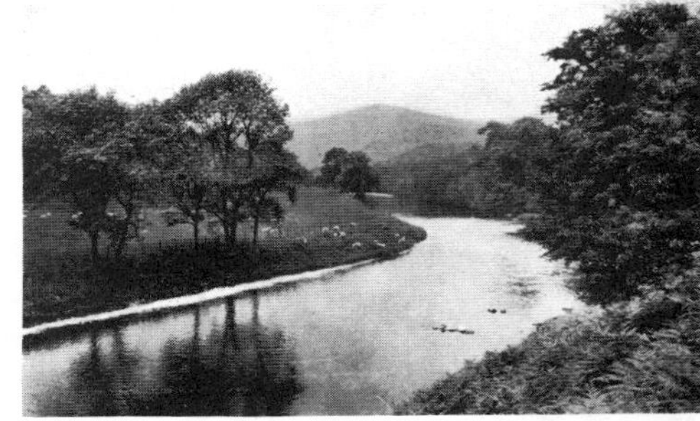

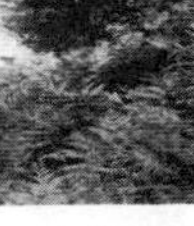

On the Teith — A, S 5937

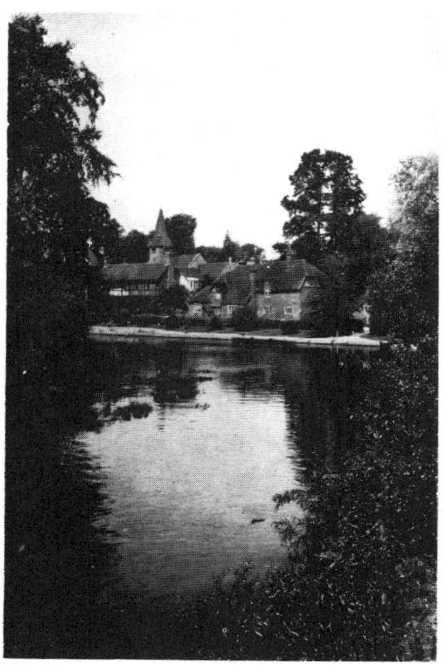

The Upper Thames — A, S 6277

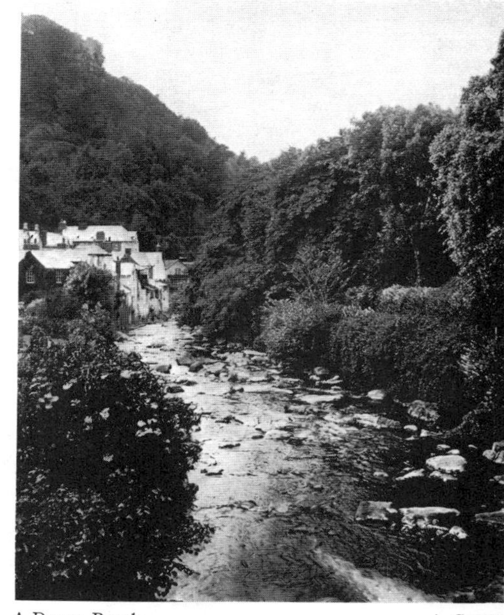

A Devon Brook — A, C 5679

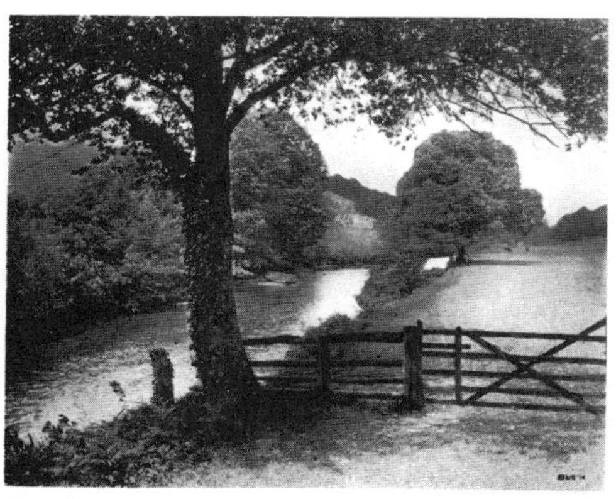

The River Meadow — A, C, E 5654

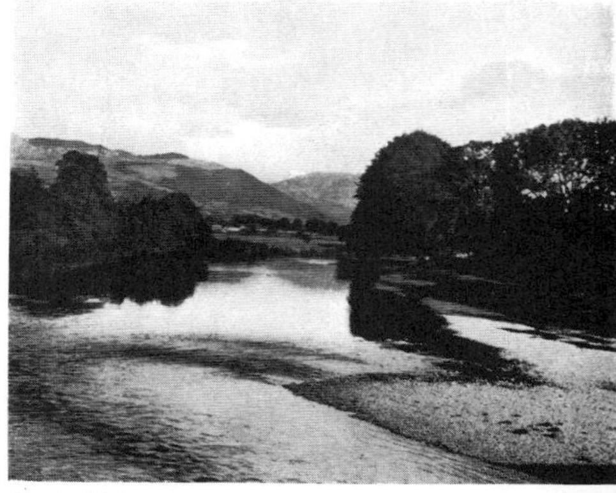

Up the Vale — E, P 6111

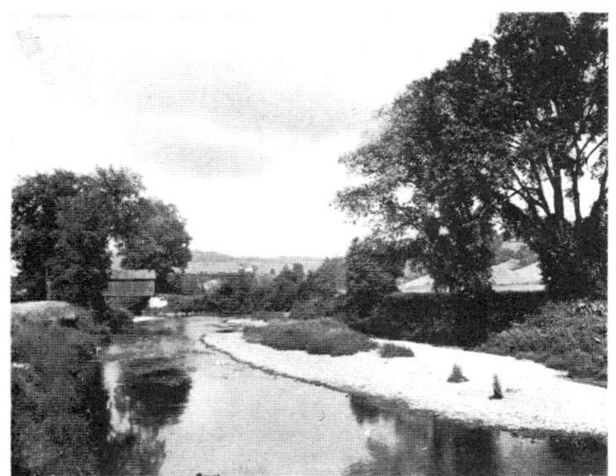

The Upper Winooski C, E 3697

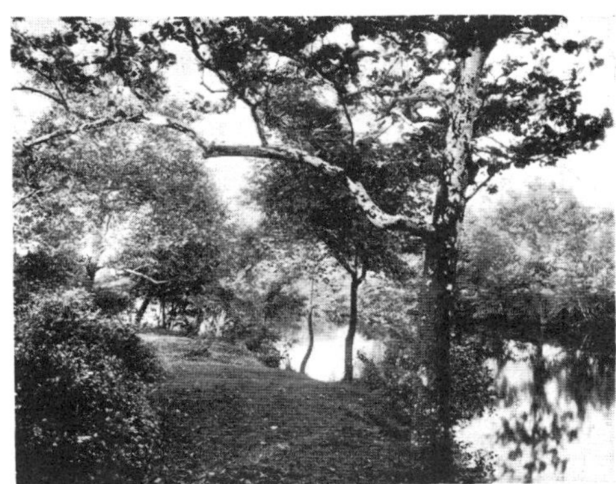

The Walk under the Buttonwoods C, E and H 8080

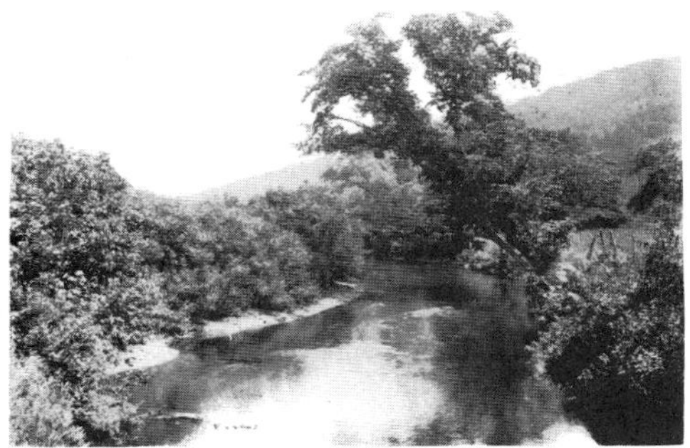

Under the Elm A, C 3757

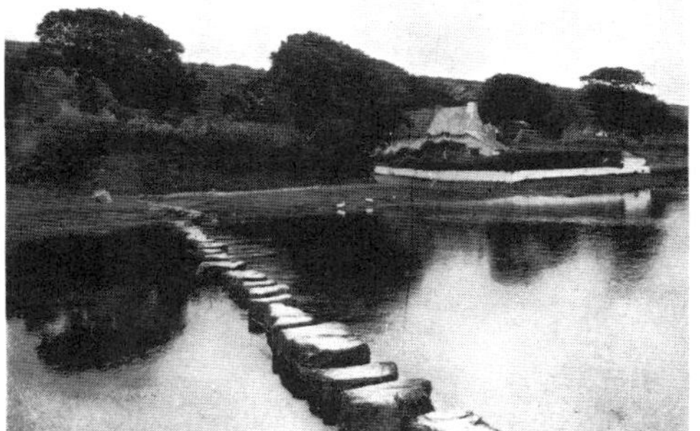

The Home Vale A, C 6403

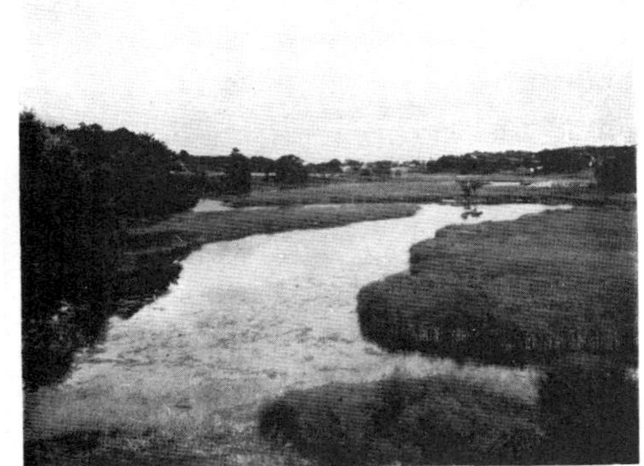

North Shore Marshes Wallace Nutting
A, Q, S, C, O, P, E 870

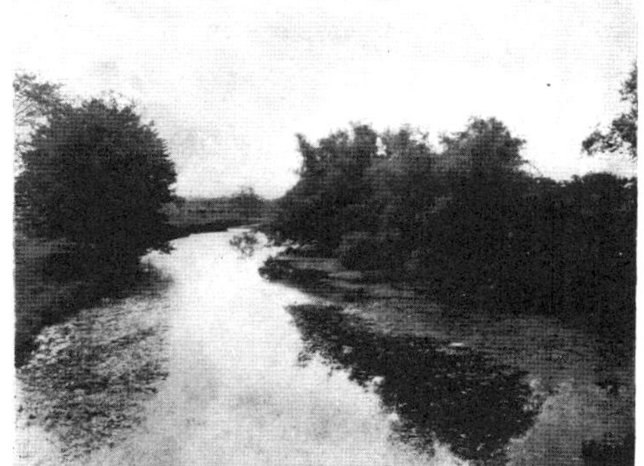

A Lane of Light C 1095 Wallace Nutting

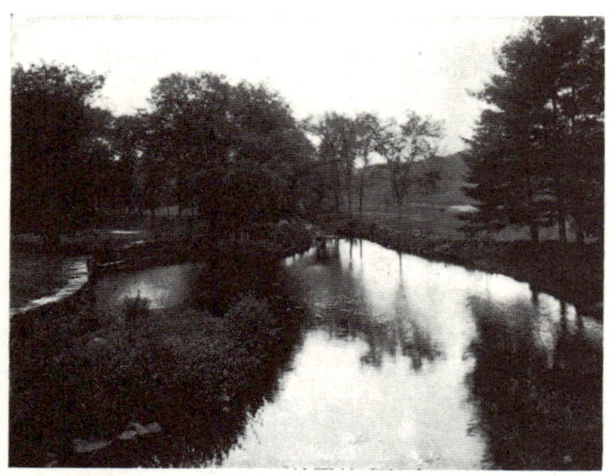
A Barre Brook Q, C, O, P, E and J 3497

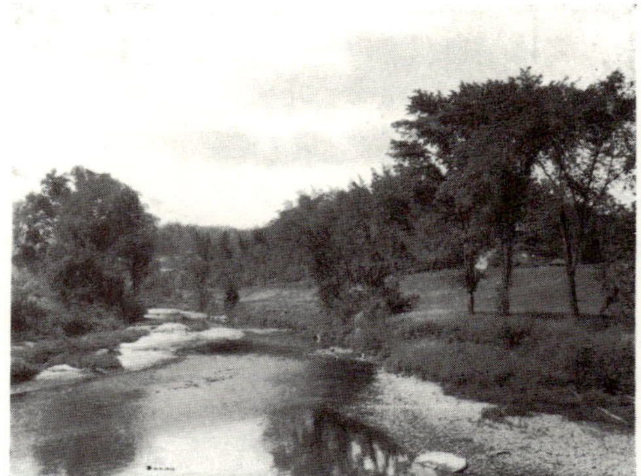
The River Valley Q, C 3715

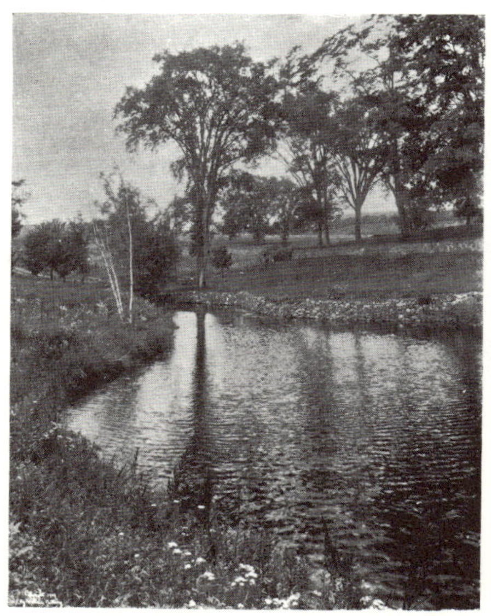
Summer Wind A, C, O, E, H or J 295

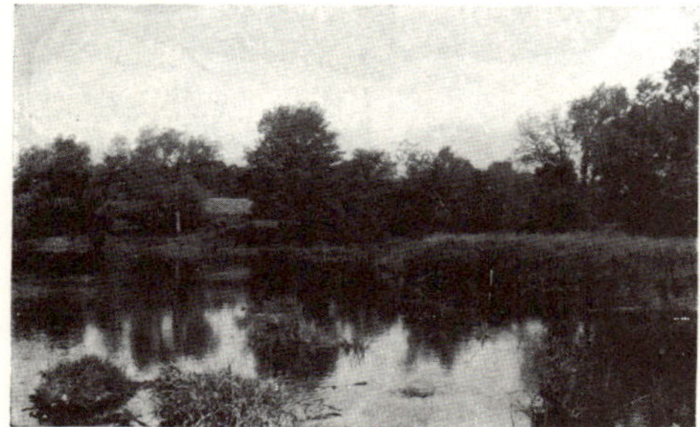
Newton Meadows Wallace Nutting
Q, S, O, P, E 1505

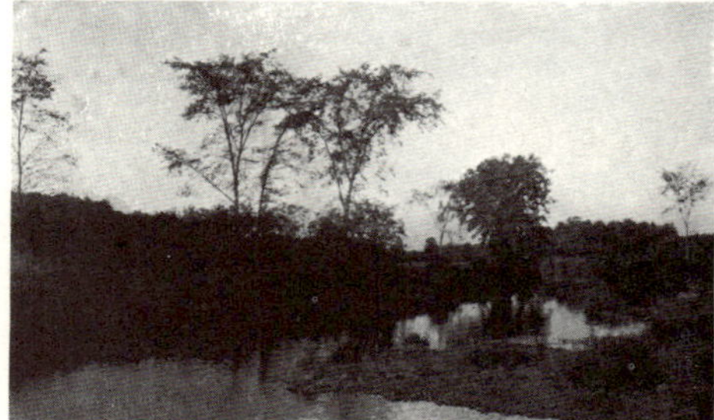
Spring in the Meadow Wallace Nutting
S 1439

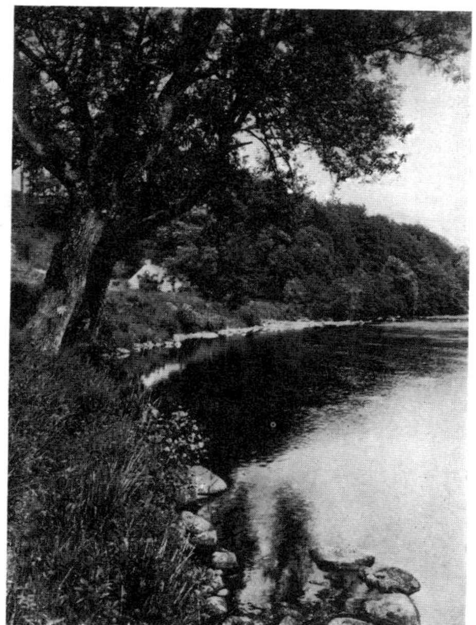

Doune Bank A, C 5964

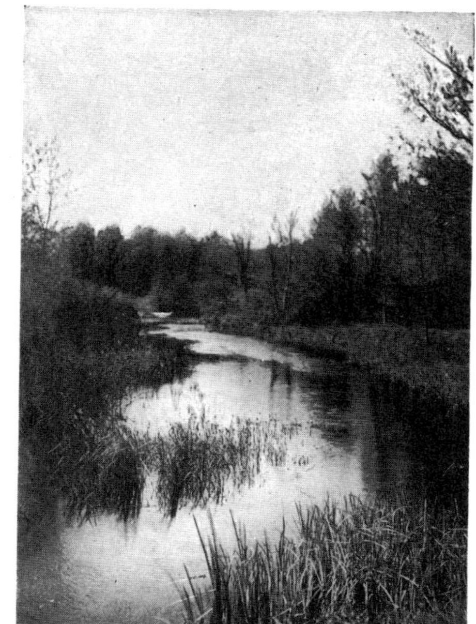

Brook Grasses A 3627

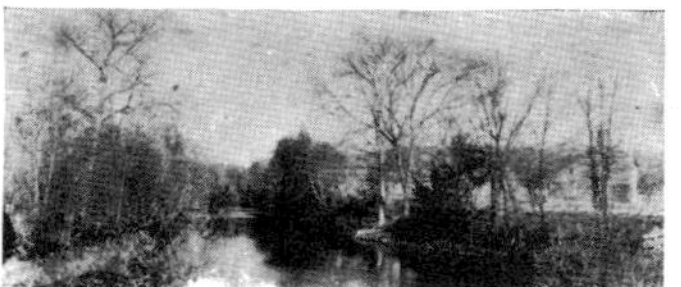

Pomperaug Banks Q 948

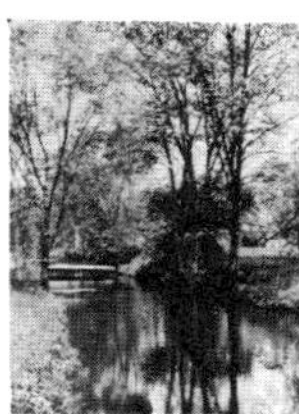

Still Depths
A 469

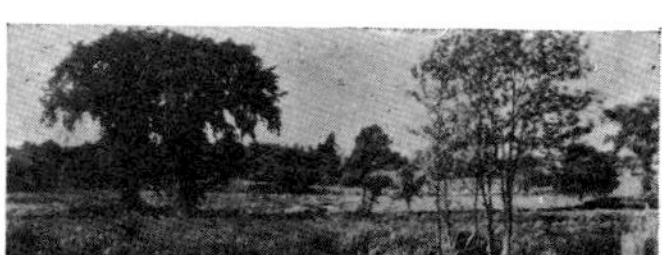

Twin Elms Q 2686

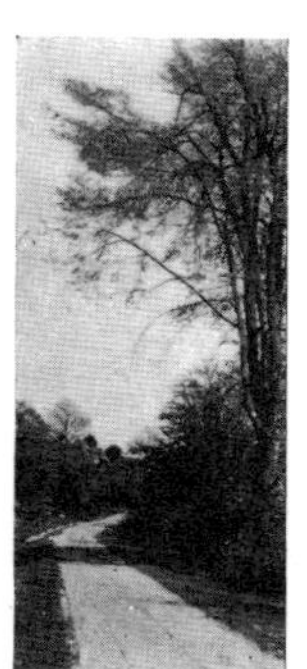

Into the West
Q 484

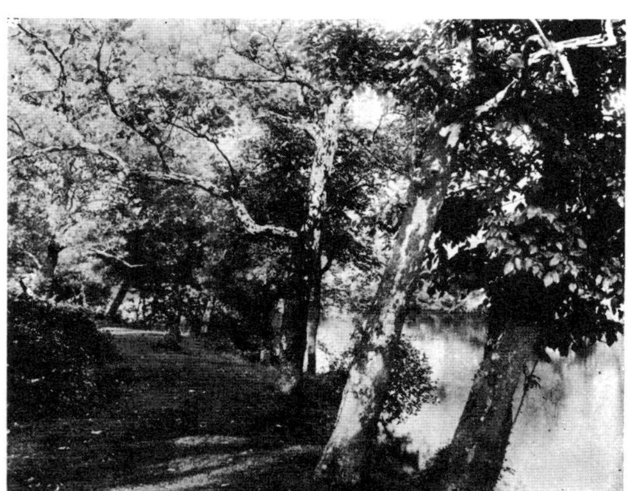

Along the Pawtuxet C, E or F 5 Wallace Nutting

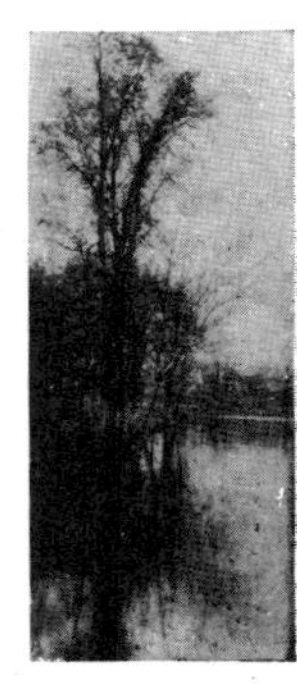

Nine-Mile Pond
Q 2

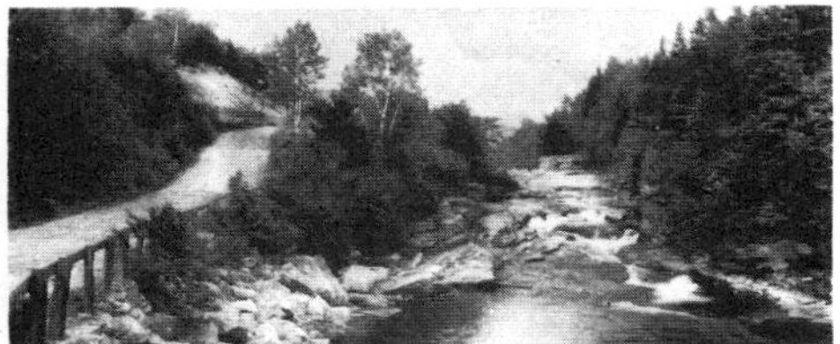
A Little River Q, O, P and T 3701

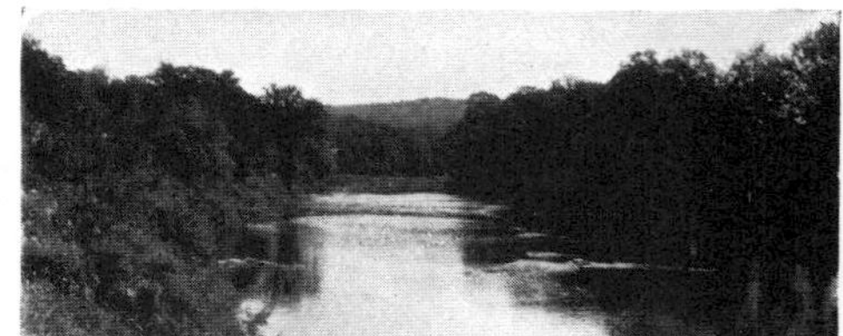
West River Q 3507

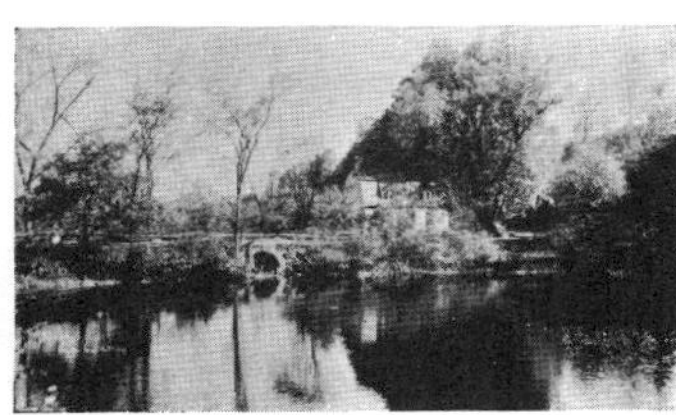
The Cottage on the Floss S 1098

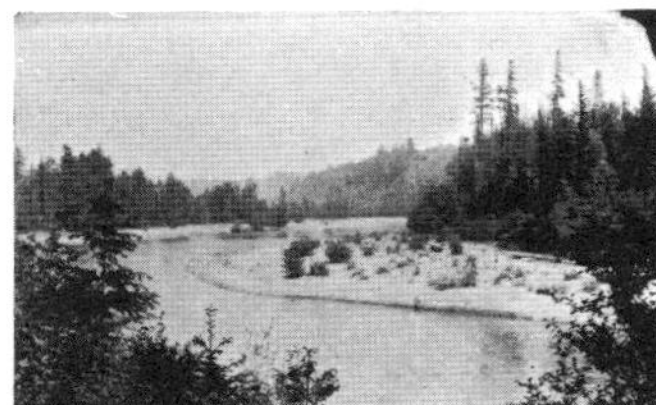
An Oregon Stream S 2462

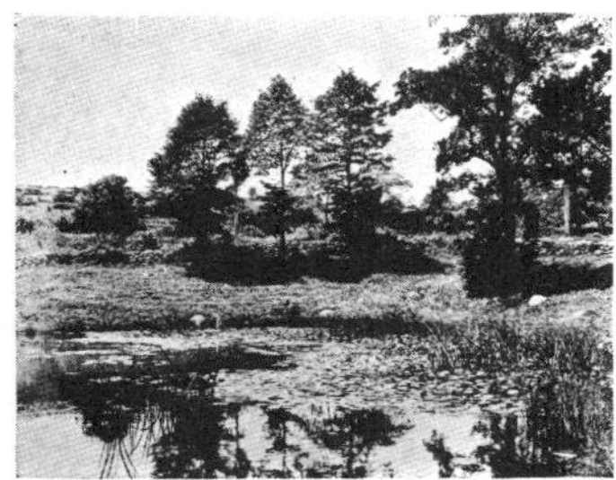
Where Lilies Blow C 1202

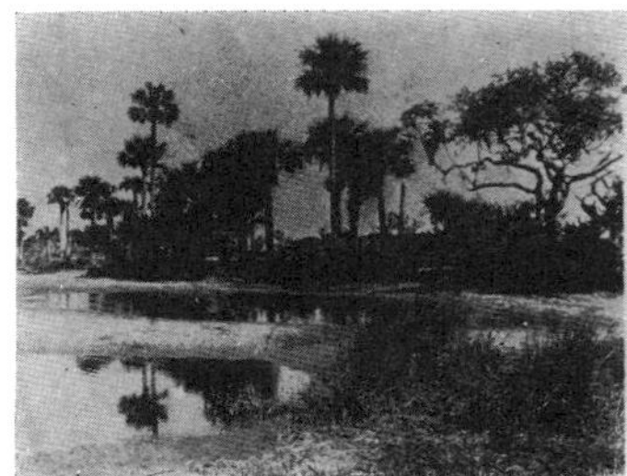
Southern Charm A or C 1125

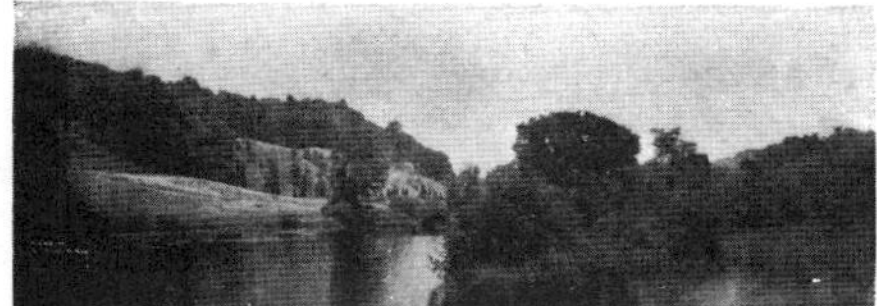
Pomperaug Water O or P 290

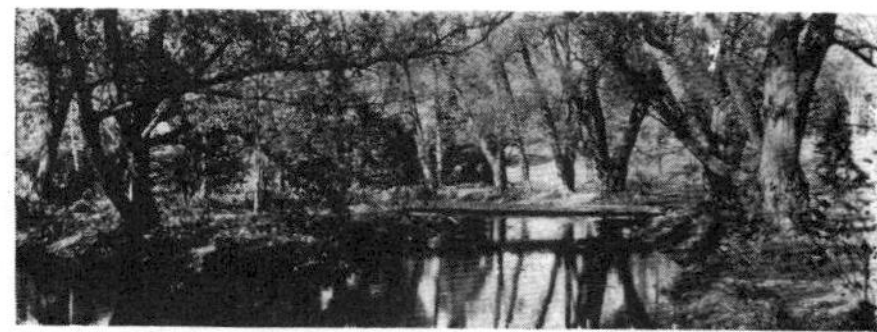
Willow Arcade O 184

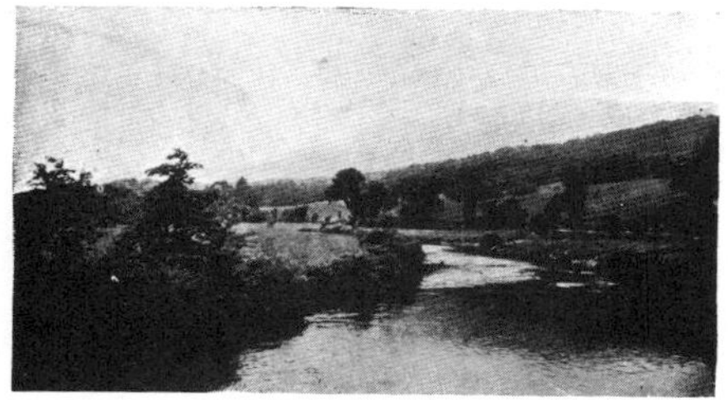
Evening at the River Bend P or E 154

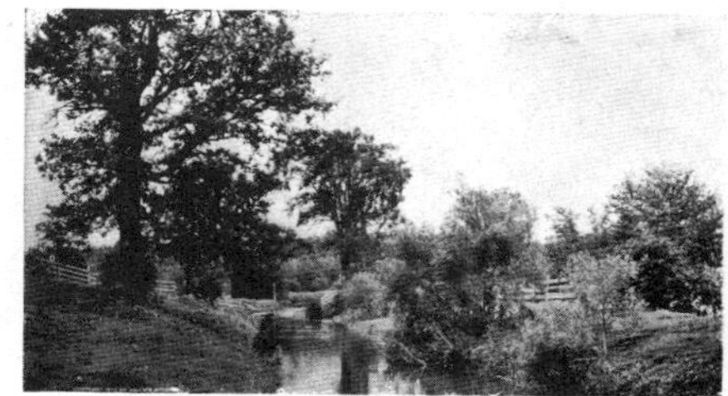
A Pasture Stream P or E 288

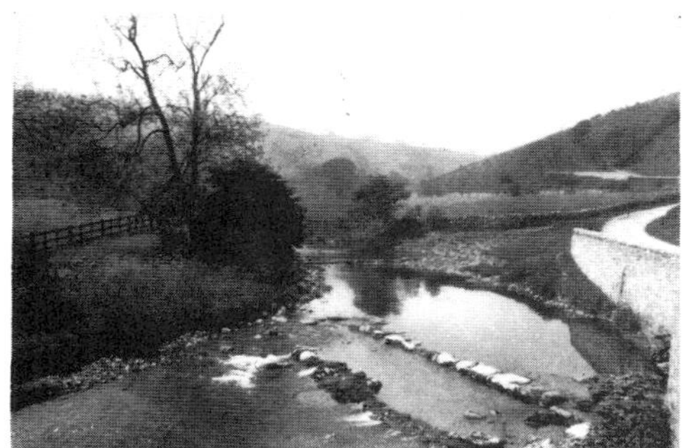
The Foot of the Moorland A, C 5832

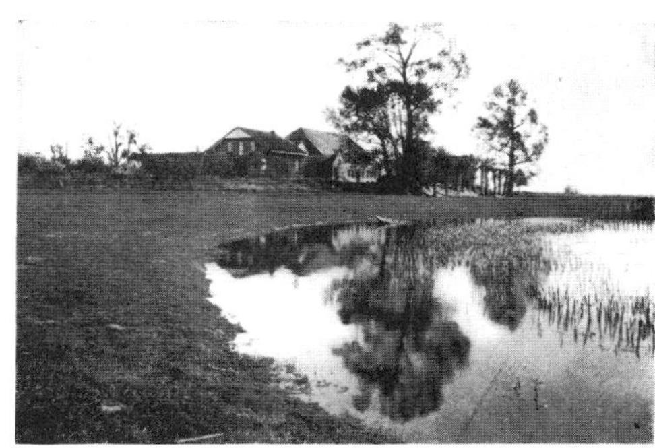
A Little Dutch Cove A, Q, C 5090

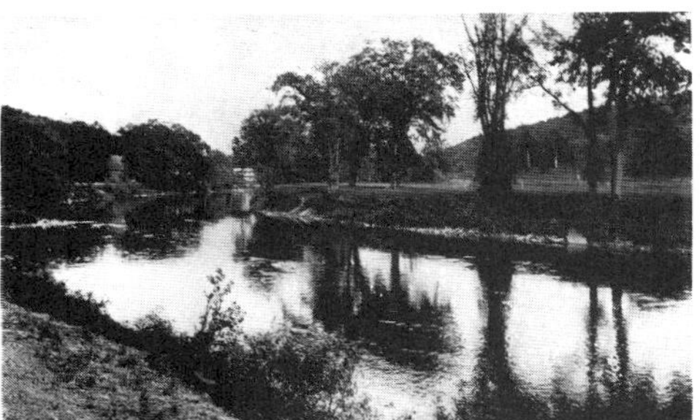
A Vermont River A and S 3551

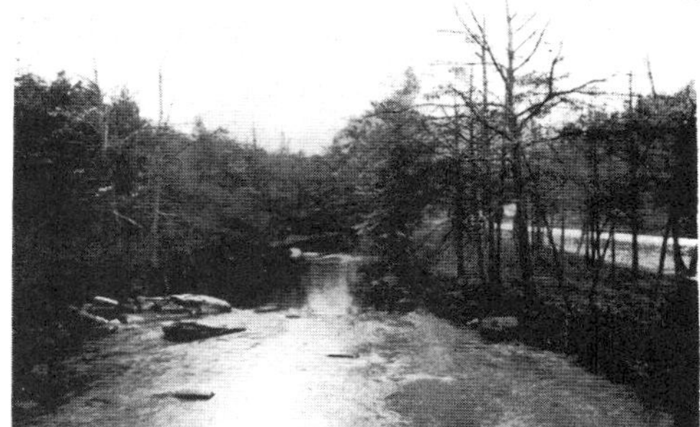
Up the Creek A 3029

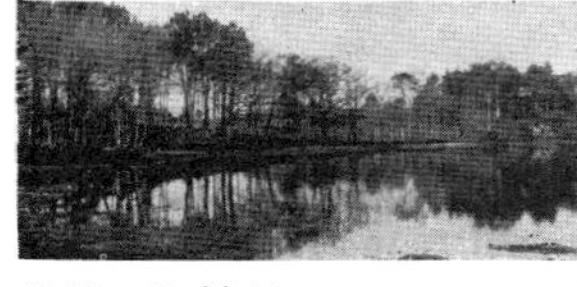
Golden Twilight Q 544

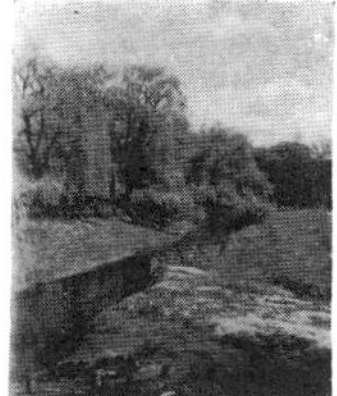
Sleepy Hollow Brook
S or C 273

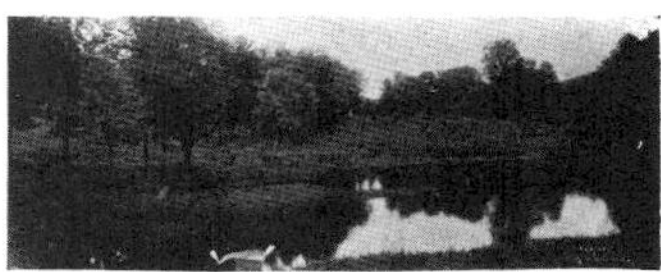
Wilder Pond Q 166

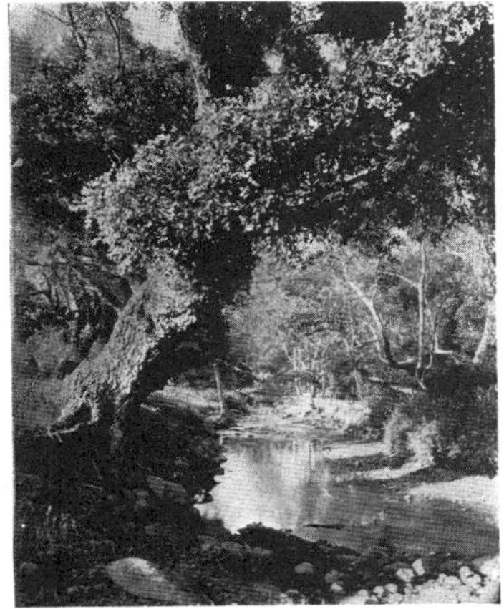
Oak Brook C or F 2442

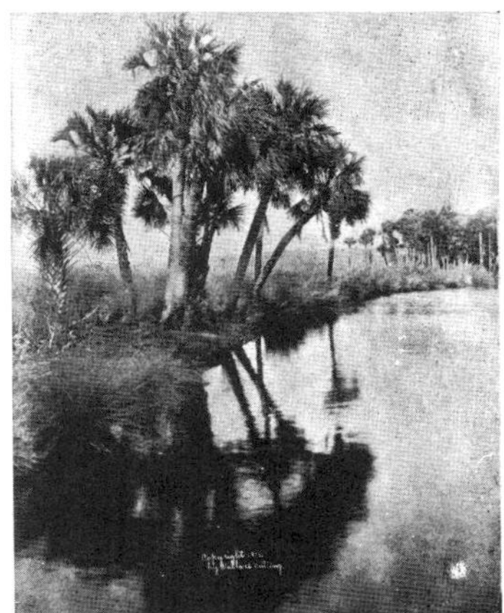
Inclining Palmettos Q, C, P or O 1070

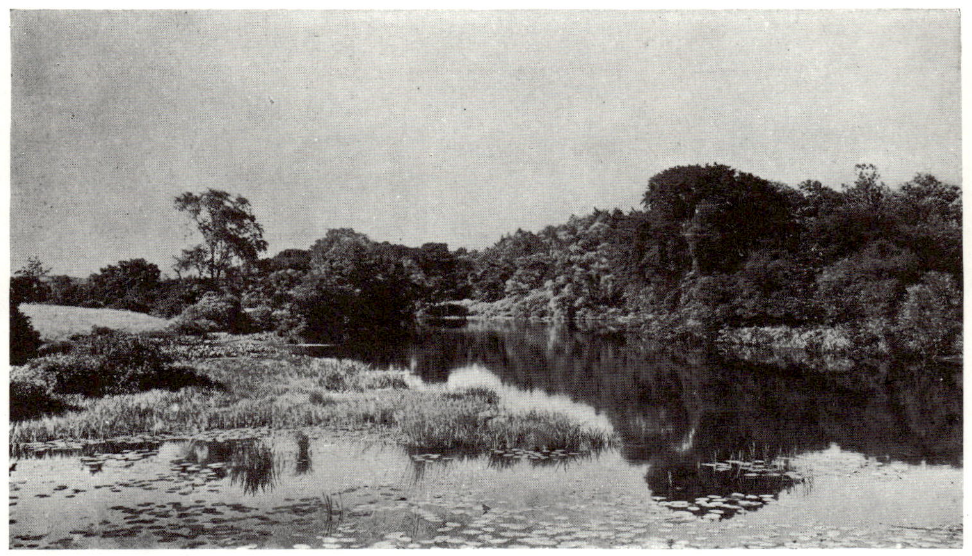

Slack Water S, O, P or W 268 Wallace Nutting
(Also now furnished in T size)

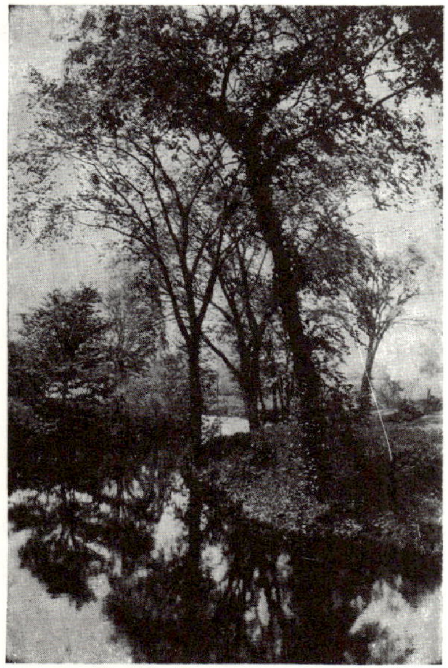

Lingering Waters Wallace Nutting
A, Q, S, C, O, P, E 668

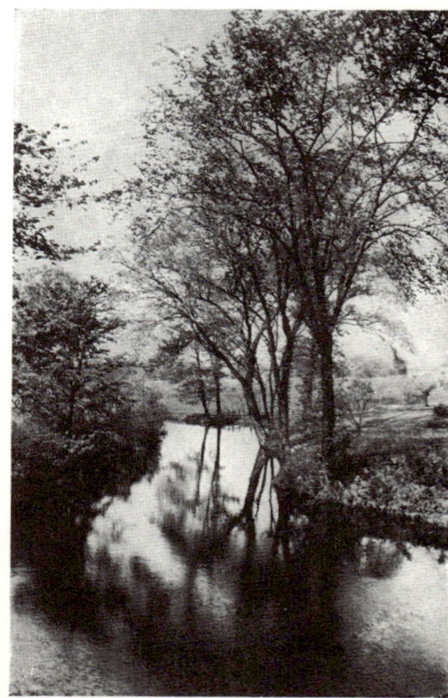

In Tender Leaf Wallace Nutting
A, Q, S, O, P, E, T 667

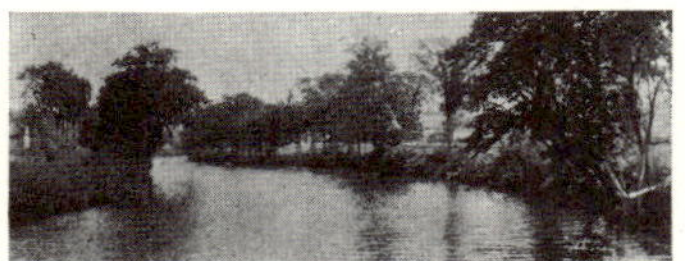

River Curves Q or C 397

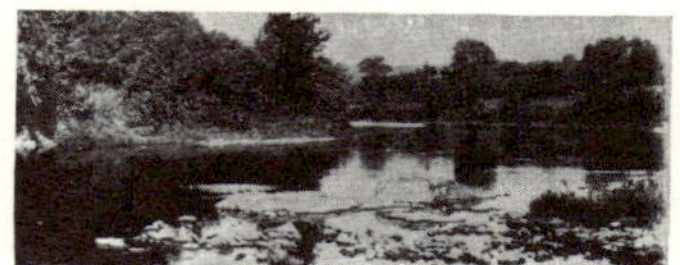

Around the Bend Q 363

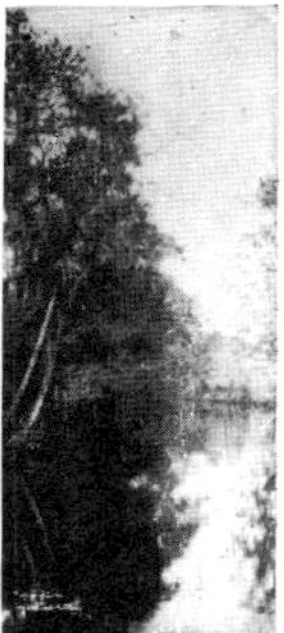

Florida Grace
Q or C 1081

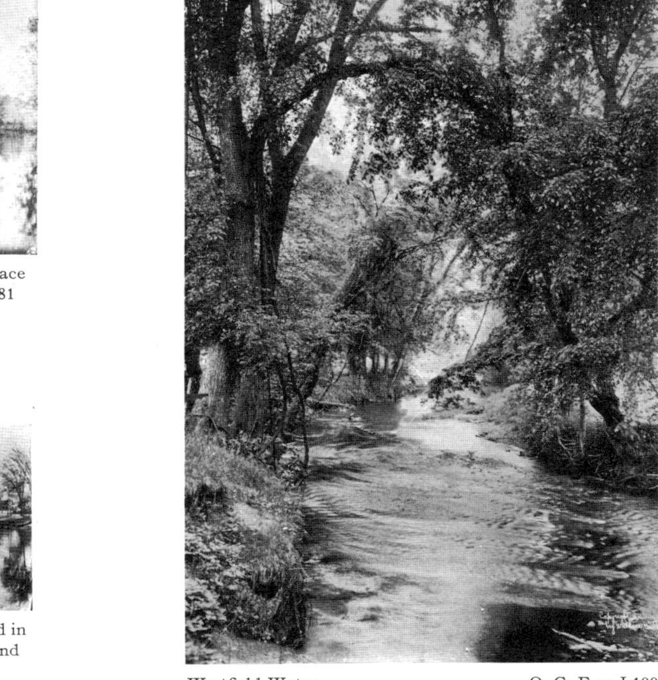

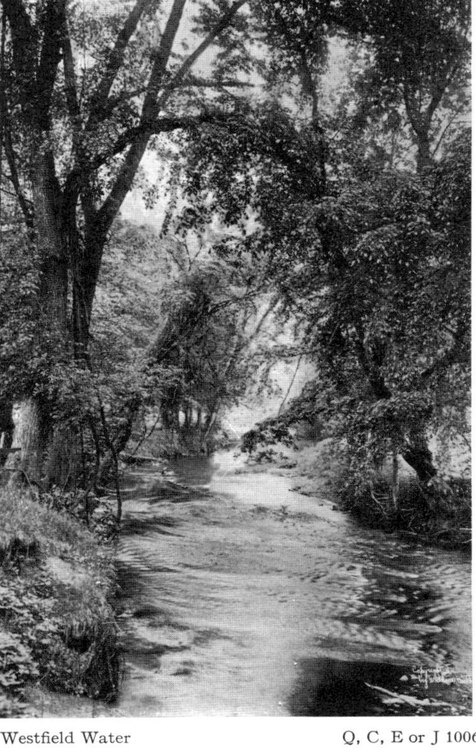

Westfield Water Q, C, E or J 1006

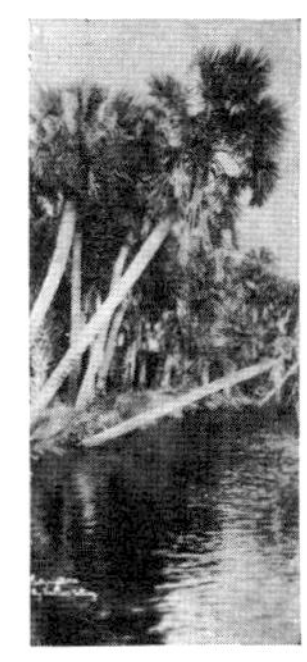

Leaning Palmettos
Q or C 1072

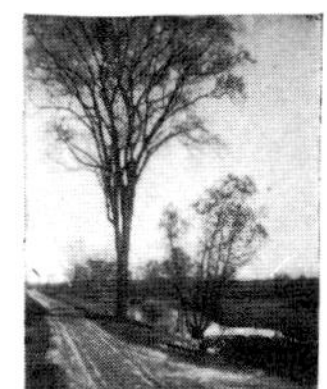

Along Shore
A 2707

Old England in
New England
A 601

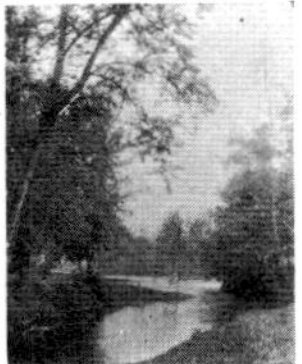

The Shade by
the Brook
A or C 1004

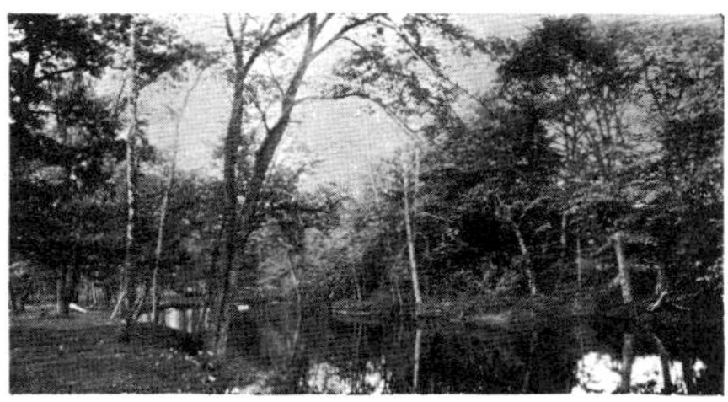

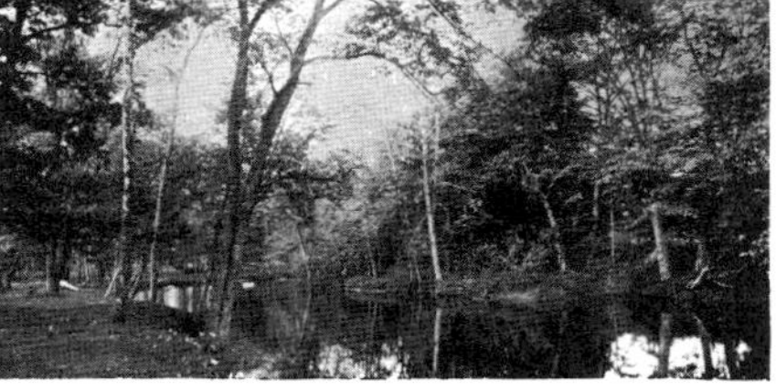

Where the River Waits C or P 1013

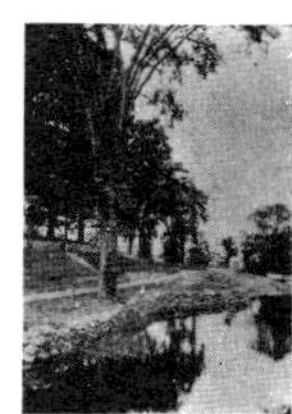

Shore Lights
A 2537

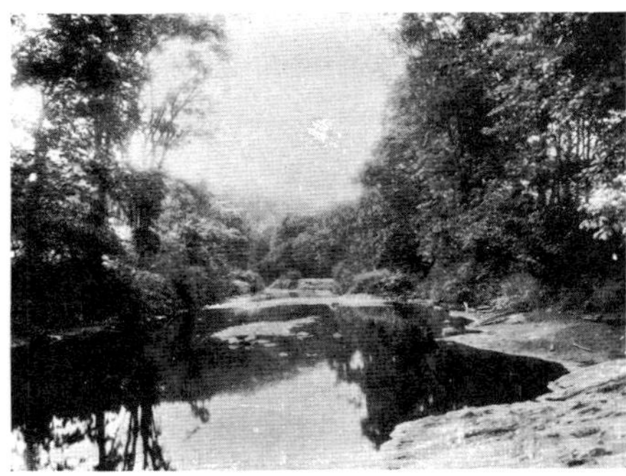

October on the River E 16

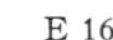

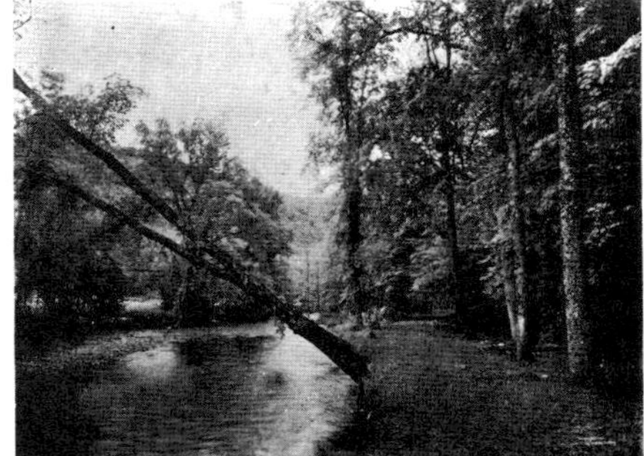

The Manchester Battenkill E 210

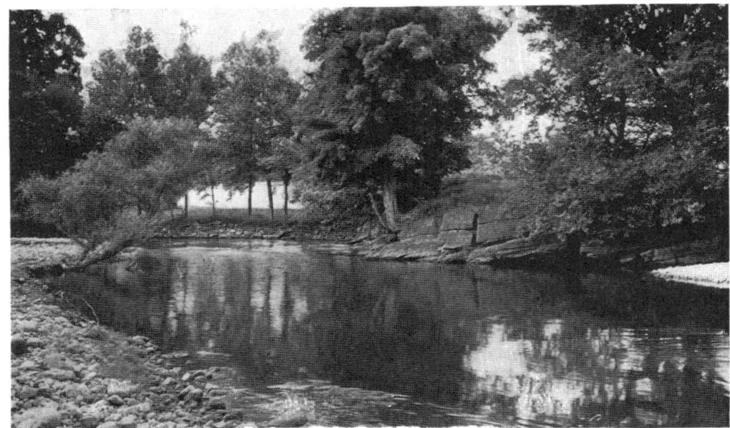

The Swimming Pool Q, S, C, O, P, E, G, H or W 220 Wallace Nutting

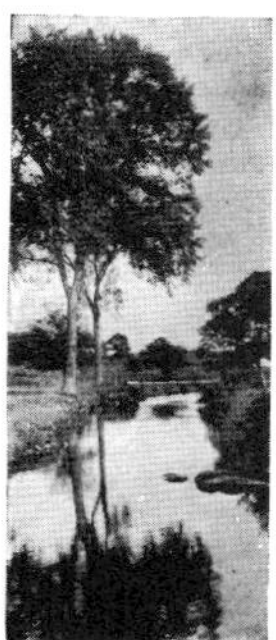

Sunset Fires
Q 2645

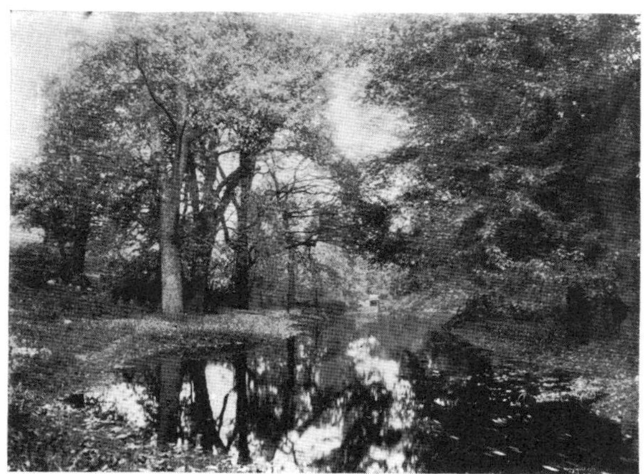

Russet and Gold (Also in C size) E 43

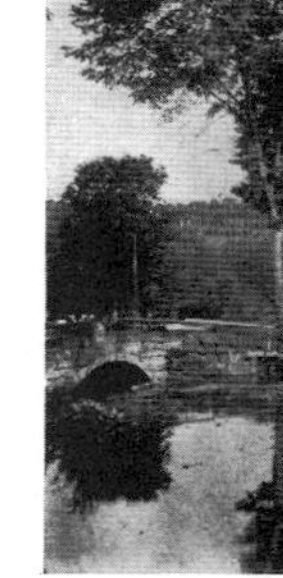

Elm and Bridge
Q or C 540

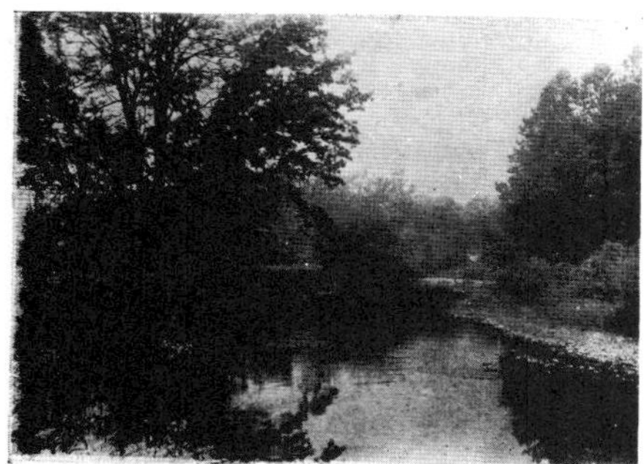

A Favorite Waterside E 342

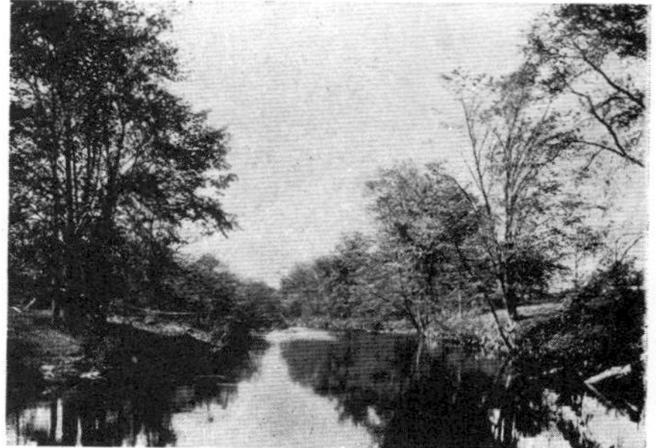

The Unbroken Flow E 228

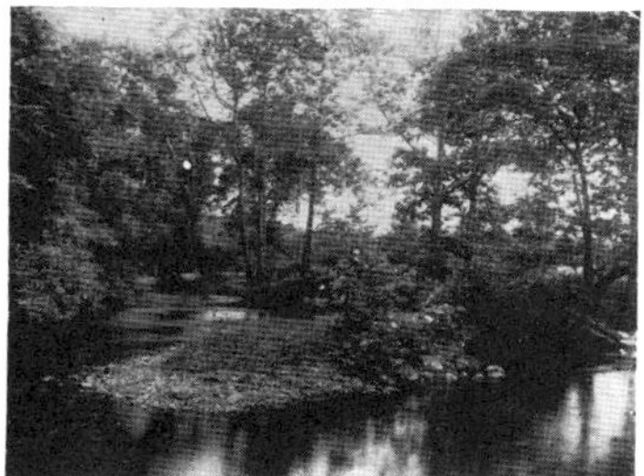
Watersmeet C 481

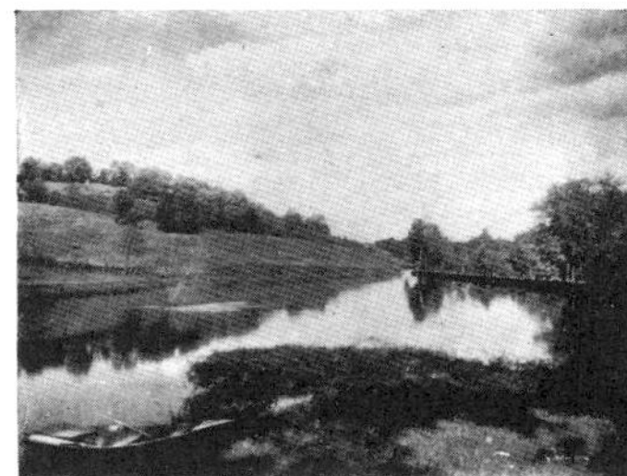
Down the Lake C 176

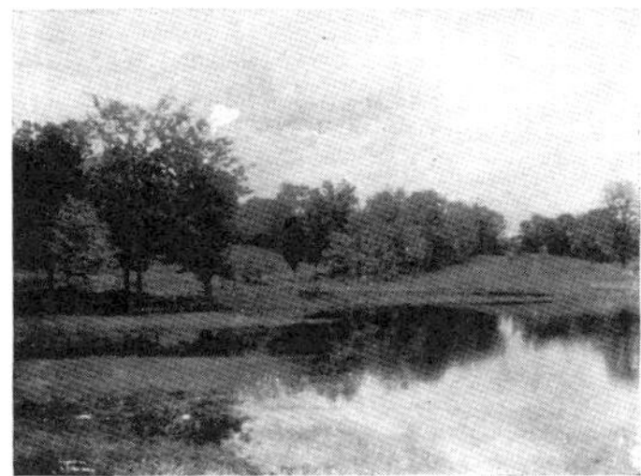
Soft Evening Lights C 153

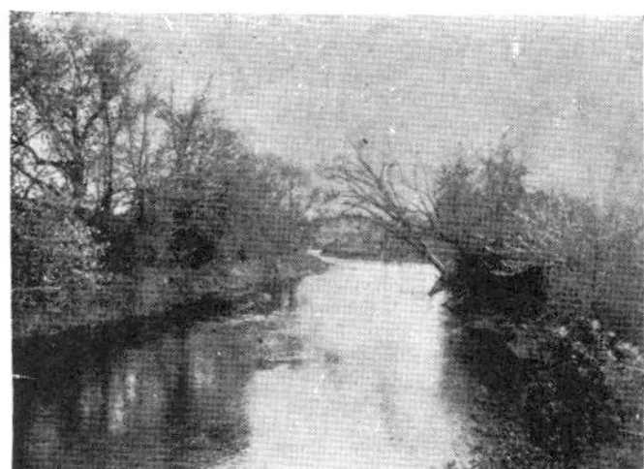
Rippling Into Silence A, Q or C 650

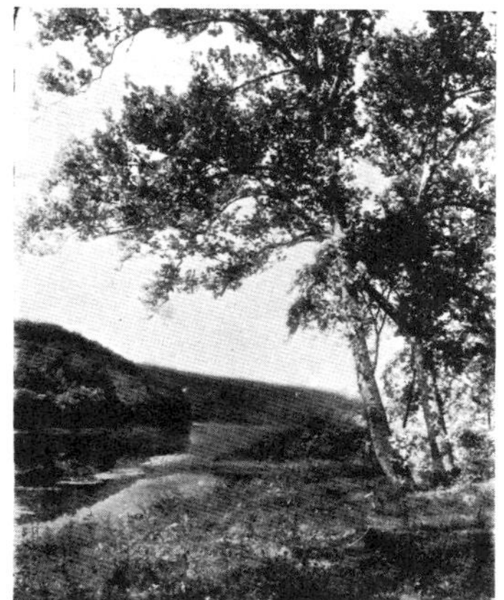
Among Litchfield Hills E 326

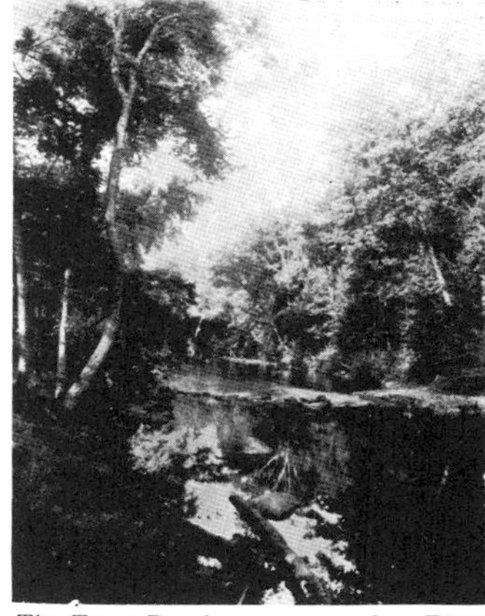
The Trout Brook O or E 219

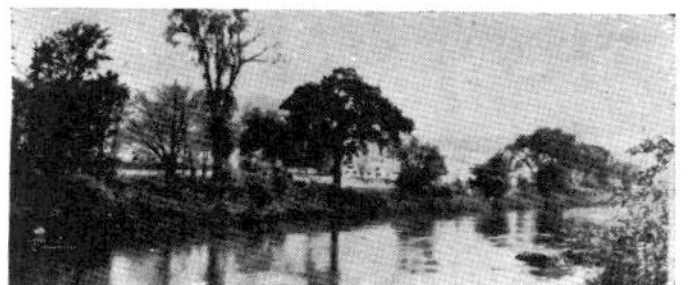
Paradise Valley Q or S 791

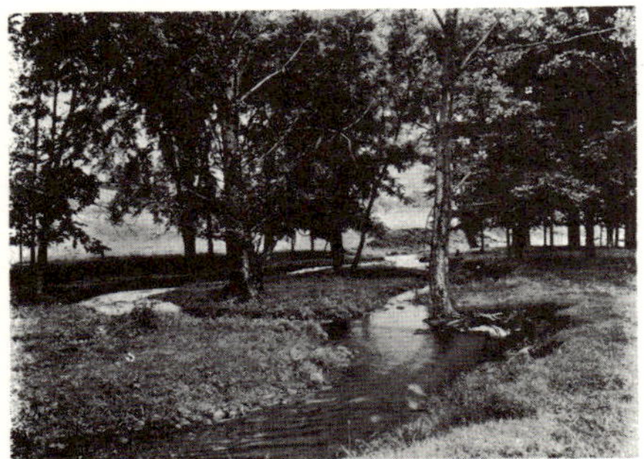
A Brook in Doubt E 253

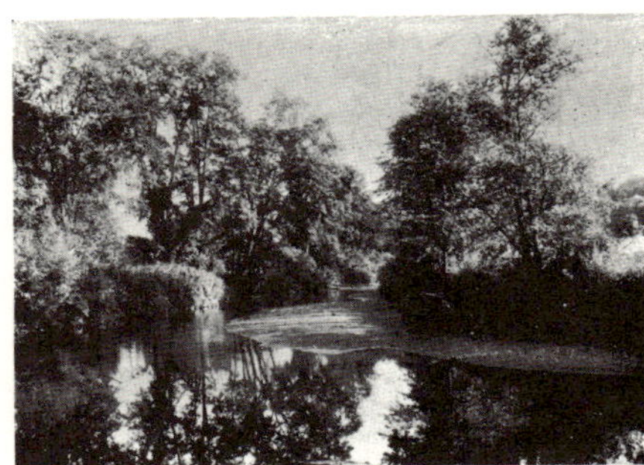
A Summer Stream E 15

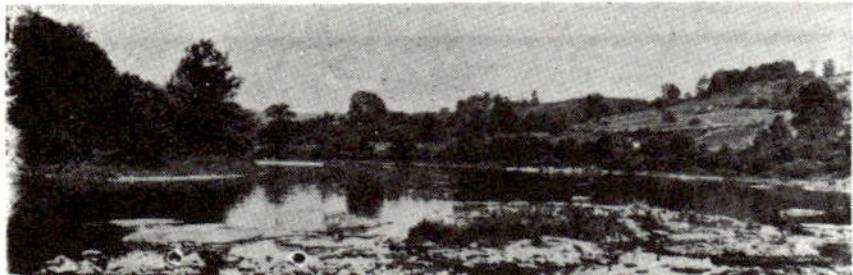
The Broads of the Housatonic O 324

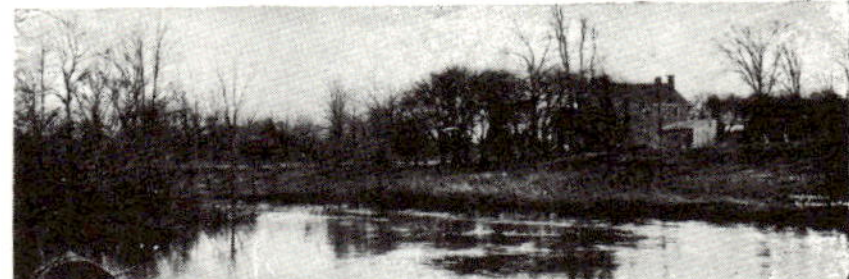
Shore Acres O 168

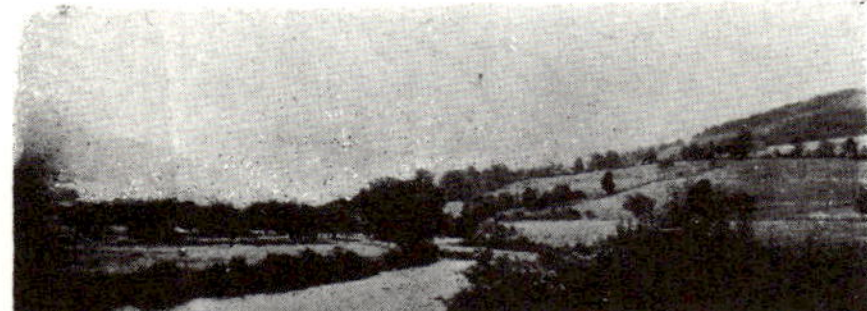
Between Cloud-crested Hills O 2665

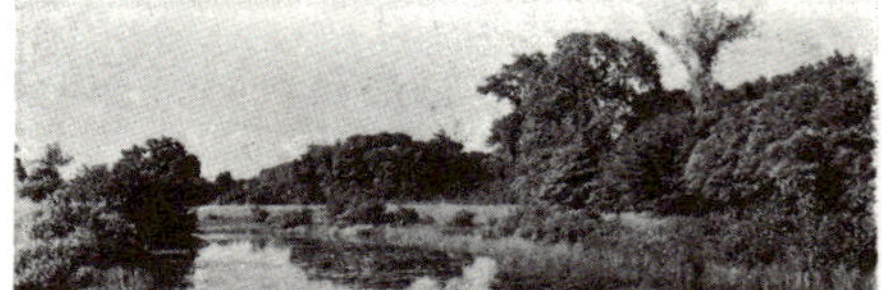
A Hint of September O, P or J 256

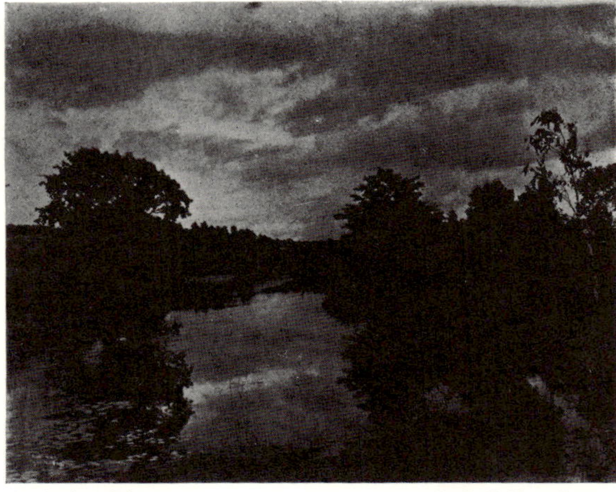
An Artist's River A, Q, C, E or G 2562

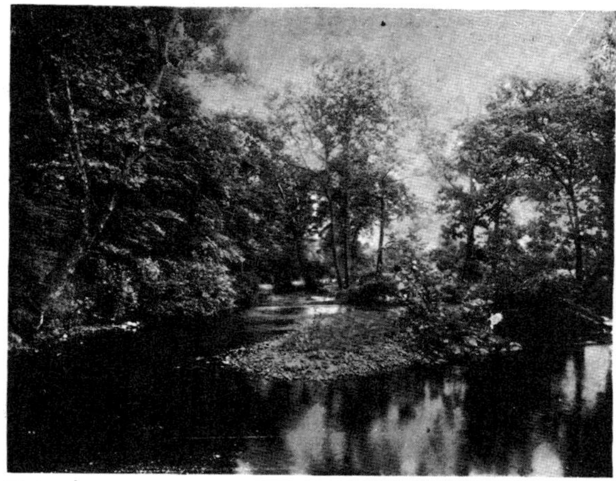

Watersmeet E, F, G 167 Wallace Nutting

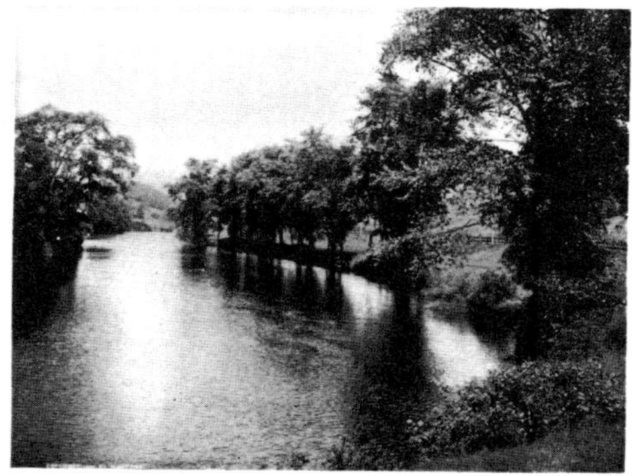

On the Passumpsic C 1838

Water scenes are probably next to blossoms and colonials in order of popularity. In the minds of many buyers they rank above the one or the other of the two last named. "Slack Water" (page 808) has had remarkable popularity in all sizes. The richness and softness of the lights and shadows give it an enduring charm. The two pictures below it are among the most beautiful of water subjects. That at the left has autumn tints and a vine in red running up the leaning tree. The other is in spring coloring, and the lights in the distance are very charming.

"Westfield Water" (page 809), with the picturesque herring-bone effect of the ripples and the perspective reaching into the shadows, is one of the most delightful and restful scenes. "The Swimming Pool" (page 810), with its rich greens of foliage and water, has enjoyed an unslacking popularity for years. "Russet and Gold," just below, with its vivid variety of fall hues, is perhaps the most striking of autumn subjects. More than one have preferred it above all other out-door subjects.

Mr. Nutting's recent European tour made splendid additions to the water subjects. "From the Mountain" (page 801), "The River Meadow" (page 802), "The Foot of the Moorland" (page 807), and "Lorna Doone Brook" (page 814), are among the most delightful of these. "On the Teith" (page 802) is a charming combination of water and pastoral subjects, — a beautiful Scotch river, with sheep feeding along the hills.

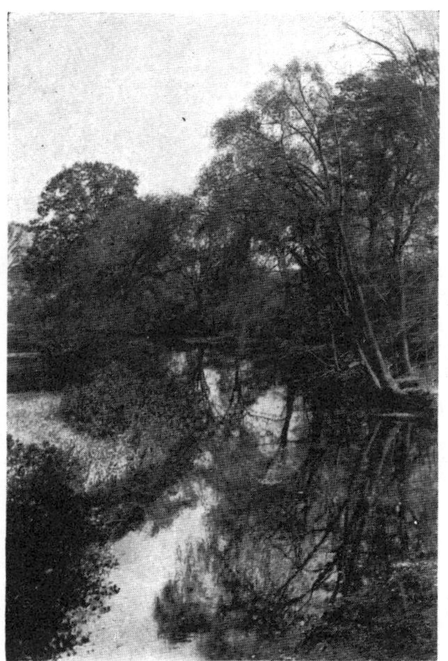

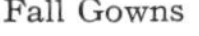
Fall Gowns C, S 3648

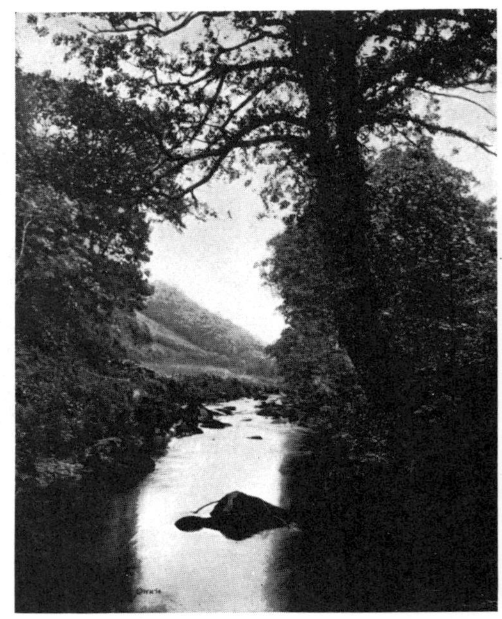

Lorna Doone Brook A, C, E 5658

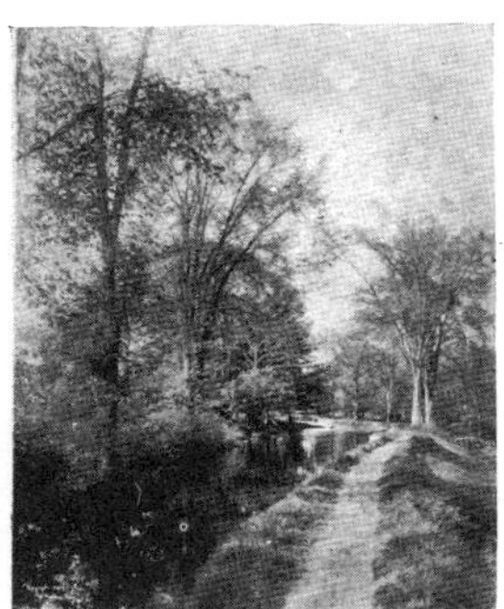

A Berkshire Water Way C 718

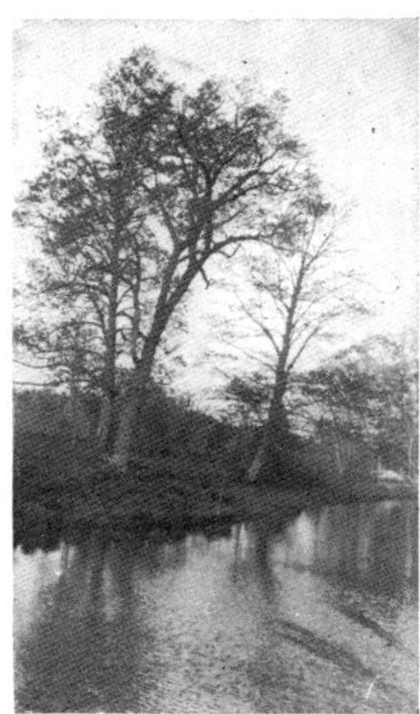

Broken Lights S or P 286

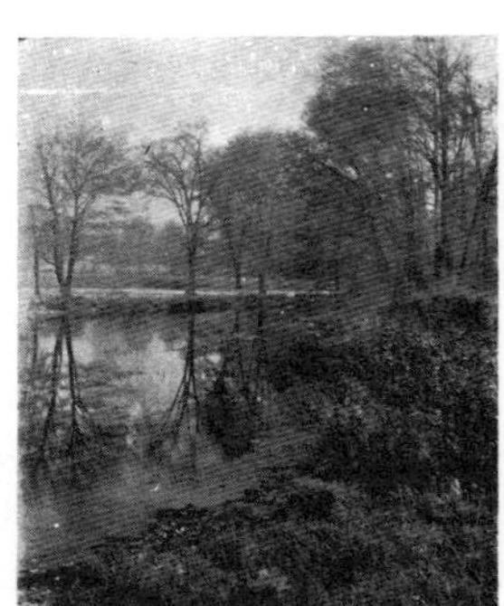

Mid-May C 272

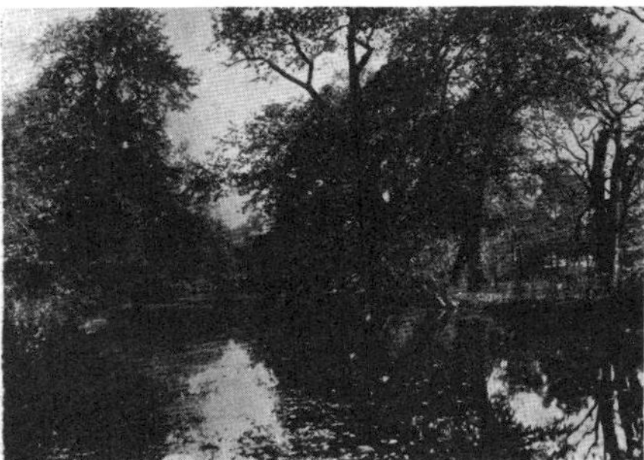

Water Maples C, E or J 50

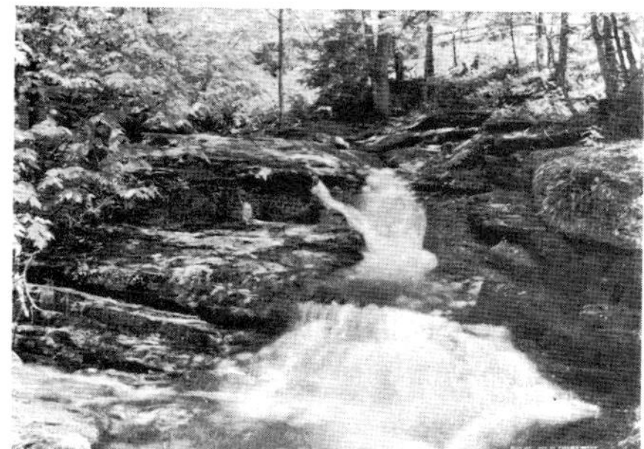

A Mossy Stair E 207

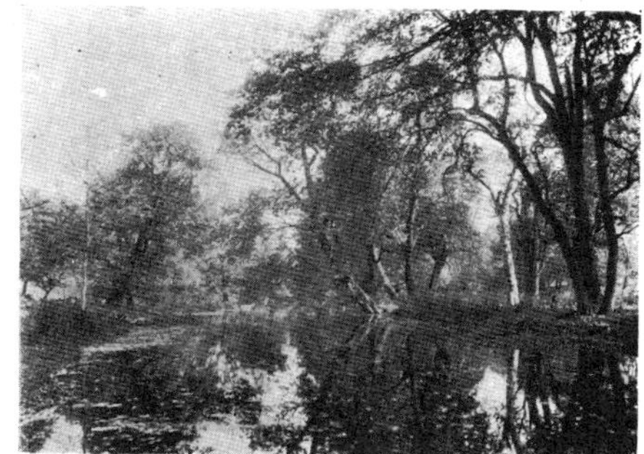

On the Pequest River E 48

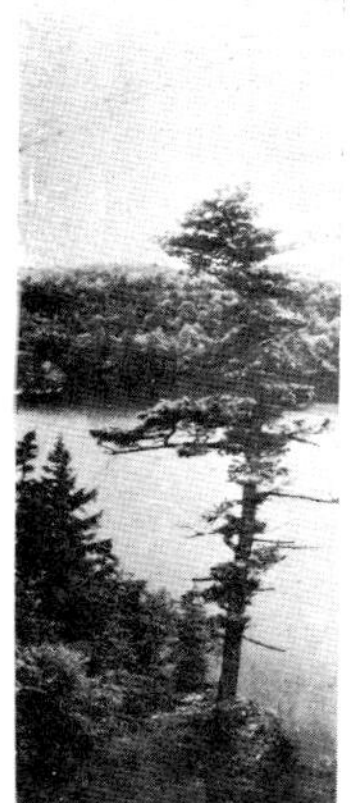

Purity O 81

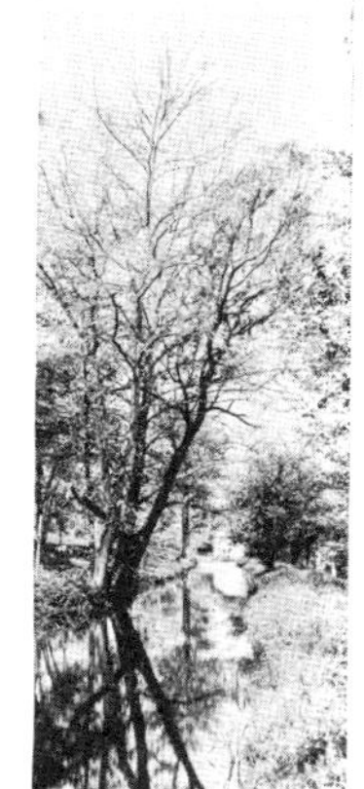

Above the Mill
O 2698

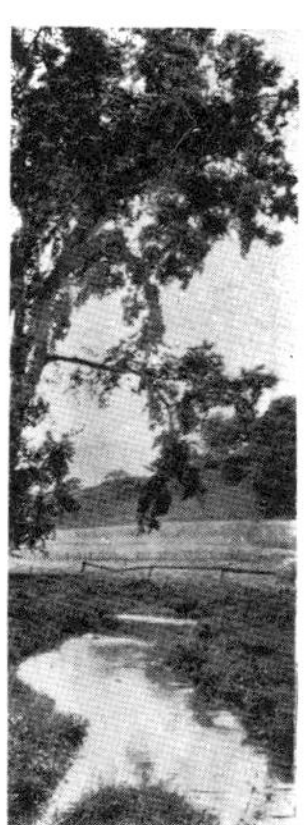

Elm Brook
Q or O 2575

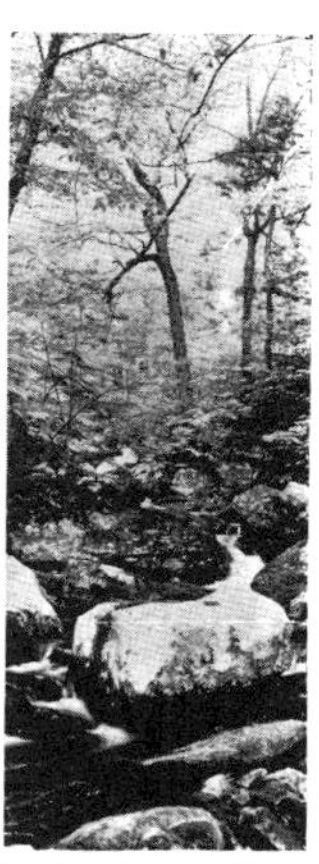

Lichen in the Glen
O, P or E 200

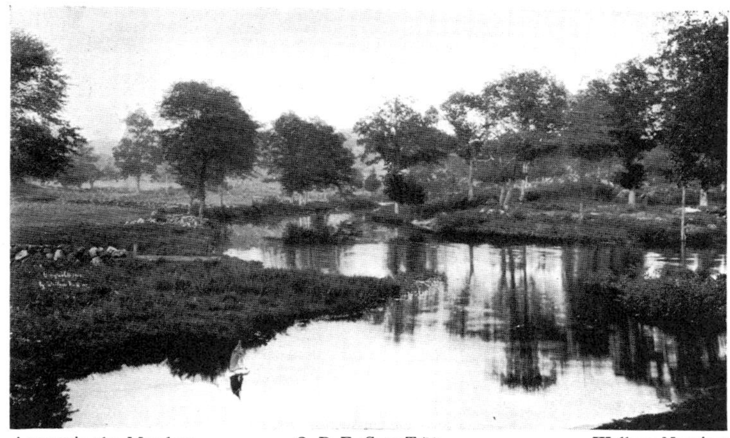

August in the Meadow O, P, E, G or T 70 Wallace Nutting

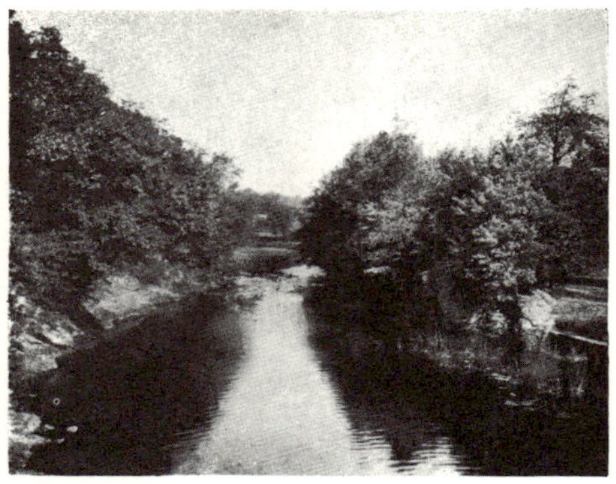

A Newton October C 1702 Wallace Nutting

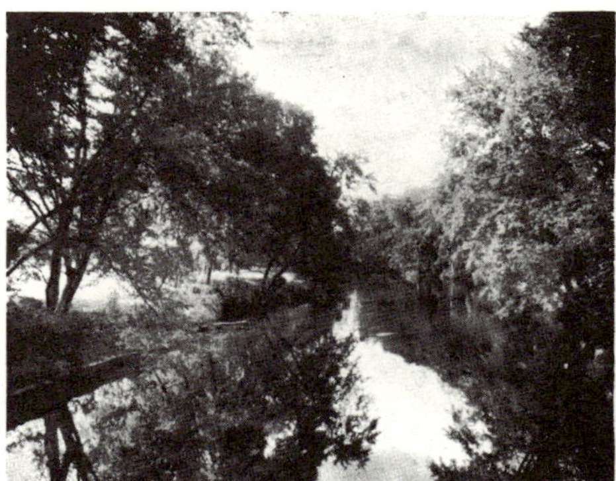

The Nashua Asleep C 1516 Wallace Nutting

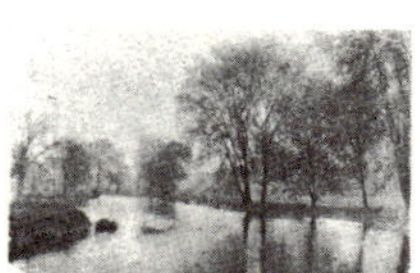

Full Stream A 881

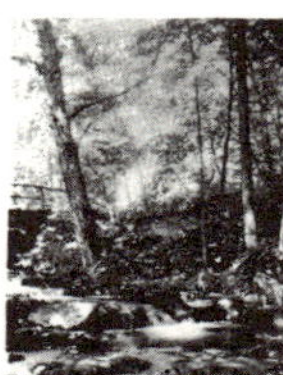

A Highland Brae
A 910

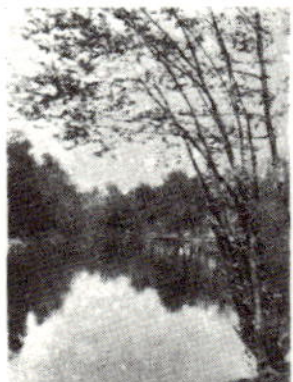

The Golden West
A 147

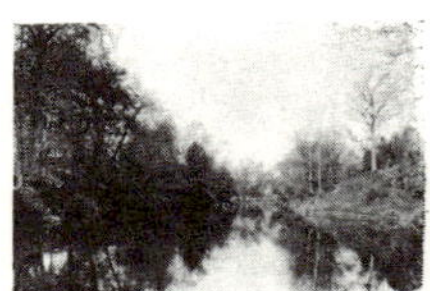

The Witching Hour
A 1175

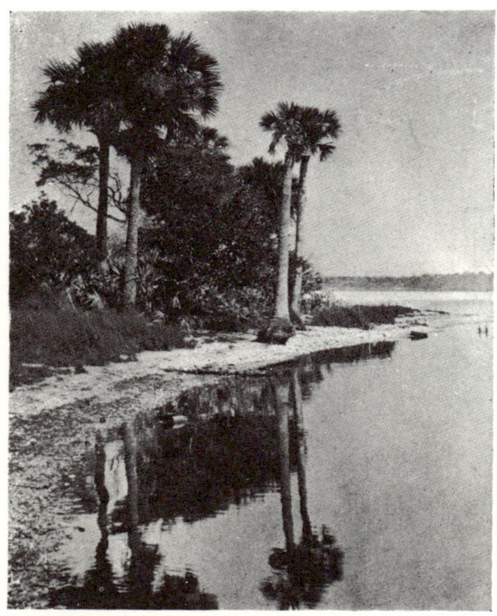

Undulating Reflections A, Q, C, O, P or E 2016

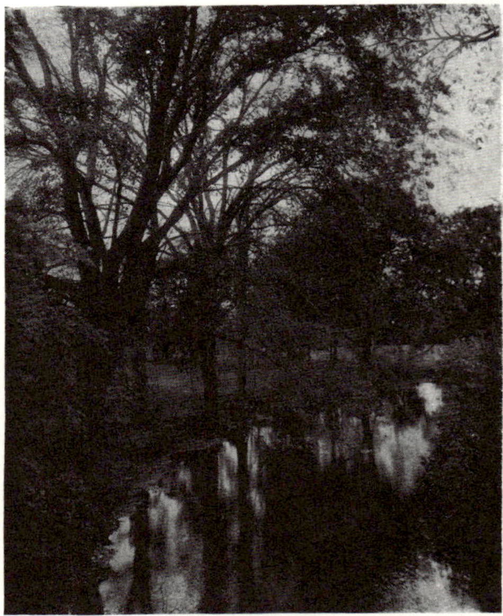

The Sudbury in October Wallace Nutting
C and E 1710

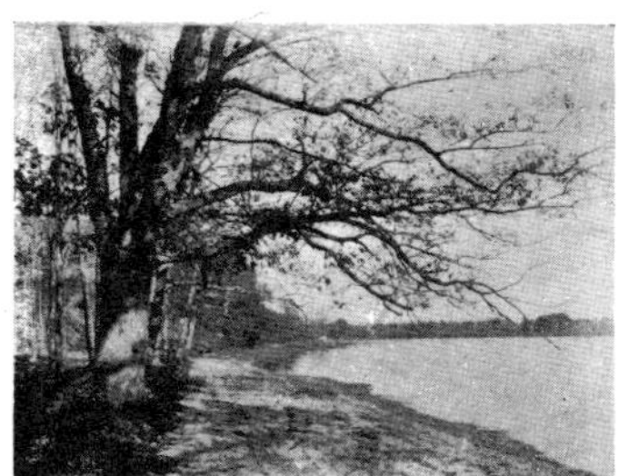

A Lake Shore Oak A or C 549

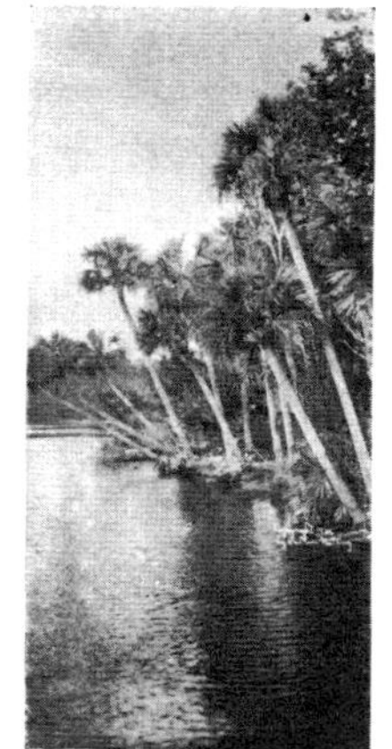

Sunset Palmettos
Q, C, P or E 1084

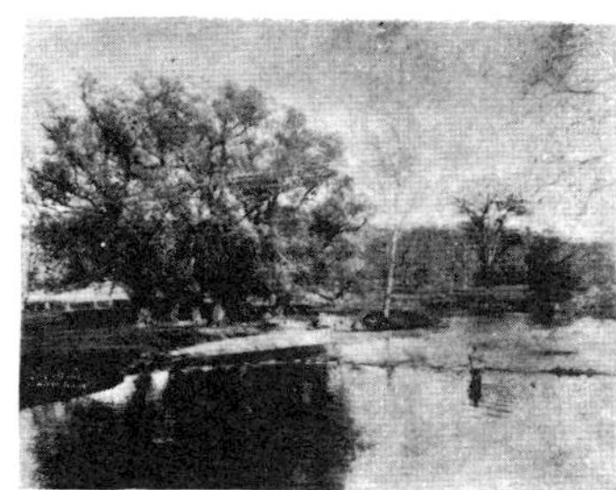

Spring Fishing A, Q or C 926

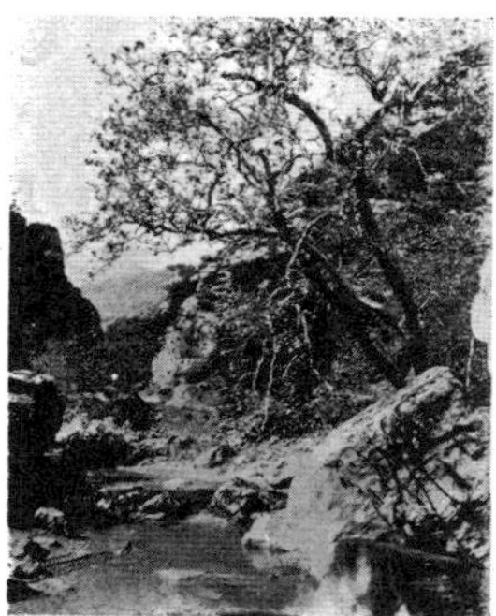

The Pass C 2261

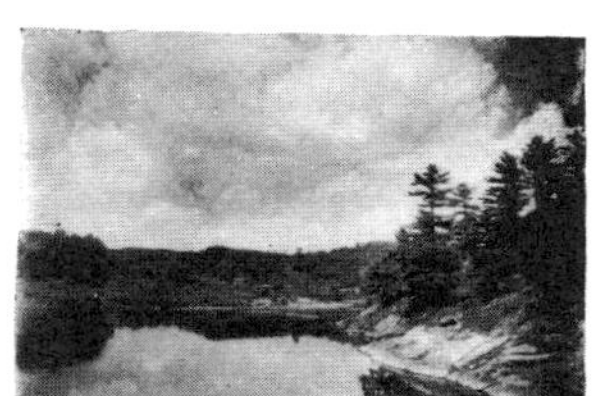

Clouds Over the Housatonic
E 337

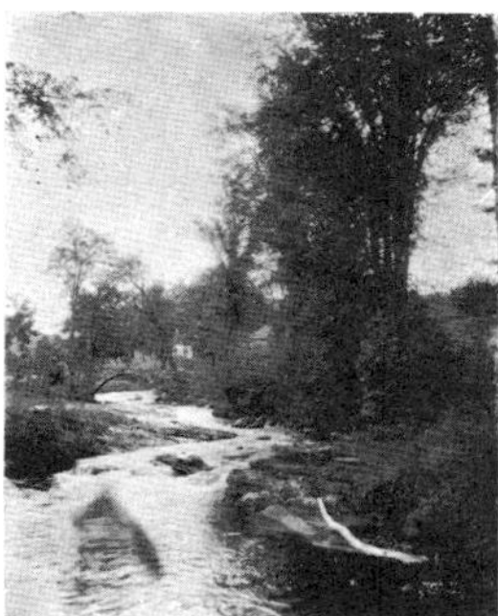

A Woodstock Arch C 151

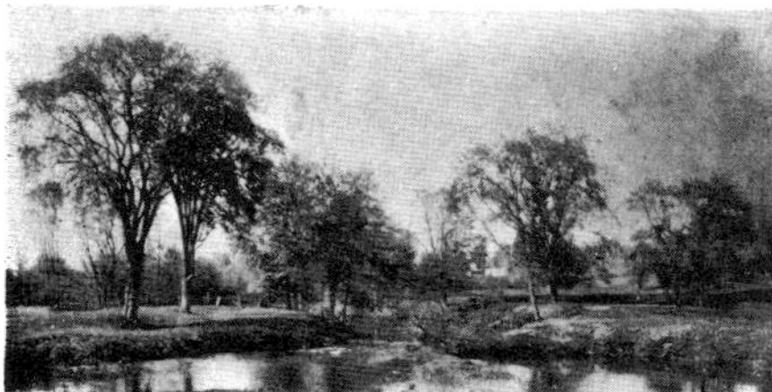

Where Streams Converge P 121

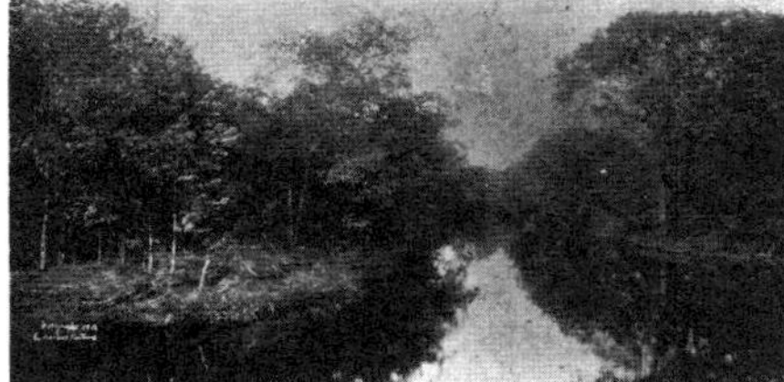

Early Summer P 186

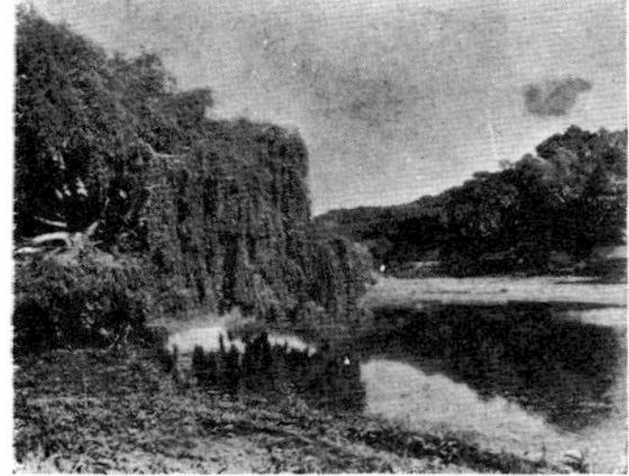

A Mystery Pool C 2316

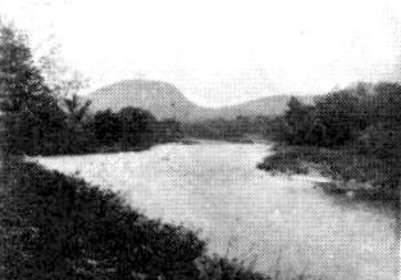

Tekoa Q, S or C 1008

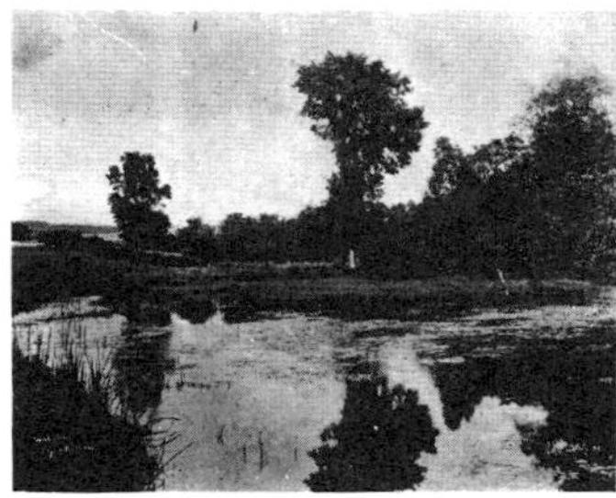

A Poet's Brook C 2553

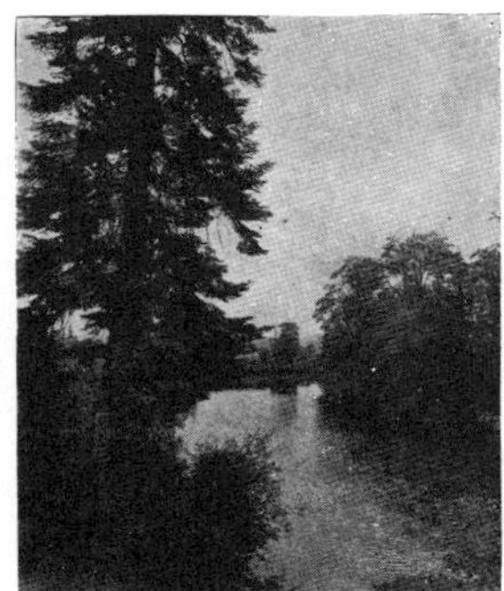

A Western Creek C 2461

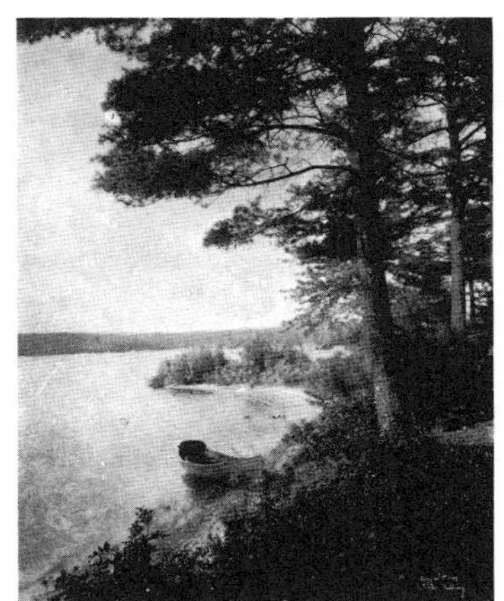

Pine Landing A, Q, C or E 437

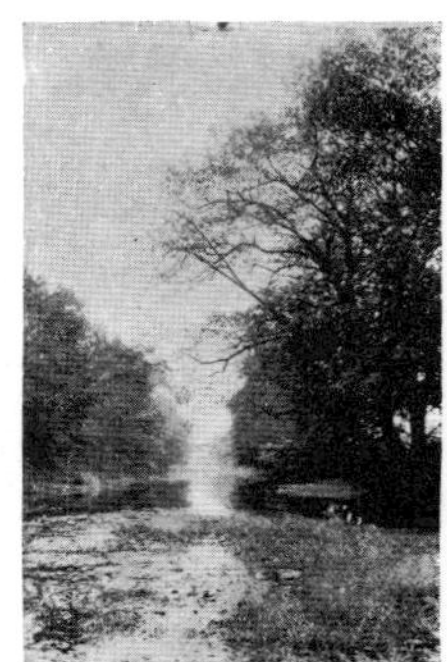

A Look Ahead S 447

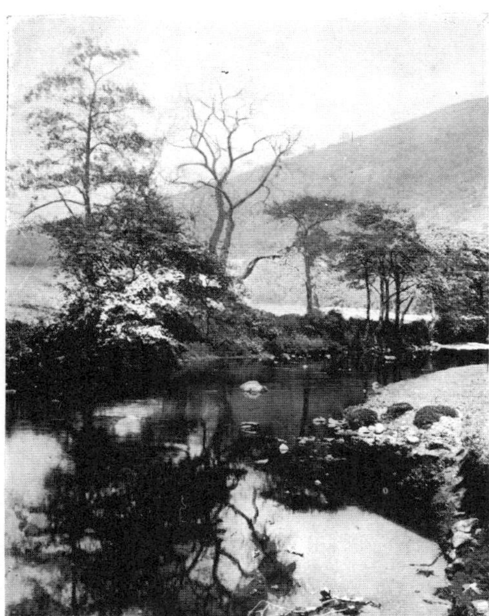

A Mountain Beck C 5805

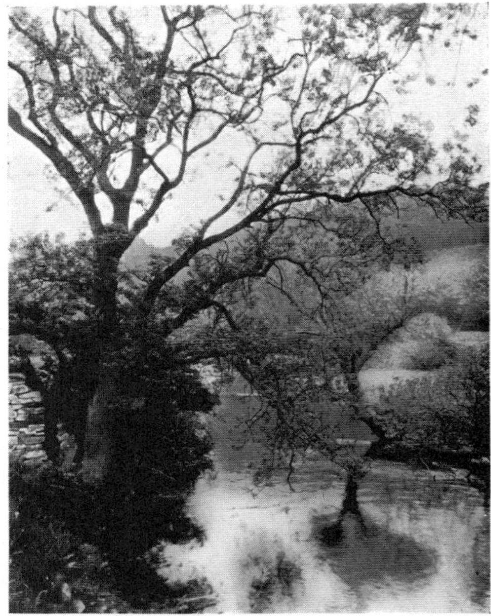

The Play of Branches C 5806

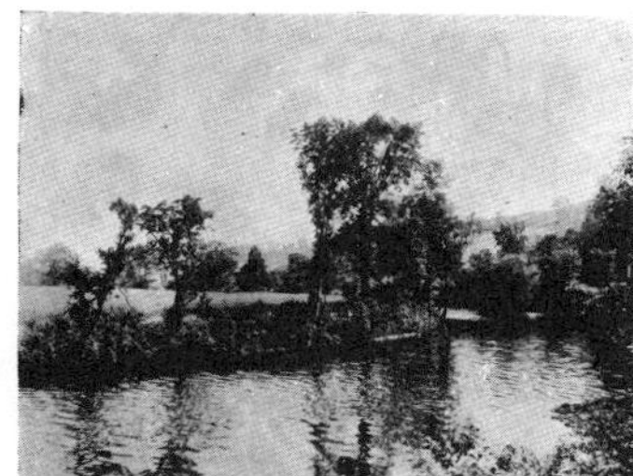

A Passumpsic Curve C 2670

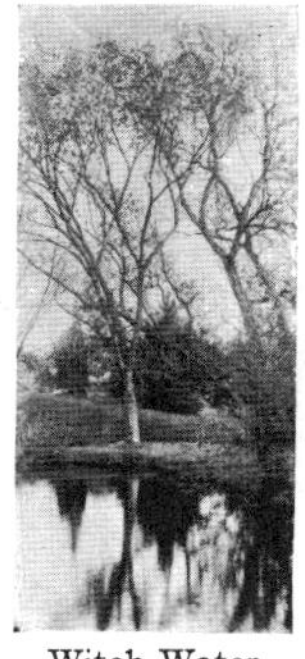

Witch Water
Q 282

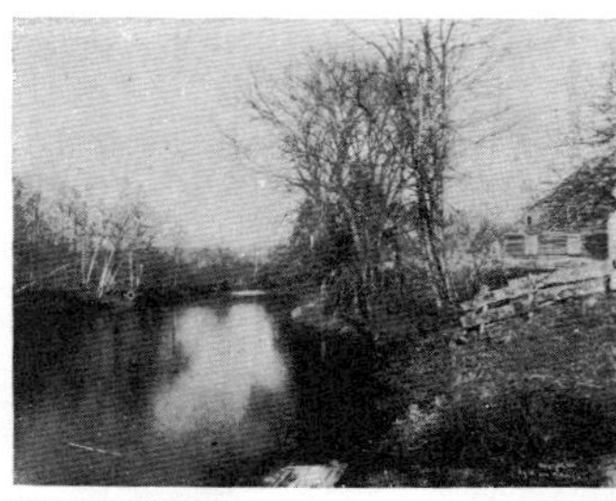

Winslow Water C 946

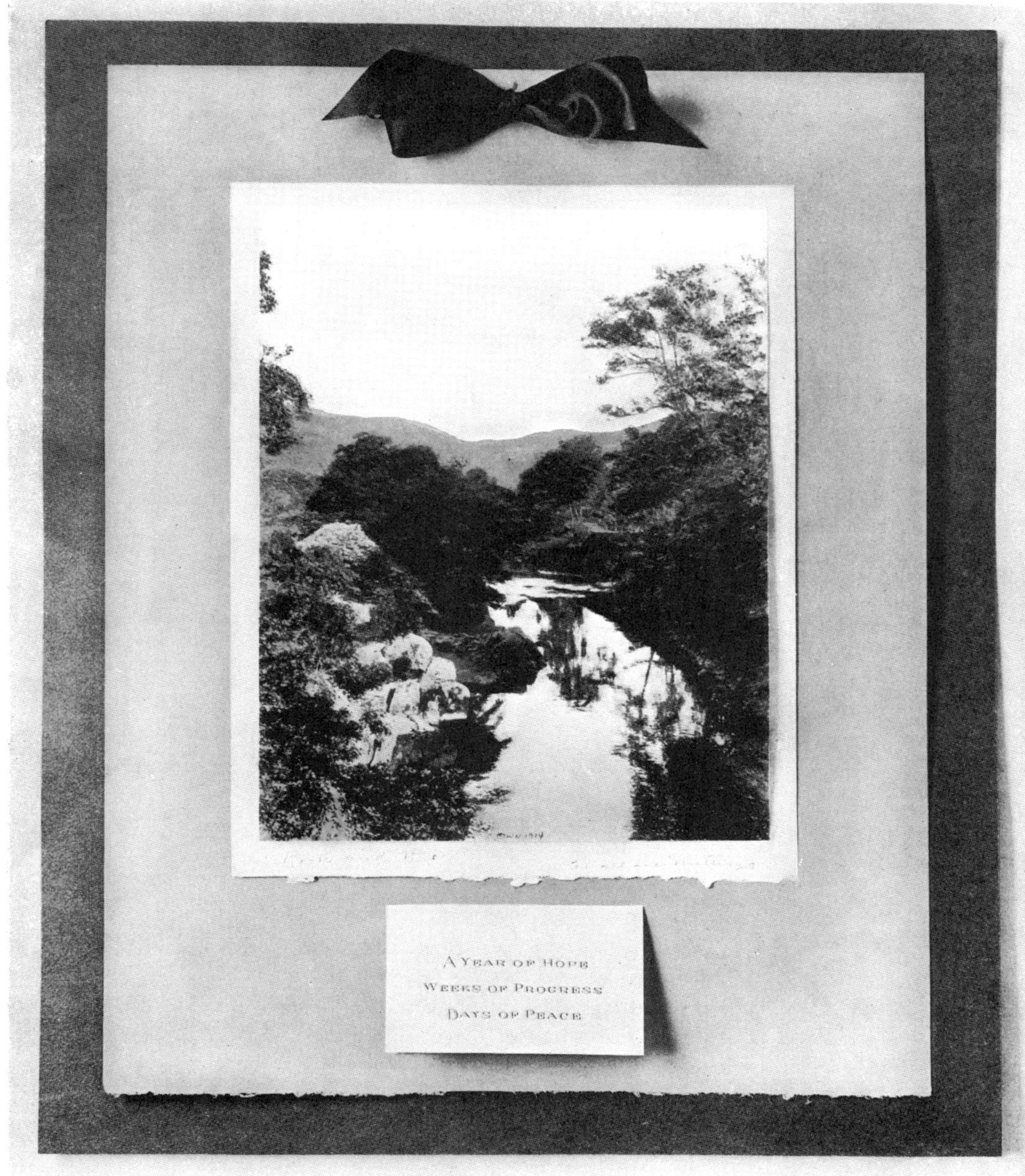

Style 487

CALENDARS

Any of our pictures can be placed on calendars to order. We add the price of making up the calendar to the price of the picture, thus a print like the above in the C size which retails at $2.50 is prepared to retail for $2.75 as a calendar. On the pages following will be found a few samples of styles illustrated, with various other styles described but not illustrated.

Style 487 (Previous page.)

Outside mounting, 14 x 17.
Any vertical picture, 8 x 10.
Base, brown.
Top, amber.
Picture overlay, cream; ribbon, brown.
Price per dozen of 13, $33.00; each, $2.75.
(Same price for all on this page.)

Style 485

Outside mounting, 14 x 17.
Any vertical picture, 8 x 10.
Base, white; overlay, green; top, white.
Picture plate marked; ribbon, green.
Sentiment pad:

"*May life flow like a river,*
With enough stones to make music
And enough depth to bear treasure
Of Friendship and Happiness."

Style 483

Outside mounting, 14 x 17.
Any horizontal picture, 8 x 10.
Base, white.
Picture plate marked; ribbon white.
Pad engraved:

" *When good friends meet the hours are fleet,*
Till then slow rolls time's cumbrous car
Whose dial is the calendar."

Style 489

Outside mounting, 14 x 17.
Any vertical picture, 8 x 10, in plate mark.
Base, white with India basket picture lining.
White cord; pad:

" *When good friends meet.*" (See style above.)

Style 488

Outside mounting, 14 x 17.
Any horizontal picture, 8 x 10, preferably autumnal, in plate mark.
Base, amber.
Top, cream; ribbon, brown.
Sentiment:

" *The soft south wind, the flowers amid the grass,*
The fragrant earth, the sweet sounds everywhere,
Seem gifts too great almost for man to bear."

William Morris.

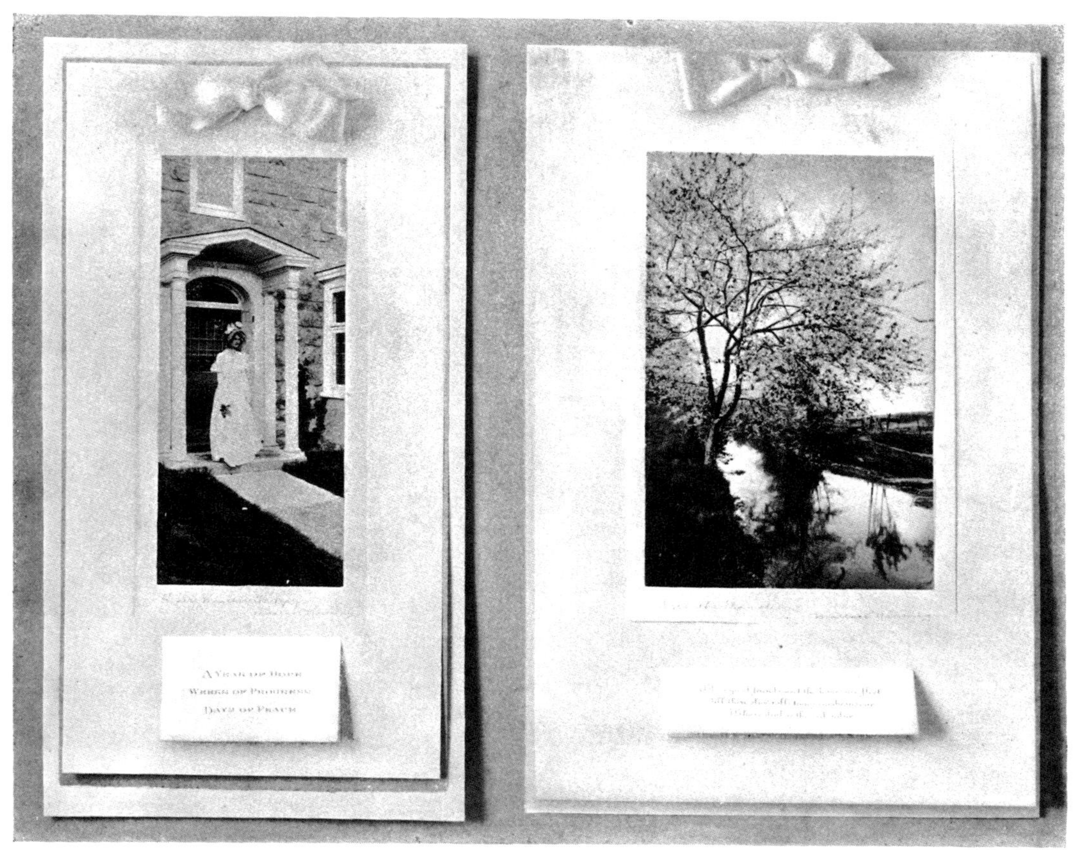

Style 466-Q picture

Style 478-S picture

Style 466

Outside mounting, 9 x 17.
Any picture, 4 x 10.
Base, white.
Overlay, gray.
Top, white.
Ribbon, white.
Price per dozen of 13, $20.00; $1.75 each.

Style 478

Outside mounting, 11 x 17.
Any picture, 6 x 10.
Base, white
Overlay, white.
Top, white.
Ribbon, pink.
Price per dozen of 13, $25.00; $2.25 each.

Style 461

Same as Style 466, except blue overlay and "Calendar 1916" pad.

Style 462

Same mounting as Style 466, with buff overlay.

Style 463

Outside mounting, 9 x 17.
Any vertical picture, 4 x 10.
Base, mottled blue; overlay, light blue.
Top, white; ribbon, light blue.
Engraved on pad:

"A Smiling Spring,
Happy Summer, Fruitful Autumn,
And Winter of Content."

Price per dozen of 13, $20.00; each, $1.75.

Style 469

Same mounting as Style 461, with green overlay, and small size pad.

Style 465

Same mounting as Style 466, except sentiment:

"A Smiling Spring,
Happy Summer, Fruitful Autumn,
And Winter of Content."

Engraved on pad; ribbon pink.

Style 476

Outside mounting, 11 x 17.
Any vertical picture, 6 x 10.
Base, gray.
Top, white; ribbon, pink.
Sentiment on pad:

" When good friends meet the hours are fleet.
Till then slow rolls time's cumbrous car
Whose dial is the calendar."

Price per dozen of 13, $25.00; each, $2.25.

Style 472

Outside mounting, 11 x 17.
Any vertical picture, 6 x 10.
Base, brown.
Top, cream.
Picture lining, cream; ribbon, yellow.
Sentiment engraved on pad:

"A Smiling Spring,
Happy Summer, Fruitful Autumn,
And Winter of Content."

Price per dozen of 13, $20.00; each, $1.75.

Style 473

Same mounting as Style 478, except sentiment pad engraved:

" May life flow like a river,
With enough stones to make music
And enough depth to bear treasure
Of Friendship and Happiness."

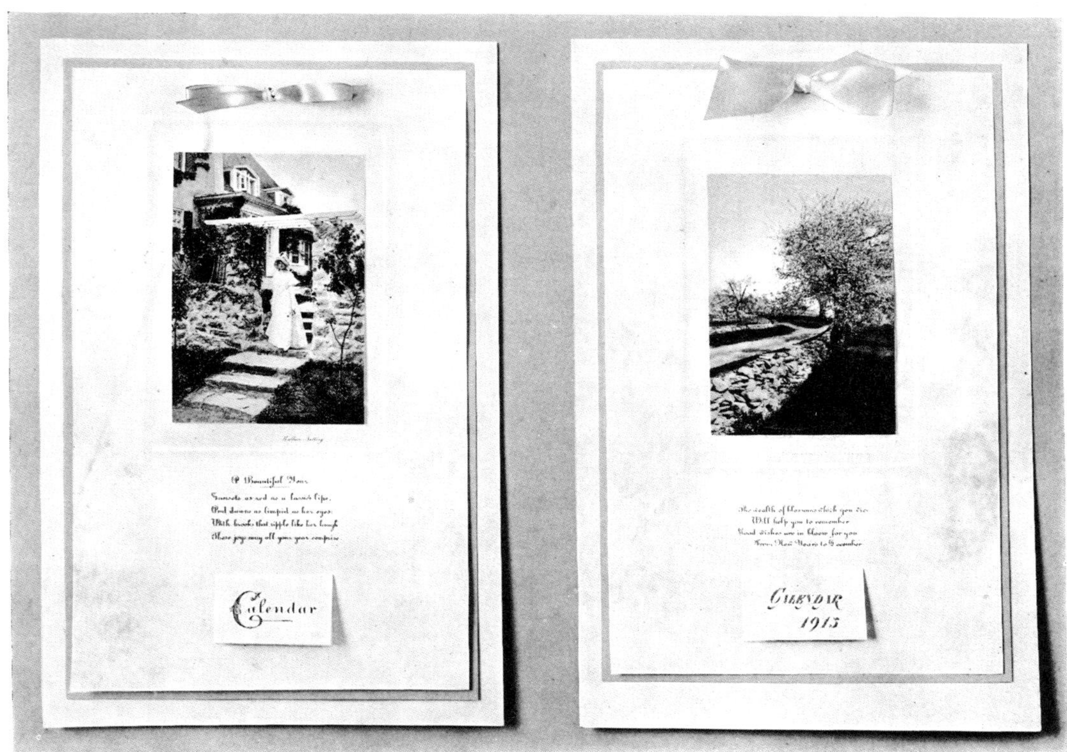

Style 458 Style 456

Style 458

Outside mounting, 11 x 17.
Any vertical picture, 5 x 7.
Base, white.
Overlay, cream.
Top, white.
Ribbon, yellow.
Price per dozen of 13, $16.00.

Style 456

Outside mounting, 11 x 17.
Only vertical blossom pictures, 5 x 7.
Base, white.
Overlay, blue.
Top, white.
Ribbon, white.
Price per dozen of 13, $16.00.

Style 457

Same mounting as style 456.
Only vertical blossom pictures, 5 x 7.
Sentiment:
"*Firm-rooted as an apple tree.*"
Price per dozen of 13, $16.00.

Style 451

Outside mounting, 11 x 17.
Any picture, 5 x 7.
Base, mottled blue; overlay, light blue.
Top, white; ribbon, blue; sentiment:

> "*I would send you richest blessings,*
> *I would keep you from all ill,*
> *I would give you life's best portion,*
> *Were the power mine to fulfill.*"

Price per dozen of 13, $16.00.

Style 452

Outside mounting, 11 x 17.
Any vertical Castle picture, 5 x 7.
Base, mottled blue; overlay, light blue.
Top, white; ribbon, white; sentiment:

> "*Our love is like a castle old,*
> *Whose wall defies the wreck of years,*
> *And graced by ivy's mantling fold,*
> *In nobler beauty still appears.*"

Price per dozen of 13, $16.00

Style 455

Outside mounting, 10 x 14.
Any horizontal picture, 5 x 7.
Base, white; top, white.
Picture overlay, white; ribbon, pink; sentiment:

> "*Thanks to the human heart by which we live,*
> *Thanks to its tenderness, its joys, and fears —*
> *To me the meanest flower that blows can give*
> *Thoughts that do often lie too deep for tears.*"

Price per dozen of 13, $16.00.

Style 460

Outside mounting, 8½ x 14.
Any vertical picture, 5 x 7.
Base, white; top, white; ribbon, white; sentiment pad:

> "*A year of hope,*
> *Weeks of progress,*
> *Days of peace.*"

Price per dozen of 13, $16.00.

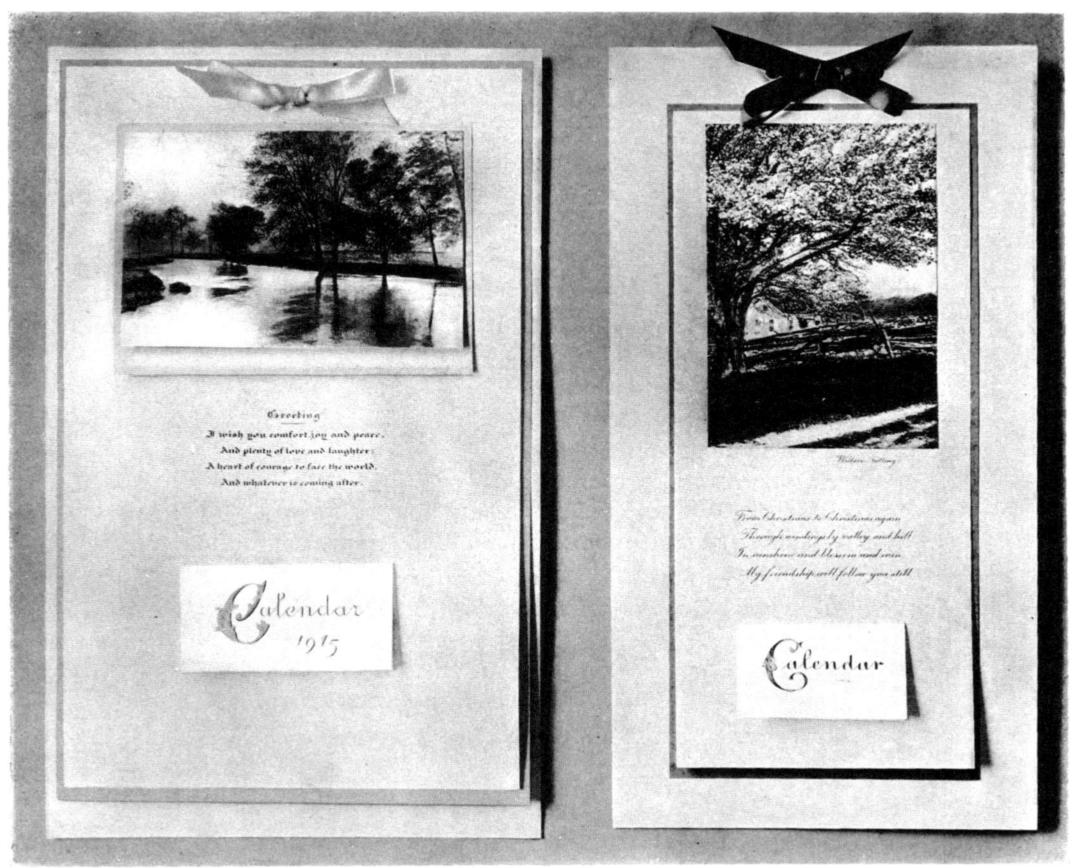

Style 354 | Style 399

Style 354

Outside mounting, 8½ x 14.
Any horizontal picture, 4 x 6.
Base, white.
Overlay, heliotrope.
Top, white.
Picture overlay, heliotrope.
Ribbon, white.
Price per dozen of 13, $12.00.

Style 399

Outside mounting, 7½ x 14.
Any vertical picture, 4 x 6.
Base, white.
Overlay, green.
Top, white.
Ribbon, green.
Price per dozen of 13, $12.00.

Style 353

Outside mounting, 8½ x 14.
Any vertical picture, 4 x 6.
Base, mottled blue; overlay, light blue.
Top, white; ribbon, blue; engraved sentiment:

"Good health, some wealth,
Good luck, much pluck,
Good fun, race won,
For you to-day."

Price per dozen of 13, $12.00.

Style 355

Outside mounting, 8½ x 14.
Any horizontal picture, 4 x 6.
Base, light blue; overlay, cream; top, white.
Picture overlay, cream; ribbon, blue; engraved sentiment:

"True Friendship.
Those ties are sweet whose strength we keep
By daily converse with a friend —
That friendship has a greater deep
Which space and silence cannot end."

Price per dozen of 13, $12.00.

Style 360

Outside mounting, 8½ x 14.
Any vertical colonial picture, 4 x 6.
Base, tea color; overlay, buff.
Top, tea color; 18-inch gray cord; sentiment:

"My Christmas wish for you: At the close of every day's work a welcoming home and the joys of friendship. And I ask you to keep a little cosy corner in your heart for me."

Price per dozen of 13, $12.00.

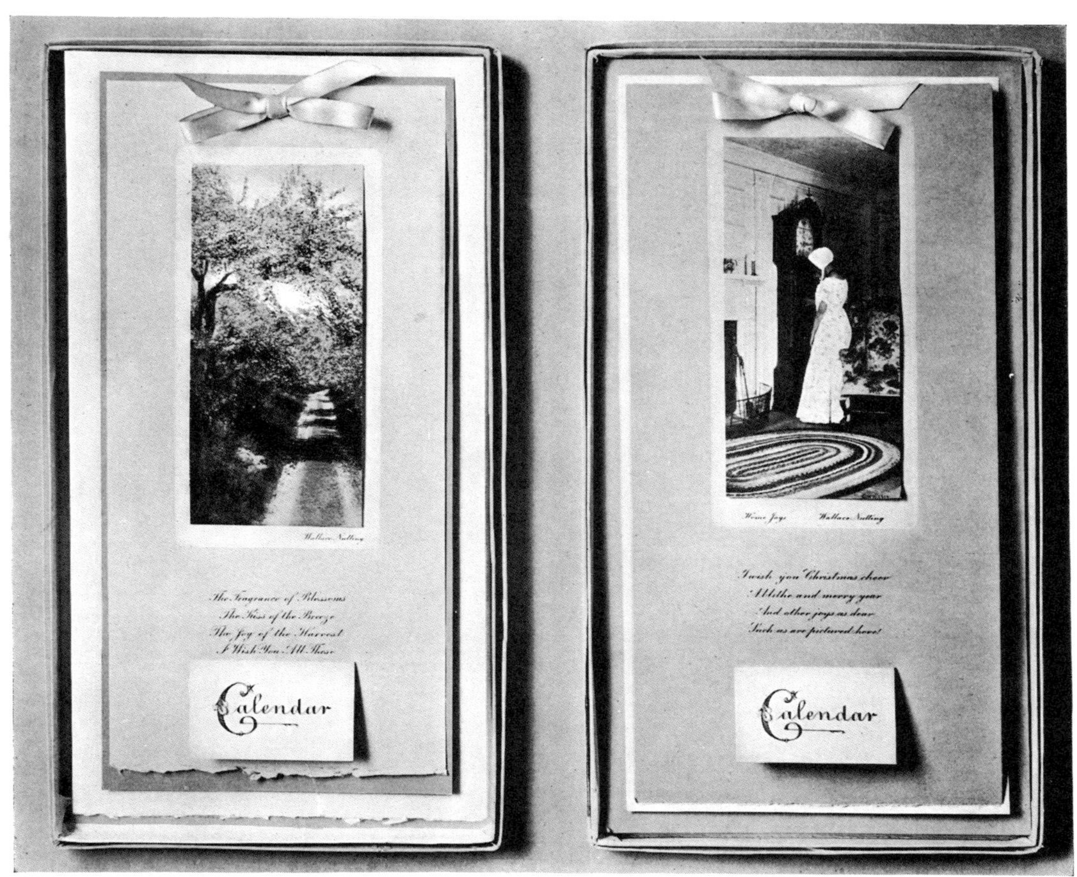

Style 285

Style 264

Style 285

Outside mounting, 7½ x 14.
Vertical Blossom pictures, 3 x 6⅝.
Base, white.
Overlay, gray.
Top, white.
Ribbon, pink.
Price per dozen of 13, $9.00;
$0.75 each.

Style 264

Outside mounting, 7½ x 14.
Vertical Colonial pictures, 3 x 6⅝.
Base, gray.
Overlay, white.
Top, gray.
Ribbon, white.
Price per dozen of 13, $9.00;
$0.75 each.

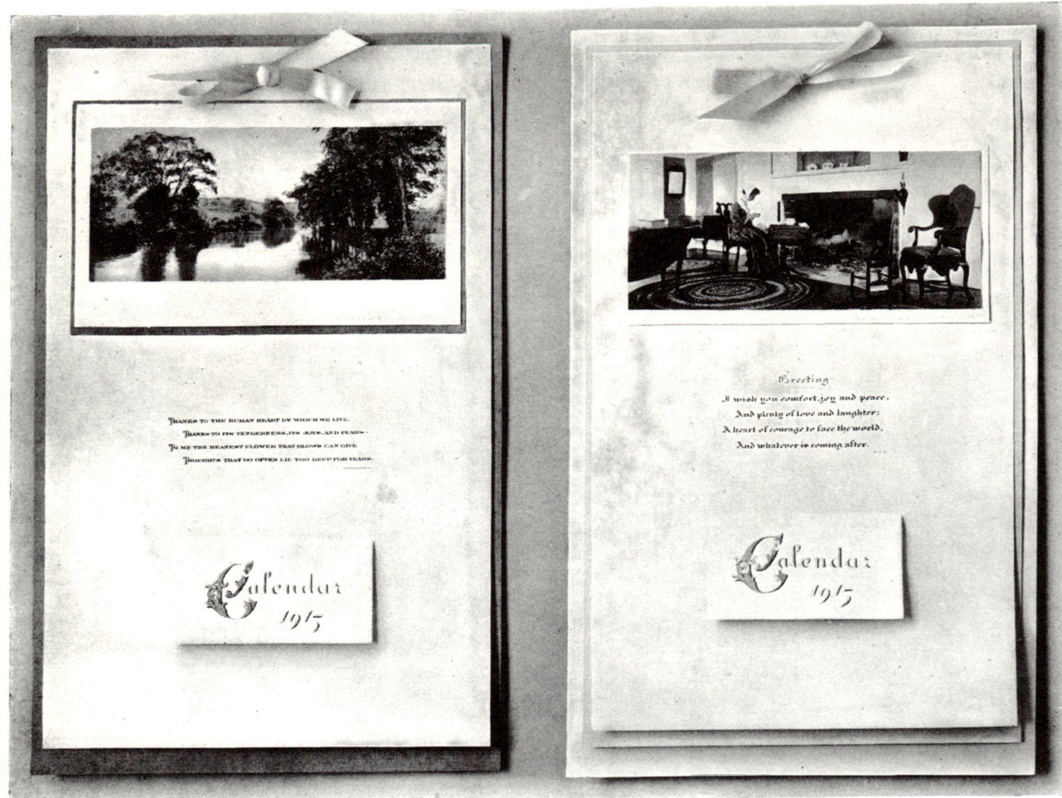

Style 260

Style 261

Style 260

Outside mounting, 8½ x 14.
Any horizontal picture, 3 x 6⅝.
Base, green.
Top, white linen.
Picture base, green.
Picture overlay, white.
Ribbon, white.
Price per dozen of 13, $9.00; $0.75 each.

Style 261

Outside mounting, 8½ x 14.
Any horizontal picture, 3 x 6⅝.
Base, white.
Overlay, blue.
Top, white.
Picture overlay, white.
Ribbon, white.
Sentiment: "*Greeting.*"
Price per dozen of 13, $9.00; $0.75 each.

Style 262

Outside mounting, 8½ x 14.
Any horizontal picture, 3 x 6⅝.
Base, white.
Overlay, green.
Top, white.
Picture overlay, white.
Ribbon, green.
Sentiment: "*Your Best,*" etc.
Price per dozen of 13, $9.00; $0.75 each.

Style 269

Outside mounting, 5 x 16.
Any vertical picture, 3 x 6⅝.
Base, white.
Top, white.
Ribbon, pink.
Sentiment: "*Greeting*"; same as Style 261.
Price per dozen of 13, $9.00; $0.75 each.

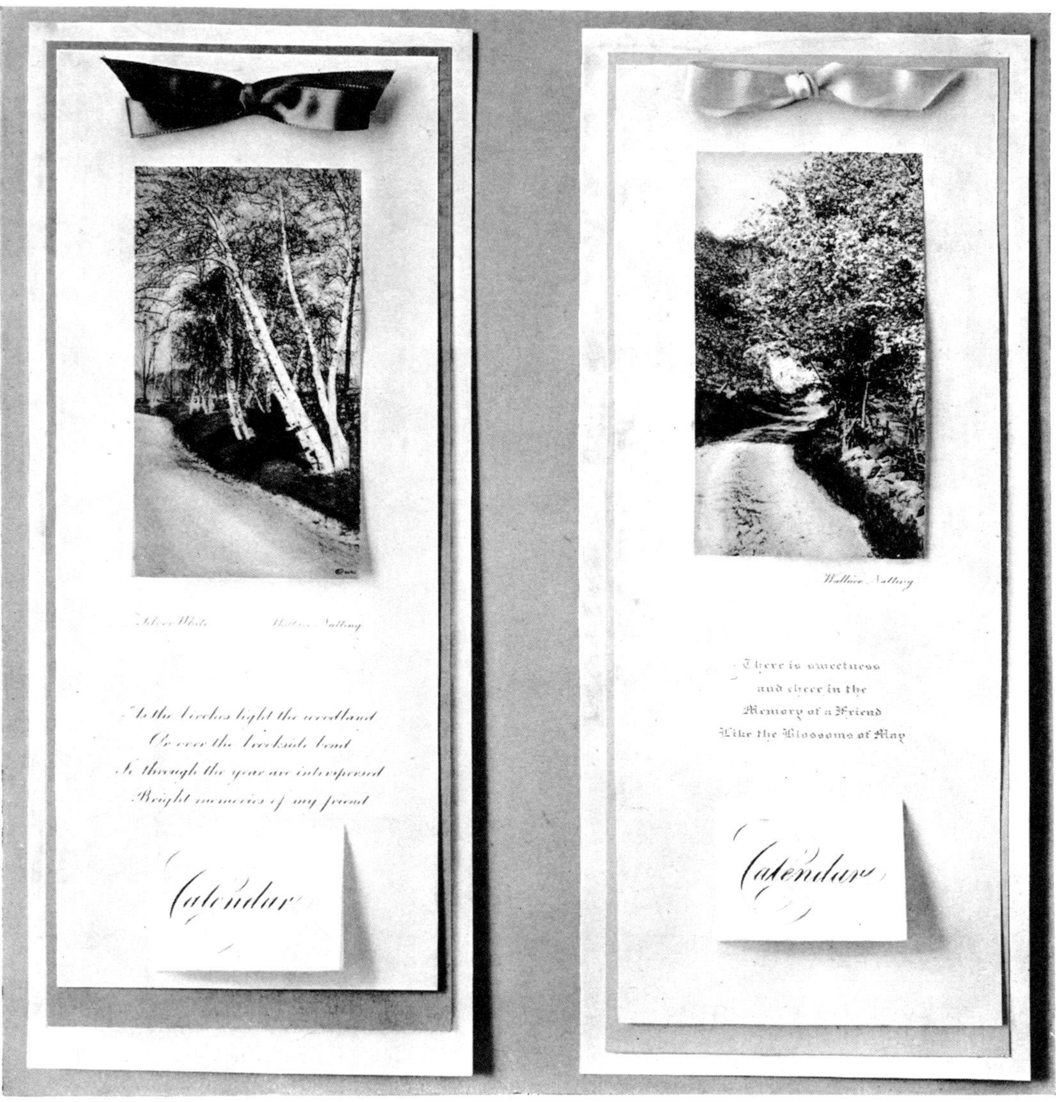

Style 123 Style 144

Style 123
Outside mounting, 5 x 12.
Vertical Birch pictures only, 2½ x 5.
Base, white.
Overlay, green.
Top, white; ribbon, green.

Style 144
Outside mounting, 5 x 12.
Vertical Blossom pictures only, 2½ x 5.
Base, white.
Overlay, heliotrope.
Top, white; ribbon, white.

Style 104
Outside mounting, 5 x 12.
Any vertical picture, 3¼ x 4.
Base, cream, overlapping at top.
Top, white; ribbon, yellow.
Sentiment: "*Good health, some wealth,*" etc.

Style 108
Outside mounting, 5 x 12.
Any vertical picture, 2½ x 5.
Base, green, overlapping at top.
Top, white; ribbon, green.
Sentiment: "*All the year,*" etc.

Price of all on this page, per dozen of 12 only, $6.00. Not less than ¼ dozen sold.

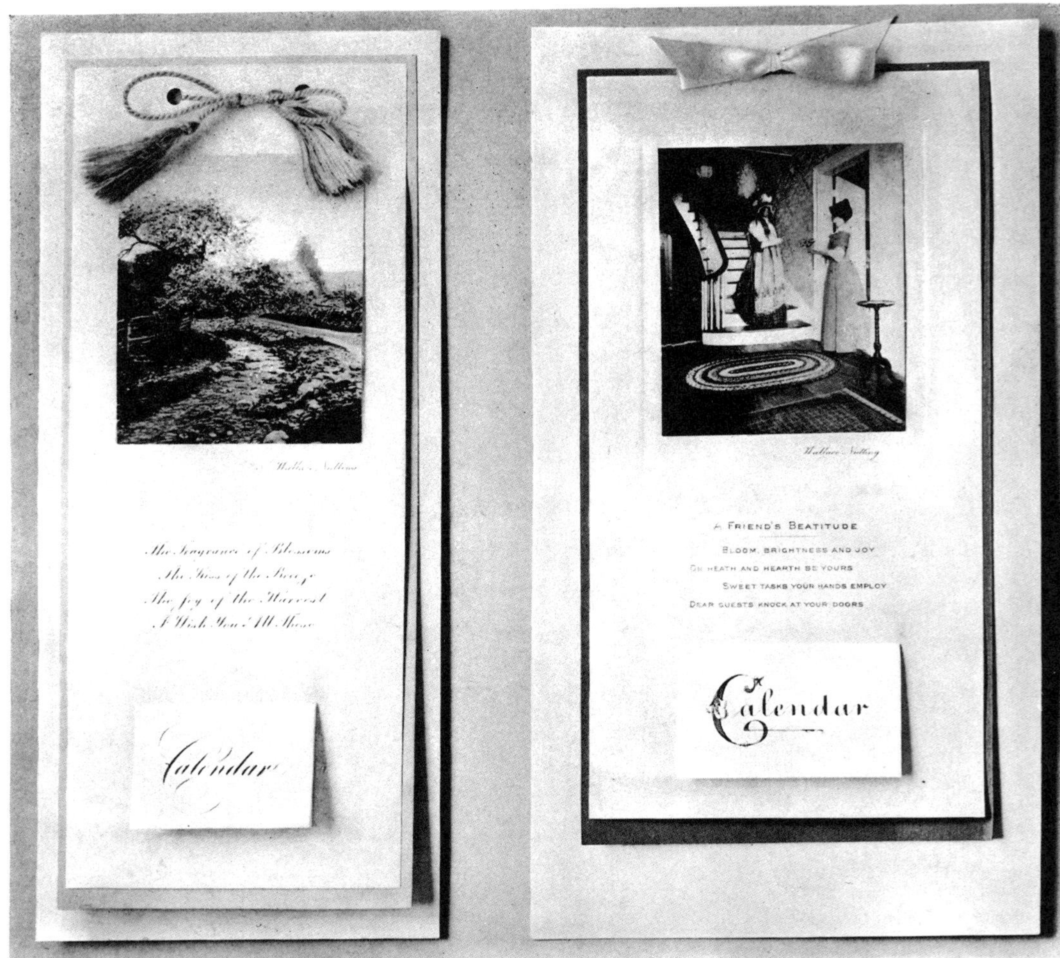

Style 164 Style 150

Style 164

Outside mounting, 5 x 12.
Any vertical picture, 3¼ x 4.
Base, white.
Overlay, lavender.
Top, white.
Lavender cord.
All Calendars are sold in white glazed boxes.
Price per dozen of 12 only, $6.00. Not less than ¼ dozen sold.

Style 155

Same mounting as 150; Figures only.
Sentiment: "*My Christmas wish for you,*" etc.
Base, white.
Overlay, gold.
Top, white.
Ribbon, white.
Price per dozen of 12 only, $6.00. Not less than ¼ dozen sold.

Style 150

Outside mounting, 6½ x 12.
Any vertical picture, 3¼ x 4.
Base, white; overlay, gold.
Top, white; ribbon, white.
Price per dozen of 12 only, $6.00. Not less than ¼ dozen sold.

Style 153

Same as Style 179, except it has a plate mark instead of picture lining. Sentiment, same as Style 164.

Style 163

Same as Style 179, except with plate mark instead of picture lining, and sentiment:

"A Beautiful Year
Sunsets as red as a lassie's lips,
And dawns as limpid as her eyes,
With brooks that ripple like her laugh,
These joys may all your year comprise."

Price per dozen of 12 only, $6.00. Not less than 1/4 dozen sold.

Style 169

Same mounting as Style 179, except ribbon is Dresden. Sentiment:

"Firm rooted as an apple tree
True friendships always are,
And the fragrance of their blossoms
May be scented from afar."

Price per dozen of 12 only, $6.00. Not less than 1/4 dozen sold.

Style 121

Same as Style 136, except picture, 3 1/4 x 4, and sentiment:

"True Friendship
Those ties are sweet whose strength we keep
By daily converse with a friend —
That friendship has a greater deep
Which space and silence cannot end."

Price per dozen of 12 only, $6.00. Not less than 1/4 dozen sold.

THE COURAGE OF CONVICTION

We are the first people to dare to mount calendars in plain white or delicate shades. Hitherto it has been said that customers wanted strong colors. We knew that such colors were not in good taste. We have proved that the public are eager to procure calendars mounted quietly but richly.

ENGRAVED SENTIMENT

There is no printing whatever on any of our special goods. Everything is in the copper or steel plate — the sentiments, the calendar pads and everything else.

This idea is original with us. Printing below one of our dainty pictures is inappropriate.

Undoubtedly our line of small goods is far more beautiful than anything hitherto offered. Dealers almost invariably sell out quickly. We do not press sales in this department.

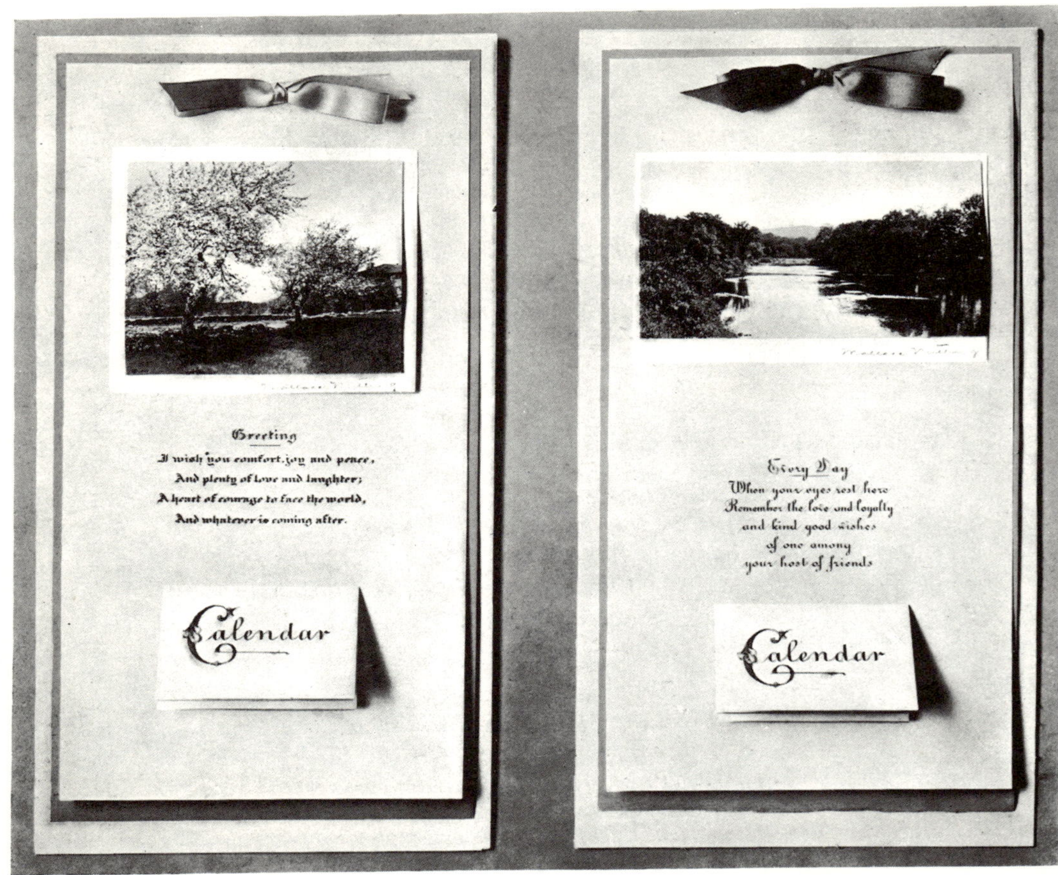

Style 179

Style 136

Style 179

Outside mounting, 6½ x 12.
Any horizontal picture, 3¼ x 4.
Base, white.
Overlay, gray.
Top, white.
Picture lining, white.
Ribbon, pink.
Price per dozen of 12 only, $6.00.
Not less than ¼ dozen sold.

Style 136

Outside mounting, 6½ x 12.
Any horizontal picture, 2½ x 5.
Base, white.
Overlay, yellow.
Top, white.
Picture lining, white.
Ribbon, yellow.
Price per dozen of 12 only, $6.00.
Not less than ¼ dozen sold.

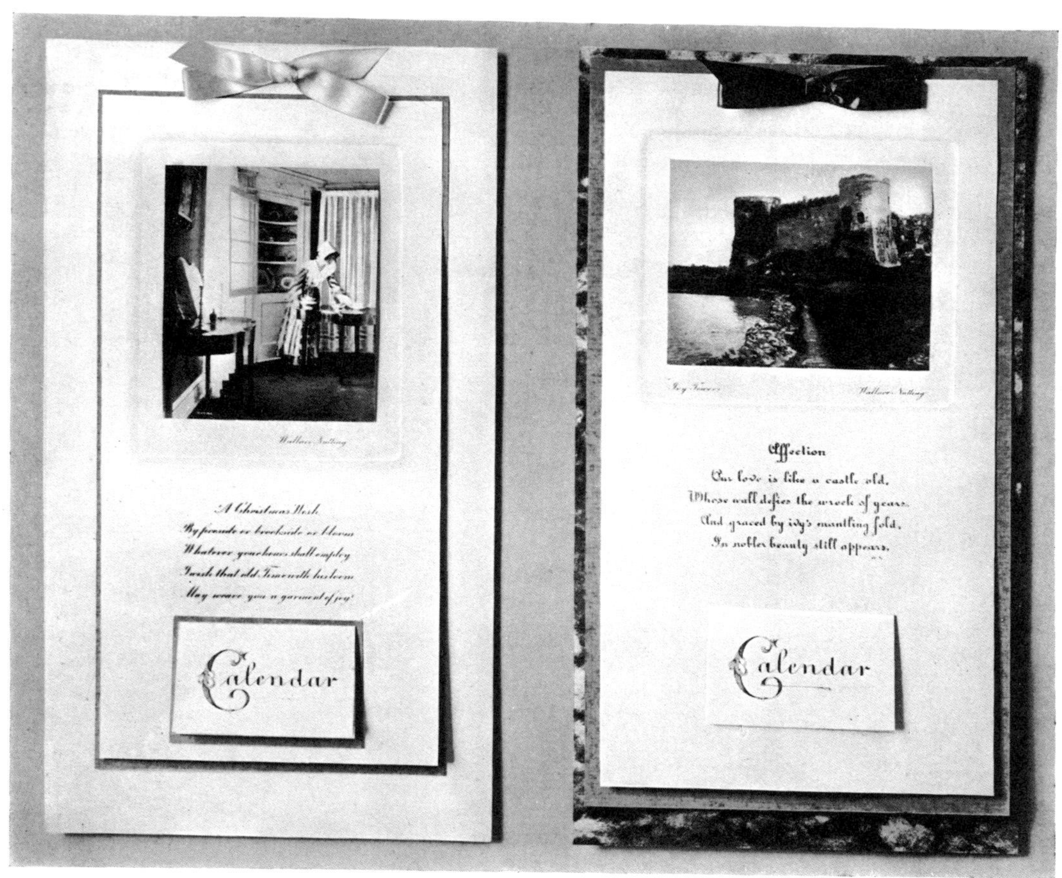

Style 156

Style 172

Style 156

Outside mounting, 6½ x 12.
Any vertical picture, 3¼ x 4.
Base, white.
Overlay, green.
Top, white.
Calendar pad lining, green.
Ribbon, white.
Price per dozen of 12 only, $6.00.
Not less than ¼ dozen sold.

Style 172

Outside mounting, 6½ x 12.
Horizontal Castle pictures only, 3¼ x 4.
Base, mottled green.
Overlay, green.
Top, white.
Ribbon, green.
Price per dozen of 12 only, $6.00.
Not less than ¼ dozen sold.

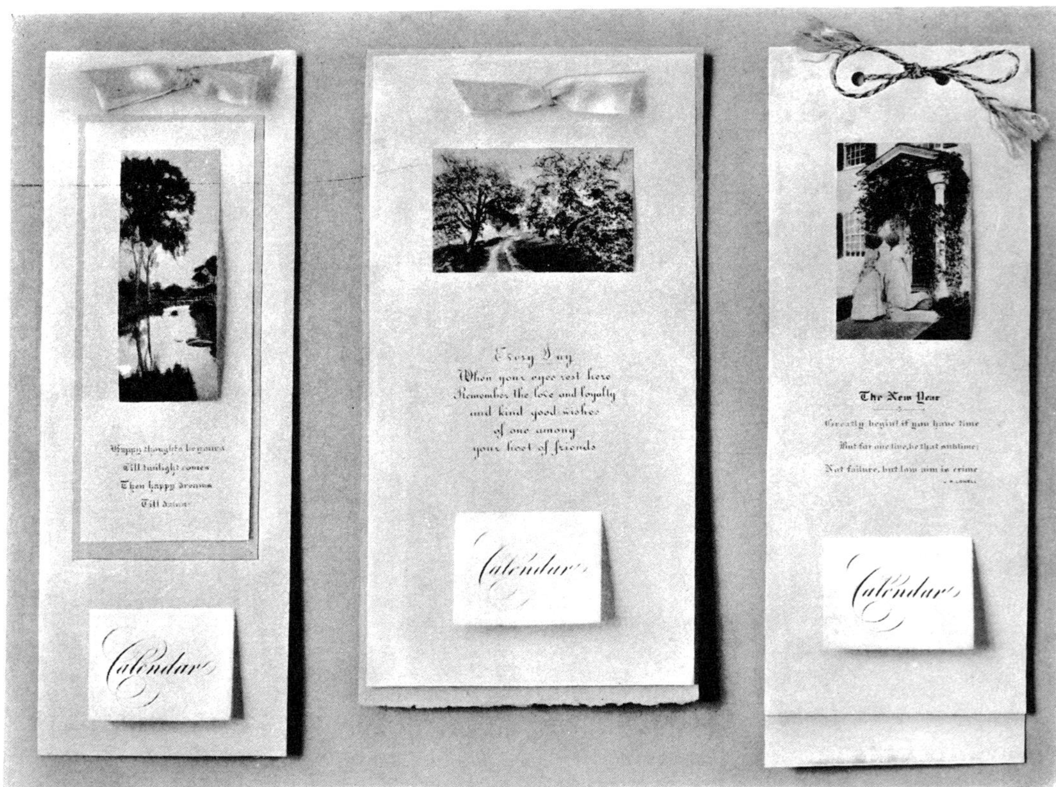

Style 437, B picture — Style 403, B picture — Style 405, B picture

Style 437

Outside mounting, 3¾ x 11.
Any vertical picture, 1½ x 4.
Base, white.
Overlay, blue.
Top, white.
Ribbon, white.
Price per dozen of 12 only, $4.00.
Not less than ½ dozen sold.

Style 403

Outside mounting, 5 x 10.
Any horizontal picture, 2 x 3.
Base, buff.
Top, white.
Ribbon, white.
Price per dozen of 12 only, $4.00.
Not less than ½ dozen sold.

Style 405

Outside mounting, 3¾ x 11.
Any vertical picture, 2 x 3.
Base, white.
Cord, yellow.
Price per dozen of 12 only, $4.00.
Not less than ½ dozen sold.

Style 401

Outside mount, 5 x 10.
Any horizontal blossom or landscape picture, 2 x 3.
Base, mottled green.
Top, white; ribbon, green; engraved sentiment:

"*All the year,*" etc.

Price per dozen of 12 only, $4.00.
Not less than ½ dozen sold.

Style 407

Outside mounting, 5 x 10.
Any horizontal colonial picture, 2 x 3.
Base, mottled green; overlay, green.
Top, white; ribbon, green; engraved sentiment:

"*At our Door and on our Settle there is Welcome for you.*"

Price per dozen of 12 only, $4.00.
Not less than ½ dozen sold.

Style 412

Outside mounting, 3¾ x 11.
Any vertical picture, 1½ x 4.
Base, cream; top, white.
Picture lining cream; white ribbon loop.
Engraved sentiment:

"*Let our Friendships.*"

Price per dozen of 12 only, $4.00.
Not less than ½ dozen sold.

Style 415

Outside mounting, 5 x 10.
Any horizontal picture, 2 x 3.
Base, light blue; top, white; ribbon, white; engraved sentiment:

"*Every Day.*"

Price per dozen of 12 only, $4.00.
Not less than ½ dozen sold.

Style 428

Outside mounting, 5 x 10.
Any vertical picture, 2 x 3.
Base, white; red and gold bordered overlay for picture.
Ribbon loop, white; sentiment pad engraved:

"*May many joys.*"

Price per dozen of 12 only, $4.00.
Not less than ½ dozen sold.

Style 429

Outside mounting, 3¾ x 11.
Any vertical picture, 1½ x 4.
Back, gray; top, white; picture overlay, gray.
Ribbon loop, pink; engraved sentiment:

"*Let our Friendships.*"

Price per dozen of 12 only, $4.00.
Not less than ½ dozen sold.

OTHER STYLES

Any sentiment will be used to order if the customer defrays cost of engraving or sends a plate, which should be of large size. No other extra charge will be made on an order for a gross. Of course the sentiment must only occupy such space as is available on the style.

CALENDARS BY FREIGHT

We recommend that all calendar orders of any size be sent by freight. They are bulky because every one is in its particular box. Allow from one week to two months for the shipment to reach you, as freights are slow. Order in the winter or spring because only on early orders are we sure to be able to ship the cheapest way, and if the present increase in the business continues, fall orders will be almost impossible to fill in full.

THE PRICE OF CALENDARS

We do not urge orders on small calendars as there is no margin of profit for us in selling them. We can make cheaper calendars, but not for the price. Every print is in platinum and all are wholly colored by hand.

Style 404

Outside mounting, 5 x 10.
Any vertical picture, 2 x 3, in plate mark.
Base, white; overlay, light blue.
Top, white; ribbon, blue; *no sentiment.*
Price $4.00 per dozen of 12.
Not less than ½ dozen sold.

Style 134

Outside mounting, 5 x 10.
Any vertical picture, 2½ x 5, in plate mark.
Base, lavender; top, white; ribbon, white; *no sentiment.*
Price $6.00 per dozen of 12.
Not less than ¼ dozen sold.

Style 124

Outside mounting, 6½ x 12.
Any vertical picture, 3¼ x 4, in plate mark.
Base, buff; top, white; ribbon, white; *no sentiment.*
Price per dozen of 12, $6.00.
Not less than ¼ dozen sold.

Style 284

Outside mounting, 7½ x 14.
Any vertical picture, 3 x 6⅝, in plate mark.
Base, white; overlay, gray; top, white.
Ribbon, pink; *no sentiment.*
Price per dozen of 13, $9.00.

Style 394

Outside mounting, 7½ x 14.
Any vertical picture, 4 x 6, in plate mark.
Base, green; top, white; ribbon, green; *no sentiment.*
Price per dozen of 13, $12.00.

Style 398

Outside mounting, 8½ x 14.
Any vertical picture, 4 x 6, in plate mark.
Base, white; overlay, cream; top, white.
Ribbon, yellow; engraved sentiment:

" Every Day
When your eyes rest here
Remember the love and loyalty
and kind good wishes
of one among
your host of friends."

Price per dozen of 13, $12.00.

Style 454

Outside mounting 11 x 17.
Any horizontal picture, 5 x 7, on cream overlay.
Base, white; overlay, cream; top, white.
Ribbon, yellow; engraved sentiment, same as style above.
Price per dozen of 13, $16.00.

PLEASE OBSERVE

Above, the five styles listed first have no sentiment. The calendar pad cover is engraved as in other styles.

PLEASE DON'T BE ORIGINAL

In respect to asking variations from the above styles buyers get into all sorts of vexatious difficulties and delays. Our styles in many cases are designed with sentiments to match a certain class of pictures. For instance, the styles " for birches only " cannot be used for other sorts of pictures. The verses only have meaning for birches. We have given this matter long and minute attention, and while we know other good styles could be designed we give enough for the utmost variety required by the largest buyer.

Another error buyers often make is in ordering picture numbers that are long vertically to be placed on styles designed for pictures that are long horizontally. It is obviously impossible to fill such an order. If the catalog is closely followed greater satisfaction will be given.

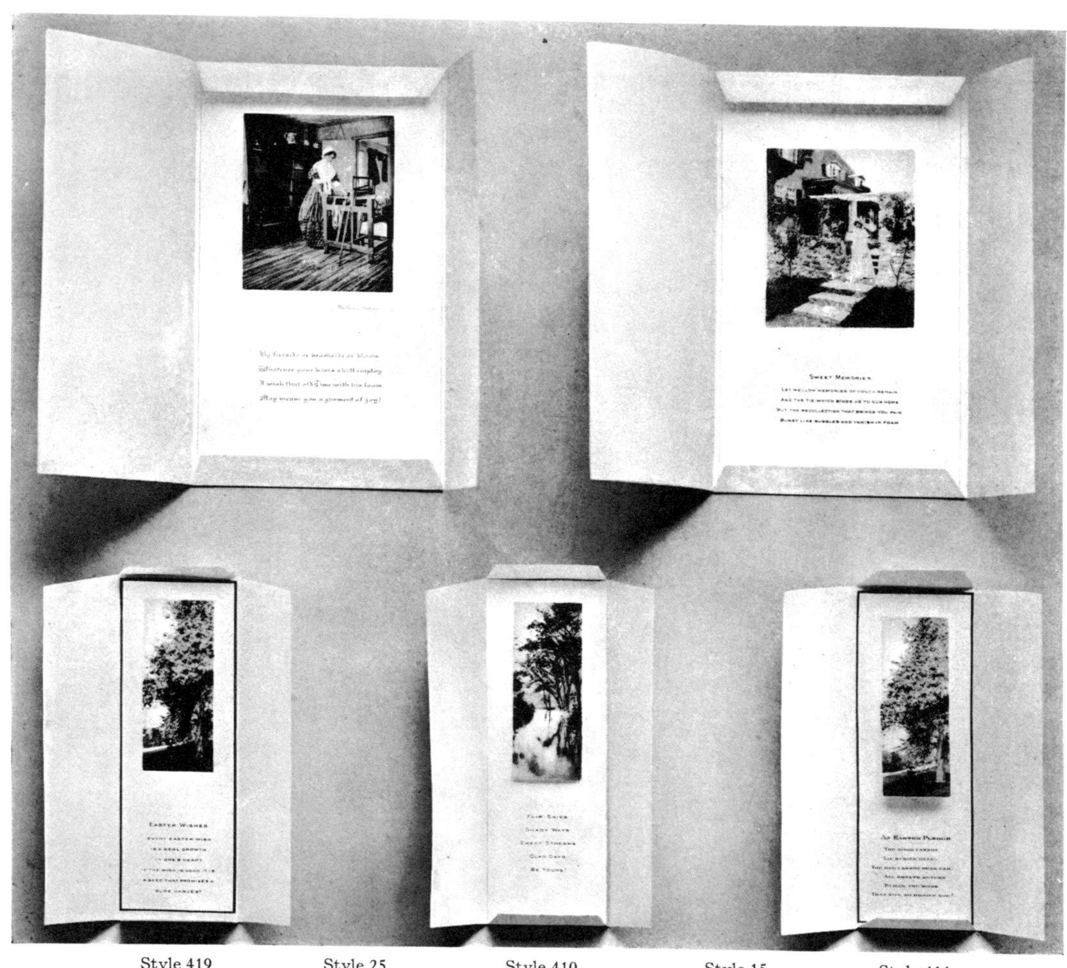

Style 419 Style 25 Style 410 Style 15 Style 414

Style 25

Outside mounting, 5 x 9.
Any picture, $3\frac{1}{4}$ x 4, mounted in plate mark on engraved white card, enclosed as shown above.
Price per dozen of 13, $6.00.

Style 15

Outside mounting, 5 x 9.
Any picture, $3\frac{1}{4}$ x 4, mounted in plate mark on engraved white card, enclosed as shown above.
Price per dozen of 13, $6.00.

Style 419

Outside mounting, $2\frac{1}{2}$ x $7\frac{1}{4}$.
Blossom picture, $1\frac{1}{2}$ x 4, mounted on green-and-gold-bordered card, enclosed as shown above.
Price per dozen of 13, $3.60.

Style 410

Outside mounting 2½ x 7¼.

Any landscape picture 1½ x 4, mounted on engraved white card enclosed as Style 419.

Price per dozen of 13, $3.60.

Style 425

Same as Style 410, except sentiment:

"A Friendship that lasts
Is a continual Thanksgiving."

Any picture, 1½ x 4.

Style 414

Same as Style 419, except sentiment:

"An Easter Pledge."

Style 427

Same as Style 410, except sentiment:

"Let our friendships
Be, not a pastime,
But a prayer;
Not for time,
But for eternity."

Style 436

Same as Style 410, except sentiment:

"In the Spring
A young man's fancy
Lightly turns
To thoughts of Love."

TENNYSON.

Booklet, Style 82

Outside 5 x 6¼.

Any horizontal 3¼ x 4 picture.

Base, light blue.

Picture overlay, white; ribbon, blue.

Engraved insert:

"On Christmas night
The stars shine bright;
On Christmas morn
The Christ is born;
A Christmas year!
God's peace be near!"

Price per dozen of 12, $6.00.

Style 438

Same as Style 410, except sentiment:

"Happy thoughts be yours
Till twilight comes,
Then happy dreams
Till dawn!"

Style 435

Same as Style 410, except sentiment:

"Sweet day, so cool,
So calm, so bright,
The bridal of
The earth and sky."

HERBERT.

Style 432

Same as Style 410, except sentiment:

"How dear to my Heart," etc.

Style 42

Same as Style 25, except sentiment:

"Life's Mirror.
Look for goodness look for gladness,
You shall meet them all the while;
If you bring a smiling visage
To the glass, you meet a smile!"

ALICE CARY.

Style 48

Same as Style 25, except sentiment:

"A Christmas Aspiration.
To hold dearest the worthiest
To seek only what will last
To know the best is yet unfolding
And we shall see it in its glory."

Style 83

Same as Style 25, except:
Blossom picture, mounted on green and gold bordered card. Sentiment:

"An Easter Greeting.
There are some plants which
Bear blossoms and fruit all the year.
I hope that may be your experience."

Style 506

White Invitation Card, 3¾ x 5¾, which reads:

"M—— Requests the pleasure of your company," etc.

Enclosed in envelopes. Price, $5.00 per hundred.

Style 512

White Gift Card, 3¾ x 5¾, which reads:

"My dear friend:
I am sending you a gift appropriate to this glad and hopeful season, a Wallace Nutting picture.
May its brightness help to cheer you through any sad or sombre days, and to enhance your pleasure when all goes well."

Enclosed in envelopes. Price $5.00 per hundred.

Style 46

Same as Style 25, except sentiment:

"Greeting
I wish you comfort, joy and peace,
And plenty of love and laughter;
A heart of courage to face the world,
And whatever is coming after."

M. W. E.

Style 4

Same as Style 25, except sentiment.
Any vertical picture, 2½ x 5.
Sentiment:

"To My Mother
The joy be yours
Of reaping the rich fruit
Of many years of hope and prayer
In the life you have brought
Into the world."

Style 29

Same as Style 25, except sentiment.
Vertical blossom or Landscape picture, 2½ x 5.
Sentiment:

"Easter
Forms of beauty and hope
Hid under snow and sod;
Ye heard the call of Love
And trembled upward to God!"

Style 11

Same as Style 25, except sentiment.
Colonial pictures, 3¼ x 4.
Sentiment:

"Stay, stay at home my heart and rest,
Home keeping hearts are happiest;
For they who wander they know not where,
Are full of sorrow and full of care.
To stay at home is best."

LONGFELLOW.

Style 10

Same as Style 25, except sentiment.
Vertical Birch pictures only, 2½ x 5.
Sentiment:

"Silver White
As the birches light the woodland
Or over the brookside bend,
So through the year are interspersed
Bright memories of my friend."

Style 21

Same as Style 10, except picture size,
Picture, 3¼ x 4.

Style 31

Same as Style 25, except sentiment.
Colonial picture, 3¼ x 4.
Sentiment:

"My Christmas wish for you: At the close of every day's work a welcoming home and the joys of friendship; and I ask you to keep a little cosy corner in your heart for me."

Style 80

Congratulation booklet.
Outside mounting, 4 x 8.
Any vertical colonial picture, 2½ x 5 on first page in plate mark.
Base, white.
Engraved sentiment on cover.
Sentiment:

"Congratulations
Two souls with but a single thought,
Two hearts that beat as one."

Enclosed in white glazed box. Price $6.00 per dozen of 13; not less than ¼ dozen sold.

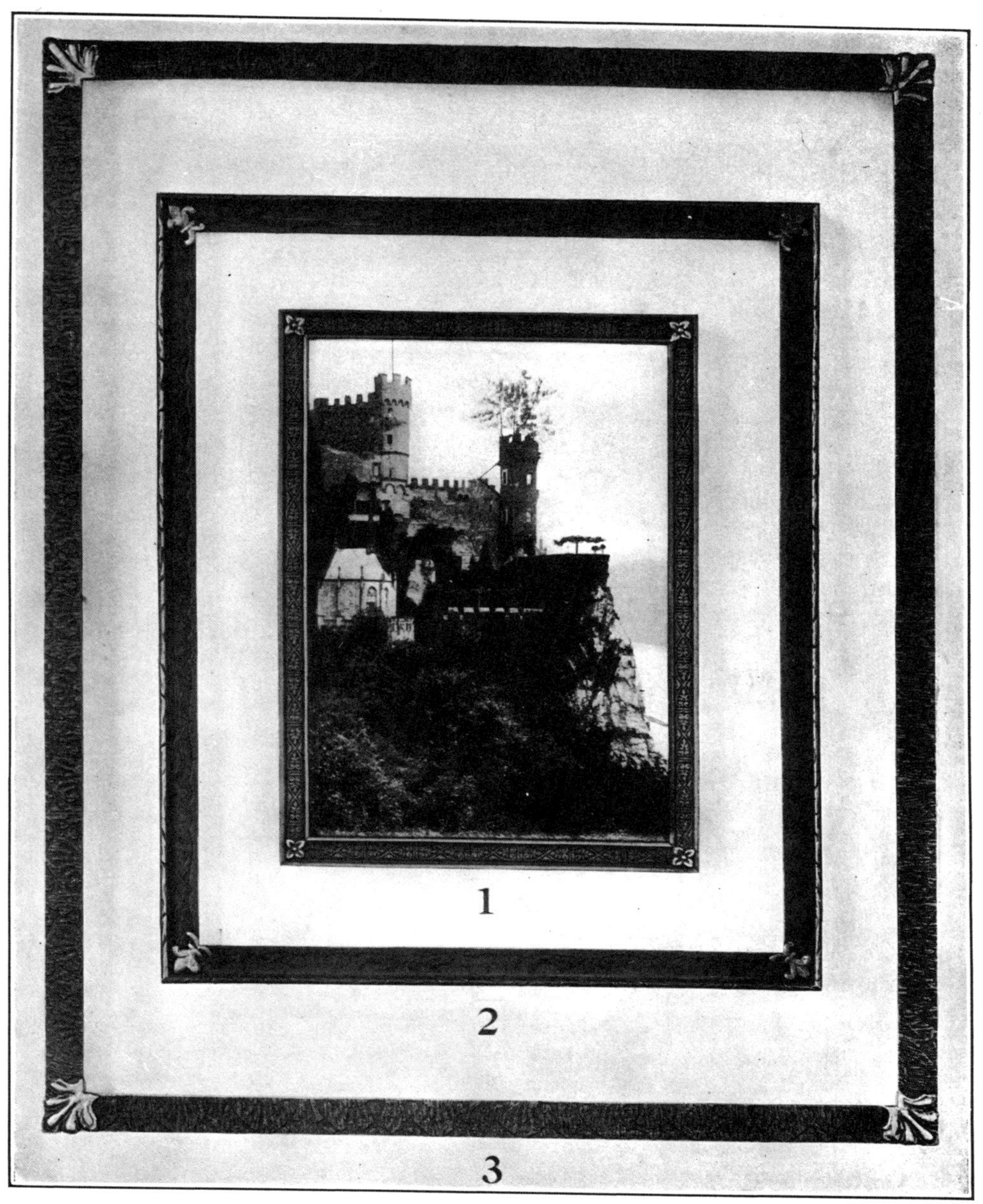

Where "framing only" or "frames only" is not specified, the prices include pictures and frames.

Frame								
Frame 1, B	size per	gross,	gilt	(5 x 7),	$125.00,	not less than	¼	gross.
1, D	"	"	"	(7 x 9),	166.00,	" " "	¼	"
1, K	"	dozen,	"	(8 x 12),	19.80,	" " "	1	dozen.
1, R	"	"	"	(10 x 12),	21.60,	" " "	1	"
2, R	"	"	green and gilt	(10 x 12),	21.60,	" " "	1	"
3, R	"	"	gilt	(10 x 12),	21.60,	" " "	1	"
3, A	"	"	" framing only	(11 x 14),	12.00,	" " "	7	pictures.
3, A	"	"	" frames only (no glass)	(11 x 14),	$6.60,	not less than	1	dozen.

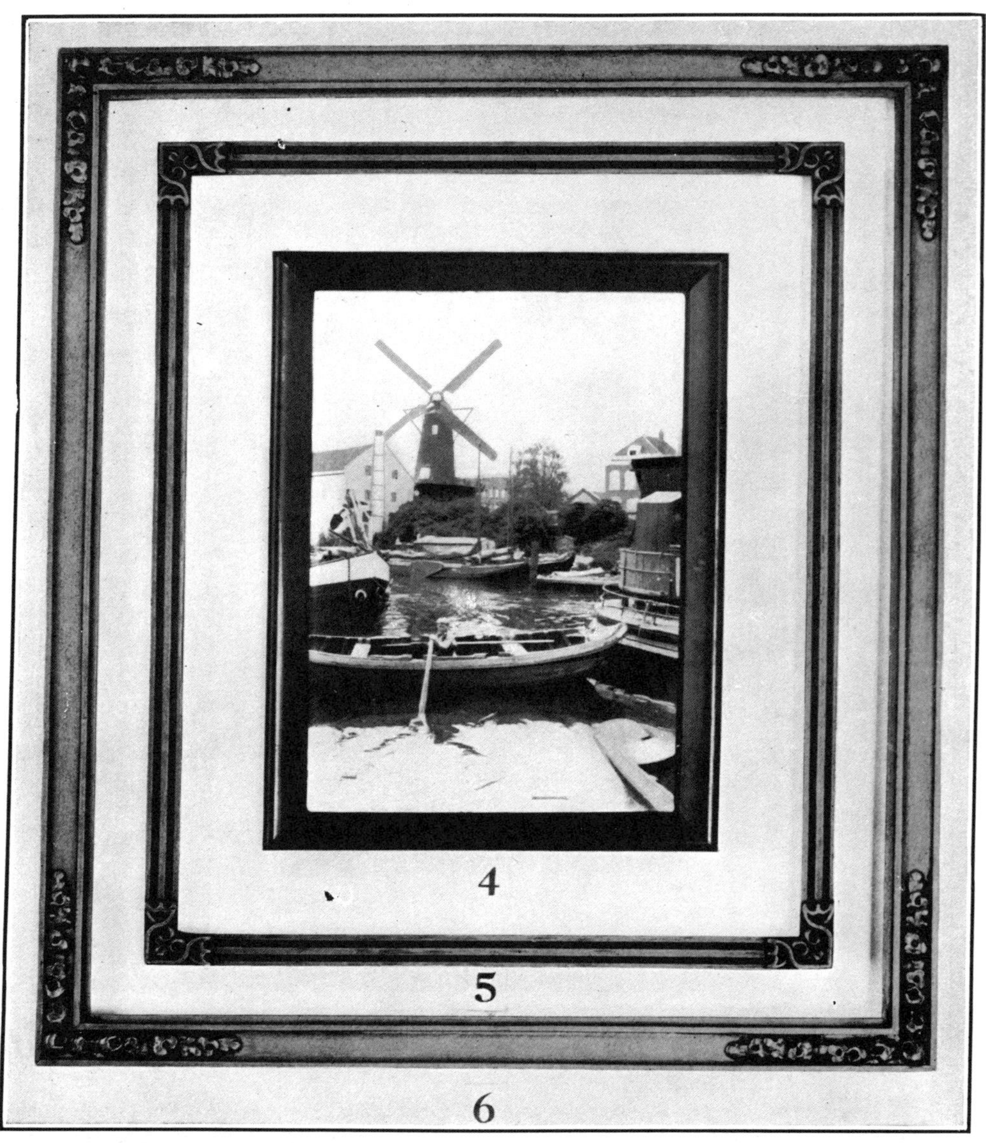

Frame 4, B size per gross, mahoganized (5 x 7), $90.00, not less than ¼ gross.
4, D " " " " (7 x 9), 127.00, " " " ¼ "
5, D " " " gilt (7 x 9), 138.00, " " " ¼ "
5, K " " dozen, " (8 x 12), 16.80, " " " 1 dozen.
5, R " " " " (10 x 12), 18.00, " " " 1 "
5, A " " " " for framing only (11 x 14), $10.80, not less than 7 pictures.
5, A " " " frames only (no glass), gilt (11 x 14), $5.40, not less than 1 dozen.
6, R " " " gold (10 x 12), $26.00, not less than 1 dozen.
6, A " " " " for framing only (11 x 14), $24.00, not less than 7 pictures.
6, A " " " frames only (no glass), gold (11 x 14), $15.00, not less than 1 doz.

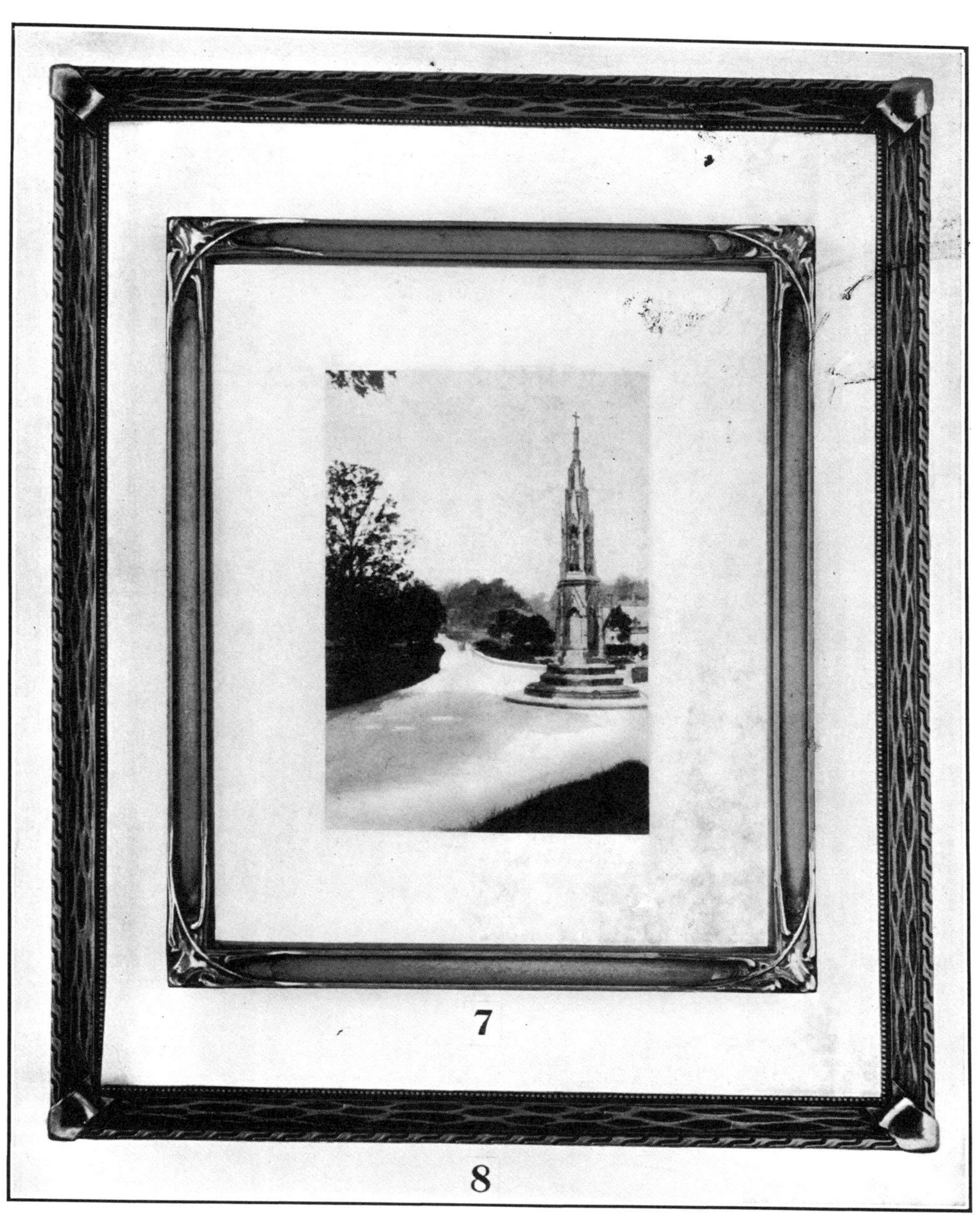

Frame	Size	Per	Description	Finish	Size (in.)	Price	Minimum
Frame 7, D	size	per gross,		gold	(7 x 9),	$130.00,	not less than ¼ gross.
7, K	"	" dozen,		"	(8 x 12),	26.00	" " " 1 dozen.
7, R	"	" "		"	(10 x 12),	28.00,	" " " 1 "
7, R	"	" "	frames only (no glass),	gold	(10 x 12),	$15.00,	not less than 1 doz.
7, A	"	" "	for framing only,	"	(11 x 14),	24.00,	" " " 7 pict.
7, A	"	" "	frames only (no glass),	"	(11 x 14),	15.00,	" " " 1 doz.
8, A	"	" "	for framing only,	gilt	(11 x 14),	11.00,	" " " 7 pict.
8, A	"	" "	frames only (no glass),	"	(11 x 14),	5.40,	" " " 1 doz.

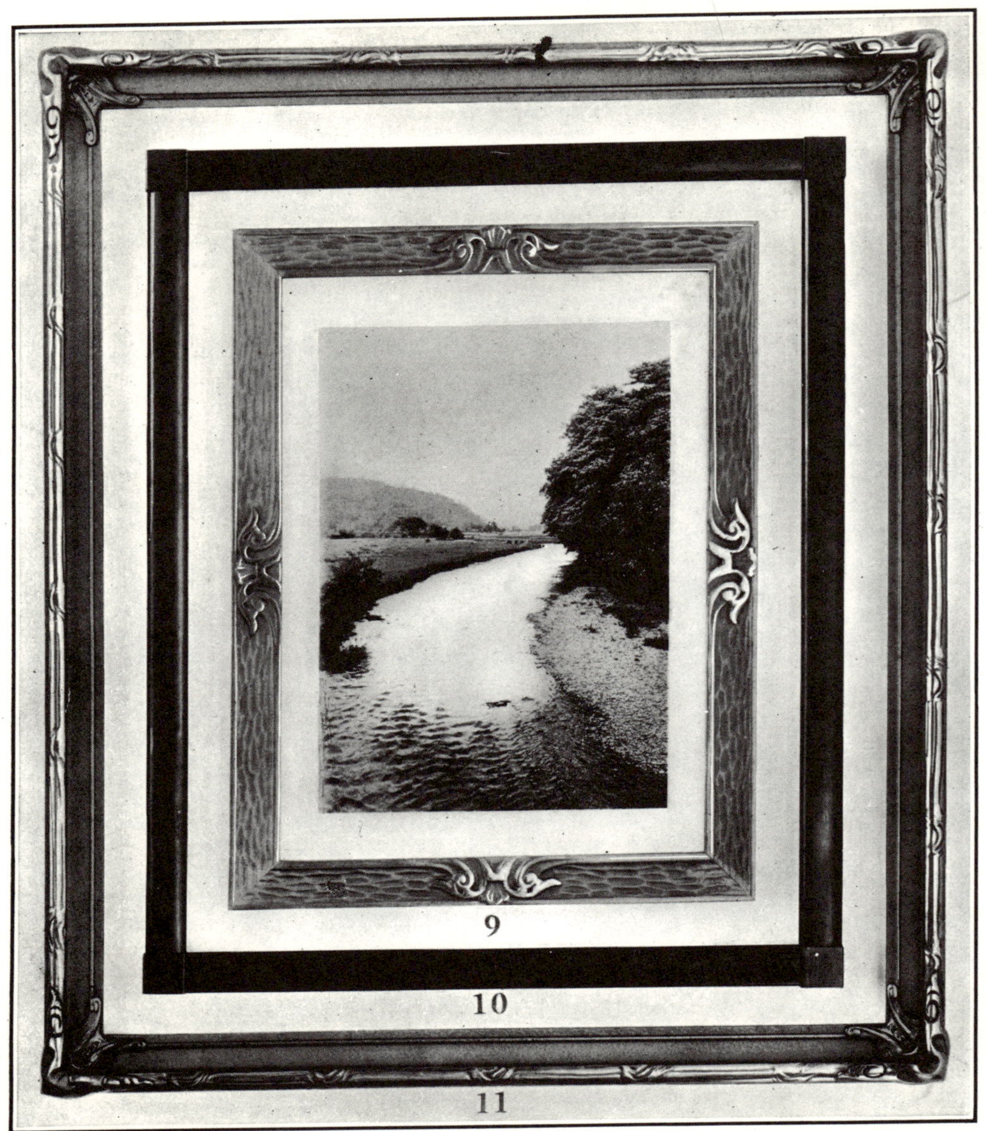

Frame 9, Q	size per doz., mahogany, for framing only	(11 x 17),	$20.	not less than 7 pictures.
9, Q	“ “ “ gold, “ “ “	(11 x 17),	20.	“ “ “ 7 “
9, Q	“ “ “ “ frames only (no glass)	(11 x 17),	14.	“ “ “ 1 doz.
9, S	“ “ “ “ or mah. for fram. only	(13 x 17).	21.	“ “ “ 7 pictures.
9, C	“ “ “ “ “ “ “ “ “	(14 x 17),	22.	“ “ “ 7 “
10, A	“ “ “ mahogany, for framing only	(11 x 14),	15.	“ “ “ 7 “
10, A	“ “ “ “ frames only (no glass)	(11 x 14),	11.	“ “ “ 1 doz.
10, Q	“ “ “ “ for framing only	(11 x 17),	17.	“ “ “ 7 pictures.
10, Q	“ “ “ “ frames only (no glass)	(11 x 17),	12.	“ “ “ 1 doz.
10, S or C	“ “ “ “ for framing only	(13 or 14 x 17),	18.	“ “ “ 7 pictures.
11, C	“ “ “ gold or mah. for framing only	(14 x 17) ,	33.	“ “ “ 7 pictures.
11, O	“ “ “ “ “ “ “ “ “	(13 x 22),	38.	“ “ “ 7 pictures.

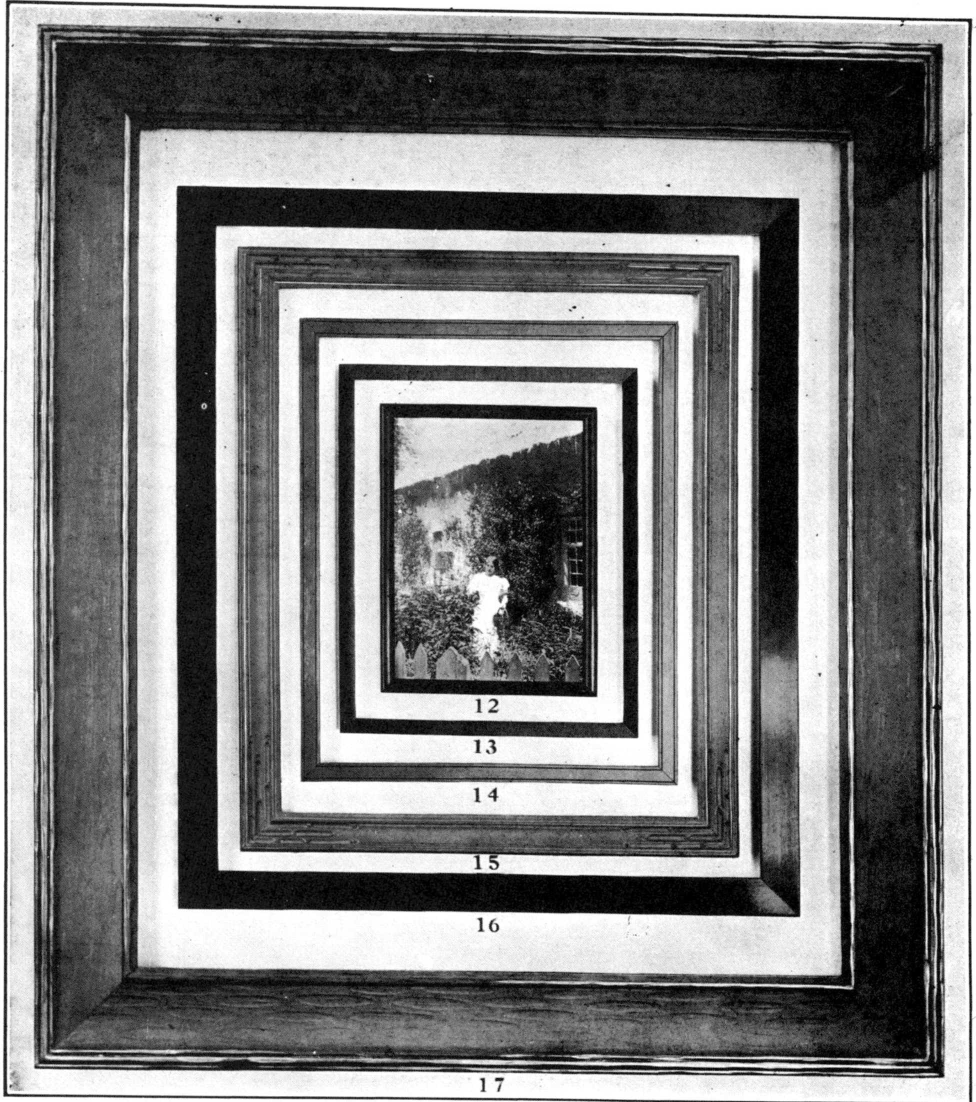

Frame	Description	Size	Width	Price	Minimum
Frame 12, B	size per gross, mahoganized	(5 x 7)	(3/8 in. wide)	$83.33 1/3,	not less than 1/4 gross.
12, D	" " " "	(7 x 9)	(3/8 " ")	120.00	" " " 1/4 "
12, K	" " dozen, "	(8 x 12)	(1/2 " ")	15.00	" " " 1 dozen.
12, R	" " " "	(10 x 12)	(1/2 " ")	16.80	" " " 1 "
13, B	" " gross, mah. veneer	(5 x 7)	(3/8 " ")	90.00	" " " 1/4 gross.
13, D	" " " " "	(7 x 9)	(3/8 " ")	127.20	" " " 1/4 "
13, K	" " dozen " "	(8 x 12)	(1/2 " ")	16.00	" " " 1 dozen.
13, R	" " " " "	(10 x 12)	(1/2 " ")	18.00	" " " 1 "
14, A	" " " green and gilt, for framing only	(11 x 14)	(1/2 in. wide)	$9.00	not less than 7 pict.
14, Q	" " " " " " " "	(11 x 17)	(3/4 " ")	11.00	" " " 7 "
14, S	or C size per dozen, green and gilt, for framing only	(13 or 14 x 17)	(3/4 or 1 in. wide)	$12.00	not less than 7 pictures.
15, A	size per dozen, gilt, for framing only	(11 x 14)	(1 in. wide)	$45.00	not less than 7 pictures.
15, Q	" " " " " " "	(11 x 17)	(1 " ")	45.00	" " " 7 "
15, S	or C size per dozen, gilt, for framing only	(13 or 14 x 17)	(1 1/2 in. wide)	$55.00	not less than 7 p.
16, A	size per dozen, mah. veneer, for framing only	(11 x 14)	(1/2 in. wide)	$12.	not less than 7 pict.
16, Q	" " " " " " " "	(11 x 17)	(1/2 " ")	14.	" " " 7 "
16, S	or C size per doz., mah. veneer, for framing only	(13 or 14 x 17)	(1/2 in. wide)	$15.	not less than 7 p.
16, O	size per dozen, mah. veneer, for framing only	(13 x 22)	(1 in. wide)	$20.	not less than 7 pict.
16, P	" " " " " " " "	(15 x 22)	(1 1/2 " ")	24.	" " " 7 "
16, E	" " " " " " " "	(18 x 22)	(1 1/2 " ")	25.	" " " 7 "
16, F	" " " " " "	(22 x 28)	(2 " ")	3. ea.	including boxing.
17, E	" per dozen, gold, " " "	(18 x 22)	(2 1/2 " ")	60.	not less than 7 pict.
17, F	" " " " "	(22 x 28)	(2 1/2 " ")	6. ea.	including boxing.
17, G	" " " " "	(26 x 30)	(2 1/2 " ")	8. ea.	" "

PLAIN MOUNTED PICTURES, B, D, K, R SIZES

These sizes are sold signed, not titled, thirteen for the price of twelve. Prices on page 5, at bottom.

SUGGESTIONS FOR FRAMING

The frames of which we sell great quantities are in the sizes B, D, K and R. These sizes are not titled, but are signed. Frame No. 12 is the simplest sort of a narrow round-edge mahogany finish and the lowest price. No. 13 is a flat surface, handsome, light veneer, which, while it is called mahogany looks more like Circassian walnut. This is very tasteful and attractive, but costs a little more.

The larger sizes, A to E inclusive, are our regular line of signed and titled sheet pictures and it will be observed that the pictures are sold as heretofore for the same prices and the prices given here for frames are extra. If less than seven are ordered, add twenty-five cents for the boxing. As the sizes F and larger are not sold in sets we quote prices for each including the boxing.

If less than the quantity named on the B, D, K and R sizes is ordered, add twenty-five cents for the box. There is no charge for boxing if sold in the quantity mentioned.

FRAMING VERY LARGE SIZES

We will quote prices for framing larger than the G size in the lists above, namely the H, J and W sizes, on request. The price will be twenty per cent. above the cost to us.

TASTE IN FRAMING

We do not believe in framing water colors in any other styles than gold or mahogany, and we advise that the frames be narrow in proportion to the size of the picture; that is to say, 3/8 inches for B and D sizes, 1/2 inch for K, R and A sizes, 3/4 inch for Q size, 3/4 or 1 inch for S and C sizes, 1 inch for O and P, and 1 to 1 1/2 inches for E sizes. Any attempt to make these pictures look like oil paintings is a mistake and contrary to the genius of the subject.

The above suggestion may be varied so far as to use a greenish gold.

The old-fashioned figure subjects look very well in a veneer. The gilt or gold frame may be placed in any room, but the mahogany is not appropriate for a parlor.

FRAMES IN BOXES

A very nice way to ship frames, either with or without pictures, is in pasteboard boxes. We supply such boxes for our 5 x 7, 7 x 9, 8 x 12 and 10 x 12 gratis. All our shipments are made in such boxes which are white and glazed and intended for the display of the framed pictures and to be sold with the picture to the consumer. In the larger sizes, A, Q, S, C, O, P and E, we also supply the frames without extra charge in pasteboard boxes, but these boxes are merely protective and not glazed; that is to say, they have not the finish or solidity of the smaller boxes, and yet are very profitable for the dealer and consumer as they avoid the danger of unskillful packing to a great extent.